MICROSOFT® WINDOWS® 2000
ACTIVE
DIRECTORY™
PROGRAMMING

Charles Oppermann

PUBLISHED BY
Microsoft Press
A Division of Microsoft Corporation
One Microsoft Way
Redmond, Washington 98052-6399

Library of Congress Cataloging-in-Publication Data
Oppermann, Charles, 1965-
    Microsoft Windows 2000 Active Directory Programming / Charles Oppermann.
       p. cm.
    Includes index.
    ISBN 0-7356-1037-1
     1. Application software--Development. 2. Directory services (Computer network
technology) 3. Microsoft Windows (Computer file) 4. Operating systems (Computers) I.
Title.

    QA76.76.D47 O67 2001
    005.4'4769--dc21

                                            00-052094

Printed and bound in the United States of America.

1 2 3 4 5 6 7 8 9   QWE   6 5 4 3 2 1

Distributed in Canada by Penguin Books Canada Limited.

A CIP catalogue record for this book is available from the British Library.

Microsoft Press books are available through booksellers and distributors worldwide. For further information about international editions, contact your local Microsoft Corporation office or contact Microsoft
Press International directly at fax (425) 936-7329. Visit our Web site at mspress.microsoft.com. Send
comments to *mspinput@microsoft.com*.

Acquisitions Editor: Danielle Bird
Project Editor: John Pierce
Technical Editor: Robert Lyon

Body Part No. X08-04896

This book is dedicated to my parents,
Carl and Suzanne Oppermann,
who always told me I could accomplish anything
and gave me the courage to try.

Contents

Contents

Part II Programming with Active Directory

Contents

Foreword

Redmond, Washington. Friday afternoon, April 9, 1999. This was a big day for us. We were going to upgrade Microsoft Corporation's Windows NT 4.0 domain to an Active Directory domain. Approximately 30,000 user accounts—most of Microsoft's employees in Redmond—depended on the success of this upgrade, and we were still months away from releasing Active Directory to the public. In case problems arose, a few of the developers, testers, and program managers from the Active Directory team would spend the night in the data center. With a touch of the Enter key by a few of the team's members, the upgrade process began. The result? Everything went smoothly. Instead of fixing bugs, those spending the night had fun watching movies until dawn. One developer summed up the experience very well: "It's like watching your child's first step." It was an incredible feeling! That day was the first that Active Directory ran in a live production environment.

Of course, everything I've described here didn't happen automatically. The Active Directory team had been preparing for this day for a long time. There is a common practice at Microsoft called "eating your own dog food," so the Active Directory team and other groups in the Windows NT development team had been running Active Directory long before D-Day. The day-to-day productivity of our team depended heavily on the availability of Active Directory servers. Developers and testers carried pagers and fixed critical problems on the spot, day or night. The consequences should Active Directory become unavailable were severe—the team would not be able to log on, check e-mail, or access secured files, file shares, or internal Web sites. The trial runs paid off, and we learned as we made progress.

Development of Active Directory and the Active Directory Service Interfaces (ADSI), the group of COM-based interfaces that provide access to Active Directory, started before the Windows 2000 project. In fact, the first time Microsoft previewed Active Directory was at the Professional Developer Conference in 1996, and the first version of ADSI predates Active Directory. I was fortunate enough to be part of the team in its early development. We were a small team, occupying only the first floor of building 26 North on Microsoft's Redmond campus. "Dynamic," "fun," and "exciting" are a few of the words that come to mind to describe this team. Everyday, it seemed, a new idea was born. New terms like *dcpromo, forest, upn, well-known guid, guid binding, object category, display specifier, dsgetdc, crackname,* or *spn* were common topics of conversations in the hallways. Although you might not recognize all of these terms, many come from ideas that were driven by customer requirements, other Microsoft groups, independent software vendors (ISVs), and the need to simplify directory information for developers, administrators, and end users.

Directory services technology itself is silent and enabling. However, together with directory-enabled applications, it produces useful solutions for customers. Active Directory is no exception. During early development, the Active Directory team worked actively with many groups within Microsoft as well as with several ISVs. Most of the ISVs' existing products ran as stand-alone applications, but when integrated with Active Directory, their products were enhanced dramatically. For example, the Domain Name System (DNS) is integrated into Active Directory to take advantage of Active Directory replication, the Distributed File System (Dfs) utilizes the Active Directory Sites topology to find the closest Dfs server, and group policy uses the hierarchical nature of Active Directory storage to govern how to apply its policies. Microsoft Exchange 2000 is also integrated with Active Directory. All these improvements enhance the customer experience and increase productivity tremendously.

Application developers have a great opportunity to enhance their existing and future applications by integrating them with Active Directory. For example, an application can store global application configuration information in Active Directory and let Active Directory take care of replication and the availability of this information. Your application can advertise its existence to the directory so that other client applications can find it. Your application can extend the Active Directory schema by including application-specific user information. Then, each time a user logs on, your application can greet the user with the specific information you store in Active Directory. These are just a few of the truly endless possibilities.

Looking forward, we don't yet see the finish line. While evidence encourages us to believe that we're heading in the right direction, there is so much work still ahead of us. Active Directory technology must continue to evolve to meet changing market requirements. In the future, you can expect our continued quest for simplicity, reliability, scalability, and seamless integration with Microsoft's .NET technologies.

In *Microsoft Windows 2000 Active Directory Programming*, Charles Oppermann walks you through Active Directory and ADSI programming with his fresh, friendly approach to explaining concepts, procedures, and code samples. He derives his explanations and expertise from his own experience at Microsoft and from conversations with developers and administrators working with this technology every day. Charles covers all the topics necessary for you to make a great Active Directory–enabled application, including ADSI, the Active Directory schema, the Active Directory user interface, searching Active Directory, and much more. For developers who need to access Active Directory or are interested in enhancing their applications by integrating them with Active Directory, this book is a must read.

Andy Harjanto
Program Manager, Active Directory
Microsoft Corporation

Acknowledgments

The most important acknowledgement goes to you—the reader—for purchasing this book. Thank you! Now allow me to introduce and acknowledge the many wonderful and talented people who played a role in making this book a reality.

From Microsoft, I first thank Andy Harjanto, Program Manager for Active Directory and ADSI, for taking the time to meet with me and for answering my many questions promptly, not to mention for writing the book's foreword! Also, Ajay Ramachandran, a Microsoft developer for ADSI, was very helpful in answering a number of questions. Special thanks to Andrew Clinick, Program Manager, Microsoft Programmability group, for reviewing and making a number of contributions to the Windows Script section in Chapter 10. Before starting this project, I had several conversations with Charles Elliot, Program Manager for Microsoft Exchange, on what makes a great computer book. I'm not sure whether I succeeded with this first effort, but at least I've kept my picture off the cover. I also want to acknowledge the influence of my former coworkers in the Microsoft Accessibility and Disabilities Group, including Greg Lowney, an excellent writer himself; Peter Kam-Ho Wong; Luanne LaLonde; and Gary Moulton. They have truly changed the world for a great number of people and continue to do so.

Many folks from around the world reviewed and contributed to this book in various ways. While there is not enough space to thank everyone, of particular note are Glenn Corbett, Greg Head, Kevin Stanush, Mark C. Smith, Gil Kirkpatrick, Neil Smith, Adam Bogan, and Tom Kiehl. Special thanks also to Andy Webb for his frontline experiences. My dear friends Gary Consolazio, John Beach, and Dave Dockery reviewed chapters and source code and offered many suggestions as well as inspiration. Help in nontechnical forms came from Karen Lee and Jennifer Nelson, without whom I would not have had the mental and physical stamina needed for this project.

Finally, and most importantly, I'd like to thank the many fine folks at Microsoft Press, including Ben Ryan and Barbara Moreland, who got this project started and who guided me in the initial steps. Jana Carter and Jennifer Brown provided administrative help, and Danielle Bird had just the right touch to save this project when it looked like it wasn't going to finish. Special thanks to Paula Gorelick, the principal page compositor, who is just as talented as her famous brother (musician Kenny G). She found countless ways to fit my verbose code comments, lengthy sidebars, and dense tables into readable form. Thanks also to Cheryl Penner, the book's skillful copy editor, and Michael Kloepfer, who produced the art.

Finally, while my name appears on the cover, I truly feel as though the book's two main editors did as much as I did to create this book. They went above and beyond the call of duty to make sure that what you are holding in your hands is readable and accurate. Technical editor Robert Lyon did an outstanding job of cleaning up overly complex passages and vetting the source code. Robert contributed his programming talents as well to a number of the sample applications and often worked throughout the night and on weekends to make sure that what I say in this book is accurate. Of course, any errors that appear are my own. John Pierce, the book's project editor, took my words and made sense of them. He patiently waited while I blew through deadline after deadline and also crafted chapters and passages to make sure I stayed on topic. This book is as much theirs as it is mine. Thank you Robert and John.

Writing this type of book is a grueling task, and while I took on the project voluntarily, my soul mate and partner for life did not. She endured many nights and weekends without me, but every step of the way she offered support and encouragement, did little things like providing flowers for my office, and helped me stay upbeat during the hardest parts. Anthea, I love you; this book would not have happened without your support.

Charles Oppermann
April, 2001
Woodinville, Washington

Introduction

Active Directory is probably the most important feature of the Microsoft Windows 2000 operating system. It can be used by organizations and enterprises to centralize network information that was previously stored in diverse and incompatible databases. It can then distribute that information throughout the network and allow access to the information in a secure, robust fashion.

However, in the year since Windows 2000 has become widely available, many network administrators and developers have come to believe that Active Directory is too complex and difficult to work with. While I've worked on this book project, I've discovered that some of their reservations are understandable, but that others are groundless. Given its scope, Active Directory is relatively straightforward and the benefits it provides far out way the initial learning curve.

Software developers should be particularly excited about the potential of Active Directory because it allows them easy access to a rich store of information about a variety of network resources. New attributes and classes can be added to Active Directory and existing information extended to suit the needs of custom applications.

The goal of this book is to provide a practical understanding of Active Directory so that developers and network administrators can produce directory-enabled applications and automate administration tasks.

What This Book Covers

Active Directory and its primary programming interface, Active Directory Service Interfaces (ADSI), is such a large topic that writing a comprehensive book would require years, and it would take up a good portion of your bookshelf. Instead of being a comprehensive A to Z reference, this book focuses on what developers need to know to get up and running quickly. Throughout the book, I provide complete samples that can be used in your own applications. All the samples are written with a style that is easy to understand and are clearly commented.

This book is broken down into three parts. In Part I, "Overview of Active Directory" (Chapters 1 through 3), I provide background that I think is helpful before starting an in-depth discussion of Active Directory. I provide some historical overview of directory services; walk through the basic architecture of Active

Directory, pointing out important concepts for developers; and then describe the fundamentals of the programming interfaces you use to communicate with Active Directory—both LDAP and ADSI.

In Part II, "Programming with Active Directory" (Chapters 4 through 8), I describe how to find and use information stored in Active Directory using ADSI and C++, Visual Basic, and VBScript. I describe common tasks faced by developers and administrators and show sample code that you can use to perform these tasks and solve common problems.

In Part III, "Special Topics" (Chapters 9 through 11), I describe how to extend Active Directory with new attributes and classes and how to perform some network administration tasks using scripts. In the final chapter, I look ahead by introducing how to program Active Directory for the Web and how Active Directory will change in the next release of Windows.

Although ADSI allows you to communicate with a variety of directory services besides Active Directory, I don't cover every aspect of ADSI; for example, I don't discuss creating ADSI providers, which allow directory vendors to produce a layer of code that allows ADSI to communicate with a proprietary directory service. For more information about using ADSI to access directories other than Active Directory, refer to the *ADSI Software Development Kit* (SDK) available on the companion CD and at *http://www.microsoft.com/adsi/* or *http://www.microsoft.com/windows2000/*.

Who This Book Is For

This book is primarily a programming book and concerns itself with how to write applications to manage the information stored in Active Directory. It will, however, appeal to a range of computing professionals. The information and samples I provide should benefit enterprise network administrators interested in automating tasks with scripts as well as developers building network management tools and full-scale directory-enabled applications with Visual Basic and C++.

For IT professionals who want a background in Active Directory before reading this book, two good references are *Understanding Active Directory Services* by Daniel Blum (Microsoft Press, 1999) and *Active Directory Services for Microsoft Windows 2000 Technical Reference* by David Iseminger (Microsoft Press, 2000).

What You Should Know Beforehand

The features of Active Directory are accessible from several programming languages and environments, but to get the most from this book, you should be able to at least write basic scripts with JavaScript or VBScript. Having a basic understanding of Visual Basic or C++ would also be helpful.

The programming interface to Active Directory used in this book is provided with the Component Object Model (COM), so the more you know about COM, the better you'll understand this book. Because Visual Basic and the scripting languages hide many of the details of COM from the developer, understanding COM is less important if you work in these environments. Still, knowing the concepts involved will help you design better applications for Active Directory. Don't worry if you are unfamiliar with COM. I provide a COM primer in Chapter 3 to help you get started.

What's On the Companion CD

The companion CD contains various files and resources that can be helpful when working with Active Directory. Here are some of the items included on the CD:

- All of the code samples presented in the book

- An electronic version of the book

- Active Directory Clients for Windows 95, Windows 98, and Windows NT 4.0

- Files from the Microsoft Platform SDK that are required to compile some of the code samples

- Software Development Kit for ADSI 2.5

- Directory Services documentation, which includes programming information for Active Directory, ADSI, and ADSI Exchange and a complete electronic reference to the Active Directory schema

- Files related to the Certified for Windows program

System Requirements

To compile the samples for this book, you will need the following:

- Windows 2000, Windows NT 4.0, or Windows 98 (Windows 2000 with Service Pack 1 is recommended.)

- Microsoft Visual C++ 6.0 (Service Pack 3 or later is recommended.)

- Microsoft Visual Basic 6.0

- Microsoft Platform SDK (Required files from the Platform SDK are included on the companion CD.)

To run the code samples, you will need one of the following configurations:

- Windows 2000 Server or Windows 2000 Advanced Server with Active Directory installed. (Windows 2000 Service Pack 1 is recommended.)

- A networked client computer running Windows 98, Windows NT 4.0, or Windows 2000 that is joined to a Windows 2000 domain. If the client computer is running Window 98 or Windows NT 4.0, the Active Directory Client must also be installed. The Active Directory Clients are available on the companion CD.

Note Some code samples require Windows 2000 and some samples require that you have administrative privileges.

Creating a Test Network and Development Environment

While writing this book, I spent many hours creating and re-creating a development environment in which to write the sample programs. The next few sections offer some guidance to help you create your own test and development network. The approach I describe is just one of many ways that a Windows 2000 domain can be set up. If you aren't familiar with Windows 2000 networking concepts and technologies such as domains, DNS, TCP/IP, DHCP, and the rest of the alphabet soup, I'd encourage you to do some background reading before working with the samples in this book. The Microsoft Domain Name System (DNS), a crucial component of a network, uses Active Directory to manage network addresses and computer names. Through experience, you'll find that even relatively minor problems in the configuration of DNS or Active Directory can cause problems later on. Planning and careful deployment are essential.

Server Setup

First you'll need an operational Windows 2000 domain. A Windows 2000 domain is different from the older Windows NT domains. If your organization is running Windows 2000 and you have security access to view and manipulate the organization's Active Directory, you have all you need, but I don't recommend using your organization's Active Directory for your development environment, particularly if you want to modify the schema. That kind of operation should always be carefully planned and deployed in a test lab environment first.

If you create your own Windows 2000 domain, or set up a child domain within an existing Windows 2000 domain, you'll need a server-class computer, one with a fast processor (500 MHz or higher) and at least 128 megabytes of memory. This should be considered the minimum configuration; working interactively at the server will require more memory. If more than one developer is going to access this domain's directory, you might consider additional servers and spread services such as DNS and DHCP to the other computers. This is particularly true if you plan on working with Microsoft Exchange 2000 Server for e-mail and collaborative applications. Windows 2000 Server should be installed on each server you use. Windows 2000 Advanced Server can also be used if support for more than four processors or clustering and failover capability is desired.

To begin the process of creating a domain, you can run Configure Your Server by clicking the Start button, pointing to Programs, pointing to Administrative Tools, and then clicking Configuring Your Server. As an alternative, you can run the DCPromo program from the Run dialog box. How you configure your server depends on many factors, such as Internet connectivity, Internet domain name registration, and personal preference. For more information, read the *Microsoft Windows 2000 Server Resource Kit* (Microsoft Press, 2000) and refer to the *Windows 2000 Planning and Deployment Guide*, which can be found at *http://www.microsoft.com/windows2000/library/planning/default.asp*.

Note I recommend running DCPromo.exe rather than using the Configure Your Server tool for creating an Active Directory domain. People seem to get less confused at the prompts the DCPromo wizard presents.

Many people starting out with Active Directory run into difficulty with the initial setup procedure. As I mentioned, Active Directory is sensitive to the DNS configuration of the network as well as the network hardware and protocols. I strongly recommend a thorough reading of the books cited previously.

Microsoft product support offers a lot of information about the issues that people encounter when upgrading from Windows NT or creating new Active Directory domains. This information can be found at *http://support.microsoft.com/support/win2000/dns.asp*.

> **Note**   Microsoft provides an updated Domain Controller Diagnostic tool (DCDiag) with new features to diagnose domain controller problems. This tool is available for download from *http://www.microsoft.com/technet/win2000/win2ksrv/dnsreq.asp*.

Development Workstation

For your development workstation, I recommend using Windows 2000 Professional, although you could use the same computer that is running Active Directory. As I mentioned earlier, you can use Windows NT 4.0 with the Active Directory Client or Windows 98 with the Active Directory Client, but I do not recommend either. When you install Windows 2000 Professional, make sure you join the domain you plan on working with. If you already have Windows 2000 running on your development computer, use the Network Identification tab under System Properties to join the domain you plan to use.

The code samples for this book were written using Visual C++ 6.0 and Visual Basic 6.0 with Service Pack 4 installed. Visual C++ developers should note that the files required for ADSI are not included in Visual C++. You can find them as part of the Platform SDK. The components of the Platform SDK that you will need are "Build Environment\Network and Directory Services\Active Directory Services Interface" and "Build Environment\Win32 API\Win32 API." You can download these components of the Platform SDK from *http://msdn.microsoft.com/downloads*. The files from the Platform SDK required to compile the code samples presented in the book are included on the companion CD. Be sure to configure Visual C++ to access these header and library files, which should be placed at the top of the directories list. The illustration below shows the Directories tab of the Options dialog box with the required Platform SDK header files at the top of the directories list.

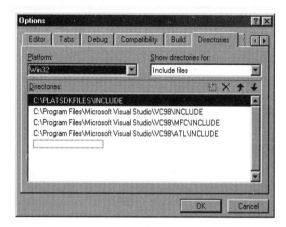

Visual Basic users will need to reference the Active DS Type Library in their Visual Basic project, as shown here.

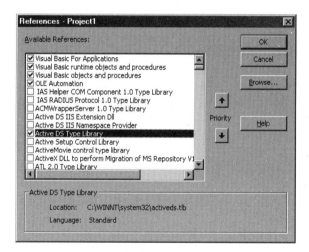

If you intend to use only the scripting examples, Visual C++ and Visual Basic are not required. The Microsoft Script Debugger can be helpful when working with scripts. It is included with Windows 2000 and is available for download from Microsoft's Web site at *http://msdn.microsoft.com/scripting/*. Other development environments, such as Borland's Delphi, might work with Active Directory; however, you are on your own, as I have used only the previously mentioned software for writing this book.

Adminpak.msi (handwritten margin note)

Support Tools (handwritten margin note)

To manage Active Directory remotely, you should install the Administration Pack on the Windows 2000 development computer by running the Adminpak.msi file found in the I386 folder on the Windows 2000 Server or Windows 2000 Advanced Server CD. This Microsoft Installer package will load the necessary management consoles that you can use to manage Active Directory. These same tools are automatically installed on the server when a domain is created. Other helpful tools are found on the Windows 2000 CD (all versions). The Windows 2000 Support Tools contain a number of good network diagnostic tools, including an LDAP browser and the powerful ADSI Edit tool. I'll describe the use of these tools in more detail near the end of Chapter 2. To install the support tools, run Setup.exe in the Support\Tools folder of the Windows 2000 CD.

Test Workstation

Although not a requirement, I recommend that you use a third workstation as your test environment. This computer should be configured similarly to the computers that most of the network users have. It should also contain only the software that's deployed in your organization. It's amazing how many programs that run fine on a development workstation crash or refuse to run on a target user's computer. This is generally the result of DLL conflicts or an assumption that a particular configuration exists.

If your programs need to run on Windows 98, Windows NT 4.0, or both, you should install the appropriate Active Directory Client (available on the companion CD). Also, make several disk partitions on this test workstation and install each operating system separately. Do not mix operating systems on the same partitions, as that will invariably cause conflicts. Each operating system partition should be clean, just as a user's will be when they get a new computer. Also, consider having multiple partitions of Windows 2000—one formatted with the FAT file system and another with NTFS. Using these multiple partitions can expose errors related to file and folder security permissions.

Good Citizenship

Microsoft for many years has tried to improve the end-user experience with its products by creating a list of guidelines for application developers. As a way of attracting vendors to use the guidelines, Microsoft created the Certified for Windows program. Applications that conform to the guidelines and pass an independent test can use the Windows logo as part of their product marketing and packaging.

As a developer, you should always adhere to the guidelines as much as possible. They take into account the needs of a broad set of users (just like the ones you're writing for) and help with the adoption of cutting-edge technologies. Additionally, customers, particularly large organizations buying in quantity, give more serious consideration to certified products. This can give your product the necessary edge that makes it more successful than a competitor's.

Developers of Active Directory–enabled products will want to take special note of the requirements contained in the *Application Specification for Microsoft Windows 2000 Server*. This specification contains information about the requirements for server applications that are integrated with Active Directory, such as how to use Active Directory appropriately and how to adhere to extensibility rules if you extend Active Directory.

For more details about the specific requirements and certification information, please refer to the Certification folder on the companion CD. Also included on the CD are test tools and a program to help document schema extensions. For up to date information on the Certified for Windows program, go to *http://msdn.microsoft.com/certification/*.

Now, let's get on with learning about Active Directory!

Part I

Overview of
Active Directory

1

Introduction to Directory Services

Active Directory is Microsoft's entry into the realm of directory services. It is designed to make network computing better and easier for all parties—users, network administrators, and developers alike. To understand the problems that Active Directory addresses and to understand how programs written for Active Directory can make managing and running a network easier, it's helpful to review the history of network computing and the evolution of directory services.

Network Computing Long Ago

Before joining Microsoft, I worked in small companies that generally employed less than a hundred people and usually didn't have a full-time information technology (IT) staff. As is the norm at many small companies, the people who liked to muck around with computers got to manage the network. The term "manage" is probably too strong—back then, network management involved connecting printers and keeping them running and performing tasks like making sure that new group assistants could access the files of the people they were assisting. Although all the computers were linked together, for the most part people worked as islands, using the network only for printing and occasionally for accessing shared files.

I started working at Microsoft in 1994 as a Program Manager for a component in Microsoft Bob. (Anyone remember that product?) At the time, I was tremendously excited at the possibility of working with more sophisticated systems. I assumed that Microsoft would have an extensive networking setup and use it to its maximum capabilities. Upon arriving, I was given four passwords—two Microsoft Windows passwords to log on to the two computers I had, a password for my Microsoft corporate network account, and, finally, a password for my Microsoft e-mail account. Each day, just to read my e-mail, I had to enter at least three different passwords. This was during the days of Microsoft Mail and Microsoft LAN Manager, so if I wanted to send e-mail to a coworker, I couldn't just type in the person's name; I had to know the "short name"—the eight characters or less that appear to the left of the @ sign in an e-mail address. If I didn't know the person's e-mail name, I could call him or her, but there was no simple way to find the phone number. My need for this information usually resulted in a call to one of the phone operators or a walk to the supply room, where I would flip through a large book called the *Microsoft Company Directory*. This printed directory was published each month and contained the full name, e-mail name, phone number, and office location of each person in the company. Figure 1-1 shows a setup in which a user needs multiple passwords to access different resources.

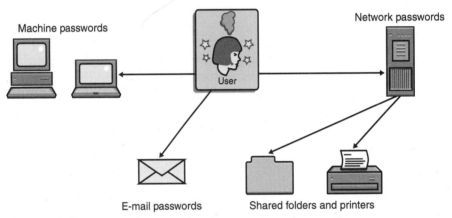

Figure 1-1 One user and many network resources and accounts.

Those hassles soon gave way to online versions of the company directory. Recognizing how personal information was being used, the group responsible for electronic mail started adding directory features to Microsoft Mail and then to Microsoft Exchange Server. The idea seemed logical: store the full name of everyone in the company, along with their e-mail name, office location, and telephone number in a special directory that was a part of Microsoft e-mail products. The directory also included the name of an employee's manager, in case the person I e-mailed didn't reply to my queries. But even with this electronic version of the company directory, I still had separate passwords for my computer and my network and e-mail accounts. With Windows NT, the security model was improved to the point where users' network accounts validated them to access both computer and network resources, but there were still separate accounts—one for the network and one for the e-mail system.

In addition, as in any company, the human resources department had large databases that stored details about each employee's salary, sick leave, performance reports, and benefit programs. So while I only needed to enter my network account information to log on and read e-mail, I had to provide a separate password to access information about my health care plan or to find out how many vacation days I had accrued. Even though Exchange provided simple hierarchical information about employees and their managers, this information couldn't be used for the official company organization chart or other purposes, usually because some necessary data was not included in the e-mail directory. Relying on the information in the e-mail directory also assumed that each employee had an e-mail account; not a problem at Microsoft, where everyone had an e-mail account, but certainly an issue for many companies at the time.

Another hassle in those days was the simple task of printing a document. If you didn't have a printer connected directly to your computer, you had to use a network printer. Some network printers offered color and duplex printing and collating, but not all of them. I would wander the halls looking at the printers stashed away in the supply rooms, make a note of the type of printer and whether it had the option I needed, and scribble down the Universal Naming Convention (UNC) name of the printer (something similar to \\prnsrv05\hpoffjet). Then I'd run back to the office, put in the name of the printer, and hope everything worked well. It rarely did, of course, and the 150-page specification output in PostScript would result in 300 pages of unreadable gobbly-gook by a printer that didn't understand PostScript.

These examples illustrate the challenges faced by the end-user. Network administrators had an even tougher job. They managed hundreds of print and file servers and tried to fit some sort of description into an 8.3-character name. They were continually called upon to make even trivial changes to user's accounts. Developers of line-of-business applications such as a human resources benefit tracking system would have to create their own databases to hold user information. Of course, whenever employees left or joined the company, moved to a new location, or changed their name, dozens of databases and directories needed to be updated. The potential for error and security violations were huge, not to mention the labor costs of maintaining all that information.

One solution to such issues is a single enterprise directory. Instead of maintaining dozens of databases on employees, a single hierarchical directory centralizes the information. The directory is available for searching from each connection point on the network. Similar to how the paper directory was printed and distributed each month, a network directory can be replicated in a matter of minutes and distributed to servers at the farthest points of the network.

Microsoft didn't invent network directories, but they have advanced the state of the art with the introduction of Active Directory, the directory and set of services included in Microsoft Windows 2000 Server. Active Directory builds on years of experience with network computing and collaboration with Windows NT, Exchange Server, and other products. To better understand Active Directory, let's further describe directories and their use in distributed computing.

What Is a Directory?

Simply put, a directory is a container of data, like the company directory I used to use. Another directory is *TV Guide*, which lists television programs and the times they are shown. These traditional directories are printed and distributed at regular intervals. They do not change but are replaced by a new issue; therefore, they can be considered *off-line directories*. Off-line directories are generally used for publishing information that is read-only.

An *online directory* is a directory that can be accessed and updated electronically over a computer network—whether that network is a local area network (LAN), wide area network (WAN), or even the Internet. Many off-line directories have an online, or electronic, counterpart. Phone companies publish their listings and yellow pages on the Web and provide an easy-to-use interface.

Other types of online directories include application directories and purpose–specific directories. An *application directory* is one that is tied to a software application—such as Lotus Notes or Novell GroupWise. Both use proprietary directories that are tailored to the specific needs of the application.

A *purpose-specific directory* can be used by any application, but it is tied to holding data for a narrow purpose. A good example of this type of directory is the Domain Name System (DNS) used by the Internet. While many different applications use DNS, the information contained within it is only useful for specific tasks—name and IP address resolution.

Network directories are online directories that store information about network resources and services. Generally, this information includes user information, security data, and lists of services available, such as printer and publishing services.

Active Directory is considered a network directory, but it has been designed to allow other data to be stored in it. For example, Microsoft has implemented the Dynamic DNS service of Windows 2000 in Active Directory. By using a standardized data model and programming interface, known as LDAP (more on that later), the directory information can be used by any application. Applications can even modify the data model to contain new classes of information for a specific purpose.

What Is a Directory Service?

When asked, "What is a directory service?" most people would answer, "The friendly telephone operator who looks up people's phone numbers for you." That is, of course, a correct answer. If the directory is the actual data—the list of people and telephone numbers—the operators and the method for calling them is the directory service. It's not all that different in the electronic world. Figure 1-2 shows a comparison of a traditional phone directory service and an electronic directory service.

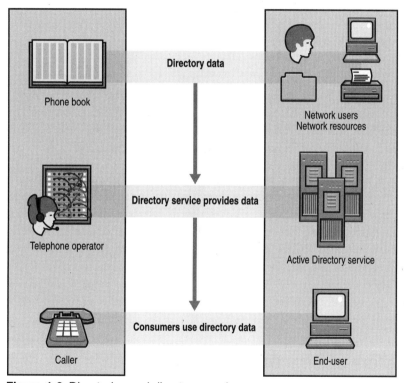

Figure 1-2 Directories and directory services.

A directory service provides for the storage and retrieval of directory information for users and applications. Areas that a directory service must address are performance, security, reliability, availability, and ease of use. ("Ease of use" means that developers can write applications to access directory information without a lot of difficult programming.)

Consider an example. Most large shopping malls have kiosks that list the stores in the mall, categorizing them by the types of products they sell. Services that the mall provides, such as restrooms, telephones, security, and information booths, are also listed and mapped. These kiosks are really directories. Now imagine that there was only one mall directory kiosk, located at the center of the mall. Dozens of people would walk up to the kiosk, everyone trying to get the information at the same time. What if it was very tiny and the text was hard to read? People would spend a lot of time searching and looking for that certain specialty store that sells only socks. (Strangely enough, this is the kind of store my girlfriend likes.) Imagine that while these people are trying to read the mall directory, a janitor walks up and takes the kiosk away to be updated or cleaned. This is an admittedly silly example, but it illustrates the need for performance, reliability, availability, and ease of use in directory services. Malls accommodate hundreds of shoppers by placing many kiosks around the shopping center and by making them easy to understand.

Network directories provide similar solutions. In order to ensure high availability, directory information is replicated to many servers (electronic "kiosks"). The computers accessing the information in the directory can do so from the nearest server, resulting in improved performance. Since directory information can be gathered and presented in a variety of ways, it's easily accessible to an end-user.

Directory services make tasks easier for developers, administrators, and end-users. If you are a developer, a directory service makes it easy to store and look up information about network resources. Applications can publish information to be stored in the network directory to be used by other applications; network administrators gain benefits that include increased security and ease of administration. Most of all, users benefit from a common security model (avoiding multiple passwords) by taking advantage of data being shared between applications and by no longer having to remember specific items for resources in the directory—like the network path to the printer down the hall.

A Brief History of Directories

It's easy to see that network directories have enormous benefits for users, information technology professionals, and developers. How those benefits came about, particularly how Active Directory evolved, is rooted in the history of network directories, specifically in the development and evolution of DNS, X.500, and LDAP, three early directory services. Figure 1-3 shows a timeline of some of the significant events in directory history.

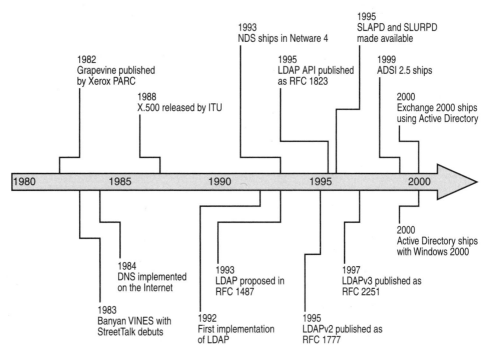

Figure 1-3 A history of directories.

Domain Name System

One of the first major electronic directories, the Domain Name System (DNS) matches domain names on the Internet with their corresponding hard-to-remember Internet Protocol (IP) addresses. Just as people have telephone numbers, computers on a TCP/IP network have IP addresses. In order for a computer to communicate with another computer on the network, it must know the other computer's IP address. The information that DNS uses is created locally and distributed globally. I can add a new computer to my network, give it the name copper1, and tell my DNS server the new computer name and IP address.

Since there are hundreds of thousands of computers on the Internet, it would be wasteful to replicate all the information to all the DNS servers. Instead, when a DNS server doesn't understand a name given to it, it refers the request to another DNS server up the chain. Eventually, the system finds the server that is responsible for the coppersoftware.com domain, asks it to look up copper1, and returns the IP address. Because DNS is incredibly robust, any computer connected to the Internet can communicate with copper1 by specifying the name copper1.coppersoftware.com, the complete domain name for my network. DNS is a good example of a purpose-specific directory. Not surprisingly, Microsoft implements its version of DNS within Active Directory.

Note   If you are setting up an Active Directory–enabled network yourself, a thorough knowledge of how DNS and Active Directory work together is useful and will help avoid common problems. Please refer to the *Windows 2000 Server Resource Kit* and to *Active Directory Services for Microsoft Windows 2000 Technical Reference* by David Iseminger, both published by Microsoft Press. In addition, for common Active Directory/DNS setup issues, refer to the Microsoft Support documents at http://support.microsoft.com/support/win2000/dns.asp.

X.500 Directory Service

The proliferation of networked applications gave rise to a need for standardized directories that implemented common programming interfaces so that multiple applications could access the same information. This era began in the mid-1980s with several large business and academic organizations searching for a common directory solution. In 1988, the International Telecommunications Union published the X.500 directory service recommendation and defined the Directory Access Protocol (DAP). This standard was the culmination of efforts by International Telephone and Telegraph Consultative Committee (CCITT, now known as ITU-T) and the International Standards Organization (ISO) to produce a global directory service standard. The X.500 standard was updated in 1993 and again in 1997.

Developed from the outset to be an all-encompassing, global directory service, X.500 and DAP were considered difficult to implement and did not receive broad commercial acceptance. Another limiting factor was the fact that X.500 depends on the Open Systems Interconnect (OSI) network protocols instead of the (now) prevalent Internet model, based on TCP/IP. Although X.500 was unique in bringing a true distributed nature and a rich searching functionality to directories, those advantages came at the expense of requiring a large amount of computing resources.

When software vendors looked at X.500, they realized that the complexity of the interface was daunting, and they didn't see the potential rewards of this powerful and open standard. Vendors didn't grasp the importance of a global directory service, and proprietary directories simply evolved along with the software they were used in. Figure 1-4 shows the components of an X.500 system.

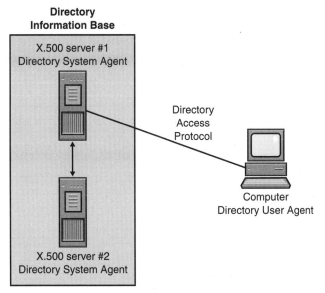

Figure 1-4 X.500 components.

Legacy Free

Working against X.500 was a widespread trend in the development of personal computing applications: build on previous technologies, make incremental technology enhancements, and preserve the customer's current investment. Whereas Windows evolved from MS-DOS, which evolved from CP/M, the X.500 standard was essentially a clean slate, requiring implementers to create a huge amount of new code. When new technologies depart significantly from those used by the majority of the installed base, they suffer slow adoption rates, regardless of their benefits. The first release of Windows NT in 1993 was poorly received, despite a major push by Microsoft to get software developers to adopt its 32-bit programming interface, a moderate jump from the 16-bit Windows API that developers were accustomed to. Microsoft, throughout its history, has learned the importance of gradually moving its installed base and software developers to new technology. Active Directory is no exception, building on technology in Windows NT and products such as Exchange Server and Microsoft Site Server.

The Advent of LDAP

Early versions of collaborative applications such as Microsoft Mail and Lotus Notes used directories, but these were proprietary in the sense that only in certain cases was interoperability with other clients available. Flexibility, security, and replication were minimal or nonexistent. Network operating systems such as Banyan VINES, Microsoft Windows NT, and Novell NetWare started implementing forms of directories to manage users and network resources. NetWare had the Bindery, and Windows NT had the Security Account Manager (SAM) database. Banyan led the way with an integrated directory service called StreetTalk, which was innovative but never achieved widespread commercial success. Each directory stored information about network users and resources, but each was geared toward security and authentication, the primary needs of the network operating system at the time.

By 1993, with the second revision of X.500 generating little commercial interest, a group of researchers at the University of Michigan (an early X.500 adoption site) were developing an alternative to the complex DAP interface in X.500. The goal was to create a simpler access protocol for X.500 directories. The group created a protocol that removed many of the X.500 elements that had blocked adoption by developers, notably the OSI network model, and that eliminated many of the unused functions of DAP. This lean and mean version of DAP started out as DIXIE (RFC 1249) and became known as Lightweight Directory Access Protocol (LDAP). Even though this first version of LDAP was a great improvement over the complex X.500 DAP, it took some time for vendors to embrace it. Not until LDAPv2 was published (in proposed form in RFC 1487 and as a standard in RFC 1777) did LDAP and open directory services really take off.

> **Note** The formal definition for LDAP is contained in documents known as *Requests For Comments*, or RFCs for short. RFCs have developed into a way of standardizing a technology to be used on the Internet. Many technologies and specifications, from DNS to how e-mail is passed around, are defined by RFC documents. The Internet Engineering Task Force (http://www.ietf.org) reviews and maintains RFC documents. A list of RFCs related to LDAP is included in Chapter 3.

At first, LDAP was simply an alternative to X.500's DAP. However, because LDAP defined the protocol, developers were free to do their own implementations of a directory service that merely complied with the requirements of LDAP and did not require X.500. The first such implementation was, unsurprisingly, at the University of Michigan, where SLAPD (stand-alone LDAP daemon) and its replication partner, SLURPD (stand-alone LDAP update replication daemon), were developed in 1995. SLAPD was a simple LDAP server that could communicate with several different databases serving as directories. SLURPD was the program that replicated the changes in the directory database to other computers acting as directory servers.

Also important to the success of LDAP was the development of the LDAP Application Programming Interface (or API) for the C language. Defined in RFC 1823, this API includes a set of functions that developers can use to access directory services. Windows NT and Windows 2000 support this API as part of the operating system to allow applications running on those platforms to access LDAP-based directories.

Parts of LDAP have been improved over the years, with a major effort directed at providing extensibility. The latest version, originally published in 1997 as RFC 2251, is known as LDAPv3. This version is a superset of LDAPv2 and includes new features such as extended controls and the ability to expose the directory data definition or schema. A major feature of LDAPv3 is the ability for LDAP directories to expose information about the services provided. Many vendors supporting LDAP do so at the v2 level, with some mixing in features from LDAPv3. Active Directory supports LDAPv2 and LDAPv3 with some custom extensions, known as controls.

Note   It's interesting that X.400, the ITU standard for network messaging, shared a similar fate as X.500. While LDAP largely supplanted X.500, the Simple Mail Transfer Protocol (SMTP) became the de facto standard for e-mail on the Internet.

The Present State of Directories

The need for large-scale directories, high connectivity between remote sites, and availability of an open and extensible programming interface pushed vendors like Microsoft into supporting LDAP and creating directory solutions based on it. Netscape, led by some of the LDAP developers from the University of Michigan, pushed its Netscape Directory Server product. Novell, which had developed a proprietary network directory called Novell Directory Services (NDS) in 1990, started to use LDAP and, eventually, some X.500 features. Microsoft implemented LDAP server support in some of its application products, notably Exchange Server 5 and Microsoft Site Server 3. Exchange 2000 Server, the latest version of Exchange, replaced its own directory structure with Active Directory. Many products incorporate support for accessing LDAP-based directories, including major e-mail applications such as Microsoft Outlook and Lotus Notes. Windows ships with a simple address book application that supports LDAP-based directories.

The trend in network directories is toward consolidating separate application directories and network operating system directories, while providing tight integration with the underlying operating system. This integration promises a reduced workload for network administrators and a better experience for the end user. It also opens opportunities for developers to create a new breed of network application. The data stored in the directory becomes universally available and is easily managed. Developers are freed from implementing their own database storage and security methods and can concentrate on the functionality of the networked application.

Active Directory Features

Active Directory is a true network directory service and includes features and benefits not available in traditional directory services. Here is an overview of the major features of Active Directory:

- **Hierarchy**   The information contained within Active Directory can be arranged in hierarchies. For example, administrators can arrange network users to follow the same organizational hierarchy that the company uses. Active Directory uses constructs called domains, trees, and forests to represent different divisions of data, all within the same directory. I'll describe these constructs in more detail in Chapter 2.

- **Scalability**   Active Directory is based on a domain model. Each domain consists of one or more workstations and servers linked together. Special servers, known as *domain controllers* (DCs), hold local copies of directory data and make it available to clients. As an organization grows, and the data contained in the directory expands, more domains can be added to meet the needs of the enterprise. I'll touch on Active Directory's ability to scale in Chapter 2.

- **Replication**   The information contained in Active Directory is replicated to all the domain controllers within the organization. Each domain can have multiple DCs for fault tolerance and load balancing. In Chapter 2 I'll describe replication and the related issues that programmers should keep in mind.

- **Interoperability**   The use of LDAP as the directory access protocol ensures that a wide range of clients can use the information stored in the directory. The Active Directory Service Interfaces (ADSI) uses LDAP to get information to and from the directory. ADSI is based on the Component Object Model (COM) and allows scripting. In Chapter 3, I'll provide an overview of LDAP and ADSI programming. Throughout the book, the code samples will show you more specific examples.

- **Security**   Each object within Active Directory can be individually secured to control access. Directory objects can have multiple levels of security, allowing certain users the ability to update some information, but not all of it. Security in Active Directory is tightly integrated with the overall Windows 2000 security model, which uses the Kerberos v5 authentication protocol. I'll touch on security issues throughout the book when describing various programming techniques.

- **Integration**   Active Directory is woven into the very essence of Windows 2000. The server management tools depend on Active Directory, and end users will notice that all applications that employ common user interface elements based on the operating system contain references for accessing and using information from Active Directory. In Chapter 8, I'll discuss some of the user interface components provided in Active Directory that developers can use when creating applications.

- **Extensibility**   Active Directory provides dozens of object classes and hundreds of attributes. Each class, such as computer, user, or printer, represents a data object. The class also specifies which attributes are available to objects of that class. Developers can add their own object classes and even add new attributes to existing classes. I discuss extending Active Directory in Chapter 9.

Microsoft is clearly headed in the right directory, uh, direction with Active Directory. The extensibility, security, and integration features alone are enough to warrant a close examination of the possibilities for developers and network administrators. In the next chapter, I'll delve into the details of Active Directory.

2

Active Directory Architecture

Active Directory is designed to be the single directory for any size organization. Active Directory works well for a small business operating out of a home office or a large conglomerate with hundreds of thousands of users. To create applications that work well with Active Directory, developers need to understand Active Directory's capabilities and the concepts it is built on. In this chapter, I'll describe the components of Active Directory, explain how Active Directory replicates information between servers in an organization, provide examples of how Active Directory is used, and then complete the chapter with a description of some of the tools you'll use to work with Active Directory.

Active Directory Concepts

Active Directory has several components that work together to provide a complete directory service. Before discussing the various systems, let's explore the concepts that Active Directory employs. Some of these concepts, such as domains, might be familiar to you, but they have different meaning with the release of Microsoft Windows 2000. Understanding these concepts is critical to successfully working with Active Directory.

Objects and Attributes

We know that network directories contain information about users, computers, and printers, but what else? The answer is "a lot." Each item in Active Directory is known as an *object*. Figure 2-1 shows some different objects in Active Directory. A *class*, sometimes called an *object class*, defines the type of object and what information is contained within it. Each class contains a list of *attributes* that comprise the information that is contained by objects of that class. *Attributes* are the properties of an object and hold information that describes the object. Some objects hold other objects. These objects are called *containers*.

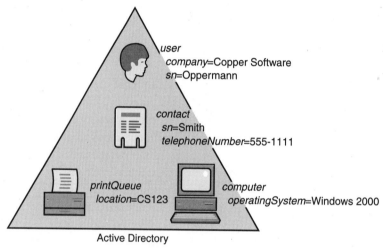

Figure 2-1 Objects and attributes in Active Directory.

Schema

The set of definitions that specify what objects and attributes can be stored in Active Directory is called the *schema*. When an Active Directory domain is initially setup, it contains a default schema known as the *base Directory Information Tree* (DIT). There are over 140 predefined classes and over 850 attributes in the base DIT. What's particularly interesting is that the schema of Active Directory is stored *within* the directory itself. That's right, the definition of the objects and their attributes is included in a special directory partition that contains the schema objects. You can browse the schema using the Active Directory Schema console, as shown in Figure 2-2. To start this console, type *schmmgmt.msc* in the Run dialog box.

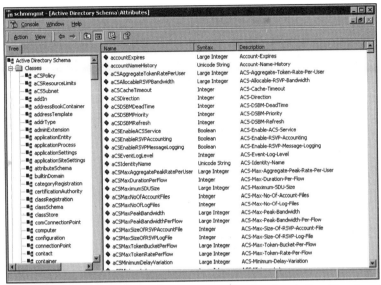

Figure 2-2 Active Directory Schema snap-in showing Active Directory classes and attributes.

While Microsoft has done a good job of implementing many different classes, they were also wise enough to know that whatever they defined, it wouldn't be enough. Developers can modify and extend the schema in several ways. New attributes can be added to existing classes and entirely new classes can be added. Best of all, since the definition of the classes is stored in the directory, other applications can discover and use new classes. Detailed information about extending the schema is covered in Chapter 9, "Active Directory Schema."

Domains

Unlike a telephone directory, Active Directory is a hierarchical directory, where objects can be grouped and separated as needed. Active Directory uses constructs such as *organizational units, domains, trees,* and *forests* to logically separate information and to help with the management of that information.

Versions of Windows NT before Windows 2000 were also based on domains, but while these domains are organizationally similar, the implementation in Windows 2000 is completely different. If you have a Windows NT background, a review of the differences between Windows NT and Windows 2000 domains is helpful.

Windows NT Domains

In Microsoft parlance, a *domain* is a collection of computers connected by a network that share user and security information. Domains are not specific to Active Directory or new to Windows 2000. From the first version, Windows NT included the concept of domains. A Windows NT domain is simply a definition of security and a grouping of computer and user accounts. For example, a Windows NT domain named Sales could be created. The Sales domain would contain all the computers and users related to the sales department.

In a Window NT domain, security information such as user accounts are stored in a directory database called the Security Accounts Manager (SAM). The SAM was the forerunner of Active Directory in that it contained directory information for the domain. The SAM resided on a computer called a *primary domain controller* (PDC), which processed requests for reading and writing to the domain database.

Although Windows NT domains are a useful way to define security boundaries, they do have some limitations. Windows NT domains aren't robust enough. The entire directory for a domain is hosted on a single PDC. The PDC contains the most current version of the directory. Backup domain controllers (BDCs) also contain a copy of the directory, but these copies are read-only in order to force updates to occur only on the PDC.

The SAM database isn't extensible. The various objects and attributes contained within it are fixed and cannot be modified. Also, new object classes or attributes can't be added.

Windows NT domains have limitations when used in large environments. In theory, a Windows NT domain can exist for an entire organization, but if the organization is large, the workload on the PDC is too great. Also, the SAM is not scalable, and once it reaches 40 megabytes, or approximately 40,000 objects, performance suffers greatly.

Creating multiple Windows NT domains increases complexity. To alleviate some of the limitations of a Windows NT domain, a *multiple master domain model* can be used. This allows several domains to be networked together, like Sales, Development, and Finance. In order to access information such as a shared file or printer on another domain, a *trust relationship* would need to be established. If Mike in the Sales department needs to access the quarterly reports from Finance, the network administrator is required to set up a trust relationship between the domains. So that everyone in the company has access, a total of six trust relationships would need to be established between the three domains. This is shown in Figure 2-3. For just six domains, thirty trust relationships are needed.

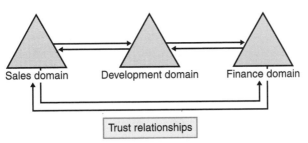

Figure 2-3 Three Windows NT domains with a total of six trust relationships.

Windows 2000 Domains

On the surface, a Windows 2000 domain is very similar to a Windows NT domain, but the implementation and functionality are very different. In fact, many organizations will simply upgrade from Windows NT domains to Windows 2000 domains, maintaining the same domain structure. Over time, however, that structure may change to take advantage of the Active Directory structure and improve network organization.

Windows 2000 and Active Directory improve greatly on the Windows NT domain model in a variety of ways. First and foremost, Windows 2000 domains are more scaleable. Active Directory has the ability to scale to millions of directory objects.

Unlike multiple Windows NT domains that are arranged in a flat structure, Windows 2000 domains use a hierarchical structure. Like Windows NT, Windows 2000 domains still contain all the necessary security and resource information. However, administrators have more control with the hierarchical structure of Active Directory to assign permissions and delegate management tasks.

A Windows 2000 domain is designed to align itself with the Internet's Domain Name System (DNS). Modeling Active Directory on a company's domain name allows for a more intuitive organization. My company, Copper Software, has registered coppersoftware.com for its Internet domain. When creating the primary domain for my network, I named it coppersoftware.com. Computers in the Copper Software network are named copper1, copper2, and so on. As shown in Figure 2-4, the full DNS name of the domain controller is copper1.coppersoftware.com. The alignment between Active Directory names and DNS names is very beneficial. It allows administrators to drop support for NetBIOS naming conventions, which required unique names for computers and devices within the entire organization. With DNS, the name of the computer or device only has to be unique within a particular domain. As an example, there can be a printer1.sales. coppersoftware.com device and a printer1.finance.coppersoftware.com device. Developers of networking applications are freed from the 15-character limitation on NetBIOS names.

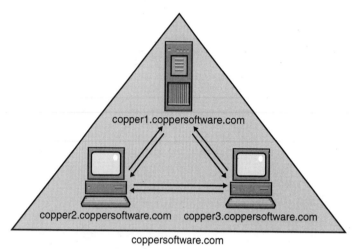

copper1.coppersoftware.com

copper2.coppersoftware.com   copper3.coppersoftware.com

coppersoftware.com

Figure 2-4 Domain with two workstations and one server.

Similar to Windows NT, the computer that processes directory service requests and keeps a local copy (a *replica*) of the directory information is called a *domain controller*. A Windows 2000 domain can have more than one domain controller, but must have at least one domain controller. The first server created in a domain is charged with being a domain controller. Designing a domain with multiple domain controllers promotes redundancy and reliability and allows it to scale as an organization grows.

Putting the Entire U.S. Phone Book into Active Directory (and then some!)

Active Directory can store millions of objects and still provide quick access. While the Windows NT SAM database started suffering severe performance problems above 40 megabytes, the only meaningful limit on the size of an Active Directory database is hard disk storage. A demonstration was created that illustrated the scalability of Active Directory. Information taken from telephone books from around the country was compiled into a directory of more than 260 gigabytes, containing over 100 million contact objects! Most organizations won't need to store 100 million objects in their directory, but some—such as an Internet Service Provider (ISP)—might need to store millions of objects. For organizations wanting to store over 10 million objects, a multidomain structure may be necessary, but it's good to know that with Active Directory you won't run out of capacity anytime soon.

Namespaces

A *namespace* is the bounded area in which a name can be resolved. The process of resolving a name to an object or another item is called *name resolution*. Just like a phone book, where you have a name and can quickly find the phone number of the person with that name, Active Directory's namespace, given the object's name, allows the referencing of any directory object regardless of where it's placed within the hierarchy of the directory.

In Active Directory, the domain is the default unit of name resolution. I can request that the directory return to me information about the user *Anthea* and it will query the directory and return the associated object. However, this process only works for a single domain. If there is an *Anthea* in a separate domain, that directory object will not be found and retrieved.

Trees and Forests

Active Directory also supports the concept of trees. A *tree* is a grouping of one or more Windows 2000 domains. A tree in Active Directory follows the structure of DNS. For example, sales.coppersoftware.com indicates that "sales" is a sub-domain, or child domain, of coppersoftware.com. The top of the tree, coppersoftware.com, is known as the *root domain*. Each domain within a tree shares the same schema and configuration, forming a larger namespace in which to resolve objects. Domain trees and a DNS structure make it easy for a company to design their Active Directory organization. Figure 2-5 illustrates a Windows 2000 domain tree.

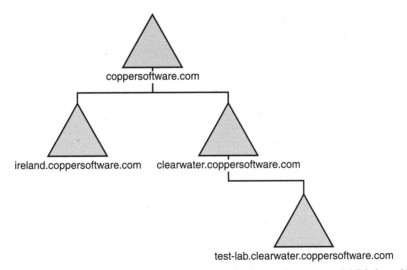

Figure 2-5 Domain tree with two child domains and one grandchild domain.

By now you might be thinking this is all very good for small companies, but what about large conglomerates with many different subsidiary companies? Actually, the single domain model scales upward very well. If geographical considerations or company policy dictates more domains, a single tree with a root and child domains can serve even a very large company well.

However, companies change constantly, divisions are spun off and new companies are formed or acquired. Managing change easily was a requirement for Active Directory. A company might have several Internet presences, for example, and desire to keep operations between them separate. In my own case, I have a separate company unrelated to software and dedicated to aviation and aircraft leasing. It's all contained within the Copper "empire," uh, enterprise, but has its own Internet domain name called *copperaviation.com*. Thus, coppersoftware and copperaviation would be considered trees. Since they are two facets of the same enterprise, there is much information contained in each tree that should be shared between them. So how can you combine two trees into one logical entity? Using a forest, of course, which you can see in Figure 2-6.

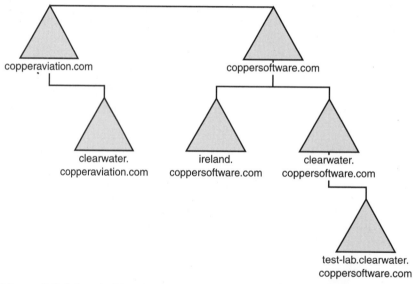

Figure 2-6 A forest of two trees.

As you would expect, a *forest* is a group of trees. In this case, the Copper enterprise consists of two independent trees, one for Copper Aviation and one for Copper Software, each containing one or more domains. All trees within the forest share a common schema, configuration, and global catalog (defined later in this chapter), but they do not allow for a contiguous namespace to resolve names. Security and replication is handled through trust relationships set up between the domain trees.

> **Note** For more information about domain trusts, refer to the excellent book *Active Directory Services for Microsoft Windows 2000 Technical Reference* by David Iseminger (Microsoft Press, 1999).

When to use trees and forests is up to network planners. Generally, child domains making up a tree are formed along geographical or physical placement considerations or both. The key is that all domain controllers within a tree share the entire directory structure, whereas domain controllers in separate trees share only the schema and configuration portions of the directory.

Organizational Units

To subdivide domains, administrators can create *organizational units* (OUs), which are containers for related objects in a domain. How OUs are related is up to the network administer. One practice is to organize the domain into organizational units that follow business structure. For example, you can have the Research OU in the clearwater.coppersoftware.com domain, as shown in Figure 2-7.

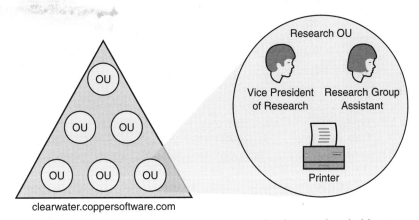

Figure 2-7 Using organizational units to group business related objects.

Most important, delegation and security rights are assigned at the OU level. For example, with the organizational unit shown in Figure 2-7, the Research group assistant could be granted rights to create new users only within the Research OU. This delegation of authority can relieve network administrators from many minor chores while ensuring security.

Security

A key goal of Active Directory is to ensure secure access to data for authorized users and to prevent unauthorized users or their client applications from accessing restricted directory information. With that in mind, all the objects in Active Directory have security settings stored with the object. This information is known as the *Access Control List* (ACL); it contains data on what operations can be performed on the object and its attributes and what entities (users, groups, and so on) are allowed to perform those operations. These security settings can also include permissions for object creation, such as creating new user or computer accounts. Active Directory also allows child objects to inherit the security settings of their parent. By using Active Directory, administrators can both tighten security over the network and relieve their own administrative burden.

Directory Partitions and Naming Contexts

Each domain controller in a forest includes what are called *directory partitions*. A directory partition is a contiguous portion of the overall directory information. By partitioning the directory data into logical groups, indexing and searching operations can be improved. Additionally, each partition can have its own replication schedule. These partitions are also called *naming contexts*. By default, the Active Directory for a enterprise consists of at least three partitions: schema, configuration, and domain partitions.

Schema Partition

The schema partition contains the definition of the type of data stored in the directory. This partition is shared by all the domains within a forest. When Active Directory adds new objects to the directory, it checks the schema partition for the definition of the object and applies consistency rules. Additionally, applications can query the schema partition to discover allowable classes and attributes.

Configuration Partition

The configuration partition is used to store configuration data for the network, such as topology, replication settings, and other network-wide services. You can view a portion of the configuration partition of Active Directory using the Active Directory Sites and Services snap-in. By default, the configuration data in the Services node is hidden. To display the Services node, click the View menu and then select Show Services Node, as shown in Figure 2-8.

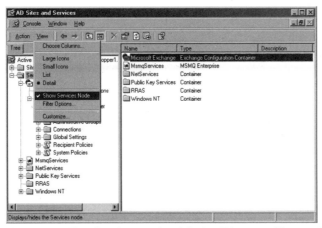

Figure 2-8 The Services node of Active Directory Sites and Services shows a portion of the data in the configuration partition.

Some network services, such as the remote access service (RAS), store their configuration data in the configuration partition. Network applications can add their own containers to this partition to store configuration information to be distributed to all the domains in the network.

Domain Partition

The domain partition is where most of the data in Active Directory for a specific domain is stored. It contains the information that is most often associated with a network directory, including information about users, computers, and various network resources such as shared printers and folders. The domain partition is also known as the *default naming context*. This partition is only shared among other domain controllers for the domain (for redundancy purposes) and not with child or parent domains.

Active Directory is really the combination of all the directory partitions for an enterprise. That includes all the individual domain partitions and one schema and configuration partition for each forest that makes up the enterprise. Since the data is partitioned and distributed throughout the enterprise, no one computer has to store all the data that makes up the Active Directory.

So how does an application find a particular piece of information? That's the purpose of the global catalog, discussed next.

Global Catalog

One way Active Directory improves searches is to maintain a global catalog. Similar to an index file of a database, the *global catalog* (GC) contains a copy of all the directory objects in an enterprise but only a subset of the attributes for each object. This is useful for the times when name resolution is required but the domain of the object is not known.

When a person logs on to a Windows 2000 domain and provides a username, the global catalog is searched to find a match between a user object and the provided username. Once found, the global catalog replica of the object is queried for the user's domain.

The global catalog replica contains only those attributes that are most commonly used when searching. Remember, in a forest configuration, each domain controller in a tree contains copies of the domain's directory partition. However, another tree has a completely different directory partition, which is shared among the domain controllers of that tree. By using the global catalog, a domain controller can quickly look up an object and provide certain attributes without deferring to other domain controllers. Compared with simply asking a domain controller to hunt down the object by making recursive calls to other domains within the forest, known as *referral chasing*, the global catalog provides real value and efficiency. I'll discuss referral chasing more in Chapter 5, "Searching Active Directory."

Multimaster Operations

In Active Directory, a copy of the domain partition is contained on each domain controller within the domain. Each domain controller is fully independent and can both read and write to its local copy of the directory. As mentioned earlier, this ability is different from Microsoft Windows NT domains, in which all updates to the SAM database are performed on the PDC and the BDCs have read-only copies of the database. The Windows NT style of updating—all changes made on one machine—is called a master-slave or single-master approach. In contrast, the approach to updating data that is used by Active Directory is known as multimaster: there is no single master domain controller and no single point of failure. If you have a complete copy of the directory on each domain controller, one domain controller does not need to send a request to another domain controller to process a request from a local user, and performance is greatly enhanced.

Flexible Single-Master Operation Roles

So, multimaster operation means that all domain controllers are created equal? Although that is the goal, in reality, there are certain dependencies on particular domain controllers. For example, in order to protect the integrity of the Active

Directory schema, modifications can be performed only on one domain controller in the entire forest. This domain controller is called the *schema operations master*. In addition, Active Directory does away with the need for a specific PDC, but allows a particular domain controller to act as a PDC emulator for backward compatibility with network workstations running Windows NT 4.0 that expect to connect to a PDC. Table 2-1 lists the various flexible single-master operation (FSMO) roles.

In a small domain, one domain controller might perform all the various operations. In a larger organization, the various FSMO roles might be distributed to other domain controllers to reduce workload on any one machine. The Ntdsutil tool (discussed later in this chapter) can be used to display and modify which domain controllers perform the various operation roles.

Role	Scope	Purpose
Schema operations master	Forest	The only domain controller that accepts changes to the schema partition. Also known as the schema master.
Domain naming master	Forest	Adds or removes new domains in the forest.
Relative ID master	Domain	Maintains relative IDs (RID), used in security IDs (SID) that are used to control access to objects.
PDC operations master	Domain	Used by clients that are not Active Directory–aware and expect to communicate with a primary domain controller. Also known as the *PDC emulator.*
Infrastructure master	Domain	Maintains references to objects in other domains.

Table 2-1 Flexible single-master operations roles.

> **Note**   Generally, you do not need to worry about which domain controller is performing a specific role. The exception is when you write a program extending the schema. Doing this requires discovering and connecting to the schema operations master. In Chapter 9, "Active Directory Schema," I'll discuss retrieving the specific name and address of the domain controller performing the schema operations master role.

Replication

A major feature of Active Directory is its ability to synchronize directory information for multiple domain controllers. The process of synchronizing directory information is known as *replication*. Replication has three primary benefits: increased performance, scalability, and fault tolerance. Performance is improved because any domain controller can search the local domain for directory information. Scalability is made easier because as the directory grows, additional domain controllers can be added to distribute the load. Fault tolerance is increased because if one domain controller is disabled, other domain controllers in the domain can handle requests using the same directory data.

From the viewpoint of an Active Directory developer, replication normally happens automatically and transparently. However, application developers need to have an understanding of the process in order to take into account the inherent latency of distributing directory data.

Replication Model

The specific replication model that Active Directory uses is called *multimaster loose consistency with convergence.* (If we were playing Buzzword Bingo that would win the pot.) So what does it mean? Here is the breakdown:

- **Multimaster**   All domain controllers in the forest can accept changes.

- **Loose consistency**   The copy of the database on any particular domain controller is not guaranteed to be consistent with any other domain controller at the same time.

- **Convergence**   Changes to the directory will ripple through all the copies and eventually converge on the same values throughout.

What's important for developers to recognize here is that at any given time, a domain controller contains only a copy, or *replica,* of the directory data. Changes made at another domain controller will eventually reach the domain controller that you might be communicating with, but you should make no assumptions about how long that process might take. Since directory data is normally updated on an infrequent basis, this latency is generally not a concern.

Triggering Replication

Whenever a change is made to directory data, Active Directory triggers an update cycle that ensures that the information is propagated to the other domain controllers that hold replicated copies.

A change occurs when an object is modified in any way—created, deleted, or moved—or when any attribute of the object is changed. Something interesting to note is that when clients make changes to the directory, the changes are made at the object level as one transaction. If any change to a particular attribute fails, all the other changes are rolled back and the transaction is cancelled. This protects the consistency of the object. However, replication occurs at the attribute level. This makes sense, since it would be incredibly wasteful to copy the entire contents of an object to many different domain controllers if only one attribute has changed.

Within a domain, the changes are replicated immediately. When a change is made to a directory object, the domain controller on which the change is made uses remote procedure calls (RPCs) over TCP/IP to inform other domain controllers within the domain of the change. In turn, the other domain controllers then make an update request to the originating domain controller. This method is known as *pull replication* and relies on domain controllers to query each other for changes. This process provides for multiple replication paths that can reduce the time it takes for all directory replicas to converge on the same set of values (to be synchronized). For example, domain controller DC1 might update DC2, which then updates DC3. However, when DC3 requests updates from DC1, it should only receive changes that it hasn't already received from other domain controllers.

Update Sequence Number

Windows NT 4.0 would only allow changes to be made to the SAM database on the PDC and would then use timestamps to determine how to update BDCs. This approach required that all domain controllers be synchronized to the same clock, and even slight timing errors could cause problems in database consistency. Active Directory in Windows 2000 uses a new method, called an *update sequence number*, to determine how to update multiple versions of the database. An update sequence number (USN) is a 64-bit value kept at the local domain controller. When an object is changed, its *uSNChanged* attribute is updated with the current USN value at the DC making the change. The DC then increments the USN by 1 and waits for the next change.

When a destination domain controller requests updates from another domain controller, it uses a value called the *high-watermark*, which is the highest USN received from the other domain controller during previous replication cycles. The originating domain controller can then search through its list of updated objects and provide only those with a higher USN, cutting down on traffic and server overhead. However, the high-watermark value by itself is not sufficient to prevent redundant updates. Domain controllers maintain a table of the most recent USN value from all other replication partners. This is known as the *up-to-dateness vector.* When replicating, the destination domain controller sends the up-to-dateness vector to the originating domain controller. If the destination and originating domain controllers have the same USN value for a particular domain controller, it can be assumed that both have the changes originating from that particular domain controller and there is no need to send updates that originated from it. While reducing replication traffic, the up-to-dateness vector also prevents changes caused by endless looping from domain controller to domain controller.

Since updates to the directory usually occur in batches, Active Directory uses *propagation damping* to prevent excessive interserver replication traffic. Each domain controller uses a built-in holdback timer to bundle directory update changes into a group. By default, this timer is set for 5 minutes and can be changed through a registry setting, although changing it is rarely necessary. This means that a domain controller will wait 5 minutes after a directory change before notifying replication partners that updates are available. In addition, domain controllers wait 30 seconds before notifying replication partners of new changes that were not originated on that server.

Topology

In the previous examples, replication occurs immediately for the various domain controllers within a domain. This works well for domain controllers that are all connected using high-speed networking, such as 100-MB Ethernet, but given the frequency and asynchronous nature of changes, the pull method of replication

---

Patience Is a Virtue

What happens when distributed networks communicate information too quickly was painfully illustrated on Monday, January 15, 1990, when AT&T's toll-free telephone network experienced a massive failure because of a simple programming mistake. It started when one of the large network switches that routes telephone calls had a minor fault and went off line temporarily. In the process, the switch notified the other switches in the network of its status, and those switches automatically routed calls around the off-line switch. When the fault was corrected, the off-line switch notified the other switches that it was now available to start accepting calls again. However, because of a misplaced *break* statement in C language code recently loaded into the switches' computers, if a switch received two calls within 1/100th of a second while it was updating its status map, it would corrupt some data. The switch would detect this corruption, send out a message indicating its status, and reboot. Once the switch had recovered, it would broadcast a message indicating that it was "OK." This caused other switches to update their status maps, putting them at higher risk of encountering the flaw. Eventually, this caused a cascading effect. During this time, business on the east coast of the U.S. was severely limited for several hours until AT&T reverted to a previous version of the switch software.

---

would be inefficient over slower connections commonly found in wide-area networks (WANs). For that scenario, Active Directory uses a different strategy, called *store-and-forward replication*. In this strategy, one domain controller is designated to hold all updates and then forward them to another domain controller.

Network administers can set up a defined topology of domains interconnected using various means. The unit Active Directory uses for this topology is known as a *site*. A site represents one or more subnets of a well-connected IP network. Normally, when I think of "well connected," I think of receiving the latest beta of Flight Simulator from my friend at Microsoft, but in this case, a "well-connected" network is a network of computers, servers, and workstations that are physically connected at LAN speeds (10 Mbps) or greater. Computers that dial in to the network using a modem or DSL connection would not be considered well connected.

For example, I show a potential site topology in Figure 2-9. In this topology, I show two domains and four sites. The domains coppersoftware.com and europe.coppersoftware.com each contain two sites, representing imaginary branch offices of Copper Software. Since the servers and workstations within a branch office are well connected, a site is defined in Active Directory to ensure that replication traffic is handled nearly immediately. I can define a schedule for replication in Active Directory with an object called a *site link*. A site link is an object that represents a set of connected sites. However, the Clearwater site might not have good connectivity to the Dublin or Reading sites, so I want to route replication traffic between the coppersoftware.com and europe.coppersoftware.com domains only between a particular server in the Home Office site and the Dublin site. For this, a *site link bridge* can be established, which is an object that represents a set of site links. A site link bridge defines the servers, path, and schedule used to route replication traffic.

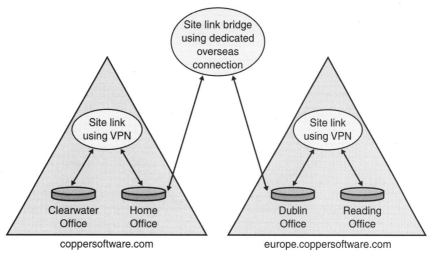

Figure 2-9 Site links and a site link bridge for a forest with two domains.

Another benefit to using sites is to help clients find directory services provided by servers that are electronically closest to them. When a user logs on to a computer using Windows 2000 Professional, the directory service client asks the nearest domain controllers to process the logon. By defining sites, network administrators reduce traffic over network routers and switches and spread directory service requests to various domain controllers. Figure 2-10 shows how sites are managed using the Active Directory Sites and Services snap-in.

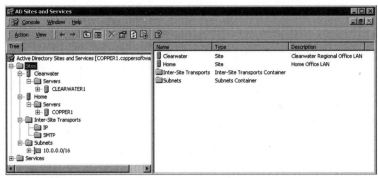

Figure 2-10 Active Directory Sites and Services snap-in showing two sites, Home and Clearwater.

Conflict Resolution

What happens when an attribute of an object is updated on one server, but before it can be replicated, it is also updated on another server? For example, a user at the Clearwater site of Copper Software forgets his password and asks the help desk to reset it. Someone at the help desk resets the user's password, updating the password attribute of the user's object. These changes are made locally on the domain controller COPPER1 located at the home site in Seattle. Just then, the user remembers the old password, logs in, and changes it to something else. This change would be made on the CLEARWATER1 domain controller at the Clearwater site. Now the system has two changes to the same attribute of the same object, but the new values are stored on different domain controllers. When replication occurs between COPPER1 and CLEARWATER1, a conflict will occur and must be resolved.

Resolution is accomplished by sending a unique stamp along with each attribute of an object that has been changed. This stamp contains the version number of the attribute, the time when the value was changed, and the globally unique identifier (GUID) of the server that was processing the change. This stamp travels with the changed attribute throughout the replication process to all domain controllers.

When COPPER1 and CLEARWATER1 connect to replicate changes, they compare the stamps applied to their versions of the same attribute. To resolve the conflict, they compare the version number of the password attribute. Since both domain controllers made changes to the same version and increased its value accordingly, the version numbers will be the same. The next tiebreaker is the time of the modification. In this example, the help desk made its change first at the COPPER1 server. Its modification time will be earlier than the change at CLEARWATER1. Active Directory's policy is to accept the change recorded last, so the value at CLEARWATER1 will be accepted, and the COPPER1 value will be discarded.

The modification time is recorded in 1-second resolution, so it's theoretically possible that two changes could occur at the same time. In that case, which change is accepted and which is discarded is arbitrary. I suspect that whichever originating domain controller has the greater GUID value wins in these cases, and GUIDs are as arbitrary as you can get. To paraphrase an old saying, "You can pick your friends, you can pick your domain names, but you can't pick your GUIDs."

Password Changes and Urgent Replication

The previous password example is actually somewhat misleading. In reality, Active Directory treats changes to password attributes differently from other changes. When a password attribute is updated on a domain controller, it immediately notifies the domain controller that is serving as the PDC operations master for the forest.

When the user attempts to log on with a newly assigned or blank password, the local domain controller checks its local copy of the *user* object. If the password matches, the user is verified. However, if the password does not match, the local domain controller refers to the PDC operations master to verify the user. Since the PDC operations master was updated immediately, the new password will be accepted. Readers experienced with Windows NT or Windows 2000 network administration will notice that until normal replication occurs, both the old and new passwords will authorize the user.

Another type of replication is known as *urgent replication*; it is trigged by security-sensitive changes. Like password changes, urgent replication does not respect predefined schedules or site links when communicating with replication partners. The following types of operations trigger urgent replication:

- Locking out a user account

- Changing the Local Security Authority (LSA) secret

- Changes to the relative identifier (RID) manager, which assigns roles to particular domain controllers

Forcing Replication

It's rarely necessary for a directory-enabled application to force a replication between domain controllers and sites. One exception is when changes have been made to the schema. It's desirable to ensure that all domain controllers get these changes as soon as possible. There are multiple ways you can initiate a replication. One way you can force a particular domain controller to replicate with a specific domain controller or all of its replication partners is by using the *DsReplicaSync* or *DsReplicaSyncAll* API functions. Network administrators and developers using scripting languages can use the Repadmin tool from the Windows 2000 Support Tools set to force a replication.

Active Directory Components

The components that make Active Directory work are relatively simple. Active Directory includes a special database to store directory data and components to manage access to the directory itself from a variety of clients. Figure 2-11 shows the basic components of Active Directory on a domain controller.

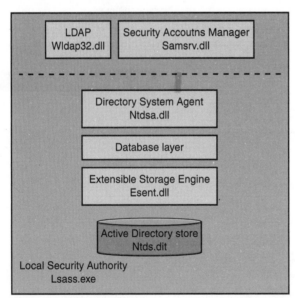

Figure 2-11 Components of Active Directory on a domain controller.

Developers working with Active Directory do not necessarily have to understand the ins and outs of the various Active Directory components. In fact, developers are purposely isolated from these details. However, an understanding of how Active Directory works as a whole will always be a benefit when creating robust, high-performance applications.

Directory System Agent

DSA, LSA

The *directory system agent* (DSA) is a collection of services and processes that run on each Windows 2000 domain controller. It's primary function is as an interface between clients requesting directory data and the directory database, known as the *store*.

The DSA executes as part of the LSA subsystem. The LSA is responsible for ensuring security for the local machine. The DSA depends on the LSA to provide security for Active Directory. Clients, both local and those external to the domain controller, access the DSA using a variety of protocols: LDAP, the Lightweight Directory Access Protocol, is the primary means for clients to interact with Active Directory. Finally, the DSA communicates with other domain controllers using remote procedure calls (RPCs).

The DSA also provides a number of Win32 APIs for local and remote clients to use. These APIs start with *DsXXX* and provide a wealth of management functions. I'll discuss some of the available APIs as we need them throughout this book. From a programming perspective, access to Active Directory will be exclusively through LDAP and provided by the Active Directory Service Interfaces (ADSI) components, which I'll introduce in Chapter 3.

Security Accounts Manager

For compatibility with older clients, Active Directory provides a translation layer. Since the Security Account Manager is now part of Active Directory, clients that use the SAM APIs are routed to the Security Accounts Manager, which translates the request for the DSA to fulfill. This mechanism ensures that older clients still function with Windows 2000 domain controllers.

Database Layer

Clients do not communicate directly with the database layer. It sits between the data store and the DSA and provides for an object-like view of the directory store. Information in the store is contained in database-like records that correspond to objects, with columns that correspond to attributes. Clients using Active Directory see an object-oriented, hierarchical view of the directory that is provided by the database layer. The database layer also applies consistency checks to new objects added to the directory and ensures that they comply with the schema in use. As a performance enhancement, the schema is loaded into a *schema cache,* an in-memory copy of the schema, while the DSA and database layer are running.

Extensible Storage Engine

The Extensible Storage Engine (ESE) is the component of Active Directory that actually stores data in and retrieves data from a physical file. Programmers familiar with Microsoft database technology might recognize ESE as the database foundation from Microsoft Exchange 4.0 and 5.0/5.5. This technology was also known as the Microsoft Jet Database Engine. Because of its replication features, the ESE technology is also used by the file replication service (FRS) and other components of Windows 2000.

The ESE maintains an Indexed Sequential Access Method (ISAM) table–driven database that supports transactions to ensure safe database operations. The database contains two tables: a link table for linked attributes such as the *memberOf* attribute, and the much larger data table for the rest of the Active Directory information. The actual file that the ESE writes for Active Directory is Ntds.dit (which stands for Windows NT Directory Services, Directory Information Tree), contained in the %SystemRoot%\NTDS folder of the domain controller.

The ESE also writes log files that are used for transaction rollback and database recovery purposes. These are circular files and are always allocated 10 MB of space. Every 12 hours, a garbage collection process runs on the domain controller. The purpose of this process is to delete unused log files and defragment the database file. This online defragmentation does not reduce the database file size, but rearranges the data to keep empty records in large blocks. Using the Ntdsutil tool (discussed later in this chapter), you can perform an offline defragmentation that will reduce the size of the Ntds.dit file.

How Big Is Active Directory?

Are you wondering how large the Ntds.dit file could get for a large company? The book *Building Enterprise Active Directory Services,* published by Microsoft Press, provides a look at a sample company storing the following types of objects in Active Directory: 100,000 users, 100,000 computers, 10,000 groups, 10,000 printers, and 10,000 volumes. The size of the resulting Ntds.dit is about 1,400 MB, or 1.4 gigabytes! This is with minimal attributes set on the objects. In Chapter 9, I'll discuss the effect of extending Active Directory with your own objects and attributes.

Examples of Services That Use Active Directory

At this point, Active Directory might seem like some sort of super-charged database, and it performs that role very well. However, Active Directory does much more than store names and phone numbers and replicate changes to this information as they are made. For application developers, Active Directory opens the new world of *service publishing*.

Network Services

One of the network services is file sharing, which allows users to access and modify files from a centralized location from any workstation. In the past, a user was required to know a long string (for example, \\copper1\documents), known as a *share*, that identified the location of files. Inflexibility resulted because the string contains the name of the specific computer (copper1) that hosts the files. What happens if the file location is moved? The same problem occurs with shared printers.

Windows 2000 solves this problem by publishing file and printer services in Active Directory. Instead of having to know a particular file share or printer path, a user can search the directory using keywords, as shown in Figure 2-12.

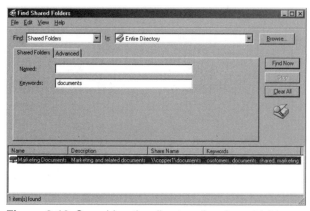

Figure 2-12 Searching the directory for shared folders.

Other network services can also publish information in Active Directory. In addition, because Active Directory is fully distributed, the services themselves are more easily distributed, making the network more service oriented than machine oriented.

Dynamic DNS Service

Another service that uses Active Directory is the Domain Name System (DNS) service. Active Directory relies on DNS to perform object lookup referrals, but the Windows 2000 implementation of DNS can use Active Directory to maintain DNS records. As I described earlier in the chapter, if the DNS service is configured to integrate with Active Directory, the resource records that bind a computer name to a TCP/IP address are stored in the directory. Previous implementations of DNS used host files—long text files with resource record entries. Updating DNS meant manually distributing revised versions of the text files to other hosts. By integrating DNS into Active Directory and using its built-in replication capabilities, updating is automatic and easy to manage. Microsoft refers to this implementation as *Dynamic DNS*.

IntelliMirror Service

Another Windows 2000 feature that uses Active Directory to publish its services is IntelliMirror, a service that makes network management easier. IntelliMirror is designed to help end users and network administrators with the task of configuring new machines, installing software, and managing user preferences. It provides the following features:

- User Data Management
- Software Installation and Maintenance
- User Settings Management

User Data Management ensures that users' documents and files follow them regardless of what machine they use. The users' My Documents folder and other folders are redirected to a network server. Placing the users' data on a server means that local storage requirements are eased and disaster recovery is enhanced because servers are backed up on a regular basis. (End users—including me—are notorious for not backing up their machines.) The users' data is not only stored on the server, but it is also synchronized to the local hard disk, providing a backup in case network connectivity is lost. The synchronization occurs transparently to the users and is configurable.

Since the data follows users, it makes sense to ensure that their applications also follow them. The Software Installation and Maintenance feature of IntelliMirror allows administrators to publish applications to a user or assign applications to a user or computer. Published applications are made available through Add/ Remove Programs in Control Panel. This gives users the option to install the software themselves. Assigned applications, on the other hand, are advertised on the computer, meaning that users see the application icons on their desktop, but initially the software is not installed. When a user runs an assigned application the first time, the software is installed from the network.

Since documents and applications follow users, it makes sense to ensure that the users' preferences or settings also roam. User Settings Management makes sure that user preferences follow the individual regardless of what workstation the network user is currently working from. Things like favorite Web sites, cookies, and color preferences are stored in a user profile and kept on a designated server.

All these IntelliMirror services are enabled via Active Directory and a *group policy.* A group policy defines a set of rules or policies that concern what users can and cannot do with their computers. Administrators use polices to provide a consistent environment for users. A *group policy object* (GPO) contains one or more policies to be enforced. GPOs are linked to objects in the directory to enforce the polices. For example, a GPO can enforce a Windows setting that prevents users from using the Run command on the Start Menu. GPOs can control a vast number of settings. A in-depth discussion of group policy is outside of the scope of this book. To learn more, refer to the *Windows 2000 Server Resource Kit.*

A wonderful example of how IntelliMirror can improve a user's productivity can be drawn from my own experience when I began writing this book. Here at Copper Software headquarters I have set up my network and laptop to utilize IntelliMirror. When I need to travel, I can simply pick up my laptop and go. By using a virtual private networking (VPN) connection to tunnel into the Copper Software network over the Internet, the laptop synchronizes the data it needs and makes my project documents and files available. When I return home, I have a painless transition back to my primary workstation, which picks up the synchronized changes to the documents.

> **Note**   When developing applications for Active Directory, it's important that you be a good network citizen by making your application work well with IntelliMirror. By using the Microsoft Windows Installer technology, you can make your applications easy to deploy. Never assume that user data or settings will be in a fixed location. If your application looks up the user's current My Documents path and statically stores that location, the application will fail or begin to behave improperly if that path is changed in the future.

Tools for Active Directory

When working with Active Directory, either as a developer or network administrator, there are various tools at your disposal. This section presents a brief summary of some of the tools available for Active Directory. I've mentioned a few of these already.

Administrative Tools

Windows 2000 contains a number of tools to manage Active Directory. They include Active Directory Domains and Trusts, Active Directory Sites and Services, and Active Directory Users and Computers. Domains and Trusts is used to administer trust relationships. Sites and Services is used to administer replication, and Users and Computers is used to administer objects in the domain partition of Active Directory. These tools are snap-ins for Microsoft Management Console (MMC) and are automatically installed on an Active Directory–enabled server. To remotely manage Active Directory, you must install the Windows 2000 Administrative Tools package (Adminpak.msi). This package can be installed from the I386 directory of the Windows 2000 Server or Windows 2000 Advanced Server CD-ROM. Once installed, these tools are accessible from the Control Panel by choosing Administrative Tools, as shown in Figure 2-13.

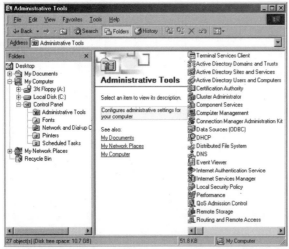

Figure 2-13 Administrative Tools folder showing icons for Active Directory Domains and Trusts, Active Directory Sites and Services, and Active Directory Users and Computers snap-ins.

> **Tip**   Some of the Active Directory snap-ins have options that control what information is presented; these options are set from the View menu in MMC. Developers and administrators should consider enabling the Advanced Features option in the Active Directory Users and Computers snap-in, which will allow containers and objects that are hidden by default to be seen. Specifically, any object that has the *showInAdvancedViewOnly* attribute set to TRUE will be hidden unless Advanced Features is enabled.

Active Directory Schema

A useful tool that is not listed in the Administrative Tools folder is the Active Directory Schema snap-in for MMC that allows you to view the Active Directory schema. Although this tool is installed with the other Active Directory snap-ins, it's not listed on the menu in order to prevent causal users from browsing the schema. To run this tool, type *schmmgmt.msc* in the Run dialog box. You can also run this tool by adding the Active Directory Schema snap-in to MMC. If the Active Directory Schema snap-in is not listed as an available snap-in, you might need to register the schema component by running Regsvr32.exe schmmgmt.dll. Figure 2-14 shows how the Active Directory Schema snap-in looks.

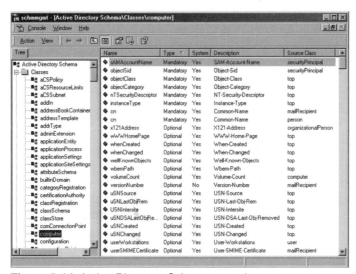

Figure 2-14 Active Directory Schema snap-in.

Creating Custom Consoles

Throughout this book you'll see screen shots of consoles. *Consoles* are collections of administrative tools that use the Microsoft Management Console (MMC) architecture. The MMC application allows anyone to add *snap-ins* or other extensions to the user interface. When developing an application for Active Directory, you might find it convenient to group all the Active Directory–related snap-ins in one console. To create your own console, follow these steps:

1. To start MMC, type *mmc* in the Run dialog box.

2. Choose Add/Remove Snap-In from the Console menu.

3. Click Add.

4. Select an Active Directory snap-in, and then click Add for each snap-in you want to add to the current console.

5. Click Close when you are finished, and then click OK.

6. To change the console name, console mode, or specify other options, choose Options on the Console menu.

7. To modify the console view, choose Customize on the View menu.

8. When you've finished, choose Save from the Console menu to save this console as an .msc (console) file. You can place this file anywhere in your system.

All the supplied snap-ins are located in the System32 folder where Windows 2000 is installed (usually C:\Winnt\System32). This folder is part of the default search path so all the snap-ins can be executed from a command prompt or from the Run dialog box. For quick access to a particular snap-in without launching a custom console, type the name of the snap-in in the Run dialog box. The following are some commonly used snap-ins and their corresponding console file names:

Active Directory Domains and Trusts	domain.msc
Active Directory Sites and Services	dssite.msc
Active Directory Users and Computers	dsa.msc
Active Directory Schema	schmmgmt.msc

ADSI Edit

The ADSI Edit tool is another snap-in for MMC that allows you to browse the directory partitions easily and retrieve attribute-level information from objects using the Active Directory Service Interfaces (ADSI), discussed in Chapter 3. You can also use ADSI Edit to create new directory objects without using the user interface of the other Active Directory snap-ins. This tool is installed with the Windows 2000 Support Tools (Support\Tools\Setup.exe) on the Windows 2000 Server or Windows 2000 Advanced Server CD-ROM. You can run ADSI Edit by selecting it from the Windows 2000 Support Tools folder on the Programs menu or by adding the ADSI Edit snap-in to MMC. Figure 2-15 shows the ADSI Edit snap-in.

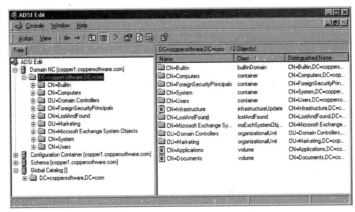

Figure 2-15 ADSI Edit snap-in.

Ldp

The Ldp tool allows you to perform low-level LDAP operations—such as connect, bind, search, modify, create, and delete—against any directory that supports LDAP. (I'll discuss LDAP in more detail in the next chapter.) Like ADSI Edit, this tool is installed with the Windows 2000 Support Tools (Support\Tools\Setup.exe) on the Windows 2000 Server or Windows 2000 Advanced Server CD-ROM. You can run Ldp by selecting Active Directory Administrative Tool (a misnomer) from the Windows 2000 Support Tools folder on the Programs menu or by running Ldp.exe. This tool is helpful when debugging difficult problems with Active Directory, but using it requires a through knowledge of LDAP. Figure 2-16 shows how Ldp looks.

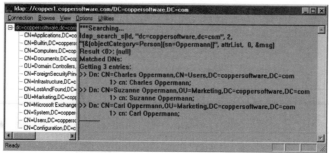

Figure 2-16 Ldp.exe.

Ntdsutil

Ntdsutil is a powerful command-line tool that allows you to perform various administrative tasks for Active Directory. Ntdsutil allows administrators to maintain the Active Directory data store, perform restoration of directory data, create new domains, and control the various operation master roles. Additionally, you can use Ntdsutil to configure the LDAP policies for a server, such as how many connections are allowed at one time. Ntdsutil is installed by default with Windows 2000 in the Winnt\System32 folder. Figure 2-17 shows Ntdsutil in action.

> **Note**   Some people use Ntdsutil to configure the LDAP policy for page size. This is not a good practice. The LDAP policy for page size controls how many results are returned at one time by the server when queried. By default, Active Directory will return up to 1,000 objects that match the search criteria. This is known as a results page. Each page is a block of records that match the query. When the application wants the next page, it requests it from Active Directory and the process continues. Pages are useful to ensure that no single application ties up the Active Directory with large searches. However, using pages adds some complexity to simple search programs. Don't be tempted to increase the default page size of an Active Directory server, particularly a server that is acting as the global catalog. Instead, use page-enabled searches, as discussed in Chapter 5, "Searching Active Directory."

```
C:\WINNT\System32\cmd.exe - ntdsutil                               _ □ ×
C:\>ntdsutil
ntdsutil: ?

?                              - Print this help information
Authoritative restore         - Authoritatively restore the DIT database
Domain management              - Prepare for new domain creation
Files                          - Manage NTDS database files
Help                           - Print this help information
IPDeny List                    - Manage LDAP IP Deny List
LDAP policies                  - Manage LDAP protocol policies
Metadata cleanup               - Clean up objects of decommissioned servers
Popups %s                      - <en/dis>able popups with "on" or "off"
Quit                           - Quit the utility
Roles                          - Manage NTDS role owner tokens
Security account management    - Manage Security Account Database - Duplicate SI
D Cleanup
Semantic database analysis     - Semantic Checker

ntdsutil: domain management
domain management: connections
server connections: connect to domain coppersoftware.com
Binding to \\copper1.coppersoftware.com ...
Connected to \\copper1.coppersoftware.com using credentials of locally logged on
user
server connections:
```

Figure 2-17 Ntdsutil.exe.

ADSI Viewer

The final tool I'll introduce is the one I find most useful in every day interaction with Active Directory. ADSI Viewer (Adsvw.exe) is part of the ADSI SDK 2.5, which is on this book's companion CD. ADSI Viewer is also a part of the Microsoft Platform SDK available from *http://msdn.microsoft.com/windows2000/*. Unlike ADSI Edit, ADSI Viewer allows searching and presents additional options for certain objects that have associated ADSI interfaces. It can also be used to communicate with other directory services and a Windows NT SAM database. Figure 2-18 shows ADSI Viewer with one window opened to a *computer* object and the bottom window showing the results of a search.

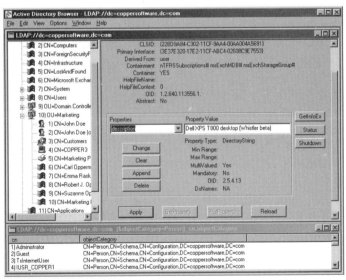

Figure 2-18 ADSI Viewer (Adsvw.exe) with object and query results shown in different windows.

Summary

Microsoft's Active Directory reflects years of experience dealing with issues of network administration and building scalable architectures. Now that we've discussed the core concepts and architecture and reviewed how Active Directory distributes directory information across the network, let's see how you write applications to access directory information.

3

Programming Interfaces for Active Directory

So far in this book I haven't presented sample source code because I wanted first to dispense information about how Active Directory is structured and provide ideas for how developers can take advantage of it. Now it's time to introduce the technologies that are used to communicate with Active Directory and write some code. In this chapter, I'll explain the various programming interfaces that developers can use with Active Directory, and I'll present some simple programs to illustrate the concepts involved in programming with Active Directory.

Incredibly Simple Sample

Using Microsoft Visual Basic Scripting Edition (VBScript) and the Windows Script Host environment built into Microsoft Windows 2000, it's easy to quickly write simple but useful scripts and programs for Active Directory. Now couple that ease with the wealth of information that Active Directory contains. The possibilities are tremendous. Listing 3-1 shows such a script, which is available on the companion CD and is named ADSIEnumTop.vbs. When you run this script, it lists the objects at the root of the Active Directory. It's just about the simplest Active Directory script you can write that is still useful.

```
' Connect to the Active Directory root object
Set adsRootDSE = GetObject("LDAP://RootDSE")

' Form a path to the top-level container of the default domain
strPath = "LDAP://" & adsRootDSE.get("defaultNamingContext")

' Display path being used
WScript.echo "Listing objects at " & strPath

' Connect to the container specified
Set adsDomain = GetObject(strPath)

' Enumerate through each object in the container
For Each adsObject In adsDomain

    ' Display the name of each object and its class
    WScript.Echo adsObject.Name & " (" & adsObject.Class & ")"

Next
```

Listing 3-1 The ADSIEnumTop.vbs sample enumerates the top-level objects in a domain's Active Directory.

Figure 3-1 shows an example of the information that will be displayed by this script when you run the command *cscript.exe adsienumtop.vbs.*

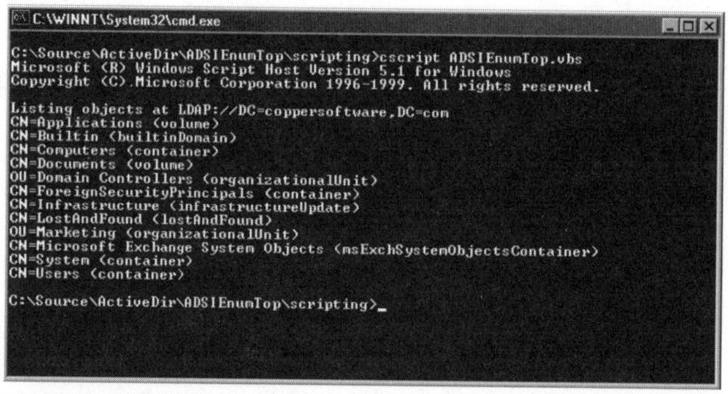

Figure 3-1 ADSIEnumTop.vbs sample output.

> **Tip**   A script for Windows Script can be executed in two ways, using the default Windows-based host or a console-based host. The Windows-based host displays dialog boxes, while the console-based host uses a command prompt window. Using a command like *cscript.exe <scriptname>* will run the specified script using the console-based host.

This simple script sets up communication with Active Directory using a special object called the *RootDSE*, which I'll discuss in the next chapter. Once connected, it retrieves the pathname of the top-level container for the directory and connects to it. The *For Each* statement instructs VBScript to step through each object in the directory at this location. The *WScript.Echo* statement displays information about the object, including its name and the type (class) of object.

The script uses seven lines of code, and almost half of them are related to setting up and displaying text. How does Active Directory accomplish this with such ease? What are the underlying technologies? I'll introduce them in the following sections.

Interfaces to Active Directory

There are two major ways to programmatically communicate with Active Directory—Lightweight Directory Access Protocol (LDAP) and Active Directory Service Interfaces (ADSI.). In the following sections, I'll provide an overview of each and describe reasons why you might choose one or the other when writing programs for Active Directory.

Lightweight Directory Access Protocol

As we discussed in the previous chapters, Active Directory is built on an LDAP foundation. The Active Directory services use the LDAP model for defining, formatting, and storing information within the directory. LDAP also defines how client applications on remote computers communicate with the directory server to read and write information in the directory.

LDAP defines and Active Directory supports nine basic protocol operations that are sent over a Transport Control Protocol (TCP) connection between the directory server and the client application. These operations are listed in Table 3-1. Most LDAP commands have a separate a request and response operation. The client makes requests of the server, and the server responds. Figure 3-2 shows how a typical LDAP session between a client and the Active Directory server works. Some operations, such as an asynchronous search, have multiple response parts, and in the case of *Unbind*, no response is necessary. This interaction is similar to what occurs between a Web browser and Web server using the Hypertext Transfer Protocol (HTTP).

Operation	Description
Bind	Initiates communication session between a client and server.
Unbind	Discontinues the session.
Abandon	Cancels any requests in progress.
Search	Searches the directory for data and returns results.
Compare	Checks whether a directory entry contains a specified attribute.
Modify	Updates a directory entry.
Add	Adds a new entry to the directory.
Delete	Removes an entry from the directory.
Modify DN (LDAPv3 only)	Renames an entry or moves an entry to a new location.
Extended (LDAPv3 only)	Used for operations not yet defined or for implementation-specific options. For example, Windows XP will use an extended operation to support dynamic directory objects.

Table 3-1 LDAP protocol operations.

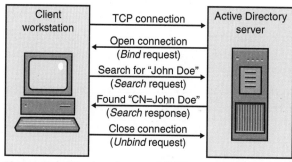

Figure 3-2 Client and server LDAP session.

Requests for Comments

The formal definition for LDAP is contained in documents known as *Requests for Comments*, or RFCs for short. RFCs have developed into a de-facto means of standardizing a technology to be used on the Internet. Many technologies and specifications, from DNS to how e-mail is passed around, are defined by RFC documents. The following is a partial listing of the important LDAP and directory related RFCs.

LDAPv3 RFCs:

- **RFC 2251**   Lightweight Directory Access Protocol (v3)
- **RFC 2252**   Lightweight Directory Access Protocol (v3): Attribute Syntax Definitions
- **RFC 2253**   Lightweight Directory Access Protocol (v3): UTF-8 String Representation of Distinguished Names
- **RFC 2254**   The String Representation of LDAP Search Filters
- **RFC 2255**   The LDAP URL Format
- **RFC 2256**   A Summary of the X.500(96) User Schema for use with LDAPv3
- **RFC 2829**   Authentication Methods for LDAP
- **RFC 2696**   LDAP Control Extension for Simple Paged Results Manipulation

Other LDAP RFCs of note:

- **RFC 1487**   X.500 Lightweight Directory Access Protocol (covers version 1, now obsolete)
- **RFC 1777**   X.500 Lightweight Directory Access Protocol (covers LDAPv2)
- **RFC 1798**   Connection-less Lightweight X.500 Directory Access Protocol
- **RFC 1823**   The LDAP Application Program Interface
- **RFC 2247**   Using Domains in LDAP/X.500 Distinguished Names
- **RFC 2377**   Naming Plan for Internet Directory-Enabled Applications

The Internet Engineering Task Force (*http://www.ietf.org*) reviews and approves all RFC documents.

How a client generates the LDAP request operation is entirely up to the developer of the application. A crude way to do this is to use low-level networking functions to form LDAP messages and send them over the TCP connection. More commonly, a developer will use a higher-level programming interface provided by the operating system or a third-party. To increase acceptance of their protocol, the creators of LDAP also defined a client interface for the C programming language. Eventually this definition became RFC 1823, "The LDAP Application Program Interface."

Microsoft provides an implementation of the LDAP API as part of Windows. This API conforms to RFC 1823 and is contained in the Wldap32.dll module. It contains a number of functions that can be used to communicate with LDAP servers. Listing 3-2 shows a C language LDAP application that searches for top level objects in Active Directory.

```c
#include <windows.h>
#include <stdio.h>
#include <winldap.h>

void main( )
{
    PLDAP pldapSession;  // LDAP session data
    PLDAPMessage plmsgSearchResponse;  // Server allocated response to
                                       // search request
    PLDAPMessage plmsgEntry;  // Server allocated response to entry request
    PCHAR pszDN;  // LDAP distinguished name string
    PCHAR* ppszDomainDN = NULL;  // Domain DN (string allocated by LDAP
                                 // library)

    // Start an LDAP session to nearest LDAP server
    pldapSession = ldap_init( NULL, LDAP_PORT );

    // Authenticate using user's current credentials
    ldap_bind_s( pldapSession, NULL, NULL, LDAP_AUTH_NEGOTIATE );

    // Search the root of the LDAP server
    ldap_search_s ( pldapSession,  // Session handle
                NULL,  // Location to start search, NULL specifies top
                       // level
                LDAP_SCOPE_BASE,  // Search only the root entry (rootDSE)
                NULL,  // Search for all objects (only one for the
                       // RootDSE)
                NULL,  // No attributes specified, return all attributes
                FALSE,  // Return attributes types and values
```

Listing 3-2 The LDAPEnumTop.c sample connects to Active Directory and searches for top-level objects.

```
                            &plmsgSearchResponse );   // Server allocates and fills
                                                      // with search results


// Using the defaultNamingContext attribute, get the distinguished
// name of the domain
ppszDomainDN = ldap_get_values( pldapSession, plmsgSearchResponse,
    "defaultNamingContext");

// Display info
printf("Listing objects at %s.\nPress CTRL+C to interrupt.\n",
    *ppszDomainDN);

// Search first level of root container
ldap_search_s ( pldapSession,   // Session handle
                *ppszDomainDN,   // Location in directory to start search
                LDAP_SCOPE_ONELEVEL,   // Search first level below the
                                       // base entry
                NULL,   // Search for all objects
                NULL,   // No attributes specified, return all attributes
                FALSE,   // Return attributes types and values
                &plmsgSearchResponse );   // Server allocates and fills
                                          // with search results


// Get the first entry from the search results
plmsgEntry = ldap_first_entry( pldapSession, plmsgSearchResponse );

while ( plmsgEntry ) {
    // Get the distinguished name of the entry
    pszDN = ldap_get_dn ( pldapSession, plmsgEntry );

    // Print the DN of the entry
    printf("%s\n", pszDN);

    // Get next entry
    plmsgEntry = ldap_next_entry( pldapSession, plmsgEntry );
    }

// Instruct the library to free the search results
ldap_msgfree( plmsgSearchResponse );

// Free string allocated by the LDAP API
ldap_value_free ( ppszDomainDN );

// Close the session
ldap_unbind( pldapSession );
}
```

> **Note** If you are running Windows 2000, I recommend installing at least Service Pack 1. SP1 fixed several problems with Wldap32.dll. For other versions of Windows, be sure that the Active Directory Client located on this book's companion CD and on the Windows 2000 CD-ROM is installed to provide current LDAP support.

Figure 3-3 shows an example of the information that will be displayed by LDAPEnumTop.c.

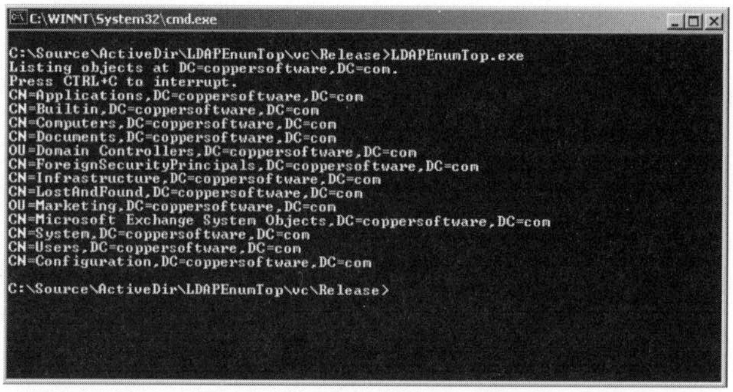

Figure 3-3 LDAPEnumTop.c sample output.

Benefits of the LDAP API

By far the greatest benefit of the LDAP API is that it provides low-level access to directory information. This access is extremely fast and requires little overhead. Compared to actually coding network messages to talk to an LDAP server, the LDAP API is a godsend.

The LDAP API also provides portability between platforms. You can take LDAP code to nearly any platform, and as long as there is an implementation of RFC 1823, the LDAP code should compile and work correctly.

Disadvantages of the LDAP API

While the LDAP API provides very low-level support, it is not object oriented, and it uses the same set of operations for all types of directory entries. Since the API is designed for C (not C++) programming, it's extremely difficult to use the API in other programming environments. There are some C++ LDAP classes available that give the LDAP API more of an object-oriented feel, but these classes are provided by third parties and aren't part of the API itself. Microsoft solves these disadvantages, not with a C++ class library, but with a COM-based solution called *Active Directory Service Interfaces*.

Active Directory Service Interfaces

Since the introduction of OLE version 2 and the Component Object Model (COM) in 1993, Microsoft has created many software technologies based on COM. A sampling of these technologies includes ActiveX Data Objects, Collaborative Data Objects, and Microsoft Active Accessibility. All provide COM objects that encapsulate functionality rather than C-language APIs that are monolithic and can be difficult to use in other programming languages.

To that end, Microsoft provides the Active Directory Service Interfaces (ADSI), which is the COM-based, object-oriented means to work with a variety of directory services, including Active Directory. Through a flexible architecture, ADSI can work with open directories based on LDAP or closed directories such as the Novell Netware bindery or the Windows NT Security Accounts Manager (SAM). The architecture can also be customized to allow ADSI-aware applications to access specialized data. This frees up the application developer from having to worry about network protocols or a specific programming interface.

Behind the scenes, the magic of working with multiple directories is made possible with ADSI's *provider* architecture. Similar to hardware device drivers, ADSI providers support standard interfaces between directory services and the applications that wish to work with them. Figure 3-4 shows the relationship between the various directory pieces. At the top are the client applications that request directory information from ADSI. The providers plug into ADSI and communicate with the respective servers. How these providers communicate with their directories is completely hidden from the client application developer. Authentication is accomplished the same way between all the providers, resolving a major headache as new encryption technologies (and the hackers to defeat them) appear.

The following sections describe the features of ADSI.

Directory Independence

ADSI can work with a variety of directory services, including LDAP, Windows NT SAM, and Novell Directory Services (NDS). While this book concentrates on Active Directory, the process of migrating applications to Active Directory might involve programming with existing and legacy directories already in use. ADSI supports the following providers:

- **LDAP** Works with any LDAP-compliant directory, including Active Directory

- **GC** Same as the LDAP provider but uses a different server port number to access the global catalog (GC) on Active Directory

- **WinNT** Used to access information stored in the SAM database on Windows NT

- **NDS**   Supports Novell Directory Services

- **NWCOMPAT**   Supports Novell NetWare 3.x versions

- **IIS**   Access to the Internet Information Services (IIS) metabase. This provider is not part of the ADSI libraries but is installed with IIS on machines running Windows NT or Windows 2000. Programmatic administration of all IIS features is accomplished with this provider.

In addition to the providers mentioned above, developers can create their own providers to allow applications using ADSI to access proprietary information stored in a directory or directory-like database. Since this book is about Active Directory, and there is already a provider available, I won't be talking about customized ADSI providers. If you'd like to read more about them, refer to the ADSI Software Developers Kit (SDK) on the companion CD.

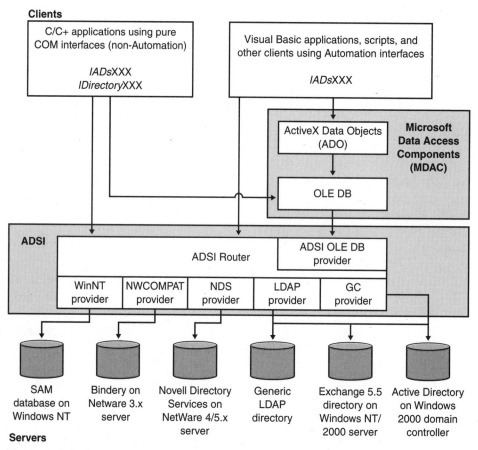

Figure 3-4 ADSI component architecture.

Providing Providers

In keeping with the provider spirit, ADSI also includes a provider for OLE DB to allow access to supported directories from any application that understands OLE DB. The programmatic name of the ADSI OLE DB provider is *ADsDSOObject*. If you have used ADO, you are familiar with OLE DB. Whereas ADSI provides a common set of interfaces to work with a variety of directories, OLE DB provides a common set of interfaces to work with data from multiple sources. This means you can use the same database technology, such as OLE DB and ADO, to access information in both a SQL database and in Active Directory. This functionality is extremely helpful when linking data stored in a SQL database and within Active Directory or when moving data from separate databases into Active Directory. It's important to note that the ADSI OLE DB provider is read-only; that is you can only use it to get information from Active Directory, not to update Active Directory. For that you must use the regular ADSI interfaces. I'll cover the ADSI OLE DB provider in more detail in Chapter 5.

Language and Technology Independent

ADSI can be used with various languages. Most ADSI interfaces support Automation (formally known as OLE Automation), which allows languages compatible with COM to access directory objects. These languages include Microsoft Visual Basic, Microsoft Visual Basic Scripting Edition (VBScript), and Microsoft JScript. Developers writing Web-based applications using either VBScript or JScript with Active Server Pages (ASP), for example, can access directory information without having to download binary code onto the client computer. C and C++ developers can choose between using the Automation interfaces or calling the object properties and methods directly. In this book, the sample applications are primarily C++, Visual Basic, and VBScript. See the upcoming "What This Book Uses" section for additional information.

ADSI supports technology independence as well. For example, ActiveX Data Objects (ADO) can be used to query and filter, but not to write directory information.

Extensible

Starting with version 2.5, ADSI includes extensibility interfaces that developers can use to further integrate their applications with directory services supported by ADSI. For example, when a new user is added to a directory, a human resources application can be invoked and can provide prompts for specific information. Active Directory has its own extension mechanism that is different from the ADSI method. In Chapter 9, I'll cover extending the Active Directory schema.

Relationship Between ADSI and Active Directory

People often confuse ADSI and Active Directory (which is understandable given their names), so being clear about the relationship between the two technologies is important because they are completely independent. We know already that ADSI can work with any directory service, thus it is not dependent on Active Directory. However, the reverse is also true: Active Directory does not depend on ADSI for programmatic access, as our LDAP sample at the start of the chapter proves. That sample uses the basic LDAP API to communicate with Active Directory.

Unfortunately, Microsoft's documentation in this area is not helpful. Since ADSI is a technology that's separate from Active Directory, its documentation is rather generic to any directory service. The Active Directory documentation, particularly material in the *Windows 2000 Server Resource Kit*, often forgets that ADSI exists and uses LDAP terms and tools based on the LDAP API. Neither is wrong, but this mix of tools and terminology can cause hours of frustration for developers searching for answers.

Deciding on the Best Interface

Both ADSI and the LDAP API have advantages and disadvantages. The following sections present various factors to consider when deciding which interface works for your situation.

The Programming Language Makes a Difference

For developers using C and C++, the choice of interfaces requires some consideration. Using the Windows LDAP API is straightforward, albeit sometimes primitive, whereas programming using the ADSI COM interfaces from C and C++ can be nightmarish to the uninitiated. However, if you are familiar with other COM components, such as ADO, working with ADSI will seem familiar and natural.

For other programming languages, using ADSI is a no-brainer, with one caveat. The language you use must support the Automation feature of COM, which Microsoft-provided languages do. Automation (discussed more thoroughly in the section "Automation" later in this chapter) is the mechanism that allows scripting languages such as VBScript and JScript to access the functionality in COM objects. Other scripting languages, such as Perl, PHP, and Rexx, are also available and can access ADSI objects.

Microsoft's Java development environment, Visual J++, works well with ADSI. However, other Java tools might not support the required COM interfaces, and Microsoft's support for Visual J++ is waning given the current push toward a new language named C# (pronounced *C sharp*) and the past legal battles with Sun Microsystems over implementation specifics.

> **Note**   JScript is Microsoft's implementation of the JavaScript language and has very little in common with the Java programming language. Specifically, JScript is the implementation of the standardized ECMAScript Edition 3, or ECMA 262, programming language. JScript is very popular in client-side HTML scripting, whereas VBScript is more popular for server-side scripting.

Platform Considerations

A deciding factor for C and C++ developers could be the client platform. ADSI is strictly a Windows-based technology. Even though Active Directory runs only on Windows 2000 servers, the information contained in a domain's Active Directory can be accessed from any platform—Windows or not—that has a network connection to the domain.

If you are creating an application that must run on Macintosh or UNIX-based systems, ADSI can't be used. If you anticipate porting your application to a non-Windows platform, you might want to use the Windows LDAP API initially on Windows. Since other operating systems have RFC 1823 implementations of the LDAP API, the porting process might be easier.

ADSI Can Be Used Regardless of Platform

Even though ADSI is only available for Windows, users of other platforms can still benefit from it. By using server-side applications such as Active Server Pages and writing ADSI code that runs on the server, the Web browser becomes a platform-independent front end to the directory application.

For companies with large investments in UNIX-based engineering workstations, this approach might be a better solution than writing separate client applications for each platform. See Chapter 11 for more information.

Performance

As a systems-level programmer, I'm always wary of technologies and languages that isolate developers from the underlying details. Usually my concern is with performance—what overhead am I paying for an object model? When I learned that the LDAP provider in ADSI calls the LDAP API functions to accomplish its work, I immediately thought that by calling those functions directly my applications would achieve a large performance boost, at the expense of a nice object model and language support. I'm happy to report that the performance overhead of ADSI is minimal. Since ADSI is an in-process COM component, method calls and property access in C and C++ are almost the same as calling a function directly.

With ADSI, performance can actually be improved over the lower-level LDAP API in some cases by caching object attribute data. In general, performance is not hampered significantly by using ADSI rather than making direct calls to the LDAP API library.

Documentation and Resources

Another consideration is the learning curve for the developer along with documentation and sample source code. Microsoft's documentation for developing with Active Directory is geared toward using ADSI. The majority of resources and sample code available use ADSI. While a number of excellent books on programming with LDAP are available, most focus on working with any LDAP directory and do not address Active Directory specifically. If you are unfamiliar with both LDAP and COM programming, I suggest that you dive into COM, as the knowledge gained will be beneficial in working with other Windows technologies now and in the future.

What This Book Uses

If you haven't already guessed, I'm an advocate of using ADSI to work with Active Directory, but I'm biased because I've been working with COM since it was originally introduced and have created my own COM objects and interfaces that ship with Windows. Trust me when I say that ADSI is easier to use and more powerful.

Also, developers no longer work in one language, and business solutions are rarely provided in a single monolithic application. This situation is a major reason for Microsoft's push toward language-independent object models and is reflected in my approach in this book.

With the exception of the LDAP sample presented earlier in this chapter, in this book I'll use ADSI from within Visual C++, Visual Basic, and Windows

Script. Note that I didn't say *programming languages*. ASP and Windows Script include engines for VBScript and JScript and can support other languages, such as Perl. When using a scripting language, I use VBScript.

But First ... a COM Primer

In practice, COM greatly reduces the amount of effort that a developer must make to get a technology working. ADSI uses the COM foundation to provide access to directory data. If you don't understand the fundamentals of COM, ADSI is going to seem unwieldy.

As I mentioned, I've been working with COM for years, and when I started, the only documentation available was two thick programmers' guides that were notorious for containing errors. I thought I understood COM after working with it for a while, but not until I created the *IAccessible* interface for Microsoft Active Accessibility did I feel I had mastered it.

Therefore, it's worthwhile to spend some time reviewing how COM works, especially with regard to ADSI and Active Directory. Even if you've been working with objects in the past, and even if you know what *QueryInterface* does, review the next several topics and brush up on COM.

> **Note**   There are several excellent books to help developers understand COM. I recommend *Inside COM* by Dale Rogerson (Microsoft Press, 1997) and *Inside Distributed COM* by Guy and Henry Eddon (Microsoft Press, 1998). Another excellent text is *Essential COM* by Don Box (Addison-Wesley, 1998).

What Is COM?

Simply put, COM is a specification that defines how binary components can communicate. Software applications tend to be monolithic, meaning large and inflexible. COM is designed to allow applications to be broken up into *components*, each component providing a set of functionality that can be reused. Components expose one or more COM objects, with each object providing some functionality.

An object, according to my dusty old copy of Ian Sommerville's *Software Engineering, Third Edition* (Addison-Wesley, 1989), is "An entity which has state and a defined set of operations to access and modify that state." This definition of an object holds true for COM's object-oriented model. A COM object encapsulates data and the code needed to modify that data into a single entity.

The data is the state of the object. Figure 3-5 shows two COM objects hosted in a component. The component is the vehicle for COM objects and is typically a dynamic-link library (DLL) or an EXE.

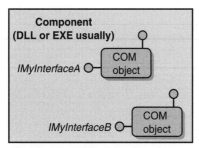

Figure 3-5 COM objects hosted in a component.

You're probably thinking, "What's so special about components? Aren't Windows DLLs the same thing as components?" (If you are thinking that, give yourself five points. There may be a test later.) There are many ways to logically separate functionality. Windows DLLs are one such way. What's special about COM is that it also specifies a strict and immutable standard for the way COM objects communicate. With a Windows DLL, you have to know at compile time what functionality is available from the DLL that you want to use for your application. Furthermore, if the DLL should change by adding new functionality, your application might fail to run because the address it used to link to the DLL would probably be different in the new version. COM solves this problem by making a "contract" of sorts between the application and the COM objects. This contract is called an *interface*.

COM Interfaces

A COM interface is the external means by which applications access the data and functionality of an object. COM objects can have more than one interface, each with a different set of operations. Each interface has a number associated with it called the Interface Identifier (IID). This number is a globally unique identifier (GUID) and is guaranteed to be unique among all computers forever. This 128-bit number is generated by the creator of the COM component and is stored in the computer registry. COM uses GUIDs to avoid naming collisions between two interfaces with the same name. Once defined, an interface cannot be changed. New interfaces can be added, but the original interface remains available. By convention, all COM interface names use mixed case and start with a capital *I*. As you can see in Figure 3-5, a COM interface is represented in a diagram with a lollipop shape that extends from a rectangular or box-shaped COM object—something Crispin Goswell, a Microsoft developer, calls "boxology."

From a C or C++ perspective, a COM interface is a group of related functions that has a specific memory structure. A COM interface is a pointer to a list of pointers that form the *virtual function table* or *vtable* for the object. If you're familiar with C++, you'll find that C++ classes and COM interfaces are very similar but not identical. Figure 3-6 shows a COM interface along with the corresponding memory structure.

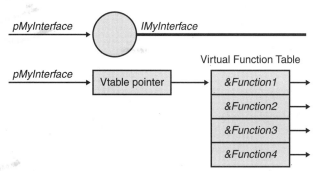

Figure 3-6 The pointer and virtual function table that make up a COM interface.

Another key point about COM interfaces is that they can inherit from one another. The derived interface inherits all the function definitions that are part of the original interface. However, COM does not support implementation inheritance and only supports interface inheritance, meaning that COM does not bring along the function code that implements the interface itself.

> **Note**   It is possible to reuse the code available in an existing COM object by having the new interface simply call the methods in the old interface to perform the requested action or by exposing the old interface as one of the interfaces in the new COM object. These techniques are known as containment and aggregation.

As defined by the COM specification, all interfaces for COM objects must inherit from an interface named *IUnknown*. In diagrams of COM objects, the *IUnknown* interface typically appears as a lollipop on top of the COM object. (See Figure 3-5.) *IUnknown* implements only three methods, *AddRef, Release*, and *QueryInterface*. The *QueryInterface* method allows an application to request any other interface that might be available from the object. *AddRef* and *Release* are used to determine when the COM object should be deleted from memory by using a reference counting technique.

Methods and Properties

As in an object-oriented model, COM objects support the concept of methods and properties. A method represents some action that an object can perform, whereas a property represents a unit of state data for an object. Applied to COM, the interface functions that perform some operation are known as *methods* and interface functions that read or modify state data are known as *properties*. Each property typically has two functions, one for reading the data (*get_*propertyname) and one for writing or modifying the data (*put_*propertyname).

Automation

Programs using Visual Basic, VBScript, and JScript can still access the functionality available in COM objects, but they do not have to concern themselves with the various COM interfaces. The mechanism that interpreted scripting languages such as VBScript and JScript use to access COM objects is named *Automation* (originally known as *OLE Automation*). Automation allows applications to call interface methods at run time without having to know the details of the object before hand. This feature is known as *late binding*, and while very flexible and lightweight, it does impose a performance penalty.

Automation is built on the COM foundation and specifies that a COM object support the *IDispatch* interface. Although a complete description of *IDispatch* is beyond the scope of this book and is a topic in itself, it can be summarized as follows: The *IDispatch* interface, composed of four methods, is constructed in such a way that a client can use this single interface and its supporting technologies to access any Automation compatible method implemented by a COM object. The four methods in *IDispatch* are *GetTypeInfoCount*, *GetTypeInfo*, *GetIDsOfNames*, and *Invoke*. These methods are used by the application hosting the Automation object to discover and use the functionality provided by the object.

Here's an example of Automation. When a VBScript program requests a property of an object, it uses a statement similar to this:

```
strName = myObj.Name
```

In this example, the program is requesting the value of the *Name* property of the object referenced by *myObj*. When this line is executed, the scripting engine calls the *GetIDsOfNames* method of the object's *IDispatch* interface, passing the string *"Name"* as a parameter. The object returns a number that is associated with the *Name* property. This number is known as the *dispatch identifier* (DISPID).

VBScript then passes the number to the *Invoke* method of *IDispatch* and requests the property value. The *Invoke* method uses the DISPID to figure out which method to call. Internally, the correct function, *get_Name*, is called to retrieve the information. VBScript will then assign the value retrieved to the variable named *strName*. If the VBScript statement was written *myObj.Name = "Carl"*, VBScript would call *Invoke* requesting the property be updated. Internally, this call maps to *put_Name* with the string *"Carl"* as a parameter.

C and C++ applications can use the *IDispatch* methods as well, but there is little reason to. With compiled languages, the exact property or method being requested is known at compile time. Instead of looking up the DISPID and then using *Invoke*, the compiler simply writes the exact address of the vtable into the program code. This mechanism is known as *early binding* and imposes very little overhead on performance. Since objects are generally loaded in the same address space as the application, calling the interface method through the vtable is like calling any other function. Even the latest versions of Visual Basic (5.0 and later) can perform early binding by referencing a file, called a *type library*, with the object and interface definitions.

COM Example

A good example of a COM component is a spelling checker. There was a time when both e-mail programs and word processing programs came with separate spelling checkers, each with its own, and usually different, dictionary. By placing the functionality of a spelling checker in a component, you can ensure that the code that verifies spelling and utilizes the dictionary can be reused by any application.

In our spell-checking component, only one object is exposed. It represents the spell-checking session and contains state data such as the current word being checked and information about the dictionary. Our simple spell-checking component could expose an interface named *ISpellCheck*, with methods named *CheckSpelling* and *AddWord*. A single read-only property, *WordsAdded*, would be defined for this interface, indicating the number of words added to the dictionary.

After developing and releasing the spell-checking component, we might want to update the *ISpellCheck::CheckSpelling* method by adding a parameter that specifies the language to be used. Since *ISpellCheck* cannot be modified after it's been published, the developer of the spell-checking component could create a new interface, named *ISpellCheck2*, that defines a *CheckSpelling* method that accepts the language parameter. Older applications would continue to work fine with the original interface, and new applications could take advantage of the new functionality and use *ISpellCheck2* instead. Figure 3-7 shows a representation of our spell-checking object.

> **Note**   Interface methods in documentation typically use C++ syntax, for
> example *ISpellCheck::CheckSpelling (parametertype name)*

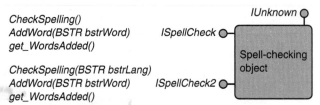

CheckSpelling()
AddWord(BSTR bstrWord)
get_WordsAdded()

CheckSpelling(BSTR bstrLang)
AddWord(BSTR bstrWord)
get_WordsAdded()

ISpellCheck

ISpellCheck2

IUnknown

Spell-checking
object

Figure 3-7 A spell-checking COM object, which has the original *ISpellCheck* interface
and the new *ISpellCheck2* interface.

Accessing Objects

The final item I want to cover in this overview of COM components is how to
actually get a reference to an object and access its interfaces. There are dozens of
ways to create objects or references to an existing object. Describing each method
is beyond the scope of this brief introduction, but I'll cover the most basic cases.

C and C++

Normally, C and C++ programs use the COM function *CoGetObject* to get a reference to an existing object. By providing a class identifier (CLSID), COM looks
up the object class in the registry, loads the proper file, and activates the object.
A CLSID is a GUID that uniquely identifies an object. If the calling program has
requested an interface other than *IUnknown*, COM calls *QueryInterface* on
IUnknown with the IID and returns a pointer to that interface to the caller.

The process for creating a new object is somewhat easier: an application
uses the *CoCreateInstance* function supplied by COM. Unlike binding to an
existing object, this creates a new object based on the object class requested.
Once you have a pointer to an interface of an object, you can access all the
exposed functionality of that object.

> **Important**   Regardless of how an interface to an object is obtained, the
> calling program is expected to call the interface's *Release* function to
> allow the object to clean up after itself.

Listing 3-3 shows a C++ sample that creates and uses the Microsoft Agent COM object.

```
#include <comdef.h>  // C++ compiler COM support
#include "AgtSvr.h"  // Microsoft Agent support
#include "AgtSvr_i.c"  // Microsoft Agent class and interface IDs

int APIENTRY WinMain(HINSTANCE hInstance,
                     HINSTANCE hPrevInstance,
                     LPSTR     lpCmdLine,
                     int       nCmdShow)
{
    HRESULT hResult;
    _variant_t varPath;
    _bstr_t bstrSpeak;
    _bstr_t bstrPlay;
    long lCharID;
    long lRequestID;
    IAgentEx *pAgentEx;
    IAgentCharacterEx *pCharacterEx = NULL;

    // Initalize COM
    CoInitialize(NULL);

    // Create an instance of the Microsoft Agent
    hResult = CoCreateInstance( CLSID_AgentServer,
                                NULL,
                                CLSCTX_SERVER,
                                IID_IAgentEx,
                                (LPVOID *)&pAgentEx);

    // Was object created?
    if ( SUCCEEDED( hResult ) )
        {
        varPath = "merlin.acs";

        // Load the merlin character
        hResult = pAgentEx->Load( varPath, &lCharID, &lRequestID );

        if ( SUCCEEDED( hResult ) )
            {
            // Get the IAgentCharacterEx interface
            pAgentEx->GetCharacterEx( lCharID, &pCharacterEx );
```

Listing 3-3 The COMAgent.cpp sample demonstrates the capabilities of COM.   *(continued)*

Listing 3-3 *continued*

```
        // Display the character
        pCharacterEx->Show( FALSE, &lRequestID );

        // Instruct the character to talk
        bstrSpeak = "COM just looks like magic.";
        pCharacterEx->Speak( bstrSpeak, NULL, &lRequestID );

        // Instruct the character to perform an action
        bstrPlay = "DoMagic2";
        pCharacterEx->Play( bstrPlay, &lRequestID );

        // Repeat, with a different phrase and action
        bstrSpeak = "Now let's learn about Active Directory!";
        pCharacterEx->Speak( bstrSpeak, NULL, &lRequestID );

        bstrPlay = "Reading";
        hResult = pCharacterEx->Play( bstrPlay, &lRequestID );

        // Wait 17 seconds to allow the Agent to finish
        Sleep(17000);

        // Stop any motion and hide the character
        hResult = pCharacterEx->Stop( lRequestID );
        hResult = pCharacterEx->Hide( FALSE, &lRequestID );

        Sleep( 5000 );
        }
    }

// Clean up
if ( pCharacterEx )
    {
    // Release the character interface
    pCharacterEx->Release();

    // Unload the character
    pAgentEx->Unload( lCharID );
    }

// Release the Agent
if ( pAgentEx )
    pAgentEx->Release();

// Unload COM
CoUninitialize();

return 0;
}
```

Visual Basic and Scripting Languages

Getting and creating objects from within Visual Basic and scripting languages is much easier than in C and C++. C and C++ developers must worry about interface pointers and releasing those interfaces; developers using Visual Basic and scripting languages are relieved of this responsibility.

To get a reference to an existing object in Visual Basic and the scripting languages you can use the *GetObject* function. To instantiate a COM object that does not already exist, you must first create the object. Visual Basic and VBScript provide the *CreateObject* function to instantiate new objects. Visual Basic developers can also create instances of objects using the *As New* option of the *Dim* statement. Developers working with JScript can create new COM objects using the *new* operator coupled with the supplied *ActiveXObject* object. Here are some examples:

```
Visual Basic/VBScript:
    Set objAgent = CreateObject("Agent.Control.2")
Visual Basic:
    Dim objAgent As New Agent.Control.2
JScript:
    objAgent = new ActiveXObject ("Agent.Control.2")
```

In all these examples, the result is a new object of the class *Agent.Control.2* and a reference to it stored in the variable *objAgent*.

Listing 3-4 shows the same Agent sample discussed in the previous section, but written in VBScript. What does it do? Well, run the COMAgent.vbs sample on the companion CD on a machine running Windows 2000 and find out!

```
Set objAgent = CreateObject("Agent.Control.2")
objAgent.Connected = True
objAgent.Characters.Load "Merlin"
With objAgent.Characters("Merlin")
   .Show
   .Speak "COM just looks like magic."
   .Play "DoMagic2"
   .Speak "Now let's learn about Active Directory!"
   .Play "Reading"
   WScript.Sleep 17000
   .Stop
   .Hide
   WScript.Sleep 5000
End With
```

Listing 3-4 The COMAgent.vbs sample demonstrates the capabilities of COM.

Now let's learn about Active Directory!

ADSI and COM

Now that we have some background on COM, let's take another look at ADSI from a COM perspective.

What Is an ADSI Object?

In most cases, when I refer to ADSI or an Active Directory object, I'm referring to a representation of a directory entry. I tend to use the term *directory entry* when referring to the unit of data stored in the directory—independent of how that data is accessed. The term *directory object* refers to the ADSI representation of a directory entry. Each directory entry is made up of one or more *attributes*, which are the named properties of the object and represent pieces of data stored in the directory object. In many cases an attribute may contain lists of data, with each piece of data known as a *value*.

You might think that there are two objects, one on the client side and the other on the server, but that isn't the case. The ADSI object always "exists" on the client, specifically in the address space of the process that requests the object. ADSI is known as a COM *in-process server*. The relationship between a directory entry and a directory object, shown in Figure 3-8, becomes apparent when changing the property value of an object. The properties are changed locally, but they must be committed before they are written to the directory and other clients can access the new values.

ADSI Interfaces

An ADSI object has multiple interfaces, some of which are specific to the class of directory entry being represented. For example, the *IADsUser* interface is available for directory objects representing a user. One interface I'll use in many of the examples in this book is the *IADs* interface. This interface provides the set of properties and methods applicable to all directory objects. In Chapter 6, I'll discuss the specifics of the *IADs* interface.

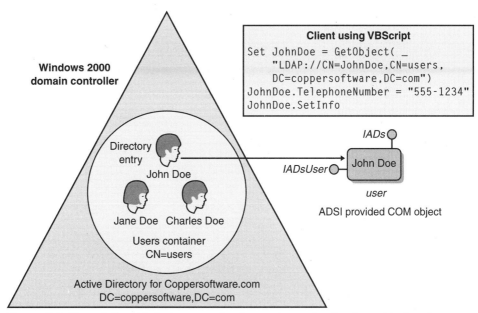

Figure 3-8 The relationship between a directory entry and a directory object.

All ADSI objects representing directory entries support the *IADs*, *IADsContainer*, *IADsDeleteOps*, *IADsObjectOptions*, *IADsOpenDSObject*, *IADsPropertyList*, *IDirectoryObject*, and *IDirectorySearch* interfaces in addition to specific interfaces. Which interfaces are available depends on the type of directory object being represented and the provider being used. Table 3-2 contains a list of ADSI interfaces available to directory objects when a program uses the LDAP provider to communicate with Active Directory.

Interface	Description
IADs	Used to identify the current object and to get and set property values. This interface is discussed in Chapter 6.
IADsClass	Used to manage the definition for a class, including identifying values, the type of class, properties for the object, inheritance settings, container settings, and help information. This interface is discussed in Chapter 9.
IADsContainer	Used to enumerate objects in a container and for creating, deleting, copying, and moving objects in a container. This interface is discussed in Chapter 6.

Table 3-2 ADSI interfaces for directory objects.   *(continued)*

Table 3-2 *continued*

Interface	Description
IADsDeleteOps	Used to delete the current object and any contained objects.
IADsGroup	Used to manage a *group* object, including adding and removing objects to the group and testing an object for membership in the group. This interface is discussed in Chapter 10.
IADsLocality	Used to manage a *locality* object. This interface contains properties related to the physical location of a network resource.
IADsMembers	Used to enumerate the members of a group. This interface is discussed in Chapter 10.
IADsO *IADsOU*	Interfaces used to manage *organization* and *organizationalUnit* objects. An *organization* object is supported but not used by default in Active Directory. An *organizationalUnit* is a special form of container used to group related objects.
IADsObjectOptions	Used to control various options of the LDAP provider.
IADsOpenDSObject	Used to supply a security context when binding to a directory object. This interface is discussed in Chapter 4.
IADsPrintQueue *IADsPrintQueue-Operations*	Interfaces used to manage printers on the network. A *printQueue* object exposes both interfaces used to identify and control a printer's job queue.
IADsProperty	Used to manage the definition of an attribute, including the object identifier, syntax, minimum and maximum range, and whether the attribute is multivalued. This interface is discussed in Chapter 9.
IADsPropertyEntry *IADsPropertyList* *IADsPropertyValue* *IADsPropertyValue2*	Family of interfaces used to examine the properties and values of a directory object. (Even though it has a similar name, the *IADsProperty* interface is different and is not part of the *IADsPropertyXXX* family of interfaces.) These interfaces are discussed in Chapter 7.
IADsSyntax	Used to get and set the Automation data type that represents the data. This interface is discussed in Chapter 9.
IADsUser	Used to manage a *user* object, including getting and setting user information, specifying the groups that this user belongs to, and changing the user's password. This interface is discussed in Chapter 10.
IDirectoryObject	Provides non-Automation clients with a low-overhead way to access directory objects. This interface is discussed in Chapter 7.
IDirectorySearch	Provides non-Automation clients with a low-overhead way to search Active Directory. This interface is discussed in Chapter 6.

The other ADSI interfaces are used for utility purposes or to conveniently manage data types. ADSI includes a large number of data type interfaces, but the LDAP provider only supports a subset of them. A list of those interfaces and objects is shown in Table 3-3. I'll discuss these objects and interfaces as needed.

Interface	Category	Description
IADsDNWithBinary	Data type	Interface to a *DNWithBinary* object. Used to map a GUID to a distinguished name.
IADsDNWithString	Data type	Interface to a *DNWithString* object. Used to associate a string with a distinguished name.
IADsExtension	Extension	Interface used to extend ADSI functionality.
IADsLargeInteger	Data type	Interface to a *LargeInteger* object. Used to manipulate 64-bit integers.
IADsSecurityDescriptor *IADsAccessControlEntry* *IADsAccessControlList*	Security	Interfaces to manage security and access-control objects. These interfaces provide a convenient means to work with the various Windows security data types.
IADsADSystemInfo	Utility	Interface to an *ADSystemInfo* object. Used to get system information about the local computer. Only available on Windows 2000; it is not supported on Windows NT, Windows 98, or Windows 95. This interface is briefly mentioned in Chapter 9.
IADsNamespaces	Core	Used to manage the installed ADSI providers. Interface to a container of namespaces available from installed providers.
IADsNameTranslate	Utility	Interface to a *NameTranslate* object. Used to translate object and account names into various formats.
IADsPathname	Utility	Interface to a *Pathname* object. Used to parse path strings into various formats.
IADsWinNTSystemInfo	Utility	Interface to a *WinNTSystemInfo* object. Used to retrieve Windows NT–style information on a computer running Windows 2000. Requires Windows 2000 or Windows NT 4 with the Active Directory Client. Not supported on Windows 95 or Windows 98.

Table 3-3 Other ADSI objects and interfaces.

Summary

This completes the overview of LDAP, ADSI, and COM. Remember that you can access information in Active Directory using either the LDAP API or the ADSI interfaces. Choosing between LDAP and ADSI depends on a number of factors, including which programming language you're using to develop your application, the platform your application will run on, and performance considerations. I recommend using ADSI because of its support of COM. If you are familiar with COM, you'll be able to work with ADSI without much trouble. Now it's time to dive into how to use ADSI to access information stored in Active Directory. We'll start covering that topic in the next chapter.

Part II

Programming with Active Directory

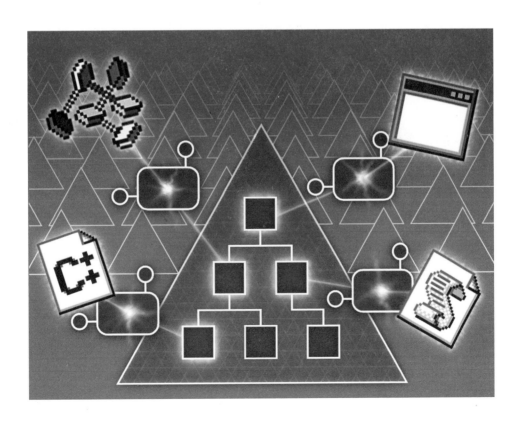

4

Connecting to Active Directory

Our focus now turns to using Active Directory with Active Directory Service Interfaces (ADSI). In this chapter, I'll describe how to use ADSI to connect to Active Directory and bind to directory objects. I'll touch on some security topics, particularly authentication. Building on the COM primer presented in Chapter 3, I'll provide more information about various ADSI interfaces and show how they are used in different programming languages. If you are familiar with Lightweight Directory Access Protocol (LDAP) programming, you'll find many of the terms similar because of the LDAP foundation that Active Directory and ADSI are built on.

Step by Step

When faced with learning a new technology, I generally want to know the process for working with it. What's the first step I have to take? What's the next? Often times, programming books and software development kits throw a bunch of information together in a seemingly random order, and not until you understand the whole do you know what specific steps to take to be productive.

The process for working with Active Directory is straightforward. Let's say you are creating an application to look up a person's telephone number in the directory and possibly change some personal information. Here is a sketch of the steps that application would follow (the terms that Active Directory and ADSI use are shown in bold).

1. Prompt the user for the name to look up.

2. **Bind** to the directory and provide authentication information if necessary.

3. **Search** the directory for entries that have the specified name.

4. **Get** the returned object's properties, in this case the telephone number and other information, possibly the full name of the person.

5. Display the information to the user and gather any changes.

6. **Put** changes into the directory object's properties.

7. **Set** changes to the object, recording them in the directory.

That covers the majority of the work with Active Directory, but of course, that's not all. I left out some things that applications tend to require because this example is so simple. Here are the other operations that are typically performed with Active Directory:

■ Enumerate objects in a container.

■ Create or delete directory objects within a container.

■ List the properties of an object when they are not known beforehand.

■ Extend the directory with new classes of objects and properties

In the following sections, I'll focus on binding to the directory. In the next chapter, I'll cover searching. In Chapter 6, I'll cover how to access directory data and modify it, enumerate directory objects, and add and delete directory objects. In Chapter 7, I'll talk about how to retrieve data without knowing property names. In Chapter 9, I'll cover how to extend Active Directory with new classes and objects.

Binding

Active Directory uses the term *binding* to describe the act of connecting to a directory object. This is the important first step in communicating with the Active Directory service. If you are familiar with COM or LDAP, you probably have come across the term *binding* before. In terms of COM, binding describes the association of a variable with an object, which can include authenticating the client. In terms of LDAP, binding describes connecting to a directory server and authenticating the client.

Getting an ADSI Object

When COM binds to an object, it can do so using a text string known as a *moniker*. We use monikers all the time while working at our computers. The following are examples of monikers:

http://www.microsoft.com/adsi/

ftp://coppersoftware.com

C:\books\activedirectory\reasonsfornotmakingdeadlines.doc

LDAP://CN=John Doe,CN=Users,DC=coppersoftware,DC=com

WinNT://coppersoftware/copper1

Uniform Resource Locators (URLs) are one form of moniker and are used by Web browsers to load the correct component and go to the specified address. In Active Directory programming, COM uses monikers to figure out which ADSI provider to load by using the portion of the moniker up to the colon character (:). COM looks up the provider, either LDAP or WinNT for the examples above, and then passes the rest of the string along. The provider parses the portion of the string passed and returns an interface to the specified object.

COM makes it easy to use monikers by supplying a function named *CoGet-Object*. Given a string and the interface identifier (IID) of the requested interface, *CoGetObject* does all the moniker and binding work for us and returns the requested interface to the object specified in the string, if the object exists. *CoGetObject* is used by the *GetObject* function in Microsoft Visual Basic, Microsoft Visual Basic Scripting Edition (VBScript), and Microsoft JScript. ADSI provides a function similar to *CoGetObject* named, appropriately enough, *ADsGetObject*, for use in C and C++ applications. The *CoGetObject* and *ADsGetObject* functions are identical in functionality, and your applications can use either. Since ADSI and Active Directory documentation use *ADsGetObject*, I'll do the same in my C and C++ samples.

Object? What Object? Where?

Something that often trips up developers working with Active Directory is the vagueness of the term *object*. Does the object exist on the client only as a COM object, but on the server as a directory entry? Are there two objects—one on the server and one created locally? I like to think there is just one object that has various states depending on whether it is being accessed or not.

Conceptually, directory data is stored on servers as entries in a database table, which are accessed and manipulated as COM objects. Each entry is made up of attribute values that describe the object, such as common name (*cn*) and category (*objectCategory*), among others. When the object is not being accessed by any clients, it is said to be in a *passive* state.

When we bind to the object in the directory, we are asking to transition the object from a passive state to a *loaded* state. This involves making a connection to the server, retrieving the object data, and loading it locally on the client machine. Specifically, the object data is copied to an in-memory property cache that ADSI creates in the address space of the application.

As the last step in binding, ADSI examines the object's data and determines what ADSI interfaces will be supported for clients. If, for example, the object represents a person, the *IADsUser* interface will be supported, in addition to the basic *IADs* interface. Once the data is loaded locally, the object is considered to be in the *running* state. In this state, the client can manipulate the object's data using the appropriate methods and properties of the ADSI interfaces.

It's important to remember that in the loaded and running states, a *copy* of the object is loaded locally. Changes made to the local data are not automatically sent to the server. To force updating the object data on the server, the *SetInfo* method of the *IADs* interface is called by the client. This writes any changes made locally back to the server.

These various states are conceptual, but they help to illustrate how directory data is stored, accessed, and manipulated. It's important to remember that when a client manipulates an object, it's doing so on a copy of the object that is loaded locally. In Chapter 6, I'll discuss manipulating object data, the *SetInfo* method, and the property cache in detail.

ADsPath

The string that is used to bind to a directory object in ADSI is named the *ADsPath*. It is central to many ADSI operations. The ADsPath is passed to the *GetObject* function in Visual Basic, VBScript, and JScript. C and C++ applications use the *ADsGetObject* function. These functions take the ADsPath string, call *CoGetObject*, and return a reference to a COM object representing the directory entry.

The format for the ADsPath depends on the ADSI provider being used. Here are the formats for the ADSI providers used in this book. Items between the square brackets are optional.

```
LDAP:[//hostname[:portnumber][/distinguishedname]]
GC:[//hostname[/distinguishedname]]
WinNT:[//domainname[/computername[/objectname[,classname]]]]
WinNT:[//domainname[/objectname[,classname]]]
WinNT:[//computername[,computer]]
```

The only required items are the provider name and a colon character. For example, if you want to access just the provider's namespace but not a specific directory object, you would use *LDAP:*. If anything does appear after the colon, a double-slash (*//*) must be included. The double-slash separates the provider and the namespace that the provider supplies.

The *hostname* is the name of the computer being accessed, while *portnumber* is the TCP/IP port number. These items are optional, but they allow ADSI to contact a specific server and port if need be. The *hostname* can be a NetBIOS name such as *COPPER1*, a fully qualified domain name such as *copper1. coppersoftware.com*, or a DNS address such as *209.20.250.168*. The *portnumber* is only needed when connecting to a TCP port other than the default of 389. One scenario that requires the use of a different port occurs when a Windows 2000 domain controller with Active Directory also hosts another LDAP server, such as Microsoft Exchange Server 5.5. Generally, the other server will be configured to use a different port number to prevent both servers from attempting to fulfill requests meant for the other. The WinNT provider allows the substitution of a domain name for a specific computer name. For example, the ADsPath *WinNT://COPPERSOFTWARE* will connect to the Security Accounts Manager (SAM) database on the primary domain controller (PDC) for the coppersoftware domain.

The remaining portion of the ADsPath identifies the desired object and is the bulk of the string. The object path is specific to the provider. LDAP uses a particular syntax that I'll discuss in the next section, "Distinguished Name and Relative Distinguished Name." WinNT and the other providers also have their own special syntaxes.

There are too many different combinations to cover in depth at this point, but Table 4-1 shows you some real world ADsPaths for the LDAP and WinNT providers.

AdsPath	Description
LDAP:	Returns a reference to the LDAP namespace object.
LDAP://CN=John Doe,CN=Users, DC=coppersoftware,DC=com	Gets the directory object named *John Doe* in the *Users* common name container in the coppersoftware.com domain.
LDAP://ldap.itd.umich.edu:389/ O=University of Michigan,C=us	Instructs the LDAP provider to contact the LDAP server at *ldap.itd.umich.edu* on port 389 and return a reference to the *University of Michigan* organization container object. The *C=us* portion indicates the organization is located in the United States.
WinNT:	Returns a reference to the WinNT namespace object.
WinNT://COPPERSOFTWARE	Uses the WinNT provider to return the *COPPERSOFTWARE* domain object.
WinNT://COPPERSOFTWARE/ Charles Oppermann,user	Uses the WinNT provider to return an object corresponding to the user *Charles Oppermann*.
WinNT://COPPERSOFTWARE/ COPPER1/Administrators,group	Uses the WinNT provider to reference the *Administrators* group on the *COPPER1* computer in the *COPPERSOFTWARE* domain.

Table 4-1 ADsPath examples.

Distinguished Name and Relative Distinguished Name

The samples in Table 4-1 for the LDAP provider uses the LDAP *distinguished name* (DN) format to identify the desired object. The distinguished name of any directory object is the concatenation of various names separated by commas. The name that uniquely identifies the desired object within the specified container is known as the *relative distinguished name* (RDN). The RDN of any object is a string that contains two parts: the naming attribute (which I'll discuss in more detail in the next section) and the value of the naming attribute, for example:

```
CN=John Doe
```

This RDN specifies that the *cn* attribute, also known as the *Common-Name* attribute, is the attribute that names this object. The value of the *cn* attribute is *John Doe*. Put them together using an equals sign, and you have a unique string that identifies the object within its container.

You could have another user named *John Doe* in a different container, but because the RDN of an object is unique within its container, the entire distinguished name remains unique, as you can see from these examples:

```
CN=John Doe,CN=New Employees
CN=John Doe,CN=Retired Employees
```

The comma serves the same role as the backslash in a file path, separating the names of the containers. The order of the names within a distinguished name starts with the child object on the left and moves right to its parent container object. This order is the opposite of the MS-DOS and UNIX file paths, in which the parent container is always listed on the left.

Naming Attributes

But what happens if two newly hired employees are both named *John Doe*? Well, first go out and get a lottery ticket since that's a rare event and it's your lucky day. Then simply give one user a *cn* like *John Doe #2*. The *cn* is just a way to name the object; other attributes hold the first name, surname, and full name of the user. A discussion of user naming conflicts appears in Chapter 9.

What's wrong with having just the string *John Doe* as the RDN of the object? Good question. The reason is that, just like a file system, the name of the object (or file) has to be unique within its container. You couldn't have two Readme.txt files in the same folder, nor could you have two objects named *John Doe*. With a file system, however, the extension is used to differentiate between types of files. So Readme.txt and Readme.doc are different and can coexist in the same file system directory. Active Directory does something similar by using the combination of the naming attribute and its value to form the RDN. For example, you could have an *ou* (organizational unit) named *Administrators* in the same container as a security group with the same name. What keeps them distinct and their RDNs unique is the attribute that's used to name them:

```
OU=Administrators
CN=Administrators
```

The object class defines which attribute is used as the naming attribute for instances of the class. For most Active Directory classes, the naming attribute is *cn*, so we'll be using it a lot. Table 4-2 lists the naming attributes for some common object classes. Classes other than those listed below use *cn* as the naming attribute.

Naming Attribute	Object Class
c	*Country*
dc	*Domain-Component*
l	*Locality*
o	*Organization*
ou	*Organizational-Unit*

Table 4-2 Naming attributes for Active Directory object classes.

Naming Top-Level Objects

If you're familiar with other LDAP directory servers, such as Netscape Directory Server or the LDAP server in Exchange Server 5.5, you'll notice that Active Directory uses a different convention for naming its top-level objects. The top-level object is the root container for a particular naming context, or what Active Directory refers to as a *partition*. The University of Michigan's LDAP directory has a top-level object with an RDN of *O=University of Michigan*. This means the name of the object is contained in the *organization* attribute of the object. The Exchange 5.5 LDAP directory also uses the *organization* attribute, while Active Directory does not.

Since Active Directory is tied to DNS domain structures, it uses the *dc* (*Domain-Component*) attribute as the naming attribute for objects of the *domain* class. Often times, you'll see an ADsPath that starts with something like this:

```
LDAP://DC=coppersoftware,DC=com
LDAP://DC=microsoft,DC=com
```

This syntax is a way of specifying each component of the fully qualified domain name. Child domains within a domain tree would have additional parts. You wouldn't want to have just *LDAP://DC=microsoft* because there may be a *microsoft.org*, *microsoft.uk*, or the feared *microsoft.gov*. (Just kidding!)

Objects and Containers

By the way, since there is such a strong parallel between ADsPath and file paths or URLs, I want to clarify something. Everything in Active Directory is an object, including containers of other objects. In a file system, it's natural to think of folders (C:\foo\) differently from files (C:\foo\foo.txt). In directory services lingo, even containers are objects and referenced as such. So, *DC=coppersoftware,DC=com* is actually a reference to a *domainDNS* object, which also happens to be a container for various objects, many of which are containers themselves. Container objects have attributes and contain data just like any other object in the directory.

Where the relationship between objects and containers becomes interesting is with a *computer* class object. This object contains attributes that describe a computer: its name, description, and so on. The RDN of a computer might be *CN=COPPER1* and the full DN might be similar to the following:

```
CN=COPPER1,CN=Computers,DC=coppersoftware,DC=com
```

Usually, a *computer* object isn't a container, but when a printer is attached to the computer, it becomes a container. The *printQueue* object associated with the printer is now contained by the *computer* object:

```
CN=HPOfficeJet,CN=COPPER1,CN=Computers,DC=coppersoftware,DC=com
```

Stringing It Together

To review what I've covered so far in this chapter; the ADsPath is the concatenation of the provider and the distinguished name of the object you're trying to access. The distinguished name itself is made up of the RDN of the object and is combined with the RDN of each of its parent containers, separated by commas. As I noted previously, the parent-child order is always right-to-left, which is opposite to the order in a URL or file path. The right-most RDN is always the parent of all other objects in the string.

Okay, now that we have an ADsPath string, what do we do with it? You pass it along...

Got Object?

I mentioned earlier that *GetObject* and *ADsGetObject* are the functions that applications use to have COM and ADSI perform their magic. *GetObject* is a function provided by Visual Basic and the scripting languages. Its purpose is to return an object reference to an existing COM object. It takes a string parameter—the ADsPath—that is used to determine which ADSI provider to load and what directory object to connect to.

GetObject

When you specify LDAP as the provider, COM loads the LDAP provider and hands it the rest of the string. The LDAP provider communicates with the LDAP server to retrieve the object and then returns a reference to that object. From that reference, you can call methods and access properties of the object. Listing 4-1 shows VBScript code, from the GetObject.vbs sample included on the companion CD, that uses the *GetObject* function. When you run this program, it contacts the server at *ldap.itd.umich.edu* and outputs the RDN of the University of Michigan's LDAP service.

```
' Specify the LDAP server at the University of Michigan
strADsPath = "LDAP://ldap.itd.umich.edu/
O=University of Michigan,C=us"

' Request a reference to the object
Set objADs = GetObject(strADsPath)

' Print the name of the object
WScript.Echo "The name of the object found is: " & objADs.Name
```

Listing 4-1 GetObject.vbs shows how to use *GetObject*.

To use this sample within the Visual Basic environment, substitute *Debug.Print* where *WScript.Echo* appears. That instructs Visual Basic to print information in the Immediate window. *WScript.Echo* is the Windows Script object method that displays text in a dialog box or in a console window if the script is run at the command prompt.

Objects in Visual Basic

With Visual Basic, the *GetObject* function will return a reference to the *IDispatch* interface of an object. However, by using the *Dim...As* statement, you can request that a different interface be returned. For example:

```
Dim objADs As IADs
Set objADs = GetObject("LDAP:")
Set obj = GetObject("LDAP:")
```

Since the variable *obj* is not explicitly declared, *GetObject* will return a reference to the *IDispatch* interface for the LDAP namespace object. By declaring the variable *objADs* using *Dim objADs As IADs*, the *GetObject* function returns a reference to the *IADs* interface.

When you specify the object type using *Dim...As*, it may be necessary to specify the object's type library. For ADSI objects, the Visual Basic project must reference the ADSI type library contained in the ActiveDS.tlb file. To reference this type library, click References on the Project menu and select Active DS Type Library as shown in Figure 4-1.

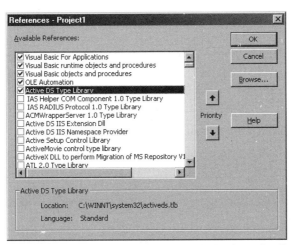

Figure 4-1 Visual Basic References dialog box showing the Active DS Type Library selected.

When Visual Basic knows about the object, based on its declaration in a *Dim...As* statement, it can provide the programmer with a list of the available properties and methods, as shown in Figure 4-2.

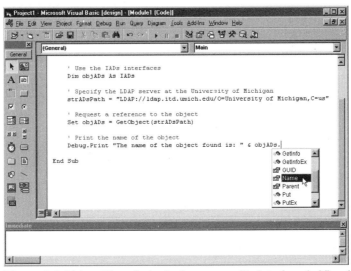

Figure 4-2 Using *Dim...As* to declare a specific interface in Visual Basic.

In addition to reducing the amount of typing Visual Basic programmers have to do, there is a performance improvement in declaring a variable using *Dim...As* with a specific interface. It allows Visual Basic to call interface functions directly. This is known as *early binding*.

When the object type is not known, Visual Basic must use a multistep process, asking the *IDispatch* interface what number (known as the *DISPID*) corresponds to a particular property or method and then calling the *Invoke* method of *IDispatch* and supplying the DISPID. *Invoke* then calls the requested method or property. This process is known as *late binding*, and while simple and effective, late binding is slower and might affect the performance of your application.

> **Note** VBScript and JScript always use late binding.

When I write Visual Basic and VBScript code, I tend to use *objADs* as the name of the variable that refers to a generic ADSI object. I use names like *objADsDomain*, *objADsUser*, and so on when referring to a specific interface. I believe in naming variables according to the object being used, so if I'm looking for users who are new employees, I might name the variable that holds the object reference *objADsNewEmployee*. Following a convention like this helps to keep track of a number of variables that might be the same data type.

ADsGetObject

The *GetObject* function is available only in Visual Basic and the scripting languages. C and C++ programmers have to use the *ADsGetObject* function, provided by ADSI. This function takes three parameters: the ADsPath string, the interface identifier for the requested COM interface, and a pointer to a pointer variable that will hold the reference to the returned object's interface. The function returns the ubiquitous COM result code, packaged in a 32-bit value known as an *HRESULT*, that contains result and error codes for COM functions.

Listing 4-2 shows code from the *ADsGetObject* sample on the companion CD, which is the C++ version of the GetObject.vbs sample presented earlier:

```
int _tmain(int /* argc */, _TCHAR /* **argv */, _TCHAR /* **envp */)
{
    IADs *pobjADs;    // Pointer to object interface
    BSTR bstrName;    // String with object name
    HRESULT hResult;  // COM result code
```

Listing 4-2 ADsGetObject.cpp shows how to use *ADsGetObject*.

```
// String to directory service
WCHAR *pstrADsPath =
    L"LDAP://ldap.itd.umich.edu/O=University of Michigan,C=us";
// Initalize COM
CoInitialize ( NULL );

// Get pointer to object's IADs interface
hResult = ADsGetObject( pstrADsPath, IID_IADs, (void**) &pobjADs);

// Check for success
if ( SUCCEEDED ( hResult ) )
    {
    // Get the Name property from the object
    hResult = pobjADs->get_Name ( &bstrName );

    // Check for success
    if ( SUCCEEDED ( hResult ) )
        {
        // Display Name property
        // (must use wide strings when working with COM)
        wcout << L"The name of the object found is: "
            << bstrName << endl;
        }
    else
        {
        wcerr << L"Error occured while getting the object  name: "
            << hResult << endl;
        }
    // When finished with the interface, call the
    // Release method to free object
    pobjADs->Release ();
    }
else
    {
    wcerr << L"Error occured while getting the object: "
        << hResult << endl;
    }

// Unload COM
CoUninitialize ();

// Return the result of any failures
return hResult;
}
```

With the scripting languages, *GetObject* always returns a reference to *IDispatch*, but with *ADsGetObject*, you can request which interface you want. For most ADSI operations, requesting the base *IADs* interface is sufficient. You can then use the *QueryInterface* method to request a different interface.

> **Note**   It's important to check the return value for all COM function calls. This is easily done with the *SUCCEEDED* or *FAILED* macros. Even if you're sure of the outcome, check the call through an *ASSERT* macro. *ASSERT*s will appear only in debug versions of your code and they ensure that your assumptions are validated. I've reluctantly omitted much error-checking code in the samples in this book in order to focus on the concepts being presented. However, your code isn't for educational purposes and will encounter many different failure scenarios. *Don't Assume—ASSERT!*

Binding Options

I often talk about Active Directory in somewhat vague terms. We know it is a database distributed to all the domain controllers within an enterprise forest. Presumably, several servers could respond to Active Directory queries. But how do you write code that talks to the appropriate server?

Serverless Binding

In many of the examples presented here, I use an ADsPath that contains *DC=coppersoftware,DC=com*, which is the distinguished name of my Active Directory domain. The LDAP provider figures out which is the closest domain controller (DC) for that domain to communicate with. Each domain can have multiple DCs, each with a replicated copy of the domain's Active Directory. Ideally, each DC is located in a particular network site that has high-speed connectivity to all the workstations in that site. (See Chapter 2 for information about subnets and sites.)

Notes on Strings in C and C++ Programs

Be aware that there are considerations when you prepare an application for an international market. Windows NT and Windows 2000 support the Unicode character set, which uses two bytes to represent a character. Windows 98 and Windows 95 use either the one-byte ANSI character set for many Western languages or the double byte character set (DBCS), also known as the multi-byte character set (MBCS), for languages that require multiple bytes to represent a single character.

To make code as portable as possible, you should use the Microsoft-specific generic-text mappings defined in Microsoft Visual C++. Generic-text mappings include definitions for various library functions so that they can be mapped at compile time to either the single-byte, double-byte, or wide-character (Unicode) variant of the function. Thus, *_tprintf* becomes *wprint* when the program is compiled with *_UNICODE* defined. This mapping extends to data types as well, so *_TCHAR chVarible* would declare *chVariable* to be a *char* (single-byte character) under ANSI, and a *wchar_t* (two-byte character) when compiled with *_UNICODE* defined. The underscore character (_) indicates that the function, macro, or datatype is not part of the Standard ANSI C/C++ language definition. Microsoft Visual C++ prefixes *_t* to all generic text macros.

To complicate matters, COM strings, including all ADSI and Active Directory strings, must be Unicode strings. That means that even if you compile the program on Windows 98 using the ANSI character set, you need to specify that the strings passed to and returned from COM functions are Unicode. For string literals in C and C++, you do this by inserting the letter *L* before the string. For example, *L"This is a wide string"* would tell the compiler to generate a Unicode string regardless of whether *_UNICODE* is defined.

I've tried to make the sample programs in this book as friendly as possible to the various platforms and character sets, but it's impossible to test under all the possible conditions. Refer to the Visual C++ documentation for more information about developing international software.

> **Note**   The exact method used to find the nearest or most suitable domain controller is complex and out of the scope of this book. ADSI and the LDAP provider use the *DsGetDcName* function, available in Windows 2000 and previous versions of Windows with the Active Directory Client (DSClient.exe) installed. The *DsGetDcName* function depends on the correct registration of DNS records in the DNS server for the network. Many difficulties faced by network administrators working with Active Directory are a result of incorrect DNS configuration or operation. If you are experiencing such problems, I recommend the *Microsoft Windows 2000 Server Resource Kit* (Microsoft Press, 2000). I also recommend articles online at *http://support.microsoft.com/support/win2000/dns.asp*.

In my network, *DC=coppersoftware,DC=com* resolves to my domain controller, *COPPER1*. The following two ADsPaths are functionally identical, retrieving the Active Directory top-level object for the coppersoftware.com domain:

```
LDAP://DC=coppersoftware,DC=com
LDAP://COPPER1
```

You should try to avoid specifying a particular server in your binding strings because doing so circumvents the built-in redundancy of Active Directory. If your application talks only to a specific server and that server is down temporarily, has been replaced, or has even been renamed, your program will fail needlessly, even though there may be another DC handling Active Directory requests.

What should you do if you don't even know the domain name, much less any server names? Active Directory has got that covered.

RootDSE

RootDSE is a special object of Active Directory that contains information about the directory service itself. *RootDSE* stands for *Root DSA-Specific Entry*. DSA is the X.500 term for *directory system agent*. *RootDSE* was introduced as part of LDAPv3 and is supported in Active Directory. Even though it is named the *RootDSE*, this object is not part of the directory tree and you cannot navigate to it. Its class and attributes are not part of the directory schema. This setup ensures that clients can access the *RootDSE* even though they might not be able to access any other part of the directory.

Using *LDAP://RootDSE* as the ADsPath binding string, you can discover a lot of useful information, such as the following:

■ The name and DNS address of the server responding

■ Versions of LDAP supported, along with any extended features, known as *extended controls*

■ The naming contexts (directory partitions) that are available on this particular server

■ The level of security and what security protocols are supported

Table 4-3 includes a complete list of *RootDSE* attributes. There are many, but you won't need to use most of them. The attribute that should interest you most at this point is *defaultNamingContext*. This attribute contains the distinguished name of the Active Directory for the current domain. You can use its value to form an ADsPath to the top-level domain object in Active Directory. The following Visual Basic function returns the Active Directory distinguished name for the user's default domain.

```
Function GetDomainDN() As String
' This function returns the distinguished name of the domain's
' Active Directory
Dim objADsRootDSE As IADs

    ' Get an IADs interface to the RootDSE
    Set objADsRootDSE = GetObject("LDAP://RootDSE")

    ' Return the naming context DN
    GetDomainDN = objADsRootDSE.Get("defaultNamingContext")
End Function
```

You can cut and paste this function into your Visual Basic programs and use it as follows:

```
Sub Main()
' Get and display the domain directory name
Dim strDomainDN As String
Dim strADsPath as String
Dim objADsDomain As IADs

    ' Get the DN for users default domain
    strDomainDN = GetDomainDN
```

(continued)

95

```
' Build ADsPath to directory
strADsPath = "LDAP://" & strDomainDN
Debug.Print "ADsPath to directory: " & strADsPath

' Access the directory
Set objADsDomain = GetObject(strADsPath)
Debug.Print "Name of the directory: " & objADsDomain.Name
End Sub
```

By always using the *RootDSE* object to discover information about the Active Directory configuration, you provide a level of flexibility in case the domain or the server name changes. Later, in the section "GUID Binding," I'll describe ways to identify objects even if they have been renamed or moved.

Attribute	Description
configurationNamingContext	The DN of the Active Directory forest configuration partition.
currentTime	Current time at the server.
defaultNamingContext	The DN of the directory partition (i.e. *DC=aviation,DC=coppersoftware,DC=com*).
dnsHostName	The DNS name of the LDAP server.
dsServiceName	The DN of the directory object that contains options for this directory service.
highestCommittedUSN	The highest update sequence number (USN). Used for directory replication.
isGlobalCatalogReady	True if this service is also a global catalog server.
isSynchronized	True or False, depending on whether this server has completed synchronizing with replication partners.
ldapServiceName	The service principal name (SPN). Used for authentication.
namingContexts	A multivalued attribute containing the DN of each directory partition (naming context) that this server contains.
rootDomainNamingContext	The DN of the top-level domain directory partition (i.e. *DC=coppersoftware,DC=com*) for the forest.
schemaNamingContext	The DN of the schema directory partition.

Table 4-3 *RootDSE* attributes.

Attribute	Description
serverName	The DN of the server processing the request.
subschemaSubentry	The DN of the object that contains information about the classes and attributes available in this service. Known as the *abstract schema* in Active Directory (discussed in Chapter 9).
supportedCapabilities	Multivalued attribute with a list of Microsoft-specific enhancements, uses object identifier (OID).
supportedControl	Multivalued attribute with a list OIDs of supported LDAP extension controls.
supportedLDAPPolicies	Multivalued attribute with a list of strings, each naming an LDAP policy for the directory service. These policies are controlled with the Ntdsutil.exe tool.
supportedLDAPVersion	Multivalued list of supported LDAP versions. Active Directory currently supports LDAP versions 2 and 3.
supportedSASLMechanisms	Multivalued list of security mechanisms supported for Simple Authentication Security Layer (SASL) negotiation. (See the LDAP RFCs.) By default, Generic Security Services API (GSSAPI) is supported.
becomeDomainMaster *becomeInfrastructureMaster* *becomePdc* *becomeRidMaster* *becomeSchemaMaster*	These operational attributes indicate that the server should take over the specified master operation role.

Note   The initial release of Windows 2000 had a problem with the LDAP module when *LDAP://RootDSE* was used as an ADsPath binding string. Service packs for Windows 2000 should fix this problem and other issues in the Wldap32.dll module. Refer to Microsoft Knowledge Base articles Q259739 and Q258507 for more information.

Global Catalog

In Chapter 2, I mentioned the global catalog (GC) as a feature that allowed for fast searches across domains. It accomplishes this by cataloging all the objects in the enterprise forest. The global catalog is not a namespace, and it does not have a hierarchy. It is simply a list of all the objects in a forest along with a partial set of attributes for those objects.

A forest represents an entire enterprise, irrespective of DNS names. Microsoft might have a forest configuration with the following trees:

microsoft.com

msn.com

hotmail.com

Each tree might have a number of subdomains, such as:

research.microsoft.com

mspress.microsoft.com

Remember that in a forest, all the domains in each tree share a common schema and configuration. That means that each domain controller replicates the schema and configuration partitions to its parent domain controller. However, the domain directory partition where objects specific to a domain reside is not replicated to parent and child domains and thus is not available across the entire enterprise.

If the domain partitions are not replicated between domains, how does my editor at Microsoft Press contact someone in Microsoft Research to verify my claims of Internet bottlenecks causing delays in submitting chapters for this book?

The Microsoft Press domain contains information only about the good, understanding, and patient folks employed in that division, like my editor, who is a pillar of patience. [Enough already – Ed.]. Searching the domain's directory partition for a colleague's e-mail address would be easy. However, the e-mail address of someone at Microsoft Research would not be contained in the Microsoft Press domain directory.

One possible solution would be to replicate the domain partitions for the forest to all the domain controllers in that forest. That way, the domain controllers for Microsoft Press would contain all object information for the folks in

Microsoft Research. However, doing that is a huge replication issue and would bog down the network with continuous replication traffic and quite possibly exceed the storage of local domain controllers. It also defeats the purpose of having distributed directory partitions in the first place.

A more elegant solution is to simply place the most requested information at a location accessible to all clients. The e-mail address, along with the full name of a person, is defined as being part of the *partial attribute set* and as such is replicated to all domain controllers that are defined as global catalog servers.

Global Catalog Servers

By default, the first domain controller created in an Active Directory site is the global catalog server for that site. By placing at least one global catalog server in each site, a client can avoid having to communicate over a potentially slow link between sites. Each domain has at least one site, which is named *Default-First-Site-Name* by default. Network administrators can control which domain controllers in a particular domain are global catalog servers in order to spread query traffic among servers. You can see the structure of the global catalog in Figure 4-3.

Accessing the Global Catalog

Since the global catalog is not a logical namespace, the global catalog server separates queries between its directory partitions and the global catalog by using a special TCP/IP port for the global catalog. To query only the global catalog, a client must make the request to port number 3268 on the global catalog server.

ADSI accommodates the global catalog using *GC:* instead of *LDAP:* for the ADsPath binding string. In reality, they both use the LDAP provider, but binding with *GC:* indicates that port 3268 of the server should be used. Why not use *LDAP://servername:3268* instead? Technically that would be the equivalent to *GC://servername* because a global catalog server responds on TCP/IP port number 3268. It's best not to request a specific global catalog server. Also, ADSI will use TCP/IP port number 3269 when performing an encrypted connection to a global catalog server. By using *GC:* instead of *LDAP:*, you can let ADSI pick which ports and servers to contact.

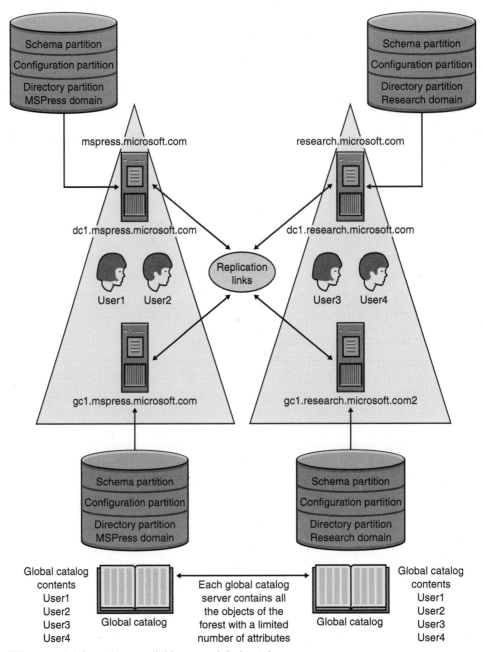

Figure 4-3 Information available on a global catalog server.

The following code snippet from the GlobalCatalog sample on the companion CD shows two methods to bind to the nearest global catalog server.

```
' Method 1 - Enumerate provider
' Bind to the global catalog root
Set objGC = GetObject("GC:")

' Enumerate the global catalog for the forest root object (can only be one)
For Each objADs In objGC
    ' Output ADsPath for global catalog
    Debug.Print objADs.ADsPath
Next

' Method 2 - Use RootDSE (faster)
' Bind to the global catalog server RootDSE object
Set objADs = GetObject("GC://RootDSE")

' Build string to forest root object
Debug.Print "GC://" & objADs.Get("rootDomainNamingContext")
```

Note that the second method uses the *RootDSE* object, which will probably be faster than the first method because it avoids the enumeration of the GC provider's container. In the next chapter, I'll show how to use the global catalog to greatly improve search speed.

GUID Binding

Another way to bind to an object in the directory is by specifying the object's globally unique identifier (GUID). Active Directory generates a new GUID for each object that it creates.

> **Note**   A GUID is a 128-bit value that, according to the gurus who invented this stuff, is guaranteed to be unique "in both space and time." I take that to mean that when my great-grandchildren are colonizing Mars, the GUIDs created by their 10-terra-bit-per-second networks will still be different from the ones my Active Directory creates.

A string representing a GUID takes the place of the distinguished name of the object in the ADsPath. Hexadecimal notation is used for each of the 16 bytes that make up a GUID. For example:

```
LDAP://<GUID=A8FCE7118CCE6647B69BB62C1B3F0DCA>
LDAP://copper1/<GUID=A8FCE7118CCE6647B69BB62C1B3F0DCA>
```

By using the object's GUID, as opposed to its name, you can locate an object even if it's been renamed or moved to a different container. If Jane Doe marries Joe Smith and changes her name to Jane Doe-Smith, the RDN and distinguished name would also change:

```
CN=Jane Doe,CN=Users,DC=coppersoftware,DC=com
CN=Jane Doe-Smith,CN=Users,DC=coppersoftware,DC=com
```

The new Mrs. Doe-Smith decides to take a leave of absence, and the *user* object is moved to a different organizational unit:

```
CN=Jane Doe-Smith,OU=Employees On Leave,DC=coppersoftware,DC=com
```

Nevertheless, the GUID for this object would remain the same throughout all the changes. This is useful for keeping track of important objects in the directory.

The GUID for every object in Active Directory is stored in the *objectGUID* attribute of each object. Applications can access the *objectGUID* attribute using the *GUID* property of the *IADs* interface. Listing 4-3 shows code from the GUIDBind sample on the companion CD. It binds to an object using a supplied distinguished name, retrieves the GUID for the object, and then binds to the object again using the LDAP GUID syntax. This sample uses the *GetDomainDN* function listed earlier in this chapter.

```
Sub Main()
Dim objADs As IADs
Dim strDomainDN As String
Dim strADsPath As String
Dim strGUID As String

    ' Get the DN for user's default domain
    strDomainDN = GetDomainDN()

    ' Get the DN of the object
    strDomainDN = InputBox("Enter the DN of an object in the directory", _
        "GUID Binding Sample", strDomainDN)

    If strDomainDN <> "" Then
        ' Build ADsPath to object
        strADsPath = "LDAP://" & strDomainDN
```

Listing 4-3 GUIDBind.bas shows how to bind to an object using its GUID.

```
                ' Display Information
                Debug.Print "Binding using " & strADsPath

                ' Bind to the object using the the DN provided
                Set objADs = GetObject(strADsPath)

                ' Display name of the object
                Debug.Print "Name: " & objADs.Name

                ' Get the GUID string of the object
                ' Using .GUID formats the GUID as a single string
                strGUID = objADs.Guid

                ' Display the GUID property string
                Debug.Print "GUID: " & strGUID

                ' Release interface
                Set objADs = Nothing

                ' Build path to same object using the GUID
                ' Note that <GUID= > syntax is unique to Active Directory
                ' and the LDAP/GC provider
                strADsPath = "LDAP://<GUID=" + strGUID + ">"

                ' Display Information
                Debug.Print "Binding using " & strADsPath

                ' Rebind to the same object
                Set objADs = GetObject(strADsPath)

                ' Display name of the object
                Debug.Print "Name: " & objADs.Name

        End If
End Sub
```

Here is example output from the GUIDBind sample in Visual Basic's Immediate window:

```
Binding using LDAP://
        CN=Charles Oppermann,CN=Users,DC=coppersoftware,DC=com
Name: CN=Charles Oppermann
GUID: 2cc16a7e5d48b64c8c313b709edd2a18
Binding using LDAP://<GUID=2cc16a7e5d48b64c8c313b709edd2a18>
Name: <GUID=2cc16a7e5d48b64c8c313b709edd2a18>
```

This output shows that the object in the directory representing me (*CN=Charles Oppermann*) has a GUID value of *2cc16a7e5d48b64c8c313b709edd2a18*.

This output also reveals an important limitation of GUID binding. Note that when you bind using the GUID syntax and then ask for the name of the object, instead of *CN=Charles Oppermann* you get *<GUID=2cc16a7e5d48b64c8c313b709edd2a18>*.

When binding using the GUID syntax, the *ADsPath*, *Name*, and *Parent* properties of the *IADs* interface do not return the same information as they do when you bind to an object using a distinguished name string. The *CopyHere*, *Create*, *Delete*, *GetObject*, and *MoveHere* methods of *IADsContainer* are similarly unsupported when the object is bound using the GUID syntax. The reason for this quirky behavior is that the intended use of GUID binding is for high-speed, low-overhead access to the object. ADSI stays out of the way and doesn't spend time utilizing class-specific ADSI interfaces.

In case you're wondering, the *objectGUID* attribute is an *indexed attribute*, meaning that Active Directory creates an index for this attribute to improve query performance. Including the *objectGUID* attribute in this index is in addition to it being part of the partial attribute set, which ensures that the GUID of each object in Active Directory is available at every global catalog server.

Internally a 128-bit GUID is stored in a data structure. To display a GUID as a string, it must be properly converted. ADSI does allow you to retrieve a GUID as a string by providing the *GUID* property of the *IADs* interface. Since the *GUID* property retrieves the *objectGUID* value, you would expect the following lines to print the same result:

```
Debug.Print objADs.Guid
Debug.Print objADs.Get("objectGUID")
```

The first line uses the *GUID* property of the *IADs* interface, whereas the second asks ADSI to retrieve the object's *objectGUID* attribute. Here is the output:

```
2cc16a7e5d48b64c8c313b709edd2a18
????????
```

The first line prints as expected, but the question marks indicate that *Debug.Print* was not able to figure out the type of information being returned by the *Get* method. *Debug.Print* was not able to print the GUID because the *objectGUID* attribute is defined as an octet string, which is a convenient way to store binary data in Active Directory. An octet is defined as an 8-bit value (aka a byte). ADSI returns an octet string as a variant array of bytes because it does not know how to interpret the contents of an octet string.

However, in the case of *objectGUID*, ADSI can assume that the octet string in this case is 16 bytes. The code that implements the *GUID* property of the *IADs* interface retrieves the *objectGUID* data, properly formats it, and passes it back to the application as a binary string (*BSTR*). A binary string is a Unicode string in which the length of the string prefixes the actual string.

Normally, you don't have to worry about formatting *objectGUID* into a usable string because the *GUID* property does the work for you. Nevertheless, if you like to tinker, here is some code that is available on the companion CD that shows how it's done.

```
Sub DisplayGUID(objADs As IADs)
Dim strGUID As String
Dim strGUIDattr As String
Dim varGUIDpart As Variant

    Debug.Print "*** DisplayGUID ***"

    ' Note that .Get("objectGUID") will return the GUID in an array
    ' of integers
    For Each varGUIDpart In objADs.Get("objectGUID")
        ' Convert number to hexidecimal string
        If varGUIDpart < 16 Then
            ' If less than 16, then only one digit is used and must
            ' be padded with a zero
            varGUIDpart = "0" & Hex(varGUIDpart)
        Else
            ' Convert number to hexidecimal string
            varGUIDpart = Hex(varGUIDpart)
        End If

        ' Build VB-style GUID string
        strGUIDattr = strGUIDattr & "&H" & varGUIDpart & " "

        ' Build version similar to .GUID property
        strGUID = strGUID & varGUIDpart
    Next

    ' Display string
    Debug.Print "VB string: " & strGUIDattr

    ' Display the GUID property string
    Debug.Print "Binding String: " & "<GUID=" & strGUID & ">"

End Sub
```

When you call this routine, it produces output similar to the following:

```
*** DisplayGUID ***
VB string: &H2C &HC1 &H6A &H7E &H5D &H48 &HB6 &H4C &H8C &H31 &H3B &H70
&H9E &HDD &H2A &H18
Binding String: <GUID=2CC16A7E5D48B64C8C313B709EDD2A18>
```

> **Note**   The GUID returned by the WinNT provider is represented in a different form from the GUID returned by the LDAP provider for the same object. Contrary to the documentation, the WinNT provider doesn't even return the GUID of an object, but returns the GUID of the *IADsXXX* interface used to manipulate the object. In short, do not use the WinNT provider to discover the GUID of an object.

Well-Known GUIDs

Being able to find an object that's been renamed or moved by using its GUID is fine, but doing that assumes you know the GUID beforehand. Whenever a new object is created in Active Directory, a GUID is automatically generated and assigned to it. For many of the containers that form the initial structure of the directory, there is a fixed set of GUIDs. These GUIDs were created by Microsoft and are documented as *well-known GUIDs*.

Let's say that you rename the *Users* container to *Employees*. All of your applications do not have to be rewritten to use the new name; they just bind to the container using the GUID constant *GUID_USERS_CONTAINER*. Table 4-4 lists directory objects and corresponding GUID constants, which are defined in the Ntdsapi.h header file, part of the Microsoft Platform SDK.

Container	GUID Constant
Users	GUID_USERS_CONTAINER_W
Computers	GUID_COMPUTRS_CONTAINER_W
System	GUID_SYSTEMS_CONTAINER_W
Domain Controllers	GUID_DOMAIN_CONTROLLERS_CONTAINER_W
Infrastructure	GUID_INFRASTRUCTURE_CONTAINER_W
Deleted Objects	GUID_DELETED_OBJECTS_CONTAINER_W
Lost and Found	GUID_LOSTANDFOUND_CONTAINER_W

Table 4-4 Well-known objects and GUID constants.

Note   You can't directly use the well-known object GUID constants listed in Table 4-4 in Visual Basic and scripting languages because they are not listed in the Active DS Type Library. To use well-known GUIDs in Visual Basic or VBScript, include the following constants in your applications:

```
Const strUserContainerGUID = "a9d1ca15768811d1aded00c04fd8d5cd"

Const strComputersContainerGUID = "aa312825768811d1aded00c04fd8d5cd"

Const strSystemsContainerGUID = "ab1d30f3768811d1aded00c04fd8d5cd"

Const strDomainControllersContainerGUID = "a361b2ffffd211d1aa4b00c04fd7d83a"

Const strInfrstructureContainerGUID = "2fbac1870ade11d297c400c04fd8d5cd"

Const strDeletedObjectContainerGUID = "18e2ea80684f11d2b9aa00c04f79f805"

Const strLostAndFoundContainerGUID = "ab8153b7768811d1aded00c04fd8d5cd"
```

To use well-known GUIDs, a variant of the GUID binding syntax is used:

```
LDAP://<WKGUID=XXX,containerDN>
```

XXX is one of the well-known GUIDs, and *containerDN* is the distinguished name of the parent container. Unlike with regular GUID binding, when binding with well-known GUIDs you must specify a parent container, which is the *domain* object. For example:

```
LDAP://<WKGUID=a9d1ca15768811d1aded00c04fd8d5cd,DC=coppersoftware,DC=com>
```

This ADsPath would bind to the *Users* container in the coppersoftware.com domain regardless of the current name of the container. It's important to note that the same limitations of GUID binding, such as unsupported methods and different property behavior, apply to binding using the well-known GUID syntax. Generally, it's best to bind first with a well-known GUID constant, retrieve the current distinguished name of the object, and then bind again using the distinguished name. In Chapter 10, I present a sample program, CreateComputer, that illustrates this technique.

Authentication

So far I've avoided the issues of security and authentication in order to keep binding simple. Obviously, Active Directory is a secure directory—most companies don't want outsiders to come in and create lists of users or delete names. Usually only certain employees have permissions to create new objects in the directory.

Active Directory keeps a list of access permissions for each object in the directory. These permissions, which determine who can access the object, can be inherited from the parent or set individually on the object. The attributes defined in the object class also carry a list of permissions. For example, a network administrator might grant most users access to the *telephoneNumber* attribute of a *user* class object, but only certain groups of users may have access to the *homePhone* attribute.

When the *GetObject* or *ADsGetObject* functions are used in a program, ADSI sends to Active Directory the *credentials* of the calling program for authentication. Credentials are typically the user name and password for the currently logged in user. When a program is started by a user, it inherits the user's *security context*. Under Windows 2000, you can change the security context for a program you are about to run by using the RunAs command, as shown in Figure 4-4.

Figure 4-4 Executing an application in the Administrator security context.

You can also change the security context for a program you are about to run by holding down the Shift key, right-clicking the program icon, and then selecting Run As from the shortcut menu. This action displays the Run As Other User dialog box, shown in Figure 4-5, where you can specify the credentials that the selected program should use.

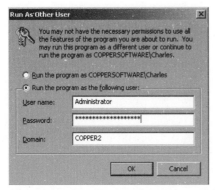

Figure 4-5 The Run As Other User dialog box displayed when Run As is chosen.

ADSI allows you to perform the same impersonation programmatically by using the *ADsOpenObject* function or the *OpenDSObject* method of the *IADsOpenDSObject* interface. Unlike *GetObject* and *ADsGetObject*, *ADsOpenObject* and *OpenDSObject* allow you to specify the user name, password, and type of security methods to be used during the session. For *ADsOpenObject*, the requested interface identifier and indirect interface pointer are the same as with *ADsGetObject*:

```
IADs *pobjADs;
HRESULT hResult;
hResult = ADsOpenObject(
    L"LDAP://CN=John Doe,CN=Users,DC=coppersoftware,DC=com",
    L"COPPERSOFTWARE\\JDoe",
    L"mypassword",
    ADS_SECURE_AUTHENTICATION,
    IID_IADs,
    (void**) &pobjADs);
```

There isn't an *ADsOpenObject* function for Visual Basic and scripting languages that depend on Automation, but ADSI does provides the *IADsOpenDSObject* interface. The *IADsOpenDSObject* interface contains a single method, named *OpenDS-Object*. This method provides a COM-based approach that has the same functionality as *ADsOpenObject*. There is no practical difference between the two functions; however, if you are working with C or C++, using *ADsOpenObject* is easier.

```
Dim objADsOpenDSObject As IADsOpenDSObject
Dim objADs As IADs

' Get any ADSI object
Set objADsOpenDSObject = GetObject("LDAP:")

' Bind using the domain\username format
Set objADs = objADsOpenDSObject.OpenDSObject( _
    "LDAP://CN=John Doe,CN=Users,DC=coppersoftware,DC=com", _
    "COPPERSOFTWARE\JDoe", _
    "mypassword", _
    ADS_SECURE_AUTHENTICATION)
```

In Visual Basic, before you can call the *OpenDSObject* method, you must already have a reference to an ADSI object. But assuming you need alternative authentication, how can you get an object before you are authenticated? This chicken-and-egg problem is solved by connecting to an object that does not require authentication in any situation. The *LDAP* object is exposed by the LDAP provider and is a container representing the LDAP namespace. This object supports the *IADsOpenDSObject* interface, and you can call the *OpenDSObject* method from it.

In two previous code snippets, I passed *COPPERSOFTWARE\JDoe* as the user name and *mypassword* as the password to be used. The user name can be specified in a number of formats, such as

user account:	JDoe
user principal name:	JDoe@coppersoftware.com
domain\username:	COPPERSOFTWARE\JDoe
distinguished name:	CN=John Doe,CN=Users,DC=coppersoftware,DC=com

Authentication Options

In the previous code snippets, I specified *ADS_SECURE_AUTHENTICATION* as the authentication type. This flag instructs the LDAP provider to use the highest level of security that can be negotiated between the client computer and the server. The LDAP client and server will negotiate the level of security they both understand, which is normally Kerberos between two computers running Windows 2000. If Kerberos security cannot be negotiated, the NTLM protocol will be used instead. In addition, you can specify data encryption options such as the Secure Sockets Layer (SSL). When using a distinguished name as the user name, you may need to use the *ADS_FAST_BIND* authentication type or set the parameter to *0*. Other authentication flags that can be used are listed in Table 4-5.

ADS_AUTHENTICATION_ENUM	Description
ADS_SECURE_AUTHENTICATION	Performs secure authentication. When connecting to Active Directory, the LDAP provider will use Kerberos if available or NTLM authentication.
ADS_USE_ENCRYPTION	Requests that ADSI use encryption for data exchange over the network.
ADS_USE_SSL	Will attempt to encrypt the communication channel using SSL. Requires that the Certificate Server be installed to support communication with Active Directory.
ADS_READONLY_SERVER	Using the LDAP provider, this flag indicates that a writeable server is not required for serverless binding. This is rarely needed with Active Directory.

Table 4-5 Authentication flags used by *ADsOpenObject* and *OpenDSObject*.

ADS_AUTHENTICATION_ENUM	Description
ADS_PROMPT_CREDENTIALS	Not used.
ADS_NO_AUTHENTICATION	Explicitly requests no authentication. Equivalent to anonymous access to the Everyone group.
ADS_FAST_BIND	When this flag is set, ADSI will only expose the base interfaces supported by all ADSI objects.
ADS_USE_SIGNING	Performs verification of sent and received data. Set in conjunction with the ADS_SECURE_AUTHENTICATION flag.
ADS_USE_SEALING	Encrypts data using Kerberos. Set in conjunction with the ADS_SECURE_AUTHENTICATION flag.
ADS_USE_DELEGATION	Allows ADSI to delegate the user's security context, which is necessary for moving objects across domains.
ADS_SERVER_BIND	Indicates the ADsPath includes a server name and allows the LDAP provider to skip a few steps when binding.

For more information on Kerberos, NTLM, and encryption, I recommend *Microsoft Windows 2000 Security Technical Reference* (Microsoft Press, 2000).

Danger, Will Robinson! Danger!

In the popular science-fiction television show "Lost in Space," when the always-curious boy, Will Robinson, was about to do something foolish, the helpful robot would warn him by waving its mechanical arms and saying "Danger, Will Robinson! Danger!" Think of me as that robot, moving my arms up and down at you with these words of caution: *Do not code the user name and password of a high-level account, such as the domain Administrator, into your applications.*

Passing alternative credentials with *ADsOpenObject* or *OpenDSObject* is convenient when the user's default credentials are not sufficient to perform a particular operation. It's tempting to place an administrator's user name and password in your application and use those credentials because administrators have broad access and the operations will rarely fail. However, I *strongly* recommend that you do not do this. The default security levels in Active Directory are well designed and allow users to manipulate their own objects without the need for greater permissions. By placing the password and user name of an account with broad permissions in your code, the risk of compromising the security of the overall network is greatly increased. Anyone with a binary editor could examine the executable program or view the source code of a scripting file to retrieve the password.

When using *ADsOpenObject* or *OpenDSObject*, you can specify that the default credentials be used, just as you do with *GetObject* and *ADsGetObject*. By specifying null as the user name and password, ADSI will instead use the security context of the current application, which is generally inherited from the user executing the program. Using *ADsOpenObject* or *OpenDSObject* and specifying null for the user name and password gives you the benefit of specifying binding options without potentially compromising security.

Security and ASP

The security risk mentioned above is especially true with Web applications. When a Web application is running under IIS, the security context is defined by the account that IIS is using. By default this account is *IUSR*_machinename. This account has limited privileges to prevent outside users from accessing network resources. A simple Web page that uses ADSI to allow users to change their own passwords would fail because the *IUSR*_machinename account does not have sufficient privileges.

Don't be tempted to use *OpenDSObject* from script code contained within Web pages; anyone who uses the View Source command in their browser will be able to see the credentials supplied. The solution is to execute the Web application in the security context of an authenticated user. In Chapter 11, I'll describe a sample Web application using Active Directory and IIS.

Performance Considerations When Binding

While making a call to *GetObject* or *ADsOpenObject* is relatively easy, internally, ADSI, COM, the client machine, and the server are performing a number of steps, from looking up DNS records to accessing the directory schema for the requested object. If your application works with a number of objects in succession, you can do a couple of things to reduce the binding overhead.

Fast Binding

When using *ADsOpenObject* or *OpenDSObject*, you can specify *ADS_FAST_BIND* as the authentication type. This flag is not really an authentication option but a directive to the LDAP provider to skip several steps in order to reduce the

binding overhead and thus improve performance. But like most performance enhancements, there is a trade-off. By specifying *ADS_FAST_BIND*, the LDAP provider will not attempt to access the object's schema information. This means that
ADSI does not know the class of the object being retrieved and the created ADSI
object will not support class-specific interfaces, such as *IADsUser*. Only the generic interfaces such as *IADs*, *IADsContainer*, *IADsPropertyList*, and a few others will be available to programs.

In addition, if you use *ADS_FAST_BIND*, ADSI and the LDAP provider will
not verify that the object requested actually exists. This saves another step. But
while *ADsOpenObject* and *OpenDSObject* will succeed, any subsequent property
or method access will fail if the object does not exist. Only use *ADS_FAST_BIND*
if you are certain the object already exists in the directory.

ADS_SERVER_BIND

Windows 2000 Service Pack 1 improves ADSI by including a handy option that
speeds access to known directory objects. Using the LDAP provider, if the binding string includes a server name, you can get better performance by using the
ADS_SERVER_BIND flag with the *ADsOpenObject* function or the *OpenDSObject*
method.

The *ADS_SERVER_BIND* flag is an option that tells ADSI not to perform a
series of steps to locate the server. Of course, since server names change, it's not
always advisable to hard code them directly into your code. The best method is
to use the *RootDSE* object and the LDAP namespace to discover the server you
want to work with at run time and then use that server name along with the
ADS_SERVER_BIND flag to achieve optimal performance.

Connection Caching

Another way of improving performance is to avoid repeatedly requesting authentication. The process of negotiating a security protocol and an encryption level
is time-consuming. Instead, keep an authenticated connection alive for as long
as you need to communicate with the same server. You do this by getting an initial
object reference, authenticating your connection to it, and reusing it as many times
as you need to. When the object is released, the connection is broken. In C and
C++, objects are released when you call the *Release* method and the reference
count for the interface goes to zero. In Visual Basic, objects are released when
the object variable is set to *Nothing*.

Summary

With this chapter, I've covered the various methods used to connect to Active Directory and access objects. Through its flexible architecture, Active Directory allows discovering and connecting securely to the most appropriate server without any prior knowledge on the part of the client. By using the global catalog and some of the binding options, you can greatly increase the performance of your application. It may seem like there is a lot to remember, but there really isn't. The vast majority of the time, you'll use the functions *GetObject* or *ADsGetObject* with few, if any options. In the next chapter, we take the process a step farther by asking the Active Directory server to search itself and return the information we're looking for.

5

Searching Active Directory

Often you need to get several pieces of information from the directory, such as the name of each person who doesn't have a telephone number listed. Other times you just need one piece of information but aren't sure where it's located. Like any database, Active Directory supports flexible searching.

In this chapter, I'll cover the search technologies for finding information in Active Directory. Searching is different from enumeration (which I'll cover in more detail in the next chapter) because in searching you're letting the server do the work for you. The client submits a query to Active Directory, the server goes through the process of finding the information and returning it, and the client processes the results. Enumeration, on the other hand, consists of retrieving an object from the server, examining its properties, and then retrieving the next object.

Search Technologies

Because searching for information is a primary function of network directories, the designers of LDAP made it a top priority. Active Directory, being a good LDAP citizen, provides excellent searching support, including some useful extensions of the LDAP specification.

This support is available to clients in various forms, the major technologies being ActiveX Data Objects (ADO) and the ADSI *IDirectorySearch* interface, both of which I'll discuss in this chapter. Generally, if you are using Microsoft Visual Basic or a scripting language, you'll use ADO technology to search Active Directory. If you're developing in C or C++, you can use ADO, *IDirectorySearch,* and other options. What's notable about the ADSI architecture is how the various technologies build on each other. The basic relationship between the search technologies is shown in Figure 5-1.

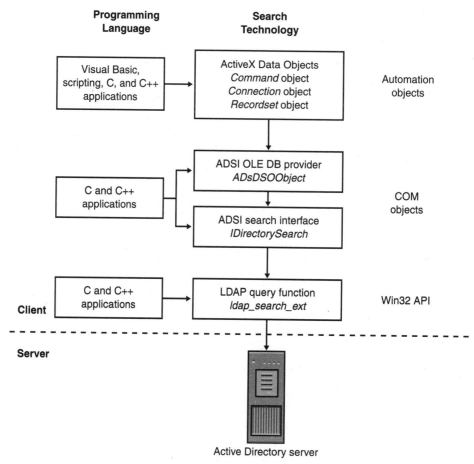

Figure 5-1 Relationships between Active Directory search technologies.

As with everything related to Active Directory, LDAP provides the foundation with the LDAP query operation. ADSI builds on this and provides the COM-based *IDirectorySearch* interface. On top of that, ADSI supplies an OLE DB provider. The formal name of this provider is the "OLE DB Provider for Microsoft Directory Services" and its programmatic name is *ADsDSOObject*. I will refer to this provider as the ADSI OLE DB provider. This provider exposes OLE DB defined interfaces that C and C++ applications can use to access Active Directory information in the same fashion as for any other database. Although similar in architecture, don't confuse the ADSI OLE DB provider with the ADSI providers for LDAP, WinNT, and others. An OLE DB provider is a component that uses OLE DB to expose data from a data source. An ADSI provider is a component that uses ADSI to expose data from a directory service.

A disadvantage of OLE DB interfaces is that they do not support Automation. In other words, they are not dual interfaces. To rectify this, Microsoft provides the set of database objects called ActiveX Data Objects. ADO is built on OLE DB, and I like to think of ADO as a high-level abstraction of OLE DB. ADO supports Automation, which allows Visual Basic and the scripting languages to access information available from OLE DB providers.

ADO uses the ADSI OLE DB provider, which in turn uses the *IDirectorySearch* interface exposed by ADSI. C and C++ applications can use *IDirectorySearch* directly, however, they lose the benefits of data source abstraction that ADO and OLE DB provide. *IDirectorySearch* provides the best performance because it is low-level and thus low-overhead.

If you are familiar with ADO or OLE DB from programming for a SQL database or even Microsoft Access and Jet databases, you'll be able to transfer that experience to searching Active Directory with ADO. In fact, you can make SQL-style queries against Active Directory.

Using the ADSI OLE DB provider does have a major limitation. It's currently restricted to read-only operations. You cannot use the SQL *UPDATE* command or any of the ADO methods that modify or delete records. This is not an issue generally because it's trivial to access the Active Directory object for updating after locating it in a search.

> **Important**   The ADSI OLE DB provider is read-only.

In the following sections , I'll cover searching Active Directory using ADO, Visual Basic, and the scripting languages. In a sample application later in the chapter, I'll demonstrate *IDirectorySearch* using C++. C and C++ developers should read the entire ADO section carefully, as many of the options and search techniques are directly applicable to *IDirectorySearch*. Of course, C and C++ developers can also use ADO or OLE DB from their applications, but they may prefer the low-level nature of *IDirectorySearch*.

A Searching Sample Using ADO and VBScript

In my opinion, the best way to teach is by example. I'll begin with a utility program that is similar to a program that was popular when I first started working at Microsoft. It pays homage to the association between Active Directory and a more traditional directory—a phone book.

This sample simply takes a last name, searches the directory for people with the same last name, and returns the full name and telephone number of the people found. For simplicity, this version is written in VBScript and is included on the companion CD. A version written in Visual Basic is also included on the companion CD.

Phone Sample

Listing 5-1 shows code from the Phone.vbs sample. Let's look at the entire program and then break it down.

```
' PHONE - Display telephone number for a specified last name
'
' Check to see if there is a command-line argument
Set objArguments = WScript.Arguments

If (objArguments.Count = 1) Then

    ' Treat the command-line argument as the name to filter on
    strPerson = objArguments(0)

Else
    ' Check to see if script is running in console
    strExecutable = LCase(WScript.Fullname)

    If InStr(strExecutable, "cscript") > 0 Then

        ' Prompt user for name
        WScript.StdOut.Write "Name to lookup (enter * for all):"

        ' Use Standard in to get name
        strPerson = WScript.Stdin.ReadLine
    Else
        ' GUI mode, use InputBox to prompt user
        strPerson = InputBox( _
            "Enter the last name of the person to lookup" & vbCrLf & _
            "(Use * to search for all people)", _
            "Lookup Telephone number")
    End If

End If

If strPerson <> "" Then
' Input box is not empty and Cancel button was not clicked
```

Listing 5-1 Phone.vbs uses ADO to search Active Directory.

```
' Build the query string
' Active Directory OLEDB Provider format has four parts separated
' by semi-colons:
' Root: which is the starting point for the search
' Filter: conditions to search on, using RFC 2254 format
' Attributes: attributes to return
' Scope: base, onelevel, or subtree for entire directory partition

' Specify the search base.
' We'll use the global catalog for performance reasons since the
' Name and Telephone number attributes are available from the GC

' First, need to discover the local global catalog server
Set objADsRootDSE = GetObject("GC://RootDSE")

' Form an ADsPath string to the DN of the root of the
' Active Directory forest
strADsPath = "GC://" & _
    objADsRootDSE.Get("rootDomainNamingContext")

' Wrap the ADsPath with angle brackets to form the base string
strBase = "<" & strADsPath & ">"

' Release the ADSI object, no longer needed
Set objADsRootDSE = Nothing

' Specify the LDAP filter
' First, indicate the category of objects to be searched
' (all people, not just users)
strObjects = "(objectCategory=person)"

' If user enters "*", then filter on all people
If (strPerson = "*") Then
    strName = "(sn=*)"
Else
    strName = "(sn=" & strPerson & "*)"
End If

' Add the two filters together
strFilter = "(&" & strObjects & strName & ")"

' Set the attributes we want the recordset to contain
' We're interested in the common name and telephone number
strAttributes = "cn,telephoneNumber"

' Specify the scope (base, onelevel, subtree)
strScope = "subtree"
```

(continued)

```
' Create ADO connection using the ADSI OLE DB provider
Set objADOConnection = CreateObject("ADODB.Connection")
objADOConnection.Open "Provider=ADsDSOObject;"

' Create ADO commmand object and associate it with the connection
Set objADOCommand = CreateObject("ADODB.Command")
objADOCommand.ActiveConnection = objADOConnection

' Create the command string using the four parts
objADOCommand.CommandText = strBase & ";" & strFilter & ";" & _
    strAttributes & ";" & strScope

' Set the number of records in the recordset logical page
objADOCommand.Properties("Page Size") = 20

' Set the maximum result size
objADOCommand.Properties("Size Limit") = 20

' Sort the results based on the cn attribute
objADOCommand.Properties("Sort On") = "cn"

' Execute the query for the user in the directory
Set objADORecordset = objADOCommand.Execute

If objADORecordset.EOF Then
    WScript.Echo "No records were found."
Else
    ' Loop through all the returned records
    While Not objADORecordset.EOF

        ' Display the row using the selected fields
        strDisplayLine = objADORecordset.Fields("cn") & vbTab

        ' Check to see if telephone number field is null
        If IsNull(objADORecordset.Fields("telephoneNumber")) Then
            strDisplayLine = strDisplayLine & "(number not listed)"
        Else
            ' Retrieve telephone number and add to line
            strDisplayLine = strDisplayLine & _
                objADORecordset.Fields("telephoneNumber")
        End If

        ' Display the line
        WScript.Echo strDisplayLine

        ' Advance to the next record
        objADORecordset.MoveNext
```

```
        Wend
    End If


    ' Close the ADO connection
    objADOConnection.Close
End If
```

You can run this sample directly from the command prompt (Cmd.exe) by typing *cscript phone.vbs*. Figure 5-2 shows an example of using Phone.vbs from the command prompt.

> **Note**   CScript is the command prompt version of Windows Script Host. Scripts executed by CScript will display their output using the command prompt window. If you include the */nologo* command-line option, CScript suppresses version and copyright information. WScript is the Windows-based version of Windows Script Host and will display output using dialog boxes. If you run Phone.vbs using WScript, each *WScript.Echo* statement will generate a dialog box.

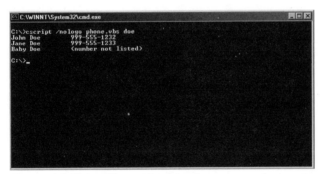

Figure 5-2 Using Phone.vbs from the command prompt.

If you just run the Phone.vbs file, it will prompt you for a name using the dialog box shown in Figure 5-3. Results are displayed, one at a time, as shown in Figure 5-4.

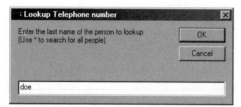

Figure 5-3 Phone.vbs prompting for input.

Figure 5-4 Phone.vbs displays each result in a dialog box.

In the following sections I'll break down this sample and explain how it connects to Active Directory and searches for information.

Gathering Input

Before getting into the details of ADO, I want to spend a moment showing off a feature of Windows Script Host. Batch files have always had the ability to examine command-line arguments, and Windows Script Host provides similar features using the *WScript.Arguments* object.

The first section of the Phone sample checks to see whether the user passed a name to search for on the command-line. Here's the code:

```
' Check to see if there is a command-line argument
Set objArguments = WScript.Arguments

If (objArguments.Count = 1 ) Then

    ' Treat the command-line argument as the name to filter on
    strPerson = objArguments(0)
```

The *Arguments* object, stored in the *objArguments* variable, is a collection of all the command-line arguments that the user enters. The *Count* property of the *Arguments* object indicates the number of arguments. If *Count* equals 1, indicating that one argument was entered after the program name on the command-line, the argument value is copied to the *strPerson* variable. Note that the *Count* property is 1-based (1, 2, 3, ...), whereas the index of the *Arguments* object is 0-based (0, 1, 2, ...).

If no argument was entered on the command-line, the sample proceeds to gather the name to be searched for by presenting a prompt to the user. If the sample is run from the Windows user interface, a dialog box is displayed (refer back to Figure 5-3) using the *InputBox* function of VBScript. While this is convenient, the *InputBox* function always uses a dialog box even if the sample is launched from the command line. However, you can detect the environment the sample is running under and adapt to that environment. Here's the code that does this.

> **Note**   With Windows Script Host, some objects and functions are provided by the VBScript or JScript engines while others are provided by Windows Script Host itself. For example, WSH provides the *Arguments* collection whereas VBScript provides the *InputBox* function. *InputBox* is not available with the JScript engine.

```
Else
    ' Check to if script is running in console
    strExecutable = LCase(WScript.Fullname)

    If InStr(strExecutable, "cscript") > 0 Then

        ' Prompt user for name
        WScript.StdOut.Write "Name to lookup (enter * for all):"

        ' Use Standard in to get name
        strPerson = WScript.StdIn.ReadLine
    Else
        ' GUI mode, use InputBox to prompt user
        strPerson = InputBox( _
            "Enter the last name of the person to lookup" & vbCrLf & _
            "(Use * to search for all people)", _
            "Lookup Telephone number")
    End If

End If
```

By checking to see whether the host is CScript.exe, you can then use the standard in (*StdIn*) and standard out (*StdOut*) streams for interaction with the user. Streams are used to redirect input and output to and from a program. Streams only work under the CScript version of Windows Script Host. If you attempt to use the *StdIn* or *StdOut* streams from WScript, Windows Script Host will report an invalid handle error. The *StdOut* stream in WSH displays output to the command prompt window. The command *WScript.StdOut.Write "Name to lookup (enter * for all):"*

is similar to the MS-DOS batch file command *ECHO Name to lookup (enter * for all):,* both of which display text in the command prompt window. The statement *WScript.StdOut.WriteLine* will display text and append a new line character as well. Similarly, by using *WScript.StdIn.ReadLine*, you can get input from the command window without using a Windows interface.

The Windows-based version of Windows Script Host is sufficient for most uses, however, I wanted to highlight the ability to truly customize your program to the environment it's running under.

Using Redirection with Streams

CScript supports the *StdIn, StdOut,* and *StdErr* streams. *StdErr* is the stream used to display error messages generated by the program being run. All the streams can be redirected from the command line using special characters. Some examples:

CScript Phone.vbs >Output.txt	Sends the output of Phone.vbs into the Output.txt file
CScript Phone.vbs >>Output.txt	Appends data to Output.txt
CScript Phone.vbs < Input.txt	Redirects input from the command prompt window and uses the text in Input.txt instead
CScript Phone.vbs 2>Errors.txt	Redirects error messages from the screen to the Errors.txt file
CScript Phone.vbs >Output.txt 2>&1	Redirects all output, including error messages, to the Output.txt file

---

Query Statement

The next portion of the sample creates the various parts of the *query statement* that will be submitted to the server. The query statement is a string that tells the server exactly what you are looking for, where to start looking for it, and what to return when it finds a match.

Given that we're using an LDAP-based directory technology combined with SQL-based data access technology, we have a choice of dialects to use when creating the query statement: LDAP or SQL.

As you would expect, the LDAP dialect is optimized toward directory data. The following is an example of a query that uses the LDAP dialect:

```
<LDAP://DC=coppersoftware,DC=com>;
(&(objectClass=user)(CN=Bob*));
ADsPath;
subTree
```

This string consists of four parts: the search base, the LDAP search filter, the attributes to return, and the scope of the search. I'll discuss each of these parts in detail in the following sections. The query statement above requests that the LDAP server for the coppersoftware.com domain examine all the *user* class objects and check to see whether the *cn* (*Common-Name*) attribute of the object starts with "Bob". It then returns the *ADsPath* attribute of all the objects meeting those criteria.

The SQL dialect, on the other hand, should look familiar to you if you've done any SQL programming. The following SQL expression is equivalent to the previous LDAP dialect query:

```
SELECT ADsPath
    FROM 'LDAP://DC=coppersoftware,DC=com'
    WHERE objectClass='user' AND CN='Bob*'
    ORDER BY sn
```

Again, this string asks the server for all the *user* objects that begin with "Bob". Using the SQL dialect, you can also specify how you want the results sorted. In this case, I used the *ORDER BY* clause to indicate that the results should be sorted by the *sn* (*Surname*) attribute. While you cannot specify a sort order directly in an LDAP dialect query string, there are other ways to get a sorted result, which I'll describe later in the section "Sorting."

Which dialect should you use? If you are using ADO or OLE DB, you can use either SQL or LDAP query statements. Just use whichever you prefer. If you are experienced with SQL queries, you might find it more convenient than the rigid LDAP search filter syntax.

Since we're talking about Active Directory, and many fine books and references already exist on SQL, I'll concentrate on the LDAP dialect for query statements in this book. However, I encourage you to use SQL if you prefer to. If you want to learn more about accessing data using SQL and ADO, Microsoft Press has a number of excellent books on Microsoft SQL Server, ADO, and database programming, including *Microsoft SQL Server 2000 Programming Step by Step,* by Rebecca Riordan, and *Programming ADO,* by David Sceppa.

If you are using *IDirectorySearch* or the LDAP *ldap_search* function directly, your only choice is to use the LDAP dialect queries.

Search Base

The first part of the LDAP query string is known as the *search base*. This ADsPath string specifies the starting point of the search. You can use whatever path you want, although it generally makes sense to reference a container object. For example, to search a particular organizational unit, you could specify the following search base:

```
LDAP://OU=users,DC=coppersoftware,DC=com
```

This statement would begin a search at the *Users* organizational unit and search only within that container. Other containers that are siblings of the *Users* container would not be searched.

More often, you want to search the entire directory, exclusive of the schema and configuration partitions. To do this, you should specify the root object of the directory partition. As I discussed in Chapter 4, various directories use different objects for the root object. For example, the University of Michigan's LDAP server uses the following distinguished name for the root:

```
O=University of Michigan,C=us
```

Normally, an Active Directory root object is the domain object and is expressed as follows:

```
DC=coppersoftware,DC=com
```

You don't need to guess the actual values, however; the *RootDSE* object provides this information in the *defaultNamingContext* and *rootDomainNaming-Context* attributes. The former will provide the distinguished name of the current domain directory partition, whereas the latter will provide the distinguished name of the forest domain directory partition.

Important Always try to use the *RootDSE* object to avoid hard coding ADsPaths and server names into your applications.

Because the Phone sample merely looks up phone numbers of users—and the *phoneNumber* attribute is a member of the partial attribute set stored in the global catalog—the sample instructs ADSI to connect to the global catalog rather than any domain controller. Doing so ensures that all the objects in the forest are searched in the most efficient manner.

```
' First, need to discover the local global catalog server
Set objADsRootDSE = GetObject("GC://RootDSE")
```

Then the sample retrieves the *rootDomainNamingContext* property of the *RootDSE* object, which is the distinguished name of the directory partition for the entire forest, not just the current domain.

```
' Form an ADsPath string to the DN of the root of the Active Directory forest
strADsPath = "GC://" & objADsRootDSE.Get("rootDomainNamingContext")
```

At this point in the sample, the variable *strADsPath* contains the root ADsPath that is used as the basis of our search. This ADsPath will be the actual root object of Active Directory, known as the domain object.

In the LDAP API, the search base is a distinguished name string. However, when using the ADSI OLE DB provider, you actually provide an ADsPath, not a distinguished name. Remember that an ADsPath string contains the ADSI provider name, *GC:* in this case, and includes a distinguished name.

To indicate to ADO that a moniker or URL (which is what an ADsPath mimics) is being passed, I wrap the ADsPath with angle brackets.

```
' Wrap the ADsPath with angle brackets to form the base string
strBase = "<" & strADsPath & ">"
```

There's no need to stay bound to the *RootDSE* object anymore, so I explicitly release the object by setting the object to the VBScript keyword *Nothing*. This removes the object from memory.

```
' Release the ADSI object, no longer needed
Set objADsRootDSE = Nothing
```

You don't need to do this for the other objects because objects are destroyed when they go out of scope. However, if you use an object early in a program and no longer need it, it's good practice to release it.

Note   For programmers using C or C++, keep in mind that Visual Basic and the scripting languages do a lot of cleanup behind the scenes that must be performed manually in a C or C++ application. When working with COM objects in C and C++, always call the object's *Release* method to instruct COM to unload the object when you are finished with it.

Search Filter

The LDAP search filter is the most complex portion of the query statement. In this part you specify the exact criteria for the search. You can use a broad range of criteria to perform extremely flexible searches. While not as readable as an equivalent SQL query, the LDAP search filter syntax is just as powerful.

> **Note**   This section covers the basic syntax for LDAP search filters. For more information, check out the definition in RFC 2254.

The LDAP search filter contains one or more strings grouped together by parentheses. Basically, the syntax goes like this:

```
(((<filtercomp1>)(<filtercomp2>) ... (<filtercompn>))
```

The *<filtercomp>* string is the combination of one or more *<filter>* strings and possibly a Boolean operator. The syntax for *<filter>* looks like this:

```
<filter1>
&(<filter1>)(<filter2>) ... (<filtern>)
|(<filter1>)(<filter2>) ... (<filtern>)
!(<filter1>)
```

Table 5-1 lists the Boolean operators.

Boolean Operator	Description
&	AND
|	OR
!	NOT

Table 5-1 Boolean operators available for LDAP search filters.

The *<filter>* string has the following syntax:

```
<attribute><comparisonoperator><value>
```

In this syntax, *<attribute>* is any attribute that might be found in the directory and *<value>* is the actual value to search for. Remember that you are searching for LDAP attributes, not ADSI properties. While these often have the same name, an attribute is the label of the data found in the directory, while a property is the label of an ADSI interface member. Keep in mind that if you misspell an attribute, the server cannot distinguish between it and an attribute that simply wasn't found. The search will be conducted, but it won't return any matches and no error will be generated.

Table 5-2 lists the comparison operators for *<comparisonoperator>*. Note that while the greater than or equal to (>=) and less than or equal to (<=) comparison operators are present, you cannot use greater than (>) or less than (<).

Comparison Operator	Description
=	Equal to.
~=	Approximately equal to. Active Directory ignores this operator and treats it the same as the Equal to (=) operator.
>=	Greater than or equal to.
<=	Less than or equal to.

Table 5-2 Comparison operators available for LDAP search filters.

The LDAP search filter syntax allows for wildcard matching using the present operator (=*) and the any operator (*). Filters that use these operators have the following syntax:

```
<attribute>=*
<attribute>=<value>*
<attribute>=<value>*<value>
<attribute>=<value>*<value>* ...
```

Search filter examples   Table 5-3 shows examples of search filter strings.

Sample Filter	Description
(objectClass=*)	Retrieves all objects. Since every object in Active Directory has an *objectClass* attribute, using the present (=*) operator will match all objects. This is the easiest way to find all the objects within a particular search scope.
(cn=Charles Oppermann)	Returns the object or objects that have a *cn* (*Common-Name*) attribute equal to "Charles Oppermann."
(!(cn=John Beach))	Returns all the objects that are *not* named "John Beach".
(sn=Oppe*)	Using the any operator (*) for wildcard matching within a string, returns all objects whose *sn* (*Surname*) attribute starts with "Oppe". This would match "Opperman," "Oppermann," and "Oppenheimer." I like this because my last name is always misspelled!

Table 5-3 Example LDAP search filter strings.   *(continued)*

Table 5-3 *continued*

Sample Filter	Description
(&(objectClass=contact) (|(givenName=Bob*) (givenName=Robert*)))	Combines two Boolean operators, AND and OR. Returns all the contact objects that have a first name of "Bob" or "Robert".
(&(objectCategory=person) (!telephoneNumber=*))	Combines AND and NOT, and returns all the objects representing people who do not have a telephone number recorded.
(showInAdvancedViewOnly=TRUE)	Uses a Boolean value to find all the objects that have the *showInAdvancedViewOnly* attribute set to *TRUE*.

Special characters   Sometimes you need to use special characters in your search, characters that are part of the syntax. For example, the following search filter string contains parentheses around the 800. If a search filter string needs to use any special characters, you might get a run-time error in your code or the search might not work as expected:

```
(telephoneNumber=(800)555-1212)
```

The characters shown in the table below are considered special characters in the LDAP search filter string.

Character	Hex Value
*	2A
(	28
)	29
\	5C
NUL	00

To use a special character, put a backslash (\) before it and then substitute the two-digit hex value. Using this method, the previous query would be appear as:

```
(telephoneNumber=\28800\29555-1212)
```

This method will work for any character, including nonprinting characters such as tab (\09) and linefeed (\0A). Whether the hex digits are uppercase or lowercase does not matter: \0a and \0A are equivalent.

Getting back to the Phone sample, I want to search all the objects in the directory that match the given last name, or surname. However, if there is someone named Bob Printer working for me, and I type *Printer* as the name to search for, I don't want all the *printQueue* objects to be returned. So in the first comparison of the filter I specify that I want to search only for objects that represent people. The *objectCategory* attribute in Active Directory provides a convenient way to specify this.

```
' Specify the LDAP filter.
' First, indicate the category of objects to be searched
' (all people, not just users)
strObjects = "(objectCategory=person)"
```

Then I add a filter for the surname. If the user chooses to search for all people by entering an asterisk (*), I use the present operator (=*), otherwise I create a filter for the specified name. People without a surname would not be returned.

```
' If the user enters "*", then filter on all people
If (strPerson = "*") Then
    strName = "(sn=*)"
Else
    strName = "(sn=" & strPerson & "*)"
End If
```

Finally, I combine the two filters into one expression using the AND operator (&).

```
' Add the two filters together
strFilter = "(&" & strObjects & strName & ")"
```

What this results in is a complete LDAP search filter string. If a user types *Doe* at the command line or when prompted, the variable *strFilter* will contain the following:

```
(&(objectCategory=person)(sn=Doe*))
```

The LDAP Search Filter

The following is the exact LDAP search filter definition from RFC 2254. It uses the Augmented Backus-Naur Form (ABNF) notation specified in RFC 2234.

```
Filter ::= CHOICE {
    and                 [0] SET OF Filter,
    or                  [1] SET OF Filter,
    not                 [2] Filter,
    equalityMatch       [3] AttributeValueAssertion,
    substrings          [4] SubstringFilter,
    greaterOrEqual      [5] AttributeValueAssertion,
    lessOrEqual         [6] AttributeValueAssertion,
    present             [7] AttributeDescription,
    approxMatch         [8] AttributeValueAssertion,
    extensibleMatch     [9] MatchingRuleAssertion
}
SubstringFilter ::= SEQUENCE {
    type    AttributeDescription,
    SEQUENCE OF CHOICE {
        initial         [0] LDAPString,
        any             [1] LDAPString,
        final           [2] LDAPString
    }
}
AttributeValueAssertion ::= SEQUENCE {
    attributeDesc   AttributeDescription,
    attributeValue  AttributeValue
}
MatchingRuleAssertion ::= SEQUENCE {
    matchingRule    [1] MatchingRuleID OPTIONAL,
    type            [2] AttributeDescription OPTIONAL,
    matchValue      [3] AssertionValue,
    dnAttributes    [4] BOOLEAN DEFAULT FALSE
}
AttributeDescription ::= LDAPString
AttributeValue ::= OCTET STRING
MatchingRuleID ::= LDAPString
AssertionValue ::= OCTET STRING
LDAPString ::= OCTET STRING
```

The following ABNF notation is the exact string representation of the LDAP search filter definition from RFC 2254.

```
filter      = "(" filtercomp ")"
filtercomp  = and / or / not / item
and         = "&" filterlist
or          = "|" filterlist
not         = "!" filter
filterlist  = 1*filter
item        = simple / present / substring / extensible
simple      = attr filtertype value
filtertype  = equal / approx / greater / less
equal       = "="
approx      = "~="
greater     = ">="
less        = "<="
extensible  = attr [":dn"] [":" matchingrule] ":=" value
              / [":dn"] ":" matchingrule ":=" value
present     = attr "=*"
substring   = attr "=" [initial] any [final]
initial     = value
any         = "*" *(value "*")
final       = value
attr        = AttributeDescription from Section 4.1.5 of RFC 2251
matchingrule = MatchingRuleId from Section 4.1.9 of RFC 2251
value       = AttributeValue from Section 4.1.6 of RFC 2251
```

Attributes to Return

The next part of the LDAP query statement specifies which attributes to return for the objects that match the search filter. Using a single asterisk (*) character, you can instruct the directory to return all the attributes of the matching objects. However, this is inefficient and wastes server and network resources. Avoiding this inefficiency is particularly important when you're working with the global catalog server because it contains only a partial set of the full attributes associated with an object. In the Phone sample, all that's required is the name of the person and their phone number.

```
' Set the attributes for the recordset to contain
' We're interested in the common name and telephone number
strAttributes = "cn,telephoneNumber"
```

The attributes are separated with commas. While it's not required for the Phone sample, if you are planning to modify any of the objects that are returned, you should specify that the *ADsPath* property be returned so you can easily bind to the object using ADSI and make any changes.

> **Note**   I've mentioned several times the differences between attributes of a directory entry and the properties of an interface. I might appear to be contradicting myself above when I say that you should ask for the *ADsPath* property in the list of attributes to return. The *ADsPath* property is not an attribute for any object in Active Directory, so how can you ask for it to be returned by the directory? The code that implements the ADSI OLE DB provider and the *IDirectorySearch* interface makes an exception for *ADsPath* and creates the value for you when the object is returned. This is only true of the *ADsPath* property of the *IADs* interface. Other properties will not be recognized and the search will report errors.

Search Scope

The last piece of the LDAP query statement is also the simplest. It specifies the scope, or the depth, of the search. Where the search base specified the starting point, the scope indicates how deep in the hierarchy the server should go when looking for objects that match the search filter. Search scope has three possible values: *base*, *onelevel*, or *subtree*.

The default value is *subtree*. It indicates that the server should search all the objects starting with the one specified in the search base. If any container objects are found, the server will also search all the objects in each container.

The *onelevel* value specifies that the server search only the children of the base object, but not the base object itself. This option is useful when you want to exclude a container from matching the filter criteria. Likewise, the *base* value specifies that the server will search only the object referenced by the search base. At most, only one object would be returned—the base object—if it matches the search filter criteria. This option is often used to verify the existence of an object.

The Phone sample, like most cases, needs to search the base object and all its containers, so it specifies the *subtree* option.

```
' Specify the scope (base, onelevel, subtree)
strScope = "subtree"
```

Note that the search scope portion of the query string is the only optional portion. If it is not provided, the ADSI OLE DB provider will default to the *subtree* option. I believe it's good coding practice to specify parameters, even default ones, because it makes your code clearer.

Using ADO

Now let's dig into ADO and treat Active Directory as a database. ADO defines several objects, as shown in Figure 5-5.

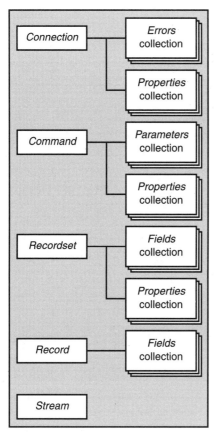

Figure 5-5 ADO object model.

The four main objects (*Connection, Command, Recordset,* and *Record*) control a search and contain the results. Each object contains a collection of other objects to hold options and various pieces of returned data.

Creating an ADO Connection

To begin a search using ADO, the Phone sample must first create an instance of the ADO *Connection* object that represents a unique session with the Active Directory server. I use the VBScript *CreateObject* function to create the *Connection* object.

```
' Create ADO connection using the ADSI OLE DB provider
Set objADOConnection = CreateObject("ADODB.Connection")
objADOConnection.Open "Provider=ADsDSOObject;"
```

> **Note** JScript does not have a *CreateObject* function. If you prefer developing with JScript, you can create a new instance of any Automation object by using the *ActiveXObject* object supplied by the JScript engine. For example *adoConnection = new ActiveXObject("ADODB.Connection");*

The *Open* method of the *Connection* object, referenced in our application with the variable *objADOConnection*, indicates which OLE DB provider should be used. A string is passed to the *Open* method that specifies the *ADsDSOObject* provider, which is, again, the programmatic name of the ADSI OLE DB provider that is used to communicate with Active Directory. The *Open* method can also accept alternative credentials, which I describe later in the section "Search Options."

Next the sample creates a new, empty ADO *Command* object that will contain the specific search options to be used. The *Connection* object is then associated with the *Command* object that will be used to carry out the search.

```
' Create ADO commmand object and associate with the connection
Set objADOCommand = CreateObject("ADODB.Command")
objADOCommand.ActiveConnection = objADOConnection
```

Specifying the Query

Now we are ready to use the LDAP query statement I created earlier. I purposely kept the four query statement sections separate and in their own string variables in order to better explain how to use them. Now it's time to "string" them together.

The ADO *Command* object has a *CommandText* property to hold the string to be passed to the data source provider. The ADSI OLE DB provider defines the format of the *CommandText* string. It requires that the four portions be separated with semi-colons.

```
' Create the command string using the four parts
objADOCommand.CommandText = strBase & ";" & strFilter & ";" & _
    strAttributes & ";" & strScope
```

Just to briefly review, the four portions of the LDAP query statement are:

■ **Root**   The ADsPath of the object, usually a container, where a program should start searching

■ **Filter**   Matching criteria expressed using the LDAP search filter syntax

■ **Attributes**   A comma-separated list of attributes to be returned for matching objects

■ **Scope**   A string with a *base, onelevel,* or *subtree* value that specifies the depth of the search (optional)

Refining the Search

The *CommandText* property specifies four options in one string. There are also additional search options that can be specified. One that's common is the *Page Size* property. The *Page Size* property is a member of the *IDirectorySearch* interface and is exposed by the ADSI OLE DB provider as a custom ADO property. To reference it, you must use the *Properties* collection of the ADO *Command* object.

```
' Set the number of records in the recordset logical page
objADOCommand.Properties("Page Size") = 20
```

A feature of the Phone sample is that if an asterisk is specified, the search filter contains *(sn=*)*. This instructs the server to return the name and phone number of all directory objects that represent people. Now imagine what happens if you do that against a directory with 100,000 names or more?

For starters, it might take a while for the server to go through the entire directory, collecting the attributes you've requested. While the server processes this query, the user is left waiting for a response. Obviously, it's a huge burden on the server as well. The server processing the search must go through all the objects, building the result set in memory with the requested attributes to return. At the same time, it might be processing requests from other clients.

Databases use the concept of *pages* to allow the server and client to work in chunks. By setting a page size of 20, the server pauses after finding 20 objects that match the search criteria and returns the results to the client. Using this setting makes the application more responsive because the client can display results before the search is fully completed, significantly reducing the workload on the server.

Active Directory by default imposes a 1000-record limit on searches that do not specify a page size. This is a common problem for programmers and IT professionals when starting out with Active Directory. A simple program or database tool uses a broad search that should return many hundreds of objects but only returns 1000. This 1000-result limit is an LDAP policy set on search servers and prevents inefficient or rouge clients from monopolizing the server and its processing resources.

You should use paging wherever possible to avoid hitting the limit. However, if using a database tool, particularly one that understands SQL queries, there is currently no way to set the page size parameter for the ADSI OLE DB provider. In a future release of ADSI, there will be a provision to use the SQL stored procedure *sp_addlinkedserver* to set the page size.

If the number of returned records could be potentially large, you could use the *Size Limit* property. *Size Limit* specifies the maximum number of records returned. When I used *Size Limit* in conjunction with the *Page Size* property, it sometimes did not work as expected, so you might need to experiment with this property. The following code shows how to set *Size Limit* to 20.

```
' Set the maximum result size
objADOCommand.Properties("Size Limit") = 20
```

Keeping the user's response time in mind, you can also set the *Time Limit* property. While I didn't use *Time Limit* in the Phone sample, it would be coded like this:

```
' Set the number of seconds for the server to spend searching
objADOCommand.Properties("Time Limit") = 5
```

This statement instructs the server to search for 5 seconds and then return whatever results it gathers in that time. The user will have to wait only a brief period to be shown a set of matching results.

We're only covering some of the several options available while searching. Other options are discussed in the section "Search Options" later in this chapter.

Note   The 1000-record limit is part of Active Directory's LDAP Policies, specifically the *MaxPageSize* policy. The maximum amount of time that Active Directory will spend searching, the *MaxQueryDuration* policy, is set at 120 seconds. The best way to change these limits is with the Ntdsutil command-line tool, which is included with Windows 2000 Server. Documentation for this utility is included with the *Windows 2000 Server Resource Kit*. Only domain administrators should use this tool. If you write efficient code, you will not have to worry about these default limits. Also, consider that some networks may be particularly busy and may have policies that are more restrictive than the defaults.

Sorting

The next line of code instructs Active Directory to sort the results for us based on the *cn* attribute:

```
' Sort the results based on the cn attribute
objADOCommand.Properties("Sort On") = "cn"
```

You can add more attributes to sort by to the list, separating them with commas. Asking for sorted results is more work for the server, but if you sort on attributes marked as indexed attributes in the directory, the server can perform the sort as it is collecting the results; otherwise it must wait until all the results are available and then sort them. Note that if you specify to sort the results, the *Page Size* setting might be ignored.

Executing the Query

I've used a couple dozen lines of code preparing to search the directory. I have all the criteria and options set, and now it's time to use ADO to have Active Directory actually perform the search. Can I get a drum-roll please?

To start the search operation, I call the *Execute* method of the ADO *Command* object. The *Execute* method returns a reference to a *Recordset* object, which we assign to the variable *objADORecordset*. I'll discuss the *Recordset* object in more detail shortly.

```
' Execute the query for the user in the directory
Set objADORecordset = objADOCommand.Execute
```

The *Execute* method passes the *CommandText* property along with the specified properties to the ADSI OLE DB provider. In turn, the provider calls *IDirectorySearch*, which eventually executes an LDAP search operation of the specified Active Directory server.

In a synchronous search (which is what we are performing now; I'll describe asynchronous searches later on), the *Execute* method returns to the application when the server has finished searching all the objects within the scope or when the number of results exceeds any specified limits, such as page size or size limit. At this point the *Recordset* object is ready to be examined.

Keep in mind, however, that if the search does not result in any matching records, the *Recordset* object is still valid. An empty result may not be intended, but it is not considered an error condition to the search engine.

Processing the Results

The ADO *Recordset* object contains an end of file (*EOF*) property that is *True* when there are no records or no more matching records. If the returned *Recordset* object is not empty, the next section of code starts a loop that will be executed

139

once for each matching object. As long as the *EOF* property is not *True*, we have not reached the end of the results and have valid results in the *Recordset* object.

```
If objADORecordset.EOF Then
    WScript.Echo "No records were found."
Else
    ' Loop through all the returned records
    While Not objADORecordset.EOF
```

At this point in the sample, I've created and executed a query that searched Active Directory's global catalog. If any objects matching the search criteria are found, the code enters a loop to retrieve each of the returned attributes.

Rows and Record Sets

As mentioned earlier, a *Recordset* object represents the results of a search. Think of the data in a *Recordset* object as a table. Each object that matches the search criteria is represented as a row. The columns contain the individual pieces of returned data. The columns are stored in a collection of *Field* objects that contain the attributes of the directory objects.

To retrieve a particular attribute from the current *Recordset* object, you must access its *Fields* collection. You specify the field using the attribute name, as shown here:

```
' Display the row using the selected fields
strDisplayLine = objADORecordSet.Fields("cn") & vbTab
```

The goal is to produce a single string containing the name and telephone number of the current record and display that to the user. In the code above, I retrieve the *cn* attribute, append a tab character, and store it in a string variable. Using a tab will separate the name from the next column, which will be the telephone number.

Something to consider in your own applications is that even though in the Phone sample we requested that the *telephoneNumber* attribute be returned, it's entirely possible that a particular object does not have a *telephoneNumber* attribute (or whatever attribute you request). This isn't because the person is a technophobe; maybe they simply didn't want to list it, or you may not have permission to access it.

What this illustrates is the need for good error checking in your code. Take, for example, the following code:

```
WScript.Echo objADORecordset.Fields("telephoneNumber")
```

If this line of code is executed on a *Recordset* object that has an empty value for the *telephoneNumber* attribute, it would generate a Type Mismatch error because it will return NULL and the *WScript.Echo* method doesn't handle null data. Using the Visual Basic or VBScript function *IsNull* we can check for that case and supply an alternative string.

```
' Check to see if telephone number field is null
If IsNull( objADORecordset.Fields("telephoneNumber") ) Then
    strDisplayLine = strDisplayLine & "(number not listed)"
Else
    ' Retrieve telephone number and add to line
    strDisplayLine = strDisplayLine & _
        objADORecordset.Fields("telephoneNumber")
End If
```

Finally, with the *strDisplayLine* variable containing the string I want to display, I call the *Echo* method of the *WScript* object. If the program is run from the command prompt, this call will display a single line of text. If the program is executed from the Windows user interface, the text will be displayed in a dialog box. (You saw this in Figure 5-4, shown earlier.)

```
' Display the line
WScript.Echo strDisplayLine
```

Now the sample moves to the next matched object using the *MoveNext* method of the *Recordset* object. Since the *MoveNext* method updates the *EOF* property, it's a convenient place to complete the loop.

```
    ' Advance to the next record
    objADORecordset.MoveNext
Wend
```

Cleaning Up

If you've moved past the last record, the *EOF* property will be set to *True* and the loop will terminate. Now it's time to clean up the application before exiting.

I call the *Close* method of the ADO *Connection* object to let ADO know that this search is finished and it can free any system resources, but it does not destroy the objects. ADO will also close the associated *Recordset* object.

```
' Close the ADO connection
objADOConnection.Close
```

If you wanted to, you could start the application over again, reusing the *Command* object. However, we've finished with the Phone sample for now.

Ideas for Improvements

The simple Phone sample is ripe for improving. Among its limitations are that it can only search using the surname, or last name, of the person. Changing it to search on a variety of name and descriptive attributes would make it more useful. Here are some suggestions:

- Allow searching on first and last names

- Return all phone numbers for the person, including fax and home numbers

- Instead of returning telephone numbers, retrieve the user's e-mail address. Using the *mailto:* protocol, it's easy to invoke the user's default e-mail program to send a message to the address.

- Use the Telephony API to allow the computer's modem to dial the number.

Using *IDirectorySearch*

By far the easiest and most common way of searching Active Directory is to use ADO and the ADSI OLE DB provider. Of course, C and C++ developers can use ADO or OLE DB from their applications, but they might prefer the ADSI *IDirectorySearch* interface, which is a low-level interface for searching Active Directory.

As I mentioned at the beginning of this chapter, the ADSI OLE DB provider uses *IDirectorySearch* to perform its work. *IDirectorySearch* and *IDirectoryObject* (explained in Chapter 7) are the only two interfaces in ADSI that don't support Automation—that is, they don't support *IDispatch*, cannot be used by the scripting languages, and are difficult to use from Visual Basic. Since this book is targeted to readers using a variety of development environments, I wanted to give an example of how you can use this interface directly using C and C++. The source code is simple enough and is similar to the VBScript version of the Phone sample. Listing 5-2 shows the code, which is also included on the companion CD.

```
#define _WIN32_WINNT 0x0500
#define _UNICODE
#include <stdio.h>
#include <tchar.h>
```

Listing 5-2 Phone.cpp uses *IDirectorySearch* to search Active Directory.

```
#include <objbase.h>
#include <activeds.h>

// Attributes to return
_TCHAR *rgpszAttributeList[] = { _TEXT("cn"), _TEXT("telephoneNumber") };

// LDAP search filter
_TCHAR *pszSearchFormat = _TEXT("(&(objectCategory=person)(sn=%s*))");

//----------------------------------------------------------------------
// wmain ( int argc, wchar_t *argv[] )
// Entry point for UNICODE console mode apps
//----------------------------------------------------------------------
void wmain( int argc, wchar_t *argv[] )
{

// Create buffer for the query string
_TCHAR *pszQuery = new _TCHAR[_MAX_PATH];

// Initialize the buffer
_tcscpy(pszQuery, _TEXT(""));

// Loop through all the command line arguments
if (argc > 1)
    {
    // Copy the name to search from the command line argument array
    _tcscpy(pszQuery, argv[1]);

    // Initialize variables
    HRESULT hResult;
    IADs *pobjIADs;
    VARIANT varDomain;

    // Initialize COM
    CoInitialize(NULL);

    // Get a base IADs object
    hResult = ADsGetObject(_TEXT("GC://rootDSE"), IID_IADs,
        (void**)&pobjIADs);

    // Use the Get method to get the default naming context
    // (directory partition)
    hResult = pobjIADs->Get(_TEXT("defaultNamingContext"), &varDomain);

    // Build LDAP path to the domain
    _TCHAR *pszLDAPPath = new _TCHAR[_MAX_PATH];
    _tcscpy(pszLDAPPath, _TEXT("GC://"));
    _tcscat(pszLDAPPath, varDomain.bstrVal);
```

(continued)

143

```
// Get the directory search interface to the domain
IDirectorySearch *pContainerToSearch = NULL;

hResult = ADsGetObject( pszLDAPPath,
    IID_IDirectorySearch,
    (void **)&pContainerToSearch);

// Create search filter in LDAP format
_TCHAR *pszSearchFilter = new _TCHAR[_MAX_PATH];

// Create LDAP format search string
_stprintf(pszSearchFilter, pszSearchFormat, pszQuery);

// Variables for column name and data
ADS_SEARCH_COLUMN colSearchColumn;

// Create search preferences structure
ADS_SEARCHPREF_INFO arSearchPrefs[3];

// Set a subtree search
arSearchPrefs[0].dwSearchPref = ADS_SEARCHPREF_SEARCH_SCOPE;
arSearchPrefs[0].vValue.dwType = ADSTYPE_INTEGER;
arSearchPrefs[0].vValue.Integer = ADS_SCOPE_SUBTREE;
// Set page size for 20 rows
arSearchPrefs[1].dwSearchPref = ADS_SEARCHPREF_PAGESIZE;
arSearchPrefs[1].vValue.dwType = ADSTYPE_INTEGER;
arSearchPrefs[1].vValue.Integer = 20;
// Turn sorting on
// Create a sort key using the cn attribute
ADS_SORTKEY adsSortKey;
adsSortKey.pszAttrType = _TEXT("cn");   // Attribute to sort on
adsSortKey.pszReserved = NULL;          // Reserved, not used
adsSortKey.fReverseorder = 0;           // Normal sort, not reversed

// Create the sort search preference
arSearchPrefs[2].dwSearchPref = ADS_SEARCHPREF_SORT_ON;
arSearchPrefs[2].vValue.dwType = ADSTYPE_PROV_SPECIFIC;
arSearchPrefs[2].vValue.ProviderSpecific.dwLength = sizeof(ADS_SORTKEY);
arSearchPrefs[2].vValue.ProviderSpecific.lpValue = (LPBYTE) &adsSortKey;

// Set the search preferences
hResult = pContainerToSearch->SetSearchPreference( &arSearchPrefs[0], 3);

// Handle to search results that is passed to other methods of
// IDirectorySearch.
ADS_SEARCH_HANDLE hSearch;
```

```
// Execute search by providing LDAP filter, attribute list, and size
// Returns handle to search
hResult = pContainerToSearch->ExecuteSearch(pszSearchFilter,
    rgpszAttributeList,
    sizeof(rgpszAttributeList) / sizeof(LPOLESTR),
    &hSearch);
if ( SUCCEEDED(hResult) )
    {
    // Call IDirectorySearch::GetNextRow() to retrieve the next
    // row of data
    hResult = pContainerToSearch->GetFirstRow(hSearch);

    if (SUCCEEDED(hResult))
        {
        // Loop through each row returned
        while (hResult != S_ADS_NOMORE_ROWS)
            {
            // Get and print the first attribute (common name)
            hResult = pContainerToSearch->GetColumn(hSearch,
                rgpszAttributeList[0], &colSearchColumn);

            if (SUCCEEDED(hResult))
                {
                // Display the cn attribute
                _tprintf(_TEXT("%s\t"),
                    colSearchColumn.pADsValues->CaseIgnoreString);

                pContainerToSearch->FreeColumn( &colSearchColumn );
                }

            // Get and print Telephone Number
            hResult = pContainerToSearch->GetColumn(hSearch,
                rgpszAttributeList[1], &colSearchColumn);

            if (SUCCEEDED(hResult))
                {
                // Display the phone number attribute
                _tprintf(_TEXT("%s"),
                    colSearchColumn.pADsValues->CaseIgnoreString);

            pContainerToSearch->FreeColumn( &colSearchColumn );
            }
        else  // Didn't get phone number, display substitute text
            _tprintf(_TEXT("(number not listed)"));
```

(continued)

145

```
                    // Start a new line
                    _tprintf(_TEXT("\n"));

                    //Get the next row
                    hResult = pContainerToSearch->GetNextRow(hSearch);
                    }
            }
        // Close the search handle to clean up
        pContainerToSearch->CloseSearchHandle(hSearch);
        }

    // Clean up objects
    if (pContainerToSearch)
        pContainerToSearch->Release();

    if (pobjIADs)
        pobjIADs->Release();

    // Uninitialize COM
    CoUninitialize();
    }
    return;
}
```

Search Options

The Phone sample demonstrates how to perform a basic search of Active Directory. Programmers can customize searching for various situations, and I'll describe some of those in this section.

Referrals

The Phone sample used the GC provider to search the global catalog. Since the global catalog contains a copy of every object in a forest of domain trees, you can be certain your search is thorough. The limitation of the global catalog is that it contains only a partial set of the attributes of each object. Sometimes it's necessary to search the entire forest for attributes not included in the global catalog, and in that case the global catalog won't be sufficient.

Since Active Directory is a distributed directory, it doesn't store information in just one place and it doesn't maintain copies of the entire directory on each domain controller. Rather, each domain controller contains the directory partition for the particular domain it hosts. Does this mean that clients are expected to query all the domain controllers in a forest, resubmitting the query to each one, looking for matches?

In a word, yes, but don't panic. The process of hunting down the information at the various domain controllers is handled transparently for the application. ADSI, or more specifically, the LDAP API library on the client machine, does the hard work of submitting the query to all relevant domain controllers. This mechanism is known as *referral chasing*.

Here's an example. Let's say you want to search all the *person* objects in the directory, looking for anyone who's employee ID is under a certain value. This information is stored in *contact* and *user* class objects under the *employeeID* attribute. Since *employeeID* is not part of the attribute set stored in the global catalog, you can't use the global catalog and must search the directory partitions of all the domains. In the Copper Software empire, employees are distributed to several domains around the world, such as

coppersoftware.com

clearwater.coppersoftware.com

dublin.coppersoftware.com

To search all the domains, you have to start at the top of the domain tree. The top can be retrieved from the *rootDomainNamingContext* from the *RootDSE* object, just as in the VBScript Phone sample. In this case, that would be *DC=coppersoftware,DC=com*. To make sure all of coppersoftware.com and its child domains are searched, you have to specify the *subtree* search scope in the query statement. Here is what the LDAP query statement would look like:

```
<LDAP://DC=coppersoftware,DC=com>;
(&(objectCategory=person)(employeeID<=9999));
name,employeeID,ADsPath;
subtree
```

This statement searches all the directory partitions looking for any *person* class objects that have an *employeeID* attribute with a value of less than 10,000. The *name* and *employeeID* attributes and the *ADsPath* property of the matching objects will be returned.

When this query is executed, the server responding on behalf of coppersoftware.com will go through all its containers looking for matching objects. As it does so, it builds a result set in memory with the requested attributes. Once all the objects in the current domain directory partition have been searched, the server will automatically add *referrals* to the result set. A referral is simply a way for the server to indicate that there might be another domain controller that contains the information you're looking for. In the example, a referral will be generated for the *clearwater.coppersoftware.com* and *dublin.coppersoftware.com* domains.

How does the server know about other servers? In the case of *clearwater. coppersoftware.com* and *dublin.coppersoftware.com*, they are child domains, also known as *subordinate* domains. The parent domain in a tree keeps information about the tree in its configuration partition and provides distinguished names to child domains in the referral.

After the referrals are added to the result set, the result set is passed back to the program performing the search. At a very low level, the LDAP API library (Wldap32.dll) processes the referral by effectively repeating the search again on the domain controllers for the referrals. Any matching objects from the other domain controllers are added to the result set and returned to the client.

> **Note** A server can generate referrals to other domain trees, even to LDAP servers on the Internet. The only requirement is that the server has a DNS name. However, unlike referrals to child domains, referrals to external domains can occur only if explicit cross-references to the domains exist in the directory. These references are established by adding a *crossRef* class object to the configuration partition of the directory. Describing external cross-references in detail is beyond this introduction to referrals, however. Most of the time, you'll be searching within a tree and won't need to be concerned with external cross-references.

As you can imagine, the process of connecting and querying the other domain controllers can be time-consuming. Active Directory will always generate referrals for a client when needed, but referral chasing by a client is turned off by default. Referral chasing is controlled using the *Chase Referrals* property of the ADSI OLE DB provider. This property is set using the ADO *Properties* object in the same fashion as the *Page Size* property. Using *IDirectorySearch*, the referral chasing option is set by building an *ADS_SEARCHPREF_INFO* structure containing the *ADS_SEARCHPREF_CHASE_REFERRALS* constant and one of the values listed in Table 5-4.

Chase Referral Option	Description
ADS_CHASE_REFERRALS_NEVER	The client will not chase any referrals generated by the server.
ADS_CHASE_REFERRALS_SUBORDINATE	The client will chase referrals to any child domain within the tree. This flag is ignored during paged searches.
ADS_CHASE_REFERRALS_EXTERNAL	The client will chase only referrals to external domains. This flag is on by default during any ADSI binding operation. This is the default for searching.
ADS_CHASE_REFERRALS_ALWAYS	The client will chase all referrals.

Table 5-4 Options for referral chasing contained in the *ADS_CHASE_REFERRALS_ENUM* enumeration.

> **Note**   In the next release of Windows, you can set up Active Directory so that it doesn't automatically generate referrals, which will improve performance. A future version of ADSI will use this option if the client won't be chasing referrals. For more information, see Chapter 11.

Asynchronous Searches

Both the VBScript and C++ version of the Phone sample perform a *synchronous* search. In other words, the client waits for results from the server before doing anything else. Since waiting for the server to search and return a result set can be very time-consuming, you don't want to force your users to be waiting during this time. Setting the *Page Size* property helps, since it reduces the result set, but even waiting for 20 results can take a while if there are a large number of objects to be searched that don't match the search filter.

With an *asynchronous* search, control is returned to the program as soon as the first result is ready. The program can display the results of the search to the user and check to see whether *EOF* was set, indicating that no more results are available. To specify an asynchronous search, you set the *Asynchronous* property, which is by default *False*, to *True*.

For a demonstration, you can modify the VBScript Phone sample with the following line and ask it to return all objects. You'll notice that results are displayed almost immediately, and performance will seem to have increased. Place this line right after the line in which you set the *Page Size* parameter:

```
objADOCommand.Properties("Asynchronous") = True
```

Authentication and Security

In Chapter 4, I discussed how to bind to an object using an alternative set of credentials. When performing searches of the directory, ADSI and the ADSI OLE DB provider use the security context of the program being run. As with the *ADsOpenObject* function, you can specify a different set of credentials to use. You can also set the level of security to use when connecting to and searching the directory.

The ADSI OLE DB provider exposes several properties that control the authentication options. These are listed in Table 5-5.

Property	Description
User ID	The name of the account to be used. The format you use is the same as for *ADsOpenObject* or the *OpenDSObject* method of the *IADsOpenDSObject* interface. See the section "Authentication" in Chapter 4.
Password	The password to match with *User ID*.
Encrypt Password	A Boolean value that specifies whether the password is encrypted. The default is *False*.
ADSI Flag	Sets the authentication options. Use one or more of the flags from the *ADS_AUTHENTICATION_ENUM* enumeration. The default is 0.

Table 5-5 ADSI OLE DB provider authentication properties.

You can set these properties in a couple of ways. The first is simply by referencing them in the *Properties* collection of the ADO *Connection* object. Here is an example:

```
objADOConnection.Properties("User ID") = "COPPERSOFTWARE\Administrator"
objADOConnection.Properties("Password") = "mypassword"
objADOConnection.Properties("Encrypt Password") = True
objADOConnection.Properties("ADSI Flag") = ADS_SECURE_AUTHENICATION
```

The second way is to use the *Open* method of the *Connection* object as the *connection string*. This method is handy when you're using data access tools that require a connection string instead of coding. The connection string uses the same property names and separates each part with a semi-colon, just like the query statement. However, only the *User ID* and *Password* properties can be set this way. For example,

```
Provider=ADsDSOObject;User ID=COPPERSOFTWARE\Administrator;
    Password=mypassword;
```

You can see that the provider name is the first property listed in the string. For the ADSI OLE DB provider, this will always be *ADsDSOObject*. To set the provider programmatically, use the *Provider* property of the *Connection* object, as follows:

```
objADOConnection.Provider = "ADsDSOObject"
```

> **Note**   For more information about credentials and connection options, refer to the section "Authentication" in Chapter 4.

Search Limits

In addition to the *Page Size* property, the ADSI OLE DB provider has other options you can include to make your applications more responsive when performing extensive searches. These are listed in Table 5-6.

ADO Property and *IDirectorySearch* Search Preference	Description
Page Size *ADS_SEARCHPREF_PAGESIZE*	Specifies the page size in a paged search.
Size Limit *ADS_SEARCHPREF_SIZE_LIMIT*	Specifies the maximum number of returned objects. If the size limit is reached, Active Directory stops searching.
Server Time Limit *ADS_SEARCHPREF_TIME_LIMIT*	Specifies the time limit (in seconds) for the search that the server should observe in a search.
Timeout *ADS_SEARCHPREF_TIMEOUT*	Specifies the time limit (in seconds) that a client is willing to wait for the server to return the result.

Table 5-6 Search limit options.   *(continued)*

Table 5-6 *continued*

ADO Property and *IDirectorySearch* Search Preference	Description
Time Limit *ADS_SEARCHPREF_PAGED_TIME_LIMIT*	Specifies the time limit (in seconds) that the server should observe to search a page of results (as opposed to the time limit for the entire search). If the limit is reached, searching stops and any results are returned. Specifying this option is also supposed to return a "cookie" that indicates the search state so that you can presumably continue searching if desired—I did not explore or test this option.

Performance

You should consider a number of pitfalls when creating queries against Active Directory. These have to do with scope and size: by keeping the scope of the search as narrow as possible and asking for as little information as necessary, Active Directory can search and return results more quickly. Here's a list of dos and don'ts:

■ Do search using indexed attributes. These attributes are kept in sorted tables within Active Directory and provide very fast response.

■ Do use paging to improve response to the user and to give the directory server a break.

■ Do use the *objectCategory* attribute. When looking for particular types of objects, use *objectCategory* instead of *objectClass*. The *objectCategory* attribute is a single-valued attribute containing the most appropriate class name for the object. Both *user* and *contact* object classes inherit from the *organizationalPerson* class, which itself inherits from the *person* class. The *objectCategory* attribute contains the value *person* for all the *user* and *contact* objects. This attribute is also indexed for even better performance.

■ Do sort on indexed attributes. If you need the server to sort the result set for you, using indexed attributes helps tremendously since the server can sort as it collects the results. Otherwise, the server must wait until all the results have been collected to sort them.

■   Don't use multivalued attributes in your searches. Attributes containing more than one value are more difficult to search. Multivalued attributes are discussed in the next chapter.

■   Don't use the *objectClass* attribute when *objectCategory* will work. The *objectClass* attribute is multivalued, thus using it reduces searching performance. But here's an exception: Querying on *(objectClass=*)* is a great way to search all objects. This type of filter is optimized within Active Directory.

■   Don't use substring searches if possible. For example *(sn=*mann)* or *(cn=*soft*)*.

■   Don't perform subtree searches against the root domain unless required. Doing this will generate referrals regardless of whether you plan on processing them.

■   Don't ask for sorting, particularly multi-attribute sorting unless absolutely required. This requires the server to collect the result set in memory.

Summary

In this chapter, I've covered most of the main topics related to searching. The VBScript Phone sample demonstrates the concepts involved with using ADO and the ADSI OLE DB provider to search Active Directory. I encourage you to use portions of this sample as boilerplate in your own projects. One area I didn't cover in-depth here is attributes and the values they contain. That's the focus of the next chapter.

6

Reading and Writing Directory Data

Now that you understand how to bind to and search for objects in Active Directory, let's move on to the subject of the data that is contained in an object and how to access and update it. In this chapter I'll cover reading and writing directory data using the Active Directory Service Interfaces (ADSI). I'll also cover the techniques involved in enumerating objects in a container and creating and deleting objects.

Directory Attributes

A directory entry is made up of various pieces of data. These pieces of data are known as *attributes* of the directory entry. Each attribute has a *name*, and the data associated with that name is the attribute's *value*. You use the attribute name when you want to retrieve data from a directory entry. Consider the following pieces of data: "Jane Clayton", "(800) 555-1111", "(800) 555-1112", "(800) 555-1113", "(800) 555-1114", "123 Main Street", "Seattle", "WA". Table 6-1 shows how this data would be stored in Active Directory. Notice that the *otherTelephone* attribute is multivalued.

Attribute Name	Attribute Value
displayName *Display-Name*	Jane Clayton
telephoneNumber *Telephone-Number*	(800) 555-1111

Table 6-1 Example attributes for an Active Directory entry. *(continued)*

Table 6-1 *continued*

Attribute Name	Attribute Value
street *Street-Address*	123 Main Street
l *Locality-Name*	Seattle
st *State-Or-Province-Name*	WA
otherTelephone *Phone-Office-Other*	(800) 555-1112 (800) 555-1113 (800) 555-1114

Naming Conventions

Active Directory uses different naming conventions for attributes, the *LDAP display name* and the *common name*. With the LDAP display name, the first character is lowercase, there are no spaces between words, and words following the first word are capitalized. The common name convention usually capitalizes the first letter of each word and separates the words with a hyphen. Let's take, for example, the telephone number attribute. The Active Directory schema defines this attribute as having an LDAP display name of *telephoneNumber* and a common name of *Telephone-Number*. Sometimes, however, the names in each convention do not map directly. Consider the state attribute. It has an LDAP display name of *st* and a common name of *State-Or-Province-Name*. Since the LDAP display name is used in source code, I typically use that naming convention in this book. When necessary, I'll use the common name.

> **Note**   The common name and LDAP display name formats also apply to object classes. For example, *organizationalUnit* is the LDAP display name for the class that has a common name of *Organizational-Unit*.

Terminology

When working with Active Directory and ADSI, you'll frequently notice differences in the terminology of the various technologies involved. ADSI is a COM technology and uses terms such as *interfaces, objects,* and *properties.* To refer to these same items, Active Directory, which is based on Lightweight Directory Access Protocol (LDAP), leans toward terms like *entries* and *attributes.* In the previous chapter, you saw that ActiveX Data Objects (ADO) uses database terminology, such as *records* and *fields.* Table 6-2 compares the terminology.

LDAP	ADSI	ADO
Entry	Object	Record
Attribute	Property	Field
Result set	Result set	Record set

Table 6-2 Terminology comparison between LDAP, ADSI, and ADO.

Attributes vs. Properties

In this chapter, the differences in terminology become very apparent when dealing with directory data. LDAP, and thus Active Directory, use the term *attribute* to refer to the named values that make up a directory entry. COM, and thus ADSI along with ADO, use the term *property* to refer to a data member of a COM object.

In this book, I'll endeavor to use *property* or *attribute* according to which is appropriate for the context. I'll use the term *attribute* when referring to the pieces of data that make up a directory object, and I'll use the term *property* when referring to the ADSI/COM representation of an attribute. However, be aware that the Active Directory documentation, ADSI documentation, and other sources of information often use *property* and *attribute* interchangeably. Usually this isn't a problem, but keep in mind that *attribute* and *property* refer to different things.

In some cases, ADSI maps Active Directory attributes to interfaces as *named properties.* A named property is simply a piece of information that is part of the definition for a particular ADSI interface. For example, the *IADsUser* interface (which I'll discuss in Chapter 10) has the *TelephoneNumber* property that corresponds to the Active Directory *telephoneNumber* attribute.

When ADSI exposes an object's attribute through a named property, it always does so by using the Automation data types. Automation defines a small set of data types that can be natively passed from object to application using an interface. In most cases, the property is defined as accepting a *binary string* or a *variant* data type.

> **Note** Briefly, a binary string, also known as a basic string, is a type of string that is prefixed with the number of characters in the string. Variants are a special data type that contain another data type, like a number, a date, a binary string, or even a reference to an object. Variants can also contain multiple values using arrays. Visual Basic handles the binary string and variant data types transparently. C and C++ developers can use the *BSTR* and *VARIANT* types to declare variables. Starting with version 6.0, Visual C++ makes working with binary strings and variants easier by using the *_bstr_t* and *_variant_t* classes, which I'll use in some of the code samples.

ADSI makes many of the commonly used attributes available as properties, however, not all attributes are directly mapped to ADSI properties. For example, the *street* attribute of the *organizationalPerson* class does not have a corresponding street property exposed on any of the ADSI interfaces. This is true of most of the 850 attributes defined in the schema. However, by using the *Get* method described later in this chapter, a program can access any attribute of an object.

Reading Attributes

ADSI makes getting the value of an object's attribute easy. The following code retrieves the *cn* (*Common-Name*) attribute using the *Name* property of the *IADs* interface.

```
strCommonName = objADs.Name
```

Using C++, you would do the same thing with this code:

```
hResult = pobjIADs->get_Name ( &bstrName );
```

In both cases, I'm using the *Name* property of the *IADs* interface. *IADs* is the base interface that applies to all ADSI objects, so regardless of the type of object, you can always call the *IADs* properties and methods. Table 6-3 and Table 6-4 list the properties and methods for *IADs*. Note that all the properties of the *IADs* interface are read-only; you can't change their value.

IADs Property	Returned Data Type	Description
ADsPath	String	The ADsPath of the object
Class	String	The name of the object's class
GUID	String	The GUID of the object as a string of two-digit hexadecimal characters
Name	String	The relative distinguished name (RDN) of the object
Parent	String	The ADsPath for the parent of the object
Schema	String	The ADsPath of the class object for this object in the schema

Table 6-3 Properties of the *IADs* interface.

IADs Method	Description
GetInfo	Retrieves all the attributes of the object from the directory and places them in the local property cache
SetInfo	Saves changes made to the object to the directory
Get	Retrieves the value of the property named
Put	Sets the value of the property named
GetEx	Retrieves the value or values of the property named and returns them as a variant array
PutEx	Adds, deletes, clears, or updates a value or values of the property named
GetInfoEx	Retrieves the values of the property named from the directory, overwriting the current cached values

Table 6-4 Methods of the *IADs* interface.

The following code is from a Visual Basic sample named IADsProperties that's included on the companion CD. This code binds to an object, reads the values of the *IADs* properties, and adds them to a list box.

```
' Bind to the object
Set objADsUser = GetObject(strADsPath)

' Gather the property values in a concatenated string
lstBox.AddItem "ADsPath:" & vbTab & objADsUser.ADsPath
lstBox.AddItem "Name:   " & vbTab & objADsUser.Name
lstBox.AddItem "Class:  " & vbTab & objADsUser.Class
lstBox.AddItem "GUID:   " & vbTab & objADsUser.Guid
lstBox.AddItem "Schema: " & vbTab & objADsUser.Schema
lstBox.AddItem "Parent: " & vbTab & objADsUser.Parent
```

When you run the code in the Visual Basic version of the IADsProperties sample, you should see something similar to Figure 6-1.

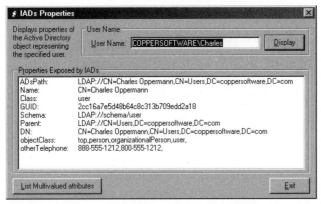

Figure 6-1 Output of the Visual Basic IADsProperties sample.

Accessing properties using C or C++ is the same in concept, but slightly different because of the nature of COM. You access interface properties using a method call that uses *get_* and the property name, as shown in the following code from the C++ version of IADsProperties.

```
// Get pointer to the user's object
IADs *pobjIADs; // Pointer to object interface
hResult = ADsGetObject(
    bstrUserADsPath,    // ADsPath of object
    IID_IADs,           // IID of interface requested
    (void**) &pobjIADs  // Pointer to interface
);
```

```
// Check for binding success
if ( SUCCEEDED ( hResult ) )
    {
    //------------------------------------------------
    // Retrieving IADs Properties
    //------------------------------------------------

    // ADSI allocates the storage for the binary string that
    // is returned for all IADs properties.  Declare variable
    // to string, must free on exit using SysFreeString()
    BSTR bstrPropertyValue;

    // ADsPath property
    hResult = pobjIADs->get_ADsPath ( &bstrPropertyValue );

    if ( SUCCEEDED ( hResult ) )
        // Display property value
      -_tprintf( _T("ADsPath: %S\n"), bstrPropertyValue);

    // Name property
    hResult = pobjIADs->get_Name ( &bstrPropertyValue );

    if ( SUCCEEDED ( hResult ) )
        // Display property value
        _tprintf( _T("Name: %S\n"), bstrPropertyValue);

    // Class property
    hResult = pobjIADs->get_Class ( &bstrPropertyValue );

    if ( SUCCEEDED ( hResult ) )
        // Display property value
        _tprintf( _T("Class: %S\n"), bstrPropertyValue );

    // GUID property
    hResult = pobjIADs->get_GUID ( &bstrPropertyValue );

    if ( SUCCEEDED ( hResult ) )
        // Display property value
        _tprintf( _T("GUID: %S\n"), bstrPropertyValue );

    // Schema property
    hResult = pobjIADs->get_Schema ( &bstrPropertyValue );

    if ( SUCCEEDED ( hResult ) )
        // Display property value
        _tprintf( _T("Schema: %S\n"), bstrPropertyValue );
```

(continued)

```
// Parent property
hResult = pobjIADs->get_Parent ( &bstrPropertyValue );

if ( SUCCEEDED ( hResult ) )
    // Display property value
    _tprintf( _T("Parent: %S\n"), bstrPropertyValue );

// Free string
SysFreeString ( bstrPropertyValue );
```

When you run the code in the C++ version of the IADsProperties sample, you should see something similar to Figure 6-2.

Figure 6-2 Output of the C++ IADsProperties sample.

Comparing the Visual Basic and C++ versions of the IADsProperties sample, it's clear why Visual Basic has become such a popular application development platform. Visual Basic reduces some of the complexities of COM and takes care of some of the error checking, which allows for more intuitive programming.

The *Get* Method

As I mentioned earlier, not all the attributes that are stored with an object are easily accessible from a named property on an ADSI interface. How do you retrieve those attributes?

The *IADs* interface provides the *Get* method for retrieving any named attribute. The *Get* method takes a string attribute name as input and returns the value of the attribute as a variant.

Here is how you would use the *IADs Get* method in Visual Basic to retrieve the *distinguishedName* attribute of an object:

```
strDN = objADs.Get("distinguishedName")
```

In C and C++, the call to the *Get* method would be as follows:

```
_variant_t var;
hResult = pobjIADs->Get( L"distinguishedName", &var );
```

You can use the *Get* method to retrieve any of the attributes associated with an object, as long as you know the name of the attribute. In Chapter 7, I'll show you ways to enumerate all the properties of an object.

> **Note**   The *Get* method is similar in appearance but different from the COM convention of using *get_PropertyName*.

Handling Errors in ADSI

ADSI is distinct among the various object-oriented technologies I've worked with in that accessing an attribute that has no value generates an Automation error. This error occurs because of the nature of the LDAP data model. To understand this point better, think of an Active Directory object simply as a collection of values, not attributes. Even if a particular attribute is allowed for a particular object, if the attribute has no value, the object has no knowledge of it. Thus, ADSI reports a "not found" error.

Specifically, if a call to the *Get* method (or to the *GetEx* method, which I'll describe in more detail later in the chapter) is asked to retrieve a property that contains no value, ADSI will return a COM result value of 0x8000500D (hexadecimal) or –2147463155 (decimal). The description supplied for this error is "The Active Directory property cannot be found in the cache." This simply means that ADSI checked the local property cache for the attribute value and did not find it. If the cache is empty, ADSI will automatically attempt to refresh the cache and check again.

This error is not a serious one; it just indicates that the particular attribute did not contain a value in the current object. It does not prevent you from assigning a value, which I'll discuss later in the chapter. However, since an error is generated by ADSI and Active Directory, you need to handle it in your code to prevent unexpected problems for a user.

Visual Basic developers can simply use the *On Error Resume Next* statement to bypass any errors. For example, if the *Get* method fails in the code shown here, code execution will resume at the next line:

```
On Error Resume Next
strTelephone = objADsUser.Get("telephoneNumber")
Debug.Print strTelephone
```

In this code, if the user doesn't have a telephone number listed in the *telephoneNumber* attribute, Visual Basic will trap the error and proceed with the *Debug.Print* statement.

This approach is handy for dealing with errors such as the "not found" error. In the IADsProperties sample application on the companion CD, I use another method, which activates error handling and directs Visual Basic to go to the *ErrorHandler* line whenever an error occurs. The *ErrorHandler* block performs a check of the *Err* object and calls a display routine if an error occurred. By placing a handler like this at the end of the function, you can quickly exit the function whenever one occurs. As a final step, you can restore normal Visual Basic error handling by using the *On Error GoTo 0* statement.

Here is a code from the Visual Basic IADsProperties sample that traps the error and calls a function named *DisplayError* to display more information:

```
Public Function ...
On Error GoTo ErrorHandler

    ' (ADSI code)

ErrorHandler:
'================================================
' Check for errors
'================================================
If Err.Number <> 0 Then
    ' Display error message
    Call DisplayError
End If

' Turn off error checking
On Error GoTo 0

End Function
```

Here is the small but handy *DisplayError* function to display error information and get a response from the user. If the user chooses the Cancel button, the application exits. This function uses the *Err* object properties to gather the error information, including a description and source module.

```
Public Function DisplayError()
'=================================================
' Display Error message box
'=================================================
Dim strError As String
Dim nAction As Long

' Build string with error information
strError = Err.Description & vbNewLine
strError = strError & "Number: " & vbTab & Hex(Err.Number) & _
    " (" & Err.Number & ")" & vbNewLine
strError = strError & "Source: " & vbTab & Err.Source & vbNewLine

' Display alert and get response
nAction = MsgBox(strError, vbExclamation + vbOKCancel, "Error")

If nAction = vbCancel Then
    ' Quit application
    Unload frmMain
End If

End Function
```

C and C++ programmers can use a COM-supplied macro to check the result code of a property or method call. The *SUCCEEDED* macro takes a COM result code, usually an *HRESULT*, and evaluates to either True or False depending on the result. In the C++ code sample, I used the *SUCCEEDED* macro as shown here:

```
// Use Get method to retrieve attribute
hResult = pobjIADs->Get( L"distinguishedName", &varDN );

if ( SUCCEEDED ( hResult ) )
    {
    // Extract the string from the variant
    BSTR bstrDN = _bstr_t(varDN);

    // Display attribute value
    _tprintf( _T("%S\n"), bstrDN );
    }
else
    // Error getting value, display
    _tprintf( _T("Error getting value: %S\n"), hResult );
```

To check for failure, you could use the *FAILED* macro, which evaluates to True if the method call resulted in an error.

All the ADSI errors are defined in the Adserr.h header file that is automatically included from the ActiveDS.h header file. In addition, other important error values, including the Win32 API result codes, are kept in the Winerror.h and Lmerr.h header files. Many LDAP-based errors are defined in the Winldap.h header file.

Note   For simplicity and explanation purposes, many of the samples shown in this book do not include graceful handling of errors, both common and esoteric. All applications, and particularly networking applications, should be able to handle errors with ease, possibly offering the user information and choices about how to proceed when unexpected events occur.

Properties and Attributes Revisited

Once again I'd like to emphasize the distinction between LDAP attribute names and ADSI property names. In the following example, the first line of code works, but the second returns an error:

```
varValue = objADs.Guid           ' Works
varValue = objADs.Get("GUID")    ' Does not work
```

The first line of code works because there is an *IADs* property named *GUID*. An error occurs in the second line because there is no attribute named *GUID* in the directory. There is an attribute named *objectGUID* and that is what the *IADs GUID* property maps to. Thus, the following two lines are nearly equivalent. They are "nearly" equivalent because the first line returns the GUID as a string and the second line returns the GUID as an octet string. (For more information on octet stings, see the section "GUID Binding" in Chapter 4.)

```
varValue = objADs.Guid
varValue = objADs.Get("objectGUID")
```

Here is an interesting exception. If you try the following code, it does execute without an error, but each line produces different results:

```
Debug.Print "Name property: " & objADs.Name
Debug.Print "Name attribute: " & objADs.Get("Name")
```

The output is something like the following:

```
Name property:  CN=Administrator
Name attribute: Administrator
```

The previous code executes without an error because most objects in Active Directory have a *name* attribute, which is different from the *Name* property supplied by *IADs*. Code in ADSI determines what the RDN of an object is and returns that as the *Name* property. The *name* attribute is usually the same as the *cn* (*Common-Name*) attribute.

Table 6-5 shows the mapping between *IADs* properties and associated Active Directory LDAP attributes. To illustrate this, the table includes real-world values from an object of the *domain* class, which is the root of the domain's directory partition. For a code sample that outputs these property and attribute mappings, see the PropertyMapping folder on the companion CD.

IADs Property	LDAP Attribute	Description
ADsPath "LDAP://DC=coppersoftware, DC=com"	*distinguishedName* "DC=coppersoftware, DC=com"	The *ADsPath* property also includes the provider string, whereas the distinguished name of an object does not.
Class "domainDNS"	*objectClass* ["top", "domain", "domainDNS"]	The *objectClass* attribute actually contains multiple values (discussed later in this chapter). ADSI uses the last value for the *Class* property.
GUID "adff8b88f6ed0a429b-0d402ac63bf704"	*objectGUID* [ad, ff, 8b, 88, f6, ed, 0a, 42, 9b, 0d, 40, 2a, c6, 3b, f7, 04]	The *objectGUID* attribute returns an array of binary values, shown in hexadecimal. The *GUID* property returns a string.
Name "DC=coppersoftware"	None	The *Name* property returns the RDN of the object, which is created dynamically by Active Directory.
Parent "LDAP://DC=com"	None	The ADSI *Parent* property dynamically creates the *ADsPath* property of the parent object.
Schema "LDAP://schema/domainDNS"	*objectCategory* "CN=Domain-DNS, CN=Schema,CN=Con-figuration,DC=copper-software,DC=com"	The *Schema* property uses an ADsPath format, whereas the *objectCategory* attribute uses a distinguished name format.

Table 6-5 Mapping *IADs* properties to LDAP attributes. Values shown in quotation marks are binary strings; values enclosed in brackets are variant arrays.

Reading Multivalued Attributes

So far we've been dealing with attributes that have a single value. Active Directory, however, allows a single attribute to have multiple values, which comes in handy for attributes that hold data that can contain one or more values of the same data type.

A good example is telephone numbers. Many people have multiple phone numbers at which they can be called. The *IADsUser* interface defines the *Telephone-Number* property, which can return a list of each number the person has in their directory entry. In Table 6-5, the *objectClass* attribute contains multiple values. Some of the common multivalued attributes associated with the *user* object are *member, memberOf, otherHomePhone, otherLoginWorkstations, otherMailbox, otherTelephone, postOfficeBox,* and *seeAlso.*

The *objectClass* attribute contains an array of string variants that correspond to the class object that the current object inherits from. Listing 6-1, from the MultiValued.bas sample on the companion CD, shows how a Visual Basic program can enumerate each of the values of the *objectClass* attribute.

```
Option Explicit

Public Sub Main()
Dim objRootDSE As IADs
Dim objADs As IADs
Dim strADsPath As String
Dim varClass As Variant
Dim varClasses As Variant

' Connect to the LDAP server's root object
Set objRootDSE = GetObject("LDAP://RootDSE")

' Form a path to a directory entry
strADsPath = "LDAP://" & objRootDSE.Get("defaultNamingContext")

' Bind to the object
Set objADs = GetObject(strADsPath)

' Use the Get method to access a multivalued attribute
varClasses = objADs.Get("objectClass")

If IsArray(varClasses) Then
    ' Enumerate and display each value for this attribute
    For Each varClass In varClasses
        ' Display the value
        Debug.Print varClass
```

Listing 6-1 MultiValued.bas showing how multivalued attributes are read in Visual Basic.

```
    Next
Else
    ' Attribute only contains a single attribute
    Debug.Print varClasses
End If

End Sub
```

In C++, reading multivalued attributes gets a little more complex because the C and C++ languages do little to protect the developer from exceeding the boundaries of an array. ADSI uses the Automation *SAFEARRAY* data type to hold the values in a multivalued attribute, as well as the upper and lower bounds of the array. You can use the *SafeArray* functions to retrieve each element in the array. Listing 6-2, from the MultiValue.cpp sample on the companion CD, shows how to read multivalued attributes using a *SAFEARRAY* data type.

```cpp
int _tmain(int /* argc */, _TCHAR /* **argv */, _TCHAR /* **envp */)
{
    IADs *pobjRootDSE;   // Pointer to RootDSE
    IADs *pobjIADs;      // Pointer to object interface
    HRESULT hResult;     // COM result code

    // Initalize COM
    CoInitialize( NULL );

    // Get the Active Directory RootDSE object
    hResult = ADsGetObject(
        L"LDAP://RootDSE", IID_IADs, (void**) &pobjRootDSE );

    // Ensure binding success before dereferencing pointer
    if ( SUCCEEDED( hResult ) )
        {
        // Distinguished name of domain directory
        _variant_t varRoot;

        // Use Get method to retrieve default naming context
        // (directory partition)
        hResult = pobjRootDSE->Get( L"defaultNamingContext", &varRoot );

        // No longer need the RootDSE object
        pobjRootDSE->Release();

        // Form a ADsPath string to the domain directory partition
        _bstr_t bstrADsPath = _bstr_t( L"LDAP://" ) +
            _bstr_t( varRoot.bstrVal );
```

Listing 6-2 MultiValue.cpp showing how multivalued attributes are read in C++.   *(continued)*

```
// Display information
_tprintf( _T("Binding to object at %s\n"),
    (const char *)bstrADsPath );

// Get a pointer to the domain object
hResult = ADsGetObject(
    bstrADsPath, IID_IADs, (void**) &pobjIADs );

// Ensure binding success before dereferencing pointer
if ( SUCCEEDED ( hResult ) )
    {
    // Value(s) for objectClass
    _variant_t varClasses;

    // Retrieve the objectClass attribute using the Get method
    hResult = pobjIADs->Get ( L"objectClass", &varClasses );

    if ( SUCCEEDED ( hResult ) )
        {
        // Display label
        _tprintf( _T("objectClass: ") );

        // Does this attribute contain multiple values?
        // Use the Automation macro to check for an array
        if ( V_ISARRAY( &varClasses ) )
            {
            // Create a safe array
            SAFEARRAY *saClasses = V_ARRAY( &varClasses );

            // Setup the upper and lower boundries of the array
            long lMin;
            long lMax;
            SafeArrayGetLBound( saClasses, 1, &lMin );
            SafeArrayGetUBound( saClasses, 1, &lMax );

            // Enumerate all the values of the array
            long lIndex;
            for ( lIndex = lMin;
                lIndex <= lMax;
                lIndex++ )
                {
                // Create a variant to hold the current value
                _variant_t varClass;
```

```
                        // Use the Automation helper function to
                        // get the value
                        hResult = SafeArrayGetElement(
                            saClasses, &lIndex, &varClass );

                        if ( SUCCEEDED( hResult ) )
                            {
                            // Display the line
                            _tprintf ( _T("%s, "), (const char *)
                                _bstr_t( varClass ) );
                            }
                        }
                    // Terminate the line
                    _tprintf ( _T("\n") );
                    }
                else
                    {
                    // Display the single value for this attribute
                    _tprintf ( _TEXT("%s\n"), (const char *)
                        _bstr_t( varClasses ) );
                    }
                }
            // Object no longer needed
            pobjIADs->Release();
            }
        }
    // Unload COM
    CoUninitialize();

    // Return the result of any failures
    return hResult;
}
```

Not all attributes can accept multiple values. The attribute definition in the schema determines whether a particular attribute can contain multiple values. You can determine whether an attribute contains multiple values dynamically by calling the *IsArray* function in Visual Basic or the Automation macro *VT_ISARRAY* in C++.

You can check the attribute's schema entry to see whether the attribute you are working with allows multiple values. Here is some code from the Visual Basic version of the IADsProperties sample that enumerates the abstract schema container, checking each defined property for whether it is multivalued. If it is, it's added to a list box for display. (I'll discuss enumerating containers in more detail later in the chapter in the section "Enumerating Containers." I'll discuss the abstract schema container in Chapter 9.)

```
'===================================================
' Display multivalued attributes in list box
'===================================================
Dim objADsSchema As IADsContainer
Dim objADsProperty As IADsProperty

' Clear the list box contents
lstProperties.Clear

' Get the abstract schema container
Set objADsSchema = GetObject("LDAP://Schema")

' Filter only properties
objADsSchema.Filter = Array("property")

' Enumerate the schema container
For Each objADsProperty In objADsSchema

    ' Check if multivalued
    If objADsProperty.MultiValued Then
        ' Add the name to the list
        lstProperties.AddItem objADsProperty.Name
    End If
Next
```

The *GetEx* Method

A major hassle in dealing with a multivalued attribute is that you must take one of two possible code paths to handle it: one for a single value, or another for multiple values. Wouldn't it be nice if you could use the same code for both single and multivalued attributes? The *GetEx* method solves this problem quite nicely.

GetEx performs the same function as *Get*, but it returns the data differently. The *Get* method returns a binary string for single values and a variant array for multiple values. The *GetEx* method always returns a variant array. Your code does not have to check for an array and can use the array code for single values as well as multiple values. The following code, from the GetExMethod.bas sample on the companion CD, demonstrates this:

```
' The GetEx method always returns a variant array even for single values
varClasses = objADs.GetEx("objectClass")
```

```
' Enumerate and display each value for this attribute
For Each varClass In varClasses
    ' Display the value
    Debug.Print varClass
Next
```

So if *GetEx* is more consistent, why does ADSI bother providing the *Get* method? For simplicity reasons. With *GetEx*, you always get an array in return, but that requires your code to enumerate the array, even if just one value exists.

> **Note**   Always use *GetEx* for multivalued attributes.

Named Properties or the *Get* Method: Which Is Better?

Even though you can access the underlying attribute easily using the *Get* method, I recommend that you use the ADSI properties wherever possible. ADSI works hard to make life easier for developers. It performs data type conversions and always returns a variant value. Generally, ADSI properties can be used without conversion in other ADSI methods.

Another advantage of using named properties is that they always exist. The *Get* or *GetEx* method will throw an error if the attribute currently has no value. (See the "Handling Errors in ADSI" section earlier in the chapter for information about error handling.) The named properties, on the other hand, will always return something, or *NULL* if there is no value. However, in some cases, an interface may define a value that isn't supported by the current provider. This will result in an *E_NOTIMPL* (not implemented) error. The ADSI documentation contains a list of the supported interfaces and properties for the ADSI LDAP provider. (See the topic titled "Provider Support of ADSI Interfaces" in the ADSI documentation.)

There is a small performance hit incurred by using *Get* rather than a named property. When you call *Get* and pass the name of the attribute as a string, ADSI must look up that attribute, which takes some additional time. Of course, since not all LDAP attributes are mapped to ADSI properties, there are times when you must use the *Get* method. In case you need more encouragement, it makes sense to use the ADSI properties in regular practice just in case the underlying structure of Active Directory changes. ADSI will likely be updated to return the correct information regardless of which attribute contains it.

Accessing Properties in Yet Another Way

In Visual Basic and VBScript, you can access object properties without explicitly calling the *Get* method. For example, the following two lines of code are functionally identical:

```
varClasses = objADs.GetEx("objectClass")
varClasses = objADs.objectClass
```

This may seem to contradict what I've been talking about, but it doesn't really. It's impossible to have a named property for every possible attribute because attributes can be added at any time by extending the Active Directory schema. However, as you saw, ADSI allows access to attributes using the *Get* method; what's new here is specifying the attribute name as a property, even though the interface, *IADs* in this case, doesn't have a named property labeled *objectClass*.

What ADSI does in this case is make an implicit call to the *Get* method, passing the property name, *objectClass*, as the attribute. This makes things convenient for developers, but it is costly for performance. Since Visual Basic does not recognize *objectClass* as a named property of the *IADs* interface, it must defer to the object implementation to figure out what to do. Specifically, Visual Basic and the scripting languages use the *IDispatch* interface to pass the property name to the object for handling.

The ADSI implementation of *IDispatch* allows for dynamic properties in addition to the properties defined for the various ADSI interfaces. However, using *IDispatch* causes Visual Basic to use late binding. This decreases performance because of calls to get the dispatch ID (*DISPID*) for the referenced property.

Because of the hoops that Visual Basic has to jump through, it's better to call the *Get* method directly, which saves Visual Basic a few steps. The performance penalty is probably negligible, particularly in light of the time required to retrieve information from the server, but to me that means it's even more important to save CPU cycles wherever possible.

The scripting languages always perform late binding, so it does not matter whether you use the *Get* method or not. For examples in this book, I'll use *Get* for properties not defined by the interfaces for consistency.

The Property Cache

You might expect that each time your application retrieves a property of an object, ADSI makes a request of the Active Directory server for the information. In reality this would be horribly inefficient, particularly over potentially slow network connections.

To minimize trips to the server and back, ADSI maintains a client-side *property cache* to hold an object's property values locally. Each entry in the cache contains information about the property's name, its data type, and its value or values. When an application requests an ADSI property or calls the *Get* or *GetEx* methods, ADSI first checks the local property cache to see whether the property is present. If it isn't, ADSI makes a request of the Active Directory server to retrieve all the object's properties at once to populate the property cache. Subsequent requests for properties are completed very quickly because ADSI does not need to return to the server for more information. Figure 6-3 illustrates the workings of the property cache.

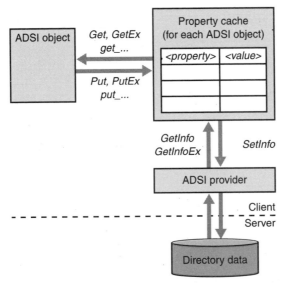

Figure 6-3 The ADSI property cache.

ADSI creates the property cache when you bind to an object but does not fill it with values until you actually request a property. The first time a property that is not already in the cache is accessed, all the attributes of that particular object are transferred from the server to the client's property cache.

The *GetInfo* Method

Your application can also force ADSI to load or refresh the property cache by using the *GetInfo* method of the *IADs* interface. Refreshing the cache retrieves the current properties from the server. If your application stays bound to an object for a long time, it's possible that another application will update the directory data. Active Directory does not automatically refresh the property cache when changes are made by another application.

The following code, from the GetInfo.bas sample on the companion CD, shows how to call *GetInfo* using Visual Basic.

```
' Bind to the object
Set objADs = GetObject(strADsPath)

' At this point, the property cache is empty
' Use GetInfo to explicitly load it
objADs.GetInfo

' Use the IADs Get method to retrieve the distinguishedName attribute
strDN = objADs.Get("distinguishedName")
```

> **Note**   Operational attributes are not retrieved by the *GetInfo* method and must be explicitly retrieved using the *GetInfoEx* method. Operational attributes are usually administrative attributes that are implemented internally by Active Directory but that don't appear in the schema. For example, many of the attributes for the *RootDSE* object are operational attributes.

The *GetInfoEx* Method

If you're like me, you cringe at the thought of all the properties of an object being loaded at the same time. What happens if the object has a large number of properties? Or from a more practical point of view, why should the property cache be loaded with all the properties of an object when you're only interested in one or a few select properties?

The clever ADSI folks think the same way, and they provided an additional method, *GetInfoEx*, to give applications control over which properties are loaded into the property cache.

GetInfoEx accepts a variant array of strings that identifies which properties of the object should be retrieved from the directory and placed in the cache. *GetInfoEx* works exactly like *GetInfo*, but it's more selective. The following code, from the GetInfoEx.bas sample on the companion CD, shows how to use *GetInfoEx* using Visual Basic.

```
' Bind to the object
Set objADs = GetObject(strADsPath)
```

```
' Fill an array with the properties we want to access
varProperties = Array("objectCategory", "distinguishedName")

' Use GetInfoEx to explicitly load only the properties listed in the array
' The second parameter is reserved for future use and must be zero
objADs.GetInfoEx varProperties, 0

' Display the properties
Debug.Print objADs.Get("objectCategory")
Debug.Print objADs.Get("distinguishedName")

' This next property isn't in the cache, so GetInfo will be
' implicitly called
Debug.Print objADs.Get("whenCreated")
```

Writing Attributes

Up until now, of course, we've just been binding to objects, retrieving values, and enumerating multivalues, but what about actually modifying attribute values in Active Directory?

ADSI makes writing to Active Directory easy with the *Put* and *PutEx* methods. Conceptually, these methods are the same as *Get* and *GetEx*, but they work in reverse. Instead of retrieving values from the property cache, they write values to the cache. Once the changes have been made to the property cache, you use the *SetInfo* method to write the data to Active Directory.

The exact steps required to update a value depend on which language you're developing in and whether the attribute is a named ADSI property or an LDAP attribute.

ADSI Properties

Some properties, such as *Name, TelephoneNumber*, and others—which I've been referring to as *named properties*—are provided by the various ADSI interfaces. When using Visual Basic or scripting languages, COM and the *IDispatch* interface take care of figuring out whether to read the value from the property or to write a new value to the property. The following code, from the ReadWrite.bas sample on the companion CD, retrieves the *TelephoneNumber* property for the current user and then uses the *InputBox* function to prompt the user to change their telephone number. To determine the current user, as well as other system information, ADSI provides the *ADSystemInfo* object and the *IADsADSystemInfo* interface, which are supported only on Windows 2000.

```
' Create ADSystemInfo object
Set objSysInfo = CreateObject("ADSystemInfo")

' Get the distinguished name of the current user
strUserDN = objSysInfo.UserName

' Prefix the users DN with the ADSI provider string to form a ADsPath
strADsPath = "LDAP://" & strUserDN

' Bind to the object
Set objADs = GetObject(strADsPath)

' Read the telephone number property
strPhoneNumber = objADs.TelephoneNumber

' Prompt string
strPrompt = "The current phone number is shown in the edit box." & _
    "Type a new number and press Enter."

' Display the number as the default, and then ask to change it
strPhoneNumber = InputBox(strPrompt, objADs.Name, strPhoneNumber)

If strPhoneNumber <> "" Then
    ' Write the new value to the object
    objADs.TelephoneNumber = strPhoneNumber

    ' Commit the change to the server
    objADs.SetInfo
End If
```

Using the *InputBox* function from the ReadWrite.bas sample is shown in Figure 6-4.

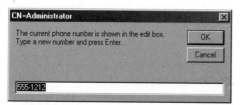

Figure 6-4 The input box created by the ReadWrite.bas sample, prompting the user for a new telephone number.

Take a closer look at these two lines from the example:

```
strPhoneNumber = objADs.TelephoneNumber
objADs.TelephoneNumber = strPhoneNumber
```

The first line reads the property, and the second line writes the property. Visual Basic, along with Automation, figures out the exact interface method to call based on the type of operation: a *get* (read) or a *put* (write).

C and C++ developers have to be more explicit with their code, calling *get_TelephoneNumber* to retrieve a property value and *put_TelephoneNumber* to set the value. Listing 6-3 shows code from the ReadWrite.cpp sample on the companion CD. The code reads the *Name* and *TelephoneNumber* properties of the current user. The program then prompts the user for a new phone number and writes that back to the directory.

```cpp
int _tmain(int /* argc */, _TCHAR /* **argv */, _TCHAR /* **envp */)
{
    // Initalize COM and result code
    HRESULT hResult = CoInitialize( NULL );

    // Create ADSystemInfo object
    IADsADSystemInfo *pobjADSysInfo;
    hResult = CoCreateInstance(
        CLSID_ADSystemInfo,
        NULL,
        CLSCTX_INPROC_SERVER,
        IID_IADsADSystemInfo,
        (void**) &pobjADSysInfo);

    if ( SUCCEEDED(hResult) )
        {
        // Get the distinguished name of the current user
        BSTR bstrUserDN = NULL;
        hResult = pobjADSysInfo->get_UserName( &bstrUserDN );

        // ADSystemInfo object no longer needed
        if ( pobjADSysInfo )
            pobjADSysInfo->Release();

        // Prefix the users DN with the ADSI provider string to
        // form a ADsPath
        _bstr_t bstrUserADsPath =
            _bstr_t(L"LDAP://") + _bstr_t(bstrUserDN);

        // Free allocated BSTR
        SysFreeString( bstrUserDN );

        // Display information
        _tprintf( _T("Binding to object at %s\n"),
            (const char *)bstrUserADsPath );
```

Listing 6-3 ReadWrite.cpp shows how to write attribute values in C++.   *(continued)*

179

```
// Get a pointer to the object using the IADsUser interface
IADsUser *pobjIADsUser;
hResult = ADsGetObject( bstrUserADsPath, IID_IADsUser,
    (void**) &pobjIADsUser );

// Ensure binding success before dereferencing pointer
if ( SUCCEEDED( hResult ) )
    {
    // Retrieve Name property into BSTR variable
    BSTR bstrPropertyValue;
    hResult = pobjIADsUser->get_Name( &bstrPropertyValue );

    if ( SUCCEEDED( hResult ) )
        {
        // Display BSTR variable - note %S to denote wide string
        _tprintf( _T("Name: %S \n"), bstrPropertyValue );
        }

    // Display current phone number
    _variant_t varPropertyValue;
    hResult = pobjIADsUser->get_TelephoneNumber(
        &varPropertyValue );

    // Always check the result in case property doesn't exist
    if ( SUCCEEDED( hResult ) )
        {
        // Display a variant string, converting to
        // null-terminated string
        _tprintf( _T("Current phone number is %s \n"),
            (const char *) _bstr_t( varPropertyValue ) );
        }
    else    // get_TelephoneNumber failed
        {
        // Possibly error 0x8000500D (E_ADS_PROPERTY_NOT_FOUND)
        _tprintf(
            _T("Could not access TelephoneNumber property.\n") );

        // Display the error code in decimal and hex forms
        _tprintf( _T("Error number %d (0x%X) \n"),
            hResult, hResult );
        }
```

```
        // Prompt for input
        _tprintf( _T("Type new phone number and press Enter: ") );

        // Get new number from console
        TCHAR  szPhoneNumber[81];
        _getts ( szPhoneNumber );

        // Copy the null-terminated string into the variant
        varPropertyValue = _variant_t( szPhoneNumber );

        // Write property back to the cache
        hResult = pobjIADsUser->put_TelephoneNumber(
            varPropertyValue );

        if ( SUCCEEDED( hResult ) )
            {
            // Commit change to the directory using SetInfo
            hResult = pobjIADsUser->SetInfo();

            if ( SUCCEEDED( hResult ) )
                {
                _tprintf( _T("Change committed.\n") );
                }
            }
        // Object no longer needed
        if ( pobjIADsUser )
            pobjIADsUser->Release();
        }
    }
// Unload COM
CoUninitialize();

// Return the result of any failures
return hResult;
}
```

Something interesting about this example is the different data types used for the *Name* and *TelephoneNumber* properties. Many interfaces use binary strings for property values, including all the *IADs* properties. However, the *TelephoneNumber* property uses a variant array. It does this because under other providers, the *TelephoneNumber* property might be an array of all the phone numbers for that particular user. In the case of the ADSI LDAP provider and Active

Directory, all the *IADsUser* phone number properties (*FaxNumber*, *TelephoneHome*, *TelephoneMobile*, *TelephoneNumber*, and *TelephonePager*) return a variant array, but with a single string element.

Note   You can't write to all the ADSI properties. As mentioned earlier in this chapter, all the *IADs* properties, such as *Name*, *ADsPath*, and so on are read-only and cannot be changed. They represent fixed information about the object.

The *Put* Method

Using the named properties of the ADSI interfaces is simple, really, and it's no different from using any other COM-based component, such as ADO or Collaboration Data Objects (CDO), that you might be familiar with.

Updating the values of the Active Directory attributes that aren't mapped to ADSI interfaces is just slightly different from the samples in the previous section. In this case you use the *Put* method to write new values, as shown in the following code, from the PutMethod.bas sample on the companion CD.

```
' Read the telephone number property
strPhoneNumber = objADs.Get("telephoneNumber")
...
' Write the new value to the object
objADs.Put "telephoneNumber", strPhoneNumber
```

Once again, updating values for Active Directory attributes that don't correspond to ADSI interfaces is more complex with C or C++, but conceptually it's the same. The following code, from the PutMethod.cpp sample on the companion CD, shows how to use the *Put* method in C++.

```
// Get current telephone number for this user
_variant_t varPropertyValue;
hResult = pobjIADs->Get( L"telephoneNumber", &varPropertyValue );
...
// Write property back to the cache using the Put method
hResult = pobjIADs->Put( L"telephoneNumber", varPropertyValue );
```

Parentheses and Visual Basic

Visual Basic and thus VBScript have a quirk regarding the use of parentheses. Basically, parentheses are required when passing parameters to a function when the function is called as part of an expression or assignment. When you do not need to check or save the return value, parentheses are not allowed. If you want your code to be consistent with regard to parentheses, use the *Call* statement. For example:

```
' Parentheses not allowed
objADs.Put "telephoneNumber", strPhoneNumber
' Parentheses required
Call objADs.Put("telephoneNumber", strPhoneNumber)
```

The *SetInfo* Method

In the previous Visual Basic and C++ samples, you'll notice that the *SetInfo* method is called. After you've finished updating an object, you must call the *SetInfo* method to save your changes to the directory.

Instead of going to the directory with each update request, changes made using ADSI properties and the *Put* method are simply made to the local property cache. You can then make bulk changes to an object without incurring a round-trip performance penalty. ADSI marks each property entry in the cache as being changed or not, so only the values that have changed will be written to the directory when you call *SetInfo*.

> **Note**   Property value changes are not saved to the directory until there is a successful call to the *SetInfo* method.

If you explicitly call *GetInfo*, the current values of the object's properties will be fetched from the directory. This is by design, since you might want to refresh the cache with the latest values and flush any uncommitted changes. However, when the cache is refreshed, any changes not saved will be overwritten. The following code writes a new value to the *telephoneNumber* attribute, but the change is lost when *GetInfo* is called.

```
Set objADs = GetObject(strADsPath)

' Write the new value to the object
objADs.Put "telephoneNumber", "800-555-1212"

' Explicit GetInfo
Call objADs.GetInfo()

' Display number - will show old number, not 800-555-1212
MsgBox objADs.TelephoneNumber
```

Writing Multivalued Attributes

So far, our examples of how to modify attribute values have used properties and attributes that accept only a single value. We can use the *Put* method to write multivalued attributes as well, with the limitation that when you call *Put* it replaces all the current values of the attribute with whatever is contained in the variant array that is passed in.

For example, let's say the *otherTelephone* attribute has the values 111-1111, 222-2222, and 333-3333. The following code would replace those values with 444-4444 and 555-5555.

```
objADs.Put "otherTelephone", Array("444-4444", "555-5555")
objADs.SetInfo
```

The *Put* method is a blunt tool. You cannot use it to slice and dice the various values in a multivalued attribute—it's all or nothing. Of course, you could read all the values into your own data structure, manipulate the structure however you choose, and then write it back en masse using *Put*. However, for those who crave more control, ADSI gives it to you in the form of the *PutEx* method.

The *PutEx* Method

The *PutEx* method is a more sophisticated version of the *Put* method. It allows you to change or remove an existing value, append a new value, or clear all the values of the attribute. One scenario for using *PutEx* would be to add the organization's new toll-free telephone number to each *user* object without disturbing the existing values.

The *PutEx* method takes three parameters. The first is the control code, which tells ADSI how to treat multivalued attributes. The next two are the attribute name and the value or values to be written, the same as with the *Put* method.

The control code value is taken from one of the constants defined in the property control code enumeration (*ADS_PROPERTY_OPERATION_ENUM*). These constants are listed in Table 6-6.

Property Control Code Constant	Description
ADS_PROPERTY_CLEAR	Removes all values from the attribute
ADS_PROPERTY_UPDATE	Replaces the current values with new values passed in (same as *Put*)
ADS_PROPERTY_APPEND	Appends the passed value to the list of values for this attribute
ADS_PROPERTY_DELETE	Removes the specified value

Table 6-6 Control codes defined in *ADS_PROPERTY_OPERATION_ENUM* used with the *PutEx* method.

Appending Values

Here is an example using the *otherTelephone* attribute, which is multivalued. The following code, from the PutEx.bas sample on the companion CD, appends an array of telephone numbers to the *otherTelephone* attribute. You must always pass a variant array to *PutEx*, even if you may be working with only one value at a time.

```
' Bind to the object
Set objADs = GetObject(strADsPath)

' Use GetEx method to save original numbers as a variant array
varOrigNumbers = objADs.GetEx("otherTelephone")

' Append new numbers to the attribute
objADs.PutEx ADS_PROPERTY_APPEND, "otherTelephone", _
    Array("800-555-1111", "800-555-2222", "800-555-3333")

' Commit the change to the directory
objADs.SetInfo
```

Active Directory will allow only a single instance of a value to exist in the attribute. If you run this code several times, it will not continue to append the phone numbers to the *otherTelephone* attribute. ADSI does not return an error code in this case.

In addition, Active Directory does not concern itself with the order of the attributes. The exact order is undefined and may vary. This is important for a series of numbers. If you write the values in a certain sequence, such as *Array(1, 2, 3, 4, 5)*, they might not be returned in the same sequence.

> **Note**   Do not depend on the order of the values in a multivalued attribute.

Removing Values

To remove a particular value from an attribute you use the *ADS_PROPERTY_DELETE* control code.

```
' Delete value
objADs.PutEx ADS_PROPERTY_DELETE, "otherTelephone", _
    Array("800-555-1111", "888-888-8888")
```

PutEx will not return an error code if one or more values did not exist.

Removing All Values

To remove all the values of a multivalued attribute, use the *ADS_PROPERTY_CLEAR* control code.

```
' Delete all the values of the attribute
objADs.PutEx ADS_PROPERTY_CLEAR, "otherTelephone", vbNullString
```

You can pass anything in the value parameter of *PutEx* because it is ignored when *ADS_PROPERTY_CLEAR* is used. After removing all the values of an attribute and updating the directory with *SetInfo*, the attribute ceases to exist for that object. Subsequent retrievals will result in a "property not found" error. This is normal. See the section "Handling Errors in ADSI" earlier in the chapter for information about how to handle this error.

Updating Values

You can replace all the values at once using the *ADS_PROPERTY_UPDATE* control code. This is the same as using the *Put* method, but it works for multivalued attributes.

```
' Update the property value
adsObj.PutEx ADS_PROPERTY_UPDATE, "otherTelephone", _
    Array("800-555-1111")
```

None of the original values will remain. In this example, if there were previously three phone number values, all would be deleted and replaced with one value.

Active Directory Attribute Oddities

The *otherTelephone* attribute is different from the *telephoneNumber* attribute, which is mapped to the *TelephoneNumber* property. The *otherTelephone* attribute is multivalued, whereas *telephoneNumber* is not. These values can be viewed and changed using the Active Directory Users and Computers administrative tool. The first illustration below shows the Properties dialog box for the Administrator with the single-valued *telephoneNumber* attribute in the Telephone Number box. The second illustration shows the Phone Number (Others) dialog box displaying values for the multivalued *otherTelephone* attribute.

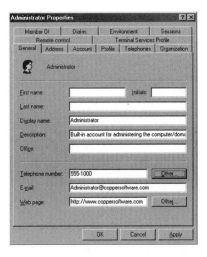

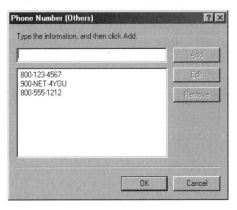

(continued)

Active Directory Attribute Oddities *continued*

You would think that if an attribute can be multivalued, there would be no need for a single-valued version. However, that's not the case. Active Directory uses a multivalued version and a single-valued version for all its phone number attributes, as well as for other attributes. Here's a list of the single-valued and multivalued phone number attributes in Active Directory.

Single-Valued Attribute	Multivalued Attribute
facsimileTelephoneNumber	*otherFacsimileTelephoneNumber*
homePhone	*otherHomePhone*
IpPhone	*otherIpPhone*
Mobile	*otherMobile*
Pager	*otherPager*
telephoneNumber	*otherTelephoneNumber*

Containers

As I've mentioned earlier in this book, in Active Directory, all objects, except the root object, are grouped under another object, known as a *container*. The container is often referred to as the *parent* object, while each object within the container is considered a *child* object. Active Directory documentation also refers to objects that have no children as *leaves* or *leaf nodes*.

In a virtual sense, a container object is simply a regular Active Directory object that is marked as a container. While the Active Directory schema provides a *container* class object, this does not mean that only *container* class objects can be containers. You need to understand the importance of this because any object can become a container object, not just objects of the class *container*. An excellent example of this is the objects representing computers on the network. These are objects of the class *computer* and are normally contained in the *Computers* or *Domain Controllers* container. When a printer is published in Active Directory, an object representing the print queue is created in the directory. The computer that physically hosts the printer is marked as a container, and the new *printQueue* object is made a child of the *computer* object.

Figure 6-5 shows a printer as a child of the *computer* object COPPER2. You need to select a View option in the Active Directory Users and Computers snap-in to show children of users, groups, and computers.

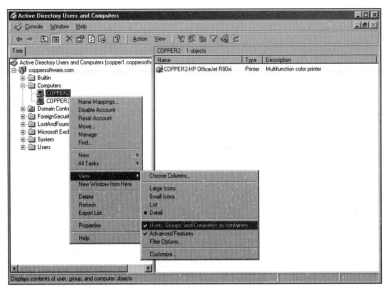

Figure 6-5 *Computer* object COPPER2 is shown as a container for a *printer* object.

The concept of containers has many benefits for developers. By allowing any object to be made a container, information that is relevant to all the child objects can be stored in the parent object. For example, information about the organizational unit, such as location information and group policy, can be stored within the parent, an *organizationalUnit* class object.

Enumerating Containers

Enumeration is the process of retrieving each object within a container. Automation, coupled with Visual Basic, makes this process very easy.

```
Set objContainer = GetObject("LDAP://CN=Users,DC=coppersoftware,DC=com")

For Each objUser in objContainer
    Debug.Print objUser.Name
Next
```

In this code, each iteration through the *For Each* loop assigns the variable *objUser* with an object that is part of the container referenced by the variable *objContainer*.

This enumeration is made possible by the *IADsContainer* interface. This interface is made available by ADSI for any object that contains other objects. *IADsContainer* is a versatile interface supplying several functions for operations such as enumerating container objects, creating and deleting objects, and moving

189

objects. Tables 6-7 and 6-8 list the properties and methods of the *IADsContainer* interface.

IADsContainer Property	Returned Data Type	Description
Count	Long	A count of the number of objects in the container. Read-only. Not supported under Active Directory.
Filter	Variant array of strings	An array of class names to filter on. When this property is set, only objects of the class that matches the filter are enumerated. The default is to enumerate all classes.
Hints	Variant array of strings	An array of attribute names to retrieve for each object when enumerating a container.
get__NewEnum (Not exposed in Visual Basic)	Object	Creates a new enumerator object that supports the *IEnumVARIANT* interface. Called indirectly from Visual Basic using the *For Each* statement. Returns an *IUnknown* interface pointer. Note that there are two underscore (_) characters in the method name.

Table 6-7 Properties of the *IADsContainer* interface.

IADsContainer Method	Description
Create	Creates a new object in the container of the class specified. Also accepts a name. Returns an *IDispatch* interface from which *IADs* properties and methods can be called. The object is not stored in the directory until the *SetInfo* method is called.
Delete	Deletes the object in the container specified by name. You must also supply the class name. The object will not be deleted from the directory until the *SetInfo* method is called.
CopyHere	Creates a new copy of the specified object in the container. Not supported under Active Directory.
GetObject	Binds to an object from the container using the provided relative name. Can also specify class name as added identification. Not required with Active Directory. Returns an *IDispatch* interface from which *IADs* properties and methods can be called.
MoveHere	Moves an object from another container to the current container, optionally providing a new name. Can be used to rename objects within the same container.

Table 6-8 Methods of the *IADsContainer* interface.

IADsContainer is unique among the ADSI interfaces in that it provides an *enumerator* object. An enumerator is a special COM object that allows a program to enumerate through a collection of other objects of the same type. Using the Visual Basic and VBScript *For Each* statement, you can use this enumerator object. JScript provides support for enumerators through the *Enumerator* object.

Visual Basic, VBScript, and JScript all handle enumerators transparently. Developers working with C or C++, as usual when it comes to COM, have a little extra work involved. Behind the scenes and hidden from the developer, Visual Basic and the scripting languages use the *get__NewEnum* property of *IADsContainer* to have ADSI create the enumerator object. In C and C++, you must call *get__NewEnum* yourself and then use *QueryInterface* to get the *IEnumVARIANT* interface. ADSI provides some help with utility functions that perform some of the steps required in working with enumerators. The *ADsBuildEnumerator*, *ADsEnumerateNext*, and *ADsFreeEnumerator* functions perform some of the work involved with calling *get__NewEnum* and the *IEnumVARIANT* interface directly. Enumeration is generic among all C and C++ programs using COM, so I won't go into the details here.

> **Note**   If you are working with C or C++, be careful to note that two underscore characters appear in *get__NewEnum*. Technically, the *IADsContainer* interface defines a read-only property called *_NewEnum,* with one underscore. The single underscore indicates a special restricted property. Since you only need to use *_NewEnum* from C or C++, and in those environments you are required to prefix method calls to properties with either *get_* or *put_,* I've listed it here as *get__NewEnum,* which is the name of the function you need to call from the *IADsContainer* interface.

Controlling Enumeration

The *IADsContainer* interface has two properties that you can set to help control the enumeration process. The *Filter* property is used when you just want to enumerate certain classes of objects. Doing this is extremely helpful when a container has a large number of objects and you are interested only in a certain type. The *Filter* property actually takes an array of strings, where each string is the class name that should be included in the enumeration.

The filtering is done on the client-side. The client must still access all the objects of the container; however, only objects matching the filter are enumerated. Filtering on the client might be a performance issue with large containers. Take, for example, the enumeration of *group* objects in the *Users* container of a company with 40,000 employees and hundreds of groups. In those kinds of cases, letting the server do the filtering is best. This approach was discussed in Chapter 5, "Searching Active Directory."

The *Hints* property is another way to increase performance. Like the *Filter* property, it takes an array of strings, each with the name of an attribute to retrieve. When enumerating, ADSI usually binds to each enumerated object and loads all the attributes of the object using the *GetInfo* method. This can be a huge waste of time if you're only interested in a certain number of attributes of the object. Listing 6-4, from the EnumContainer.bas sample on the companion CD, shows how to use the *Filter* and *Hints* properties in Visual Basic to enumerate all the *Organizational Unit* containers in the directory. By removing or commenting the line *varClasses = Array("organizationalUnit")* and by deleting the reference to *varClasses(0)* in the *Debug.Print* line, you can enumerate all objects in the directory recursively. (For a C++ sample that shows how to enumerate objects in a container, see the EnumContainers folder on the companion CD.)

```
Option Explicit
Dim nIndentLevel As Double ' Global variable to track nesting level

Public Sub Main()
' Enumerate all the containers in the directory partion
Dim objRootDSE As IADs
Dim strPath As String
Dim objContainer As IADsContainer
Dim varClasses As Variant

    ' Connect to the LDAP server's root object
    Set objRootDSE = GetObject("LDAP://RootDSE")

    ' Form a ADsPath string to the name of the default domain
    strPath = "LDAP://" + objRootDSE.Get("defaultNamingContext")

    ' Connect to the directory specified in the path
    Set objContainer = GetObject(strPath)

    ' Display the name of the object
    Debug.Print objContainer.Name

    ' Setup array of classes to enumerate
    varClasses = Array("organizationalUnit")

    ' Display ADsPath being used
    Debug.Print "Listing " & varClasses(0) & " objects at " _
        & strPath & "..."
```

Listing 6-4 EnumContainer.bas shows how to use the *Filter* and *Hints* properties to enumerate all the *Organizational Unit* containers in the directory.

```
        ' Enumerate the container
    Call EnumContainer(objContainer, varClasses)

End Sub

Public Function EnumContainer(objContainer As IADsContainer, _
varSchemaClasses As Variant)

Dim objADs As IADs
Dim objClass As IADsClass

    ' Increase the indent level
    nIndentLevel = nIndentLevel + 1

    ' Only enumerate certain classes
    objContainer.Filter = varSchemaClasses

    ' Retrieve only the Name and Schema attributes
    objContainer.Hints = Array("Name", "Schema")

    ' Loop through each object in the container
    For Each objADs In objContainer

        ' Indent text according the nesting level
        Debug.Print String(nIndentLevel, vbTab);

        ' Display the name of the object
        Debug.Print objADs.Name

        ' Get the class of object
        Set objClass = GetObject(objADs.Schema)

        ' Check whether this class is a container
        If (objClass.Container = True) Then

            ' Recurse to enumerate this container
            Call EnumContainer(objADs, varSchemaClasses)
        End If
    Next

    ' After going through a container, reduce the indent level
    nIndentLevel = nIndentLevel - 1

End Function
```

Adding Objects

The *IADsContainer* interface is also the interface you use to add objects to the directory. Once again, ADSI makes this a near trivial task. The function below accepts two strings, one a name for the new object and the other the class name for the new object. Active Directory uses the class name to determine what attributes are available for the object. You must call *SetInfo* to update the directory, otherwise the object is only created locally and will be discarded when the object reference is released.

The name of an object is given as the RDN for the new object. Generally this is "CN=MyObject". In the case of an *Organizational Unit* container, this would be "OU=MyOrgUnit". The following function shows how to create new objects in a container:

```
' Creates a new object in the container specified
Public Function CreateObject(strClass As String, strName As String, _
strADsPath As String) As IADs

Dim objContainer As IADsContainer
Dim objClass As IADsClass
Dim objNewObject As IADs

    ' Bind to the object at the path given
    Set objContainer = GetObject(strADsPath)

    ' Get the class of object
    Set objClass = GetObject(objContainer.Schema)

    ' Check whether this class is a container
    If (objClass.Container = True) Then

        ' Create new object in the container
        Set objNewObject = objContainer.Create(strClass, strName)

        ' Write the new object to the directory
        objNewObject.SetInfo

        ' Return the new object back to the caller
        Set CreateObject = objNewObject

    Else
        ' Not a container, exit
        Debug.Print objContainer.Name & " at "; _
            strADsPath; " is not a container."
        CreateObject = Nothing
    End If

End Function
```

Deleting Objects

Deleting an object is nearly identical to creating one. Once again, the class name and RDN are used to identify the object within the container. Actually, under Active Directory and the ADSI LDAP provider, the object's RDN is sufficient to uniquely identify the object within a container. However, other directory services require both parameters and, as such, both are required when you call the *Delete* method of the *IADsContainer* interface.

To delete an object, you must ask the object's container to delete the object; you cannot perform the operation directly on the object itself. In the following function, the object to be deleted is named *objADsToDelete*, and I use its *Parent* method (from the *IADs* interface) to get the distinguished name string to its parent container. Then I use the *Class* and *Name* properties to identify the object to the container when calling the *Delete* method.

```
' Deletes the object
Public Function DeleteObject(objADsToDelete As IADs)

Dim objContainer As IADsContainer

    ' Get the parent of the object
    Set objContainer = GetObject(objADsToDelete.Parent)

    ' Call the parent container's Delete method
    ' Specify object class and name
    objContainer.Delete objADsToDelete.Class, objADsToDelete.Name

    ' Explicitly discard object reference, no longer valid
    Set objADsToDelete = Nothing

    ' Update the directory
    objContainer.SetInfo

End Function
```

If the object is a container itself, it must be empty or Active Directory will report an error. You must delete all the contained objects first. Fortunately, ADSI helps out again, supplying an interface you can use to wipe out the container and all the objects contained within it: the *IADsDeleteOps* interface.

Easy Deleting with *IADsDeleteOps*

The *IADsDeleteOps* interface is used for performing sweeping deletion operations in the directory. It can delete the current object and all objects contained within it, which is useful for removing chunks of the directory tree without having to enumerate each child object and delete it using the *Delete* method of *IADsContainer*.

The *IADsDeleteOps* interface has only one member, the *DeleteObject* method. This method uses the current object—which supports the *IADsDeleteOps* interface—enumerates any child objects and deletes the current object. After the call to *DeleteObject*, the reference to the object is no longer valid and should be released by setting the variable to *Nothing* (in Visual Basic and VBScript) or by calling the *Release* method (in C or C++).

The *DeleteObject* method accepts a number as a parameter, but at this time the parameter is unused. You can use 0 when calling *DeleteObject*. The following function shows how to use the *IADsDeleteOps* interface and the *DeleteObject* method.

```
' Deletes the current object and any subobjects
Public Function DeleteTree(objTreeToDelete As IADsDeleteOps)

    ' Call the parent containers Delete method
    ' Specify object class and name
    objTreeToDelete.DeleteObject (0)

    ' Explicitly discard object reference, no longer valid
    Set objTreeToDelete = Nothing

End Function
```

Creating and Deleting Objects Sample

The following code, from the CreateDelete sample on the companion CD, shows how to call the functions shown earlier to create and delete objects. It creates two randomly named organizational unit containers in the root of Active Directory and then proceeds to delete them.

```
Option Explicit

' Create then delete a series of objects
Sub Main()

Dim objRootDSE As IADs
Dim strADsPath As String
Dim objContainer As IADsContainer
Dim objADs As IADs
Dim strName As String
```

```
' Connect to the LDAP server's root object
Set objRootDSE = GetObject("LDAP://RootDSE")

' Form an ADsPath string to the name of the default domain
strADsPath = "LDAP://" + adsRootDSE.Get("defaultNamingContext")

' Connect to the directory specified in the path
Set objContainer = GetObject(strADsPath)

' Display the name of the object
Debug.Print objContainer.Name

' Create, then delete 2 organizational unit objects in the
' directory root
Dim X As Long
For X = 1 To 2
    ' Assign a name to the new object using a random number
    Randomize
    strName = "Test" & Int((1000 * Rnd) + 1)

    ' Call function to create object
    ' Note that name must be an RDN
    Set objADs = CreateObject("organizationalUnit", _
        "OU=" & strName, strADsPath)

    ' Display info about new object
    Debug.Print objADs.Name, objADs.Guid

    ' Delete the object
    Call DeleteObject(objADs)

    ' Delete the object and all objects contained within it
    'Call DeleteTree(objADs)

    ' Discard the reference
    Set objADs = Nothing

Next X

End Sub
```

Summary

In this chapter, I've shown how to use the properties and methods of the *IADs* interface to work with the attributes and values of directory objects. Active Directory and directory services are different from most databases in that each object might have a different set of attributes and, even if an attribute is allowed for an object class, it might not exist for the particular instance of that class. The *IADs* interface is supported on all directory objects and is the one you'll use the most when developing applications with Active Directory. I've also shown how to enumerate, create, and delete objects, which in Visual Basic is made very easy by ADSI.

In the next chapter, I'll provide more details about attributes and values, showing how to manipulate the local property cache and use *IDirectoryObject*, the lean-and-mean version of *IADs*.

7

Advanced Properties and Values

In the previous chapter I described how to read data from and write data to Active Directory using ADSI. In this chapter, I'll show you a set of interfaces you can use to manipulate directory objects locally through the property cache. I'll describe how to work with the details of properties, their types, and the values they contain. Later in the chapter, in keeping with the data access theme, I'll describe how C and C++ developers can access Active Directory objects directly with the *IDirectoryObject* interface.

> **Note** To avoid confusion over terminology in this chapter, I refer to Active Directory data as *properties* since the data is represented by ADSI COM objects using COM data types. When working directly with Active Directory using C or C++ data types and structures, the term *attributes* is more appropriate.

Trolling for Properties

Previously I've described using the *Get* and *GetEx* methods of the *IADs* interface to return individual properties by name. Active Directory, however, is a dynamic database with an extensible schema. This means that new properties can be defined for any object in the directory. You might not know the names of these properties or the types of values they contain, but you might need to examine them nonetheless. Utility applications that browse Active Directory need this capability in particular.

The properties of an Active Directory object fall into two categories: The properties that *can be* contained within an object, and the properties that *are* contained within an object. Of course, the latter group will be a subset of the former group. First I'll cover those properties which are available to an object, and then I'll discuss how to manipulate the properties and values currently associated with a particular object.

One way to determine which properties can be contained within an object is to examine the object's class definition in the Active Directory schema. The object's class defines the set of properties the object could contain, not those that it actually does contain. Listing 7-1 shows code from the ClassProperties.bas sample on the companion CD. This sample uses the *Schema* property of the *IADs* interface to return an ADsPath to the schema object for the class of the object we're examining. The code enumerates the list of mandatory and optional properties of the *domainDNS* class, displaying the value of each if it exists within the object. Since I'm using the *Get* method, each existing property value is returned as a variant. If a property doesn't exist, the *On Error Resume Next* statement keeps the program moving to the next possible property.

```
Public Sub Main()

' Define which ADSI interfaces to use
Dim objRootDSE As IADs
Dim objADs As IADs
Dim strValue As String
Dim strADsPath as String
Dim varProperty as Variant

' Connect to the LDAP server's root object
Set objRootDSE = GetObject("LDAP://RootDSE")

' Form a path to the root domain object
strADsPath = "LDAP://" & objRootDSE.Get("defaultNamingContext")

' Bind to the object
Set objADs = GetObject(strADsPath)

' Get the schema class for the object
Dim objADsSchemaClass As IADsClass
Set objADsSchemaClass = GetObject(objADs.Schema)

' Display object information
Debug.Print "Name:    " & objADs.Name
Debug.Print "Class:   " & objADs.Class
```

Listing 7-1 ClassProperties.bas enumerates all properties of the *domainDNS* class.

```
' Enumerate all the mandatory properties for this class
Debug.Print "---Mandatory Properties---"

For Each varProperty In objADsSchemaClass.MandatoryProperties
    ' Display property name and value for the object
    Debug.Print vbTab & varProperty & ": ";

    ' Trap errors since not all attributes will be
    ' contained in a particular instance of the class
    On Error Resume Next

    ' Display the current value for this property
    strValue = objADs.Get(varProperty)

    If Err.Number = 0 Then
        Debug.Print strValue
    Else
        Debug.Print
    End If

    ' Turn off error checking
    On Error GoTo 0
Next

' Enumerate all the optional properties
Debug.Print "---Optional properties---"

For Each varProperty In objADsSchemaClass.OptionalProperties
    ' Display property name and value for the object
    Debug.Print vbTab & varProperty & ": ";

    ' Trap errors since not all attributes will be
    ' contained in a particular instance of the class
    On Error Resume Next
    ' Display the current value for this property
    strValue = objADs.Get(varProperty)

    If Err.Number = 0 Then
        Debug.Print strValue
    Else
        Debug.Print
    End If

    ' Turn off error checking
    On Error GoTo 0
Next

End Sub
```

When you run the code in Listing 7-1, you'll see a long list of mandatory and optional properties for the *domainDNS* class. The following shows an abbreviated sample output. The exact values will vary from server to server.

```
Name:    DC=coppersoftware
Class:   domainDNS
---Mandatory Properties---
    dc: coppersoftware
    instanceType: 5
    nTSecurityDescriptor:
    objectCategory: CN=Domain-DNS,CN=Schema,CN=Configuration,
        DC=coppersoftware,DC=com
    objectClass:
---Optional properties---
    adminDescription:
    adminDisplayName:
    allowedAttributes:
    allowedAttributesEffective:
    allowedChildClasses:
    ...
    whenChanged: 1/1/2001 9:34:00 AM
    whenCreated: 1/1/2001 9:27:20 AM
    wWWHomePage:
```

You can use the *IADs* methods to access and manipulate the properties of an object, but you must know the property names. In the sample shown in Listing 7-1, the names of the properties are provided by the schema class of the object, whether or not a value is assigned to the property. To provide more flexibility when working with properties in the cache, some of which might be unknown to you, ADSI supplies the *IADsPropertyXXX* family of interfaces, also known as the *property cache interfaces*. These interfaces enable a program to browse the local property cache and determine the values of each object property.

The Property Cache Interfaces

In the majority of your dealings with ADSI, you won't need to work with the property cache directly. The *IADs* interface provides all the functionality that is required to read, modify, and delete object property values. However, it's useful to understand how ADSI works under the covers, which always comes in handy when your code isn't working as expected.

The *IADsPropertyXXX* family of interfaces are a convenient way to examine the properties and values of a directory object contained in the cache. They also allow a program to create and remove cache entries that can then be applied to the object on the server. However, the property cache interfaces work only on the local property cache. Changes are not saved, nor is new data retrieved, unless you specifically request it. To make working with the property cache easier, ADSI exposes it as a collection of entries, one for each property of the object that contains a value. The property list is managed using the *IADsPropertyList* interface. Each entry is a *PropertyEntry* object that supports the *IADsPropertyEntry* interface. Likewise, the entries contain one or more values. Each value is packaged with its own *PropertyValue* object that supports two interfaces: *IADsPropertyValue* and *IADsPropertyValue2*. Table 7-1 describes the function of each of these interfaces.

> **Note** Another ADSI interface, named *IADsProperty,* represents the schema definition of an attribute in the directory. Despite its name, this interface is not related to the local property cache. I'll discuss *IADsProperty* in Chapter 9, but I mention it now to avoid confusion with the *IADsPropertyXXX* family of interfaces.

IADsPropertyXXX Interface	Description
IADsPropertyList	Manages the list of *PropertyEntry* objects in the property cache of an object. Used to enumerate the list of properties, read and modify property values, and add and remove properties from the property cache.
IADsPropertyEntry	Used to read, modify, and delete property values for an entry in the property cache. Supported by the *PropertyEntry* object.
IADsPropertyValue	Used to read and write a property value as a specific data type. Supported by the *PropertyValue* object.
IADsPropertyValue2	Used to read and write a property value as a specific data type. Similar to *IADsPropertyValue*, this interface supports any data type, including custom data types. Supported by the *PropertyValue* object.

Table 7-1 The *IADsPropertyXXX* family of interfaces.

To get an idea of the relationship between the property cache interfaces and which parts of the property cache they are associated with, Figure 7-1 shows a loose representation of these interfaces and their corresponding objects in the property cache.

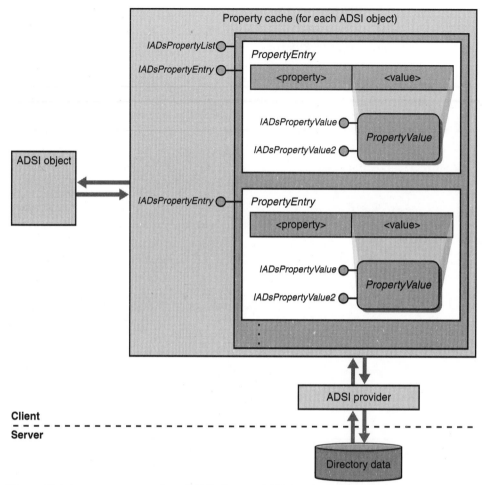

Figure 7-1 Loose representation of *IADsPropertyXXX* interfaces and the property cache.

IADsPropertyList

When ADSI populates the property cache with information from the server, it creates a *PropertyEntry* object in the cache for each property that's associated with the current object. ADSI exposes the property cache as a list of *PropertyEntry* objects. Using the *IADsPropertyList* interface, your application can manage the property cache—reading, modifying, adding, and removing *PropertyEntry* objects independently of the server.

Remember that the property cache is a snapshot of the properties of the object in the directory at the time when the *IADs GetInfo* method was called (either explicitly or implicitly). When working with the local cache, everything occurs within the confines of your application. Only when you call the *IADs SetInfo* method is Active Directory contacted and the object updated *en masse* with property and value data from the cache. Only at that time does Active Directory validate any changes. Keep this in mind because a change to a property in one place in a program might cause an error in a separate part of the application that calls *SetInfo*. This kind of error can happen if you delete a property from the cache that is required by the object class, resulting in a "Constraint Violation" when *SetInfo* is called. It's also wise to keep the local cache refreshed using the *GetInfo* or *GetInfoEx* methods because your application won't be notified of changes made by other clients to the same object.

Table 7-2 lists the methods of the *IADsPropertyList* interface. Note that the interface refers to property entries as *items*.

IADsPropertyList Method	Description
Next	Returns the next property item in the list.
Skip	Skips a specified number of property items in the list.
Reset	Moves back to the start of the list.
Item	Returns the property item specified by name or index (zero based).
GetPropertyItem	Returns the property item specified by name. The item is returned by specifying a particular data type.
PutPropertyItem	Updates or adds a property item in the list.
ResetPropertyItem	Removes the property item specified by name or index (zero-based).
PurgePropertyList	Removes all items from the list.

Table 7-2 Methods for the *IADsPropertyList* interface.

The *IADsPropertyList* interface has one property, named *PropertyCount*. This property is read-only and indicates the number of items in the list. Its data type is a Long.

The *IADsPropertyList* interface does not support enumerator objects or the *IEnumVARIANT* interface, which allows enumeration using the Visual Basic and VBScript *For Each* statement. Instead, to enumerate the entries, you must use a *For Next* loop starting at 0 for the first item (a zero-based index) and loop up to *PropertyCount*–1 for the last item. The *PropertyCount* value will change as you delete or add entries to the list.

PropertyEntry and *PropertyValue* Objects

The *IADsPropertyList* methods *Next*, *Item*, and *GetPropertyItem* all return a reference to an ADSI *PropertyEntry* object, which represents a single property of the current directory object. The *PropertyEntry* object is different from other ADSI objects we've worked with earlier because it is not contained in the directory itself; it only exists locally. The *PropertyEntry* object supports the Automation interface *IADsPropertyEntry* with four properties that describe and control the entry. All of these properties can be read and written to. Table 7-3 lists the properties of the *IADsPropertyEntry* interface.

IADsPropertyEntry Property	Type	Description
Name	String	The name of the property. In Active Directory, this will be the LDAP display name of the attribute (i.e. *adminDescription*).
ADsType	Long	The data type of the entry. See the *ADSTYPEENUM* enumeration (Table 7-5) later in this chapter for a list of supported data types.
ControlCode	Long	Controls how the property should be treated when being written to the server. Uses one of the constants defined by the *ADS_PROPERTY_OPERATION_ENUM* enumeration: *ADS_PROPERTY_APPEND* *ADS_PROPERTY_CLEAR* *ADS_PROPERTY_DELETE* *ADS_PROPERTY_UPDATE* These control codes are described in more detail in Chapter 6.
Values	Variant array	Variant array of *PropertyValue* objects containing the individual values for this property.

Table 7-3 *IADsPropertyEntry* properties.

New *PropertyEntry* objects can be created using the *New* keyword or the *CreateObject* function in Visual Basic. In VBScript the *CreateObject* function can be used. C and C++ developers can use the COM function *CoCreateInstance*. A new *PropertyEntry* object can be added to the property list using the *PutPropertyItem* method of the *IADsPropertyList* interface. The directory object is updated with the new property when the *SetInfo* method is called.

The *Values* property returns a collection of one or more *PropertyValue* objects that represent the value or values of the property. The *PropertyValue* object represents a single value of the property. Multivalued attributes will be represented with an array of *PropertyValue* objects, each exposing the *IADsPropertyValue* interface. In addition to containing the actual value of the property, the *PropertyValue* object contains information about the data type of the value.

The data type is stored in the *ADsType* property of the *IADsPropertyValue* interface. The contents of this property correspond to a data type defined in the *ADSTYPEENUM* enumeration. Depending on the data type returned, you retrieve the value using the appropriate *IADsPropertyValue* property. For example, if the *ADsType* property is equal to the number defined by *ADSTYPE_OCTET_STRING*, you should use the *OctetString* property to retrieve and set the value. In some cases, the value is represented as another object, such as a *LargeInteger* object supplied by ADSI. In those cases, the value returned by the appropriate method is a reference to an object representing the value. I'll discuss the data types and interfaces in the next section. Table 7-4 lists the properties of the *IADsPropertyValue* interface.

IADsPropertyValue Property	Type	Description
ADsType	Long	The data type of the value. One of the constants defined by *ADSTYPEENUM* (Table 7-5).
Boolean	Long	Returns the value as a Boolean (*ADSTYPE_BOOLEAN*).
CaseExactString	String	Returns the value as a case-sensitive string (*ADSTYPE_CASE_EXACT_STRING*).
CaseIgnoreString	String	Returns the value as a case-insensitive string (*ADSTYPE_CASE_IGNORE_STRING*).
DNString	String	Returns the value as a distinguished name (*ADSTYPE_DN_STRING*).
Integer	Long	Returns the value as an integer (*ADSTYPE_INTEGER*).
LargeInteger	Object	Returns the value as a *LargeInteger* object (*ADSTYPE_LARGE_INTEGER*).
NumericString	String	Returns the value as a string of numeric characters (*ADSTYPE_NUMERIC_STRING*).

Table 7-4 *IADsPropertyValue* properties. *(continued)*

Table 7-4 *continued*

IADsPropertyValue Property	Type	Description
OctetString	Variant array of single-byte characters	Returns the value as a byte array (*ADSTYPE_OCTET_STRING*).
PrintableString	String	Returns the value as a printable string (*ADSTYPE_PRINTABLE_STRING*).
SecurityDescriptor	Object	Returns the value as a *SecurityDescriptor* object. (*ADSTYPE_NT_SECURITY_DESCRIPTOR*).
UTCTime	Date	Returns the value as a coordinated universal time (*ADSTYPE_UTC_TIME*).

The *IADsPropertyValue* interface has one method, named *Clear*, which clears the *PropertyValue* object's current value. Calling any of the other properties after clearing the object will return empty strings or variants.

Value Data Types

In a number of places, the old school of LDAP and the more modern world of COM collide and result in confusion. LDAP, and thus Active Directory, supports data types known as *syntaxes*. A syntax defines what kind of data a particular directory attribute can contain. Active Directory defines 23 different syntaxes, such as an integer, printable string, and octet string, to name a few. (I discuss Active Directory syntaxes in more detail in Chapter 9.) Automation, on the other hand, supports a limited number of data types, such as binary string and variant, that can contain one of several other major data types, such as date, string, array, and so on.

Since Automation supports a limited number of data types and Active Directory supports a larger, and sometimes overlapping, set, ADSI must map and convert the two sets of data types. Additionally, since ADSI supports other directory services, each with their own unique data types, there are a lot of data types floating around. It's easy to get confused.

> **Note** Adding to the confusion is the fact that both the *IADsPropertyEntry* and *IADsPropertyValue* interfaces have an *ADsType* property. When working with Active Directory, each value of a property must have the same type, so *ADsType* must be the same for both interfaces. In the future, it's possible that Active Directory or another directory service will support multiple values of different types, but that is not the case currently.

ADSI manages this data type problem using a generic set of data types for directory services. This set is defined in a series of constants specified in the *ADSTYPEENUM* enumeration shown in Table 7-5.

> **Note**   The *ADSTYPEENUM* enumeration contains many more types in addition to those listed in Table 7-5; only those types supported by the LDAP provider and Active Directory are listed.

ADSTYPEENUM Constant	Description
ADSTYPE_BOOLEAN	Boolean value
ADSTYPE_CASE_EXACT_STRING	Case-sensitive string
ADSTYPE_CASE_IGNORE_STRING	Case-insensitive string
ADSTYPE_DN_STRING	String containing a distinguished name
ADSTYPE_DN_WITH_BINARY	Structure (*ADS_DN_WITH_BINARY*) that associates a fixed GUID with a distinguished name of a directory object
ADSTYPE_DN_WITH_STRING	Structure (*ADS_DN_WITH_STRING*) that associates a constant string with a distinguished name of a directory object
ADSTYPE_INTEGER	Integer value
ADSTYPE_INVALID	The data is of an invalid type
ADSTYPE_LARGE_INTEGER	64-bit (long) integer value
ADSTYPE_NT_SECURITY_DESCRIPTOR	Windows NT/Windows 2000 security descriptor
ADSTYPE_NUMERIC_STRING	String containing numerical characters
ADSTYPE_OCTET_STRING	String of bytes representing binary data
ADSTYPE_PRINTABLE_STRING	String containing characters that are safe to print and display (i.e. no control codes)
ADSTYPE_PROV_SPECIFIC	The type is specific to the ADSI provider
ADSTYPE_UNKNOWN	Unknown or undefined type
ADSTYPE_UTC_TIME	Structure (*SYSTEMTIME*) containing a coordinated universal time (UTC) value

Table 7-5 The *ADSTYPEENUM* constants supported by the LDAP provider and Active Directory.

IADsPropertyValue2

In addition to the *IADsPropertyValue* interface, the *PropertyValue* object also supports the *IADsPropertyValue2* interface, which can return values as variants of a particular subtype. Instead of having a fixed list of properties based on the data type of the value, the *GetObjectProperty* and *PutObjectProperty* methods of *IADsPropertyValue2* accept the data type as a parameter. Since new data types might appear in the future, having this flexibility is the better way to go. This is already true of the *ADSTYPE_DN_WITH_BINARY* type, used by Active Directory to associate a GUID with a distinguished name to provide the well-known GUIDs functionality described in Chapter 4. The *IADsPropertyValue2* methods are listed in Table 7-6.

IADsPropertyValue2 Method	Description
GetObjectProperty	Returns the value as a variant. The exact type is specified by an *ADSTYPE* value. For example, passing in *ADS_UTC_TIME* returns a *VT_DATE* variant.
PutObjectProperty	Sets the value of the object using the *ADSTYPE* supplied.

Table 7-6   *IADsPropertyValue2* methods.

> **Note**   You can use the *IADsPropertyValue2* interface to perform some data conversion between different types. For example, if a *PropertyValue* object contains a security descriptor (*ADSTYPE_NT_SECURITY_DESCRIPTOR*), you can ask ADSI to return the value as a different type instead of as a reference to an *IADsSecurityDescriptor* interface. To return the value as an octet string, call *GetObjectProperty* with *ADSTYPE_OCTET_STRING*. However, there are many limitations. I thought that by passing in *ADSTYPE_UTC_TIME* to the value of the *lastLogon* property, I could get ADSI to do the complex work of converting the *LargeInteger* data type to a date variant. Unfortunately, *IADsPropertyValue2* won't do that.

Data Type Objects

Some ADSI types are contained in structures while others are represented using ADSI objects. Representations such as this are made when a single value cannot be easily expressed using the basic data types available or when the value contains multiple parts. A value defined as an *ADS_LARGE_INTEGER* data type, for example, actually returns a reference to an ADSI *LargeInteger* object from which you can use the *IADsLargeInteger* interface to manipulate the 64-bit number represented. The same is true for the *ADSTYPE_NT_SECURITY_DESCRIPTOR* type that returns a reference to a *SecurityDescriptor* object. A security descriptor contains the security information associated with an object. It is actually a structure defined by Win32 that contains arrays of other structures. The *IADsSecurityDescriptor* interface makes working with *SecurityDescriptor* objects easy, however.

Care must be taken when working with data types that are represented by objects. You cannot immediately use the value returned by the *IADsPropertyValue* or *IADsPropertyValue2* interfaces; they are object references, and the actual property value is retrieved using the properties and methods of the associated interface. Table 7-7 lists the data type objects supported by Active Directory.

ADSTYPE	Object and Interface	Description
ADSTYPE_LARGE_INTEGER	*LargeInteger* *IADsLargeInteger*	Represents a 64-bit integer value. Often used to contain values in the *FILETIME* Win32 structure.
ADSTYPE_NT_SECURITY_DESCRIPTOR	*SecurityDescriptor* *IADsSecurityDescriptor*	Represents a security descriptor containing Access Control Lists (ACL) and Access Control Entries (ACE).
ADSTYPE_DN_WITH_BINARY	*DNWithBinary* *IADsDNWithBinary*	Represents distinguished name and GUID pairing. Used by Active Directory for updating well-known GUIDs.
ADSTYPE_DN_WITH_STRING	*DNWithString* *IADsDNWithString*	Represents a distinguished name with another, fixed string. Available but not used by the default Active Directory objects.

Table 7-7 Active Directory data types represented by ADSI objects.

Monster Property Cache Interfaces Sample

The best way to illustrate how to use the various *IADsPropertyXXX* interfaces is with a program. Listing 7-2, from PropertyList.bas on the companion CD, shows a sample that does it all. It's a good starting point for learning how to work with the *IADsPropertyXXX* interfaces. The PropertyList.bas sample does the following:

- Displays the type and value of each property in the property cache

- Deletes all entries in the property cache

- Adds an entry to the property cache

- Removes properties one by one

- Deletes an entry from the property cache

   Here's the code:

```
' Property List Navigation Example'
' Shows the use of IADsPropertyList, IADsPropertyEntry,
' IADsPropertyValue and IADsPropertyValue2
'
Public Sub Main()

' Define which ADSI interfaces to use
Dim objRootDSE As IADs
Dim objADs As IADs
Dim objADsPropList As IADsPropertyList
Dim objADsPropEntry As PropertyEntry
Dim objADsPropValue As PropertyValue
Dim objADsPropValue2 As IADsPropertyValue2

' Data type interfaces
Dim objADsLargeInteger As LargeInteger
Dim objADsSecurityDescriptor As SecurityDescriptor
Dim objADsDNWithString As DNWithString
Dim objADsDNWithBinary As DNWithBinary

Dim strADsPath As String
Dim nPropCount As Long
Dim nPropIndex As Long
Dim strOperationCode As String
```

Listing 7-2 PropertyList.bas demonstrates some of the capabilities of the *IADsPropertyXXX* interfaces.

```
Dim varVal As Variant
Dim strValue As String
Dim strType As String
Dim strName As String

' Connect to the LDAP server's root object
Set objRootDSE = GetObject("LDAP://RootDSE")

' Form a path to the root domain object
strADsPath = "LDAP://" & objRootDSE.Get("defaultNamingContext")

' Bind to the object
Set objADs = GetObject(strADsPath)

' Explicitly call GetInfo to populate the cache
objADs.GetInfo

' Get the IADsPropertyList interface for the bound object
Set objADsPropList = objADs

' PropertyCount is the current number of attributes in the cache
nPropCount = objADsPropList.PropertyCount

' Display some information
Debug.Print "Object " & objADs.Name & " at " & objADs.ADsPath
Debug.Print "Cache contains " & nPropCount

' Loop through all the properties
For nPropIndex = 0 To nPropCount - 1

    ' The Item method accepts a text name or index number
    ' and returns a IADsPropertyEntry object
    Set objADsPropEntry = objADsPropList.Item(nPropIndex)

    With objADsPropEntry
        ' Display PropertyEntry information
        Debug.Print "Name/Type/Code:" & vbTab;
        Debug.Print .Name & " / " & .ADsType & " / ";

        ' What is the status of the property?
        ' If non-zero, then the entry has been updated but not committed
        Select Case .ControlCode
            Case 0:
                strOperationCode = "Property entry has not been updated"
            Case ADS_PROPERTY_CLEAR:
                strOperationCode = "ADS_PROPERTY_CLEAR"
```

(continued)

Listing 7-2 *continued*

```
            Case ADS_PROPERTY_UPDATE:
                strOperationCode = "ADS_PROPERTY_UPDATE"
            Case ADS_PROPERTY_APPEND
                strOperationCode = "ADS_PROPERTY_APPEND"
            Case ADS_PROPERTY_DELETE
                strOperationCode = "ADS_PROPERTY_DELETE"
            Case Else
                strOperationCode = "Unknown ADSI property operation"
    End Select
    ' Display the text name of the status/control code
    Debug.Print strOperationCode

    ' Display PropertyValue information
    Debug.Print "Type / Value:  " & vbTab;

    ' Loop through each value for this property
    For Each varVal In .Values

        ' Check for types that returned as objects
        Select Case .ADsType

            ' 64-bit number
            Case ADSTYPE_LARGE_INTEGER:
                ' Use IADsPropertyValue for this type
                Set objADsPropValue = varVal

                ' Store the value in a LargeInteger object
                Set objADsLargeInteger = objADsPropValue.LargeInteger

                ' Convert the LargeInteger object to a string
                strValue = "&H" & Hex(objADsLargeInteger.HighPart) & _
                    Hex(objADsLargeInteger.LowPart)
                strType = "ADSTYPE_LARGE_INTEGER"

            ' String representing a Windows NT/Windows 2000
            ' security descriptor
            Case ADSTYPE_NT_SECURITY_DESCRIPTOR:
                ' Use IADsPropertyValue for this type
                Set objADsPropValue = varVal

                ' Store the value in a SecurityDescriptor object
                Set objADsSecurityDescriptor = _
                    objADsPropValue.SecurityDescriptor
```

```
                    ' Build string with information from object
                    strValue = objADsSecurityDescriptor.Owner & _
                        " of group " & objADsSecurityDescriptor.Group
                    strType = "ADSTYPE_NT_SECURITY_DESCRIPTOR"

                Case ADSTYPE_DN_WITH_STRING:
                    ' NOTE:  Default Active Directory schema does not
                    ' use this syntax.

                    ' Type not supported by IADsPropertyValue, use
                    ' IADsPropertyValue2
                    Set objADsPropValue2 = varVal

                    ' Use GetObjectProperty to return a reference
                    Set objADsDNWithString = _
                        objADsPropValue2.GetObjectProperty(.ADsType)

                    ' Get the string and binary portions
                    strValue = "DN: '" & objADsDNWithString.DNString & _
                        "' String: '" & objADsDNWithString.StringValue
                    strType = "ADSTYPE_DN_WITH_STRING"

                Case ADSTYPE_DN_WITH_BINARY:
                    ' Type not exposed by IADsPropertyValue, use
                    ' IADsPropertyValue2
                    Set objADsPropValue2 = varVal

                    ' Use GetObjectProperty to return a reference
                    Set objADsDNWithBinary = _
                        objADsPropValue2.GetObjectProperty(.ADsType)

                    ' Get the string and binary portions
                    strValue = objADsDNWithBinary.DNString & " (" & _
                        objADsDNWithBinary.BinaryValue & ")"
                    strType = "ADSTYPE_DN_WITH_BINARY"

                Case Else:
                    ' Use the IADsPropertyValue2 interface to get all
                    ' other types of variants
                    Set objADsPropValue2 = varVal

                    ' Use GetObjectProperty to return a variant
                    strValue = objADsPropValue2.GetObjectProperty(.ADsType)
                    strType = TypeName( _
                        objADsPropValue2.GetObjectProperty(.ADsType))
            End Select
```

(continued)

Listing 7-2 *continued*

```
                ' Print the type and value
                Debug.Print strType & " / " & strValue

                ' Indent the next line
                Debug.Print String(4, vbTab);
            Next
            ' End of values, terminate the list
            Debug.Print
        End With
    Next

    ' Purge the property cache
    '
    ' Example of the PurgePropertyList
    ' method to dump the entire cache
    '----------------------------------
    Debug.Print "Purging the cache..."

    ' Purge the property cache
    objADsPropList.PurgePropertyList

    ' Display number of items in property list cache
    Debug.Print "Property list has " & objADsPropList.PropertyCount & _
        " entries."

    ' Add an entry to the property list
    '
    ' Example of creating new property entries
    ' and associated values in the local cache
    '-----------------------------------------
    Debug.Print "Add an entry to the property list..."

    ' We'll use the description attribute, which is multivalued
    strName = "description"
    strValue = ">>> Temporary attribute - Safe to delete <<<"

    ' Create new entry object and fill in the properties
    Set objADsPropEntry = New PropertyEntry

    ' Set the attribute name
    objADsPropEntry.Name = strName

    ' Specify to add new values to an existing set
    objADsPropEntry.ControlCode = ADS_PROPERTY_APPEND
```

```
' The values will be a case-insensitive string
objADsPropEntry.ADsType = ADSTYPE_CASE_IGNORE_STRING

' Create a value for this entry
Set objADsPropValue = New PropertyValue

' Set the data type based on the property entry
objADsPropValue.ADsType = objADsPropEntry.ADsType

' Set the value using the type property
objADsPropValue.CaseIgnoreString = strValue

' Add the value to the entry
objADsPropEntry.Values = Array(objADsPropValue)

' Add this property entry to the property list
objADsPropList.PutPropertyItem objADsPropEntry

' Count should now be 1
Debug.Print "Property list has " & objADsPropList.PropertyCount & _
    " entries."

' Entries and values are not saved until SetInfo is called
Debug.Print "Saving new entry to server..."
objADs.SetInfo

' Saving resets the property cache, use GetInfoEx to reload specific
' properties
objADs.GetInfoEx Array("description", "name", "distinguishedName"), 0

' Count should now be 3
Debug.Print "Property list has " & objADsPropList.PropertyCount & _
    " entries."

' Remove property entries one-by-one
'
' Example of how to loop through the property cache
' using the Next property and delete entries using
' the ResetPropertyItem method
'-----------------------------------------------------
Debug.Print "Move to start of list, then remove each entry..."

' Start at the beginning of the cache
objADsPropList.Reset
```

(continued)

217

Listing 7-2 *continued*

```
' The Next property fails at the end, must trap this error
On Error Resume Next

' Loop through the entire cache using Next property
' Note, cannot use For loop with index since the number of items will
' be changing
Set objADsPropEntry = objADsPropList.Next

' Ensure we got an entry by checking for no error
While (Err.Number = 0)

    ' Turn off error checking
    On Error GoTo 0

    ' Display the unsaved property entry
    Debug.Print "Property Entry: " & objADsPropEntry.Name

    ' Remove the entry from the list
    ' This only removes the entry from the cache, not from the server object
    objADsPropList.ResetPropertyItem (objADsPropEntry.Name)

    On Error Resume Next
    ' Get the next entry in the cache
    Set objADsPropEntry = objADsPropList.Next
Wend

' Turn off error checking
On Error GoTo 0

' Display number of items in property list cache
Debug.Print "Property list has " & objADsPropList.PropertyCount & _
    " entries."

' Refresh Cache
'
'---------------
Debug.Print "Refresh cache with GetInfo..."

' Explicit call to GetInfo will overwrite dirty entry
objADs.GetInfo

' Display number of items in property list cache
Debug.Print "Property list has " & objADsPropList.PropertyCount & _
    " entries."
```

```
' Delete a property value
'
' Example showing how to delete the value
' we added to description.  Very similar
' to adding values, but with a different
' operations control code.
'----------------------------------------
' Get the entry we added earlier
Set objADsPropEntry = objADsPropList.GetPropertyItem( _
    strName, ADSTYPE_CASE_IGNORE_STRING)

' Specify to remove values from an existing set
objADsPropEntry.ControlCode = ADS_PROPERTY_DELETE

' Create a value for this entry
Set objADsPropValue = New PropertyValue

' Specify the value to remove without regard to case
objADsPropValue.CaseIgnoreString = strValue

' Set the data type based on the property entry
objADsPropValue.ADsType = objADsPropEntry.ADsType

' Add the value to the entry
objADsPropEntry.Values = Array(objADsPropValue)

' Remove this property entry from the property list
objADsPropList.PutPropertyItem objADsPropEntry

' Commit changes of the property list to the directory
objADs.SetInfo

End Sub
```

When you run the code in Listing 7-2, you'll see a long list related to the properties of the object and the progress of manipulating the property cache. The following is an abbreviated example of the output.

```
Object DC=coppersoftware at LDAP://DC=coppersoftware,DC=com
Cache contains 39
Name/Type/Code: masteredBy / 1 / Property entry has not been updated
Type / Value:   String / CN=NTDS Settings,CN=COPPER1,CN=Servers,
    CN=Default-First-Site-Name,CN=Sites,CN=Configuration,
    DC=coppersoftware,DC=com
```

(continued)

219

```
Name/Type/Code: auditingPolicy / 8 /
 Property entry has not been updated
Type / Value:   Byte() / A

Name/Type/Code: creationTime / 10 /
 Property entry has not been updated
Type / Value:   ADSTYPE_LARGE_INTEGER / &H1C073D5A2D6E216


...


Name/Type/Code: wellKnownObjects / 27 /
 Property entry has not been updated
Type / Value:   ADSTYPE_DN_WITH_BINARY /
    CN=Deleted Objects,DC=coppersoftware,DC=com (????????)
                ADSTYPE_DN_WITH_BINARY /
    CN=Infrastructure,DC=coppersoftware,DC=com (????????)
                ADSTYPE_DN_WITH_BINARY /
    CN=LostAndFound,DC= coppersoftware,DC=com (????????)
                ADSTYPE_DN_WITH_BINARY /
    CN=System,DC= coppersoftware,DC=com (????????)
                ADSTYPE_DN_WITH_BINARY /
    OU=Domain Controllers,DC= coppersoftware,DC=com (????????)
                ADSTYPE_DN_WITH_BINARY /
    CN=Computers,DC= coppersoftware,DC=com (????????)
                ADSTYPE_DN_WITH_BINARY /
    CN=Users,DC= coppersoftware,DC=com (????????)

Name/Type/Code: whenChanged / 9 / Property entry has not been updated
Type / Value:   Date / 1/1/2001 9:34:00 AM

Name/Type/Code: whenCreated / 9 / Property entry has not been updated
Type / Value:   Date / 1/1/2001 9:27:20 AM

Purging the cache...
Property list has 0 entries.
Add an entry to the property list...
Property list has 1 entries.
Saving new entry to server...
Property list has 3 entries.
Move to start of list, then remove each entry...
Property Entry: description
Property Entry: distinguishedName
Property Entry: name
Property list has 0 entries.
Refresh cache with GetInfo...
Property list has 40 entries.
```

That's how you deal with objects in the property cache and the interfaces that manage it. Now let's turn our attention to an ADSI interface that ignores the property cache altogether and accesses Active Directory objects directly.

IDirectoryObject

Developers using Visual Basic or a scripting language are insulated from having to specifically request the *IADs* interface since COM and ADSI provide access to all the properties and methods of an object dynamically using the *IDispatch* mechanism in Automation. However, Microsoft giveth, and Microsoft taketh away. When you're given simplicity, reduced performance is usually the cost. Since ADSI is an *in-process* COM component, calling interface methods can be very fast if the application uses early binding. Still, the code supporting both early binding and late binding using the *IDispatch* mechanism incurs a slight performance penalty. In addition, the ADSI interfaces mold LDAP attribute types into COM data types such as binary strings and variants.

Realizing that C and C++ developers generally want the fastest possible performance, ADSI provides the *IDirectoryObject* interface for more direct access to directory objects. In this section I'll focus on how to use *IDirectoryObject* with C and C++.

Using *IDirectoryObject* from C and C++

IDirectoryObject is the best interface to use when a program requires low-level, low-overhead access to directory objects. Similar in purpose and functionality to *IADs*, *IDirectoryObject* complements the *IDirectorySearch* interface described in Chapter 5.

The *IDirectoryObject* interface is not a dual interface; in other words, it does not support *IDispatch* and thus cannot be used from the scripting languages. Although the later versions of Visual Basic can read type libraries and use them for early binding, getting Visual Basic to understand C/C++ data structures is prohibitive.

In addition to trimming away the overhead of supporting dual interfaces, *IDirectoryObject* also does away with the local property cache. While the property cache is a performance enhancement in most cases, *IDirectoryObject* provides direct access to the information in the directory and gives the developer control over exactly how often the directory is accessed. This is an "on-the-wire" access protocol, meaning that each method call results in an LDAP operation over the network from the client to the server. Table 7-8 lists the methods for the *IDirectoryObject* interface.

IDirectoryObject Method	Description
GetObjectInformation	Returns an *ADS_OBJECT_INFO* structure with members that contain fixed information about the object itself. Similar to the *IADs* properties such as *Name* and *Class*.
GetObjectAttributes	Returns an array of *ADS_ATTR_INFO* structures with members that contain information about the requested attributes of the object. Similar to the *IADs GetEx* method.
SetObjectAttributes	Accepts an array of *ADS_ATTR_INFO* structures with which to update the object. Similar to the *PutEx* and *SetInfo* methods.
CreateDSObject	Creates a new directory object as a child of the current object. Accepts a distinguished name string and an array of *ADS_ATTR_INFO* structures with the attributes that make up the new object. Similar to the *IADsContainer Create* method.
DeleteDSObject	Deletes a directory object. Accepts a relative distinguished name string of a leaf object to delete. Similar to the *IADsContainer Delete* method.

Table 7-8 *IDirectoryObject* methods.

Although *IDirectoryObject* doesn't use the property cache or the property cache interfaces, you'll see that much of what follows is similar to the discussion earlier in this chapter. For example, both the property cache interfaces and *IDirectoryObject* are designed to be low-level and to work more directly with the data. Also, *IDirectoryObject* uses structures (*ADS_ATTR_INFO* and *ADSVALUE*) that have similarities to the *PropertyEntry* and *PropertyValue* objects.

IDirectoryObject might be friendlier to C and C++ developers because it uses structures rather than COM interface properties to work with data. Instead of using binary strings and variants, *IDirectoryObject* uses its own data type, known as an *ADSTYPE*, that, like a variant, stores various types of data. However, *ADSTYPE* is very specific and is optimized for directory service data.

In some ways, it's surprising that *IDirectoryObject* is a COM interface at all. It feels like a group of Win32 API functions. It you are comfortable working with the LDAP API but want some of the benefits that ADSI can provide, the *IDirectoryObject* interface is a natural stepping stone.

Listing 7-3, from IDirectoryObject.cpp on the companion CD, is a sample program that shows how the *GetObjectInformation* and *GetObjectAttributes* methods of the *IDirectoryObject* interface can be used to retrieve information about a specified object.

```
#include <stdio.h>        // Standard I/O
#include <comdef.h>       // COM definitions
#include <activeds.h>     // ADSI definitions

// The following must be updated to point to your own Active Directory domain
#define ADSPATH L"LDAP://CN=Administrator,CN=Users,DC=coppersoftware,DC=com"

int main(int argc, char **argv , char  **envp )
{
    // Initalize COM
    HRESULT hResult = CoInitialize ( NULL );

    // Get pointer to object's IDirectoryObject interface
    IDirectoryObject   *pdsoUser = NULL;
    hResult = ADsGetObject( ADSPATH , IID_IDirectoryObject,
        (void**) &pdsoUser );

    // Check for binding success
    if ( SUCCEEDED ( hResult ) )
        {
        // Retrieve and display object information
        ADS_OBJECT_INFO *padsObjInfo;

        hResult = pdsoUser->GetObjectInformation( &padsObjInfo );

        if ( SUCCEEDED( hResult ) )
            {
            printf("Relative Distinguished Name: %S\n",
                padsObjInfo->pszRDN);
            printf("Distinguished Name: %S\n", padsObjInfo->pszObjectDN);
            printf("Parent: %S\n", padsObjInfo->pszParentDN);
            printf("Class: %S\n", padsObjInfo->pszClassName);
            printf("Schema: %S\n", padsObjInfo->pszSchemaDN);

            // ADSI allocates the info structure and the app must
            // free it
            FreeADsMem( padsObjInfo );
            }

        // Get specified values
        ADS_ATTR_INFO    *pdsoAttributeInfo;
        DWORD   dwReturn;
        LPWSTR    pdsoAttributeNames[] =
```

Listing 7-3 IDirectoryObject.cpp demonstrates accessing directory *(continued)*
attributes using the *IDirectoryObject* interface.

Listing 7-3 *continued*

```
        {
        L"sn",
        L"otherTelephone",
        L"whenChanged"
        };
DWORD   dwNumAttr = sizeof( pdsoAttributeNames ) /
    sizeof( LPWSTR );

hResult = pdsoUser->GetObjectAttributes( pdsoAttributeNames,
    dwNumAttr,
    &pdsoAttributeInfo,
    &dwReturn );

if ( SUCCEEDED( hResult ) )
    {
    // Loop through all the returned attributes
    for ( DWORD curAttribute = 0;
        curAttribute < dwReturn;
        curAttribute++, pdsoAttributeInfo++ )
        {
        // Display attribute name
        printf( "%S: ", pdsoAttributeInfo->pszAttrName );

        // Loop through all values of current attribute
        for ( DWORD curValue = 0;
            curValue < pdsoAttributeInfo->dwNumValues;
            curValue++, pdsoAttributeInfo->pADsValues++ )
            {
            // Retrieve attribute value based on ADSTYPE
            switch (pdsoAttributeInfo->dwADsType)
                {
                case ADSTYPE_CASE_IGNORE_STRING:
                    printf ( "%S\n", pdsoAttributeInfo->
                        pADsValues->CaseIgnoreString );
                    break;

                case ADSTYPE_UTC_TIME:
                    printf ( "%02d/%02d/%04d %02d:%02d:%02d\n",
                        pdsoAttributeInfo->pADsValues->
                            UTCTime.wMonth,
                        pdsoAttributeInfo->pADsValues->
                            UTCTime.wDay,
                        pdsoAttributeInfo->pADsValues->
                            UTCTime.wYear,
```

```
                                    pdsoAttributeInfo->pADsValues->
                                        UTCTime.wHour,
                                    pdsoAttributeInfo->pADsValues->
                                        UTCTime.wMinute,
                                    pdsoAttributeInfo->pADsValues->
                                        UTCTime.wSecond );
                            break;

                        default:
                            printf ( "Unsupported data type (%#0.2x)\n",
                                pdsoAttributeInfo->dwADsType );
                            break;
                        }
                    }
                }
            }
        // Allocated by ADSI, must free
        FreeADsMem( pdsoAttributeInfo );
        }

    // Release interface if allocated
    if (pdsoUser)
        pdsoUser->Release ();

    // Unload COM
    CoUninitialize ();

    // Return the result of any failures
    return hResult;
}
```

When you run this code, you should see something similar to Figure 7-2.

Figure 7-2 Output of IDirectoryObject.cpp sample.

GetObjectInformation

The *GetObjectInformation* method of *IDirectoryObject* is defined using the following prototype:

```
HRESULT GetObjectInformation (
    PADS_OBJECT_INFO *ppObjInfo );
```

GetObjectInformation uses the *ADS_OBJECT_INFO* structure to store several pieces of fixed information about the directory object. The members of the *ADS_OBJECT_INFO* structure are listed in Table 7-9. The members are very similar to the *IADs* read-only properties, which are *Name, ADsPath, Parent, Schema,* and *Class.*

ADS_OBJECT_INFO Members	C/C++ Data Type	Description
pszRDN	*LPWSTR*	Relative distinguished name of the object
pszObjectDN	*LPWSTR*	Distinguished name (DN) of the object
pszParentDN	*LPWSTR*	DN of the object's parent
pszSchemaDN	*LPWSTR*	DN of the object representing the schema for the current object
pszClassName	*LPWSTR*	Name of the class of which this object is an instance

Table 7-9 Members of the *ADS_OBJECT_INFO* structure.

To use *GetObjectInformation* you must create a pointer variable of type *ADS_OBJECT_INFO.* You then pass the address of the pointer (double indirection) as the parameter to *GetObjectInformation.* The function will allocate memory and adjust the passed pointer variable to point to the object information. When the function returns, use the pointer to dereference the *ADS_OBJECT_INFO* members for the object's information.

```
// Retrieve and display object information
ADS_OBJECT_INFO *padsObjInfo;

hResult = pdsoUser->GetObjectInformation( &padsObjInfo );

if ( SUCCEEDED( hResult ) )
    {
    printf("Relative Distinguished Name: %S\n", padsObjInfo->pszRDN);
    printf("Distinguished Name: %S\n", padsObjInfo->pszObjectDN);
    printf("Parent: %S\n", padsObjInfo->pszParentDN);
    printf("Class: %S\n", padsObjInfo->pszClassName);
```

```
printf("Schema: %S\n", padsObjInfo->pszSchemaDN);

// ADSI allocates the info structure
// and the app must free it
FreeADsMem( padsObjInfo );
}
```

All the *ADS_OBJECT_INFO* members are pointers to null-terminated, wide-character strings. With the exception of *pszClassName*, they all use some form of an LDAP distinguished name, not an ADsPath however.

Important   Since ADSI allocates memory automatically on your application's behalf; you must manually free the memory when you are finished with it. Use the *FreeADsMem* function to accomplish this.

GetObjectAttributes

The *GetObjectAttributes* method is used to gather the object's attributes and values into an array. Similar to the property cache but without the COM-style interfaces, *GetObjectAttributes* is defined using the following prototype:

```
HRESULT GetObjectAttributes (
    LPWSTR          *pAttributeNames,
    DWORD           dwNumberAttributes,
    PADS_ATTR_INFO  *ppAttributeEntries,
    DWORD           *pdwNumAttributesReturned );
```

GetObjectAttributes accepts an array of attribute names to be retrieved from the server. A pointer to the array of names is passed using the *pAttributeNames* parameter along with the number of names in the *dwNumberAttributes* parameter. When called, ADSI queries the server for the attributes requested. The function returns a pointer to the array of *ADS_ATTR_INFO* structures containing the attribute information in the *ppAttributeEntries* parameter. The value of the *DWORD* variable pointed to by *pdwNumAttributesReturned* is updated with the number of attributes collected. If no attributes are found, *E_ADS_PROPERTY_NOT_FOUND* is returned as the result code.

The *ADS_ATTR_INFO* structure is the *IDirectoryObject* version of the *PropertyEntry* object. It contains the same information, including the data type of the property and the series of values for that property. The members of the *ADS_ATTR_INFO* structure are listed in Table 7-10.

ADS_ATTR_INFO Member	Win32 Type	Description
pszAttrName	LPWSTR	Pointer to a string with the name of the attribute.
dwControlCode	DWORD	Indicates how the attribute should be modified. Value corresponds to one of the following update control code constants:
		ADS_ATTR_APPEND ADS_ATTR_CLEAR ADS_ATTR_DELETE ADS_ATTR_UPDATE
		These are equivalent to the similarly named ADS_PROPERTY_OPERATION_ENUM enumeration.
dwADsType	ADSTYPE	Indicates the data type of the attribute. Corresponds to constants defined in the ADSTYPEENUM enumeration (Table 7-5).
pADsValues	PADSVALUE	Pointer to an array of ADSVALUE structures that contain values for the attribute. (See Table 7-11.)
dwNumValues	DWORD	Number of ADSVALUE structures in the array.

Table 7-10 Members of the *ADS_ATTR_INFO* structure.

Setting up a call to *GetObjectAttributes* involves creating an array of attribute names. You also need to pass the number of attributes you're looking for.

```
// Get specified values
ADS_ATTR_INFO   *pdsoAttributeInfo;
DWORD   dwReturn;
LPWSTR   pdsoAttributeNames[] =
    {
    L"sn",
    L"otherTelephone",
    L"whenChanged"
    };
DWORD   dwNumAttr = sizeof( pdsoAttributeNames ) / sizeof( LPWSTR );

hResult = pdsoUser->GetObjectAttributes(
    pdsoAttributeNames,
    dwNumAttr,
    &pdsoAttributeInfo,
    &dwReturn );
```

In this example, I've requested that the *sn* (*Surname*), *otherTelephone*, and *whenChanged* attributes be returned. Because of the lack of a local property cache, you must specify the attributes by name. There is no provision for enumerating unknown attributes of an object when it is accessed through *IDirectoryObject*.

If *GetObjectAttributes* returns successfully (*S_OK*), *pdsoAttributeInfo* will point to three *ADS_ATTR_INFO* structures. By dereferencing this pointer, you can access the value of the attribute directly.

```
printf( "%S: ", pdsoAttributeInfo->pszAttrName );

// Loop through all values of current attribute
for ( DWORD curValue = 0;
    curValue < pdsoAttributeInfo->dwNumValues;
    curValue++, pdsoAttributeInfo->pADsValues++)
    {
    ...
    }
```

The *dwNumValue* member contains the number of values that a particular attribute contains. Before accessing the value, however, you must check the data type and choose the *ADSVALUE* union member that corresponds to the correct data type. The easiest way to do this is with a *switch* statement.

```
// Retrieve attribute value based on ADSTYPE
switch (pdsoAttributeInfo->dwADsType)
    {
    case ADSTYPE_CASE_IGNORE_STRING:
        ...
        break;
    }
```

IDirectoryObject uses the same set of data types as the *IADsPropertyEntry* interface, which are defined in the *ADSTYPEENUM* enumeration. See Table 7-5 for a list of these data types.

After you know what data type the particular value is, you can use the *ADSVALUE* union member to access the value, just like the *IADsPropertyValue* interface.

```
printf ( "%S\n", pdsoAttributeInfo->pADsValues->CaseIgnoreString );
```

Table 7-11 lists members of the *ADSVALUE* structure that are used by Active Directory. Table 7-12 lists the corresponding Win32 data type for each ADSI data type.

ADSVALUE Member	ADSI Data Type	Description
dwType	*ADSTYPE*	The data type of the value. One of the constants defined by *ADSTYPEENUM* (Table 7-5).
Boolean	*ADS_BOOLEAN*	Boolean value.
CaseExactString	*ADS_CASE_EXACT_STRING*	Case-sensitive string.
CaseIgnoreString	*ADS_CASE_IGNORE_STRING*	Case-insensitive string.
DNString	*ADS_DN_STRING*	String containing a distinguished name.
Integer	*ADS_INTEGER*	Integer value.
LargeInteger	*ADS_LARGE_INTEGER*	Long integer value.
NumericString	*ADS_NUMERIC_STRING*	String containing numerical characters.
OctetString	*ADS_OCTET_STRING*	String of bytes representing binary data.
pDNWithBinary	*PADS_DN_WITH_BINARY*	Pointer to an *ADS_DN_WITH_BINARY* structure that associates a fixed GUID with a distinguished name of a directory object.
pDNWithString	*PADS_DN_WITH_STRING*	Pointer to an *ADS_DN_WITH_STRING* structure that associates a constant string with a distinguished name of a directory object.
PrintableString	*ADS_PRINTABLE_STRING*	String containing characters that are safe to print and display (i.e. no control codes).
ProviderSpecific	*ADS_PROV_SPECIFIC*	Provider-specific structure.
SecurityDescriptor	*ADS_NT_SECURITY_DESCRIPTOR*	Windows NT/Windows 2000 security descriptor.
UTCTime	*ADS_UTC_TIME*	Time interval value expressed in coordinated universal time (UTC).

Table 7-11 Members of the *ADSVALUE* structure that are used by Active Directory.

ADSI Data Type	Win32 Data Type
ADS_BOOLEAN	*DWORD*
ADS_CASE_EXACT_STRING	*LPWSTR*
ADS_CASE_IGNORE_STRING	*LPWSTR*
ADS_DN_STRING	*LPWSTR*
ADS_DN_WITH_BINARY *PADS_DN_WITH_BINARY*	*typedef struct {* *DWORD dwLength;* *LPBYTE lpBinaryValue;* *LPWSTR pszDNString;};*
ADS_DN_WITH_STRING *PADS_DN_WITH_STRING*	*typedef struct {* *LPWSTR pszStringValue;* *LPWSTR pszDNString;};*
ADS_INTEGER	*DWORD*
ADS_LARGE_INTEGER	*LARGE_INTEGER*
ADS_NT_SECURITY_DESCRIPTOR	*typedef struct {* *DWORD dwLength;* *LPBYTE lpValue;};*
ADS_NUMERIC_STRING	*LPWSTR*
ADS_OCTET_STRING	*typedef struct {* *DWORD dwLength;* *LPBYTE lpValue;};*
ADS_PRINTABLE_STRING	*LPWSTR*
ADS_PROV_SPECIFIC	*typedef struct {* *DWORD dwLength;* *LPBYTE lpValue;};*
ADS_UTC_TIME	*SYSTEMTIME*
ADSTYPE	*DWORD*

Table 7-12 ADSI data types and corresponding Win32 data types.

Writing Attributes with *SetObjectAttributes*

The *SetObjectAttributes* method is used to add, delete, or modify an attribute or value of an object. *SetObjectAttributes* is defined using the following prototype:

```
HRESULT SetObjectAttributes (
    PADS_ATTR_INFO   pAttributeEntries,
    DWORD            dwNumAttributes,
    DWORD            *pdwNumAttributesModified ) ;
```

To update the directory attributes, simply change the values contained in the *ADSVALUE* structure and update the *dwControlCode* member of the *ADS_ATTR_INFO* structure with the type of operation requested: update, append, delete, or clear.

Pass the *ADS_ATTR_INFO* pointer in the *pAttributeEntries* parameter along with the number of attributes you'd like to have updated. When the update is finished, the *DWORD* variable pointed to by the *pdwNumAttributesModified* parameter will contain the actual number of attributes modified.

> **Note**   Two methods not shown in the sample code above are the *CreateDSObject* and *DeleteDSObject* methods, which are used to create and delete objects within containers. The functionality of these methods is the same as provided with the *IADsContainer* interface, which I described in Chapter 6.

Summary

This chapter has covered two ways that ADSI and Active Directory present object data using properties, values, and data types. The property cache and *IDirectoryObject* interfaces are powerful features that can be used to manipulate the wide range of information and data types available in Active Directory. Personally, I prefer working with *IADs* and the property cache interfaces to using the *IDirectoryObject* interface. I'm biased towards COM technology, although I'm certain that many C++ and most C developers will feel more familiar with *IDirectoryObject* than with the "pure COM" interfaces.

In the next chapter, we tackle user interface issues and how to implement the user interface elements supplied by Active Directory.

8

The Active Directory User Interface

Active Directory stores directory data, and ADSI helps retrieve it. It's up to your application to present the information to users in a meaningful and useful way. In this chapter, I'll show how to take advantage of the user interface components that Active Directory provides. I've also included some C++ code that you can use to invoke the dialog boxes that the Active Directory snap-ins and the Microsoft Windows shell use for viewing and administering Active Directory.

The user interface (UI) components that Active Directory provides fall into two broad categories: common dialog boxes for selecting domains, containers, or objects, and various other user interface elements customized for individual object classes. These elements include property pages, context menus, and wizards that walk users through the creation of a new object.

But First, a Note from Our Sponsor...

All the Active Directory user interface elements interact with the Windows shell in some fashion or another. While I won't get into the nitty-gritty of working with the shell or shell extensions, you might want to review the shell documentation in the Microsoft Platform SDK. Also, the components, objects, and programming interfaces described in this chapter are provided by Active Directory components, not ADSI components. You'll notice that, in addition to the ActiveDS.h header file, the samples include references to DSClient.h, DSAdmin.h, and ObjSel.h. These files are not part of the ADSI SDK, and you must install the Platform SDK to ensure the correct header and library files are available. The components of the Platform SDK that you will need are "Build Environment\Network and Directory

Services\Active Directory Services Interface" and "Build Environment\Win32 API\Win32 API." You can download these components of the Platform SDK from *http://msdn.microsoft.com/downloads/*. The header and library files required to compile the code samples for this chapter are included on the companion CD. Additionally, for Windows 95, Windows 98, and Windows NT 4.0, the Active Directory Client (DSClient.exe) must be installed. Installers for these clients are included on the companion CD.

Since the Active Directory user interface components don't support Automation, the scripting languages cannot use them. This is truly unfortunate because so many administrative tasks could be simplified by allowing scripts to utilize familiar Active Directory dialog boxes. Another limitation of the Active Directory components is the C/C++ style of the interfaces, which requires working with large structures containing arrays of structures. These structures are inconvenient to use from Microsoft Visual Basic and nearly impossible from scripting languages. So I'll stick to using C++ in this chapter.

OK, with that bit of housekeeping aside, on to the Active Directory common dialogs boxes and how to use them in your applications.

Common Dialog Boxes

Active Directory provides common dialog boxes that you can use from within your application to present lists of directory objects and to select, or allow users to select, the directory objects your program will work with. These dialog boxes include the container browser dialog box, the domain browser dialog box, and the object picker dialog box. The common dialog boxes are similar in purpose to the common Open and Save As dialog boxes that Windows provides.

You could create your own dialog boxes to present directory information and gather object selections, but why reinvent the wheel? Plus, the dialog boxes that Active Directory provides will be updated in future versions of Windows to use the latest in user interface design. I'm going to describe the container browser dialog box first because the method used to invoke it is a little different from the one used with the domain browser and object picker dialog boxes.

Container Browser Dialog Box

The container browser dialog box presents a list of containers in a tree view. A user can expand or collapse the various nodes of the tree and select a container. This type of dialog box is used mostly when a user needs to choose a location to copy or move an object to or perform some other operation that involves a container (rather than an individual object). Figure 8-1 shows the container browser in action.

Figure 8-1 Active Directory container browser dialog box.

The container browser dialog box is presented to the user by calling the *DsBrowseForContainer* function and passing it a *DSBROWSEINFO* structure with the options you want. When the user makes a selection and closes the dialog box, this function returns the ADsPath of the selected object in the *pszPath* member of the *DSBROWSEINFO* structure. The declaration for *DsBrowseForContainer* and the *DSBROWSEINFO* structure are as follows:

```
int DsBrowseForContainer(
    PDSBROWSEINFO pInfo
);

typedef struct DSBROWSEINFOW {
    DWORD        cbStruct;
    HWND         hwndOwner;
    LPCWSTR      pszCaption;
    LPCWSTR      pszTitle;
    LPCWSTR      pszRoot;
    LPWSTR       pszPath;
    ULONG        cchPath;
    DWORD        dwFlags;
    BFFCALLBACK  pfnCallback;
    LPARAM       lParam;
    DWORD        dwReturnFormat;
    LPCWSTR      pUserName;
    LPCWSTR      pPassword;
    LPWSTR       pszObjectClass;
    ULONG        cchObjectClass;
} DSBROWSEINFOW, *PDSBROWSEINFOW;
```

While *DSBROWSEINFO* contains many members, the only ones that are required to be set are *pszPath* and *ccPath*. The rest can be initialized to 0 to accept the default behavior for the dialog box. For *DsBrowseForContainer* to return the ADsPath of the selected object, the calling application must allocate a character buffer to hold the ADsPath. The ADsPath is returned in Unicode even on ANSI systems, so the buffer must allocate space based on wide characters. The number of characters is returned in the *cchPath* member, which tells *DsBrowseForContainer* how much space is available. This value is expressed in characters, not bytes.

Many options are available to customize the behavior and appearance of the dialog box. They are set in the *dwFlags* member of *DSBROWSEINFO* and can be any combination of the flags listed in Table 8-1, all of which start with *DSBI*.

DsBrowseForContainer Option	Description
DSBI_CHECKBOXES	Not currently implemented. If set, turns on the checkbox style for the tree view (*TVS_CHECKBOXES*).
DSBI_ENTIREDIRECTORY	When specified, includes all the trusted domains on the server specified in *pszPath* (or the domain that the user is logged on to).
DSBI_EXPANDONOPEN	Instructs the tree view to expand to the level specified in *pszPath*.
DSBI_HASCREDENTIALS	When set, *DsBrowseForContainer* will use the credentials specified in *pUserName* and *pPassword*. Otherwise, default credentials are ignored.
DSBI_IGNORETREATASLEAF	Shows all container objects. Otherwise, the *treatAsLeaf* attribute for the *displaySpecifier* class is used to determine whether an object is a container and should be shown.
DSBI_INCLUDEHIDDEN	Shows all objects, including those with the *showInAdvancedViewOnly* attribute set.
DSBI_NOBUTTONS	Does not display expand (+) and collapse (-) symbols next to items.
DSBI_NOLINES	Does not display lines between objects.
DSBI_NOLINESATROOT	Does not display lines between root objects.
DSBI_NOROOT	Does not display the root object.

Table 8-1 Possible flags for the *dwFlags* member of *DSBROWSEINFO*.

DsBrowseForContainer Option	Description
DSBI_RETURN_FORMAT	When set, *DsBrowseForContainer* will return the ADsPath string in the format specified in the *dwReturnFormat* member. Can be any of the *ADS_FORMAT* constants. The default is to use *ADS_FORMAT_X500*.
DSBI_RETURNOBJECTCLASS	When set, *DsBrowseForContainer* will also return the class name of the selected object. The calling application must allocate buffer space and put the address of the buffer into the *pszObjectClass* member, along with the number of characters allocated into the *cchObjectClass* member.
DSBI_SIMPLEAUTHENTICATE	Indicates that secure authentication is not needed when calling *ADsOpenObject*.

After creating and initializing the *DSBROWSEINFO* structure, you call *DsBrowseForContainer* with the structure address. The dialog box will then be displayed to the user. When the user closes the dialog box, the return code will be either *IDOK* for success or *IDCANCEL* if the user pressed the Escape key or clicked the Cancel button. All other errors return −1. Listing 8-1 shows code from the DsBrowseForContainer sample included on the companion CD, which shows how to use the *DsBrowseForContainer* function. When the container dialog box is closed, the results are displayed in a message box.

```
//--------------------------------------------------------------------------
// Filename:     DsBrowseForContainer.cpp
// Description:  Example using Active Directory DsBrowseForContainer
//               function
// Platform:     Win32 Application
//--------------------------------------------------------------------------
#define UNICODE
#define _UNICODE
// C++ and Compiler Support
#include <crtdbg.h>             // C-runtime debugging support
#include <tchar.h>              // Generic text handling
#include <stdio.h>              // Standard C I/O routines
#include <comdef.h>             // COM definitions
```

Listing 8-1 Using the *DsBrowseForContainer* function.   *(continued)*

Listing 8-1 *continued*

```
// Windows Platform Support
#include <objbase.h>           // COM base object support
#include <shlobj.h>            // Shell support (dsclient req'd)
#include <initguid.h>          // GUID support (dsadmin req'd)
// Active Directory Support
#include <activeds.h>          // ADSI object support
#include <dsclient.h>          // Active Directory UI object support
#include <dsadmin.h>           // Active Directory Admin object support
#include <objsel.h>            // DsObjectPicker support
// Set compiler options
#pragma warning( push, 4 ) // Warning level 4 for this code
#pragma comment( lib, "activeds.lib" ) // Link to ADSI library
#pragma comment( lib, "adsiid.lib"  ) // Link to ADSI interface GUIDs
#pragma comment( lib, "dsuiext.lib" ) // Link to Active Directory UI
// Handy macro to return number of elements in array (good for strings)
#define ARRAYSIZE(a)    (sizeof(a)/sizeof(a[0]))


//-----------------------------------------------------------------------
// Function: _tWinMain
//           Entry point for Win32 applications
// Inputs:   HINSTANCE hInstance  Handle to current instance
//           HINSTANCE hPrevInstance  Previous instance (always NULL)
//           LPSTR lpCmdLine  Pointer to command line string
//           int nCmdShow  Show state (SW_xxx)
// Returns:  int  Program exit code 0 = no errors
// Notes:    _tWinMain is the character-set independent version of
//           WinMain.  Resolves to either WinMain or wWinMain, depending
//           on character set in use.
//           Parameter names not used are commented out to avoid
//           compiler warning C4100; "unreferenced formal parameter"
//-----------------------------------------------------------------------
int WINAPI _tWinMain( HINSTANCE/*hInstance*/,
                      HINSTANCE/*hPrevInstance*/,
                      LPSTR/*lpCmdLine*/, int/*nCmdShow*/)
{
    // Initialize COM
    HRESULT hResult;
    CoInitialize( NULL );


    //---------------------------------------------:--
    // Set options for the dialog
    //---------------------------------------------
    DSBROWSEINFO dsbInfo = { NULL };  // Set all members to default
    dsbInfo.cbStruct = sizeof( dsbInfo );  // Set size for version purpose
    dsbInfo.hwndOwner = NULL;  // Window handle
```

```
dsbInfo.pszCaption = _T("Container Browser");  // Text for title bar
dsbInfo.pszTitle = _T("This example presents this dialog and
    displays the ADsPath of the chosen container. Please pick from
    the list below...");  // Additional text
dsbInfo.pszRoot = NULL;  // Do not specify a root object
dsbInfo.dwFlags =  // Option flags
    DSBI_ENTIREDIRECTORY |  // Include all trusted domains
    DSBI_EXPANDONOPEN |  // Expand tree to pszPath
    DSBI_IGNORETREATASLEAF |  // Show all objects, vs. just containers
    DSBI_RETURN_FORMAT |  // Format paths based on ADS_FORMAT_*
    DSBI_RETURNOBJECTCLASS;  // Fill in pszObject class
// Function to call back
dsbInfo.pfnCallback = *DsBrowseCallBack;
// Format ADsPaths using X.500
dsbInfo.dwReturnFormat = ADS_FORMAT_X500;
dsbInfo.pUserName = NULL;  // Specify current user name
dsbInfo.pPassword = NULL;  // Specify current user password


//---------------------------------------------
// Allocate buffers to hold return values
//---------------------------------------------
// Class and ADsPath are always UNICODE
WCHAR pszObjectClass[MAX_PATH] = { NULL };
// Buffer to hold class name
dsbInfo.pszObjectClass = pszObjectClass;
// Size of classname buffer
dsbInfo.cchObjectClass = ARRAYSIZE(pszObjectClass);


// ADsPath to hold results
WCHAR pszResult[MAX_PATH] = { NULL };
// Place result in here
dsbInfo.pszPath = pszResult;
// Size of path string
dsbInfo.cchPath = ARRAYSIZE(pszResult);


// Display browser dialog
hResult = DsBrowseForContainer( &dsbInfo );

if ( hResult == IDOK )
    {
    //---------------------------------------------
    // Display returned object ADsPath
    //---------------------------------------------
    // Format information string
    _TCHAR pszMessage[1024] = { NULL };
```

(continued)

Listing 8-1 *continued*

```
        _stprintf( pszMessage,
            _T("ADsPath: \t%ls \nClass Name: \t%ls \n"),
            pszResult,
            pszObjectClass);
        MessageBox( NULL,
            pszMessage,
            _T("DsBrowseForContainer Results"),
            MB_OK | MB_ICONINFORMATION );
        }
    // Uninitialize COM
    CoUninitialize ();

    // Exit with any lingering hResult
    return ( hResult );
}
```

Another powerful feature of the *DsBrowseForContainer* function is the ability to have messages sent to a function you specify. You specify the address of the callback function in the *pfnCallback* member of the *DSBROWSEINFO* structure. The callback function receives a message in the *msg* parameter along with data in the *lParam* and *lpData* parameters. The *msg* parameter will be one of the *DSBM* messages listed in Table 8-2.

Callback Function Message	Description
DSBM_CHANGEIMAGESTATE	This message is documented as being sent when the image state in the tree view is changed. However, this message is currently not used.
DSBM_CONTEXTMENU	Sent whenever a user requests a context menu by right-clicking the mouse or, if using the keyboard, by pressing Shift+F10 or the Application key. However, a context menu is not displayed by default. You can then use the Windows *TrackPopupMenu* API to display a context menu at the location of the selected item.
DSBM_HELP	Sent whenever a user presses F1 or uses the Help button on the dialog box's title bar. The application can choose to display a ToolTip with additional information about the item selected.
DSBM_QUERYINSERT	Sent whenever the tree view is building a list of items. You can modify the item being added or filter it entirely.

Table 8-2 Messages for the *DsBrowseForContainer* callback function.

Listing 8-2 shows a framework of the callback function, displaying message information in the debug window. The complete source code is available on the companion CD.

> **Note**   Here's some information on an undocumented feature. In addition to the *DSBM* messages, the callback function is also called whenever the user changes his or her selection. The *msg* parameter is set to 0x02 and *lpData* points to an ADsPath of the item being selected, followed by the class name. In Listing 8-2, whenever the selection changes, the code sets the text above the tree control to show the ADsPath of the selected object. The dialog box's title bar is also set to the class name. Interestingly enough, the ADsPath string is always returned using the *ADS_FORMAT_WINDOWS_NO_SERVER* style, regardless of the *DSBROWSEINFO dwReturnFormat* setting. As always, be extremely careful using undocumented features, as they are generally undocumented for a good reason, including being unsupported or being subject to change in the future. As a former Microsoft developer, I can be trusted on this.

```
// Disable "conditional expression is constant"
// generated by _RPTx macros
#pragma warning( disable : 4127 )


//-----------------------------------------------------------------
// Function:    DsBrowseCallBack
//              Callback to filter and modify directory browser
// Inputs:      HWND hwnd   Window handle of dialog
//              UINT msg    Message number (DSBM_*)
//              LPARAM lpData   Pointer to data, depends on message type
//              LPARAM lParam   Instance data specified by caller
// Notes:       Parameter names not used are commented out to avoid
//              compiler warning C4100; "unreferenced formal parameter"
//-----------------------------------------------------------------
int CALLBACK DsBrowseCallBack( HWND/*hwnd*/, UINT msg, LPARAM lpData,
    LPARAM/*lParam*/)

{
    PDSBITEM    pdsbItem = NULL;  // For DSBM_QUERYINSERT
    LPHELPINFO  phlpInfo = NULL;  // For DSBM_HELP
    HWND        hWnd = NULL;      // For DSBM_CONTEXTMENU
    BOOL        bResult = FALSE;  // Default result is to ignore message
```

Listing 8-2 A framework of the callback function.   *(continued)*

Listing 8-2 *continued*

```
switch ( msg )
    {
    case DSBM_CONTEXTMENU:
        // User requested a context menu
        // lpData contains the HWND of the window,
        // the dialog box to the callback function
        // lpData contains the HWND of the item

        // Display information
        hWnd = (HWND)lpData;

        // Create popup menu
        _RPT1( _CRT_WARN, "DSBM_CONTEXTMENU: %x \n", hWnd );

        bResult = FALSE;
        break;

    case DSBM_HELP:
        // Used to forward the WM_HELP message from the
        // dialog box to the callback function
        // lpData points to a HELPINFO structure

        // Display the X/Y location of mouse when help is selected
        // Can use this information to query the tree view control
        phlpInfo = (LPHELPINFO)lpData;
        _RPT2( _CRT_WARN, "DSBM_HELP: %u/%u\n",
            phlpInfo->MousePos.x,
            phlpInfo->MousePos.y );
        break;

    case DSBM_QUERYINSERT:
        // Called before each item is inserted into
        // the display. Can modify the name, icon, and state.

        // lpData points to DBSITEM structure
        _ASSERT(lpData);
        // Display item name
        pdsbItem = (PDSBITEM)lpData;
        _RPT2( _CRT_WARN, "DSBM_QUERYINSERT %d: %ls\n", msg,
            pdsbItem->szDisplayName );

        // Return indicates item was not modified
        bResult = FALSE;
        break;
```

```
        case DSBM_QUERYINSERTA:
            // Called in addition to DSBM_QUERYINSERTW with
            // ANSI version of DSBITEM
            bResult = FALSE;
            break;

        case 0x02:
            // UNDOCUMENTED
            // Called whenever selection changes
            // lpData contains pointer to selected item as a
            // UNICODE ADsPath using ADS_FORMAT_WINDOWS_NO_SERVER
            // After the ADsPath string NULL character,
            // the class name of the object always follows
            if (lpData)
                {
                WCHAR* pszADsPath = (WCHAR*)lpData;
                WCHAR* pszClassName = pszADsPath +
                    _tcslen(pszADsPath) + 1;
                _RPT3( _CRT_WARN, "DSBM_??? %d: %ls %ls\n", msg,
                    pszADsPath, pszClassName );

                // Copy the ADsPath to the banner text using the
                // DSBID_BANNER control ID
                SendDlgItemMessage(
                    hwnd,  // Windows handle of dialog box
                    DSBID_BANNER,  // Specify banner label control
                    WM_SETTEXT,  // Send message to change text
                    0,   // Not used
                    (LPARAM)pszADsPath);  // Set banner to ADsPath
                // Set the dialog caption to the class name
                SetWindowText(hwnd, pszClassName);
                }
            bResult = TRUE; //DEBUG
            break;

        default:
            // Unknown message, display in debug
            _RPT1( _CRT_WARN, "DsBrowseCallBack: %d\n", msg );
            break;
        }

    // Return the result
    return ( bResult );

}
#pragma warning( default : 4127 )  // Restore default behavior
```

> **Note** Listing 8-2 uses a couple of features from the Microsoft Visual C++
> run-time library. The _RPTx macros are handy for displaying *printf* style
> messages in the debugging window or for forcing an assert dialog box.
> However, they generate C4127 warnings, so I use a #pragma statement
> to disable those messages while retaining the warning level specified
> in the project settings.

Domain Browser Dialog Box

The domain browser dialog box is similar to the container browser dialog box.
I won't cover this dialog box in as much detail because you are unlikely to use
it as often. Instead of using a function, as the container browser dialog box does,
the domain browser uses the *IDsBrowseDomainTree* interface. The user is shown
a dialog box with just the specified domains, including any trusted domains, as
shown in Figure 8-2.

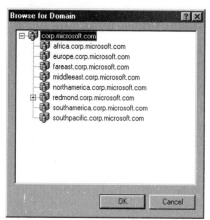

Figure 8-2 Active Directory domain browser dialog box.

Listing 8-3 shows how to invoke the domain browser dialog box using the
BrowseTo method of the *IDsBrowseDomainTree* interface.

```
int WINAPI _tWinMain( HINSTANCE/*hInstance*/,
    HINSTANCE/*hPrevInstance*/,
    LPSTR/*lpCmdLine*/, int/*nCmdShow*/)
{
    // Initialize COM
    CoInitialize( NULL );
```

Listing 8-3 DsBrowseDomain.cpp showing how to invoke the domain browser dialog
box using the *BrowseTo* method of the *IDsBrowseDomainTree* interface.

```
//--------------------------------------------
// Create an instance of the domain browser
//--------------------------------------------
IDsBrowseDomainTree *pobjDSBDomain = NULL;
HRESULT hResult = CoCreateInstance( CLSID_DsDomainTreeBrowser,
    NULL,
    CLSCTX_INPROC_SERVER,
    IID_IDsBrowseDomainTree,
    (void **) &pobjDSBDomain);
// Ensure object was created
if ( SUCCEEDED( hResult ) )
    {
    //--------------------------------------------
    // Display domain browser dialog
    //--------------------------------------------
    LPWSTR pszDomainName;
    hResult = pobjDSBDomain->BrowseTo(
        NULL,  // Owner window
        &pszDomainName,  // Pointer to hold returned domain name
        DBDTF_RETURNFQDN |  // Return fully qualified domain name
        DBDTF_RETURNMIXEDDOMAINS |  // Show downlevel trust domains
        DBDTF_RETURNEXTERNAL |  // Show external trust domains
     // DBDTF_RETURNINBOUND |  // Show trusting domains instead of
                                // trusted domains
        DBDTF_RETURNINOUTBOUND );  // Show both trusted and
                                   // trusting domains

    if ( pszDomainName != NULL )
        // Display users selection
        MessageBox(NULL, pszDomainName,
            _T("User selected the following domain"), MB_OK |
            MB_ICONINFORMATION);

    // Free memory allocated for target string
    if ( pszDomainName )
        CoTaskMemFree ( pszDomainName );
    }

// No longer need the object, release the interface
if ( pobjDSBDomain )
    pobjDSBDomain->Release ();

// Uninitialize COM and exit
CoUninitialize ();

// Exit with any lingering hResult
return (hResult);
}
```

Object Picker Dialog Box

It's impossible to work with Active Directory and not have used the object picker dialog box. The Windows 2000 administrative tools use the object picker extensively when modifying groups and security settings. Selecting *user* objects is the most common use of this component; however, it does much more than that. Figure 8-3 shows an example of the object picker dialog box.

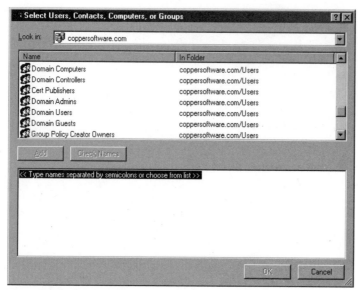

Figure 8-3 Object picker dialog box.

The object picker dialog box is an extremely useful component for developers of Active Directory–enabled applications. Instead of having to create a custom user interface, developer's lives are made easier because all the work of displaying objects and gathering input is wrapped up in a single COM object named *DsObjectPicker*.

Think of *DsObjectPicker* as the Active Directory version of the common Open dialog box provided by the Windows shell and used in most Windows-based applications. Unlike the container and domain browser dialog boxes, the object picker does not display the directory hierarchy. The *DsObjectPicker* is optimized for directory objects and is simplified for that task.

IDsObjectPicker

The *DsObjectPicker* object exposes a simple COM interface, *IDsObjectPicker*, which has two methods. The first is the *Initialize* method, which you use to set options for the dialog box, including scopes and filters, which I'll define shortly.

The second is *InvokeDialog*, which displays the dialog box and returns the user's selections via the *IDataObject* interface.

When using *DsObjectPicker*, you specify the location in the directory to display, which object classes to show, and whether the user is allowed to pick multiple objects. The location is defined with a *scope*. There are two kinds of scope: *up-level* for Windows 2000 domains, and *down-level* for mixed-mode domains with Windows NT 4.0 or earlier domain controllers. The mechanism used to specify which objects to display for a scope is called a *filter*. The dialog box options are set using a *DSOP_INIT_INFO* structure, each containing an array of *DSOP_SCOPE_INIT_INFO* structures for each scope to be used. Filters are set per-scope by using the *DSOP_FILTER_FLAGS* and *DSOP_UPLEVEL_FILTER_FLAGS* structures.

After a user has made his or her choice of objects and clicks the OK button, information about the objects selected is returned via the COM *IDataObject* interface. *IDataObject* is a generic interface used to pass a data object between processes. In this case, the data object is formatted as a *DS_SELECTION_LIST* structure. This structure contains an array of *DS_SELECTION* structures, which is listed below.

```
typedef struct _DS_SELECTION {
    PWSTR    pwzName;
    PWSTR    pwzADsPath;
    PWSTR    pwzClass;
    PWSTR    pwzUPN;
    VARIANT *pvarFetchedAttributes;
    ULONG    flScopeType;
} DS_SELECTION, *PDS_SELECTION;
```

Object Picker Sample

Listing 8-4 shows how to use the object picker dialog box from C++. This application opens the object picker dialog box and allows the user to select one or more users, contacts, or computers. When the user clicks OK, the name, class, ADsPath, and user principal name (UPN) for each object is displayed in a message box. Figure 8-4 shows a sample of the output.

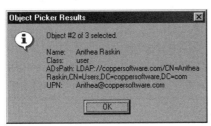

Figure 8-4 Information displayed for the object selected in the object picker.

The sample calls the *Initialize* method of the *IDsObjectPicker* interface with a pointer to a *DSOP_INIT_INFO* structure that defines the scope and filter for the object picker. Then the sample invokes the object picker dialog box using the *InvokeDialog* method of the *IDsObjectPicker* interface. Finally, the sample processes the returned *IDataObject* objects and displays a message box with information about each object.

```cpp
int WINAPI _tWinMain( HINSTANCE/*hInstance*/,
    HINSTANCE/*hPrevInstance*/,
    LPSTR/*lpCmdLine*/, int/*nCmdShow*/)
{
    // Initialize COM
    CoInitialize( NULL );

    //--------------------------------------------------
    // Create an instance of the object picker.
    //--------------------------------------------------
    IDsObjectPicker *pobjDSOPicker = NULL;
    HRESULT hResult = CoCreateInstance( CLSID_DsObjectPicker,
        NULL,
        CLSCTX_INPROC_SERVER,
        IID_IDsObjectPicker,
        (void **) &pobjDSOPicker);
    // Ensure object was created
    if ( SUCCEEDED( hResult ) )
        {
        //--------------------------------------------------
        // Initialize DsObjectPicker parameters
        //--------------------------------------------------

        // Initialize an array of scopes
        static const int SCOPE_INIT_COUNT = 1;
        DSOP_SCOPE_INIT_INFO rgScopeInit[ SCOPE_INIT_COUNT ];

        // Set structure members to zero to indicate default
        ZeroMemory( rgScopeInit,
            sizeof( DSOP_SCOPE_INIT_INFO ) * SCOPE_INIT_COUNT);

        //--------------------------------------------------
        // Set scope options
        //--------------------------------------------------

        // Set scope size (used to check version)
        rgScopeInit[0].cbSize = sizeof( DSOP_SCOPE_INIT_INFO );
```

Listing 8-4 DsObjectPicker.cpp showing how to use the object picker dialog box.

```
// Set scope type to entire forest (i.e. enterprise)
rgScopeInit[0].flType = DSOP_SCOPE_TYPE_ENTERPRISE_DOMAIN;

// Returned objects should have ADsPath with the LDAP provider
rgScopeInit[0].flScope = DSOP_SCOPE_FLAG_WANT_PROVIDER_LDAP;

//-------------------------------------------------------------
// Set Filter options to show users, computers, and contacts
//-------------------------------------------------------------

// Uplevel scope supports Active Directory
rgScopeInit[0].FilterFlags.Uplevel.flBothModes =
    // Native or mixed mode domains
    // Show groups
//  DSOP_FILTER_BUILTIN_GROUPS |
    // Show computers
    DSOP_FILTER_COMPUTERS |
    // Show contacts
    DSOP_FILTER_CONTACTS |
    // Show local distribution groups
//  DSOP_FILTER_DOMAIN_LOCAL_GROUPS_DL |
    // Show local security groups
//  DSOP_FILTER_DOMAIN_LOCAL_GROUPS_SE |
    // Show global distribution groups
//  DSOP_FILTER_GLOBAL_GROUPS_DL |
    // Show global security groups
//  DSOP_FILTER_GLOBAL_GROUPS_SE |
    // Show showInAdvancedViewOnly objects
//  DSOP_FILTER_INCLUDE_ADVANCED_VIEW |
    // Show universal distribution groups
//  DSOP_FILTER_UNIVERSAL_GROUPS_DL |
    // Show universal security groups
//  DSOP_FILTER_UNIVERSAL_GROUPS_SE |
    // Show users
    DSOP_FILTER_USERS ;    // Show users
    // Include well-known security principals
//  DSOP_FILTER_WELL_KNOWN_PRINCIPALS

// Downlevel scope supports Windows NT 4.0
rgScopeInit[0].FilterFlags.flDownlevel =
    DSOP_DOWNLEVEL_FILTER_COMPUTERS |  // Show computers
    DSOP_DOWNLEVEL_FILTER_USERS;       // Show users

//---------------------------------------------
// Create Initialization Structure
//---------------------------------------------
```

(continued)

Listing 8-4 *continued*

```
        // Initialize the DSOP_INIT_INFO structure.
        DSOP_INIT_INFO   dsopInitInfo;
        ZeroMemory( &dsopInitInfo, sizeof( dsopInitInfo ) );

        // Set size of structure (used to check version)
        dsopInitInfo.cbSize = sizeof( dsopInitInfo );

        // Use local computer to determine domain
        dsopInitInfo.pwzTargetComputer = NULL;

        // Set the number of scopes that are part of this structure
        dsopInitInfo.cDsScopeInfos = SCOPE_INIT_COUNT;

        // Add scope(s) to structure
        dsopInitInfo.aDsScopeInfos = rgScopeInit;

        // Allow the user to select multiple objects
        dsopInitInfo.flOptions = DSOP_FLAG_MULTISELECT;

        // DsObjectPicker can retrieve certain attributes of
        // selected objects
        // Not shown in this example. Instead, use the returned
        // ADsPath to bind and work with selected objects.
#if defined(USE_ATTR_NAMES)
        // For each object, retrieve the lDAPDisplayName attribute
        PCWSTR pcwszAttrNames[] = { L"lDAPDisplayName" };
        dsopInitInfo.cAttributesToFetch = 1;
        dsopInitInfo.apwzAttributeNames = &pcwszAttrNames[0];
#else
        // Specify no attributes be returned (ADsPath is always available)
        dsopInitInfo.cAttributesToFetch = 0;
        dsopInitInfo.apwzAttributeNames = NULL;
#endif
        //-----------------------------------------------
        // Initialize DsObjectPicker
        //-----------------------------------------------

        // Initialize the object picker with the DS_INIT_INFO structure
        hResult = pobjDSOPicker->Initialize ( &dsopInitInfo );

        if ( SUCCEEDED ( hResult ) )
            {
            //-----------------------------------------------
            // Display object picker dialog
            //-----------------------------------------------
```

```
// Register the results data object format
CLIPFORMAT cfDsObjectPicker = (CLIPFORMAT)
    RegisterClipboardFormat( CFSTR_DSOP_DS_SELECTION_LIST );

// Display the picker dialog, and return a IDataObject interface
IDataObject *pobjDataObject = NULL;
hResult = pobjDSOPicker->InvokeDialog( NULL, &pobjDataObject );

if ( SUCCEEDED ( hResult ) )
    {
    // If not S_OK, user pressed Cancel button
    if ( hResult == S_OK )
        {
        //---------------------------------------------
        // Get the user's selections
        //---------------------------------------------

        // Important to fill in all members of STGMEDIUM and
        // FORMATETC structures before calling GetData method
        STGMEDIUM stgmedium = {  // Storage medium information
            TYMED_HGLOBAL,  // Use global memory to hold data
            NULL,  // Global memory handle
            NULL };  // Indicate receiver will release medium

        FORMATETC formatetc = {  // Data format information
            cfDsObjectPicker,  // Registered clipboard format
                               // value

            NULL,  // Independence device for data
            DVASPECT_CONTENT,  // We want the content itself
            -1,  // No boundary break
            TYMED_HGLOBAL };  // Use global memory to hold data

        // Get the global memory block containing a user's
        // selections
        hResult = pobjDataObject->GetData(
            &formatetc, &stgmedium );

        if ( SUCCEEDED( hResult ) )
            {
            //---------------------------------------------
            // Process selections
            //---------------------------------------------
```

(continued)

Listing 8-4 *continued*

```
                    // Get a pointer to the data contained in
                    // DS_SELECTION_LIST structure
                    DS_SELECTION_LIST *pdsslSelectedObjects = NULL;
                    pdsslSelectedObjects = (DS_SELECTION_LIST*)
                        GlobalLock( stgmedium.hGlobal );

                    // Verify valid data
                    if ( pdsslSelectedObjects )
                        {
                        // Loop through array of selected objects
                        ULONG ulIndex;
                        for ( ulIndex = 0;
                            ulIndex < pdsslSelectedObjects->cItems;
                            ulIndex++)
                            {
                            // Display information for each object
                            // selected
                            _TCHAR pszMessage[1024] = { NULL };
                            _stprintf( pszMessage,
                                _T("Object #%u of %u selected.
                                \n\nName:\t%ws \nClass:\t%ws
                                \nADsPath:\t%ws \nUPN:\t%ws \n"),
                                ulIndex + 1,
                                pdsslSelectedObjects->cItems,
                                pdsslSelectedObjects->
                                aDsSelection[ulIndex].pwzName,
                                pdsslSelectedObjects->
                                aDsSelection[ulIndex].pwzClass,
                                pdsslSelectedObjects->
                                aDsSelection[ulIndex].pwzADsPath,
                                pdsslSelectedObjects->
                                aDsSelection[ulIndex].pwzUPN);
                        MessageBox( NULL,
                            pszMessage,
                            _T("Object Picker Results"),
                            MB_OK | MB_ICONINFORMATION );
                            }
                        // Release the data
                        GlobalUnlock( stgmedium.hGlobal );
                        }
                    }
                // Release the storage medium
                ReleaseStgMedium( &stgmedium );
                }
```

```
        else // Success, but not S_OK; user pressed Cancel button
            {
            MessageBox( NULL,
                _T("User pressed Cancel button."),
                _T("Object Picker Results"),
                MB_OK | MB_ICONINFORMATION );
            }
        // No longer need the selections; release
        // IDataObject interface
        if ( pobjDataObject )
            pobjDataObject->Release ();
        }
    }
}
// No longer need the DsObjectPicker; release IDsObjectPicker interface
if ( pobjDSOPicker )
    pobjDSOPicker->Release ();

// Uninitialize COM and exit
CoUninitialize ();

// Exit with any lingering hResult
return (hResult);
}
```

Display Specifiers

Active Directory objects contain a lot of data. Just a single *user* object has over 200 possible attributes. Presenting information about an Active Directory object to end users and administrators is quite a challenge. Each object class in Active Directory has a number of user interface elements you can use when working with objects of that class. They include the following:

- Property pages
- Context menu items
- Icons
- Display names
- Display options
- Creation wizards

Network administrators have probably already worked with some of these components when setting up Active Directory. These components are also part of various Active Directory Microsoft Management Console (MMC) snap-ins such as Active Directory Users and Computers. Figures 8-5 and 8-6 illustrate how Active Directory objects are presented and manipulated using the MMC snap-ins.

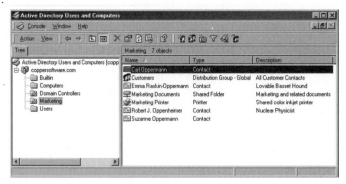

Figure 8-5 Active Directory Users and Computers console showing various user interface elements for objects.

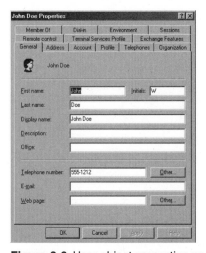

Figure 8-6 User object properties page.

Windows Shell Integration

Administrators and developers are not the only users who can view the contents of the directory. Active Directory extends Windows to enable viewing the directory by end users. For example, users can use tools such as Windows Explorer and the common dialog boxes to browse and search the directory. The following illustration shows the same directory location as Figure 8-5 does, but this view is in Windows Explorer.

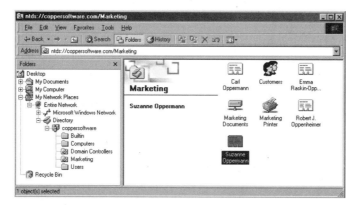

Property pages for directory objects are displayed differently in the Windows shell from what they are in MMC. Here's a property page presented by the Windows shell. It's for the same user as shown in Figure 8-6, but the information is presented in a form more suitable for end users than administrators. Of course, an end user cannot change anything that he or she does not have access to.

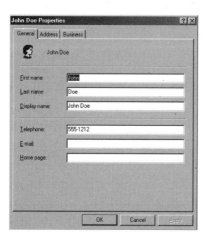

Display Specifiers Background

Each object class in Active Directory has a schema object that defines the properties of the class. However, information about the user interface elements associated with objects of a class are not stored in the schema. Instead, information about the user interface elements available for a particular object class (including property pages, context menus, and creation wizards) is stored in objects known as *display specifiers*. The *displaySpecifier* class contains a number of attributes, listed in Table 8-3, that allow applications to load property pages, display icons and context menus, and map displayable field labels and attribute names.

displaySpecifier Attribute	Description
adminContextMenu	Context menus for administrative tools. Each value is the CLSID of a COM context menu object and the loading order. Each context menu object can supply one or more menu items. Alternatively, a command line can be used to launch an application. (This attribute is multivalued.)
adminPropertyPages	Property pages for administrative tools. Each value is the CLSID of a COM property page object. Can also specify the position number and optional data to be passed to a property page. (This attribute is multivalued.)
attributeDisplayNames	Display names for class attributes. Each value is a Unicode string with the attribute name and the localized, friendly display name. (This attribute is multivalued.)
classDisplayName	Unicode string with localized, friendly display name of the class.
contextMenu	Context menus for shell and nonadministrative tools. Each value is the loading order number and CLSID of a COM object supporting the *IContextMenu* and *IShellExtInit* interfaces. Each context menu object can supply one or more menu items. Alternatively, a command line can be used to launch an application. (This attribute is multivalued.)
createDialog	Used to control how the User and Contact creation wizards format the Full Name field and thus the *cn* attribute for new objects.

Table 8-3 Attributes of the *displaySpecifier* class.

displaySpecifier Attribute	Description
createWizardExt	Creation wizards for objects of this class. Each value is the CLSID of a COM object supporting the *IDsAdminNewObjExt* interface.
creationWizard	Primary creation wizard for objects of this class. Value is the CLSID of a COM object supporting the *IDsAdminNewObjExt* interface.
iconPath	Icons representing this class. Each value contains the state of the icon, the path to the resource file, and the resource index.
queryFilter	Unknown
scopeFlags	Unknown
shellContextMenu	Not used and incorrectly documented. Use *contextMenu* instead.
shellPropertyPages	Property pages for shell and nonadministrative tools. Each value is the CLSID of a COM property page object. Can also specify the position number and optional data to be passed to property page. (This attribute is multivalued.)
treatAsLeaf	This attribute indicates that although the class might be defined in the schema as a container, it should not be shown as one by the user interface. The *computer* class has this attribute set.

Using the *createDialog* Attribute

The purpose of the *createDialog* attribute is not described in the Active Directory documentation and none of the default display specifiers use it. However, Microsoft Knowledge Base article Q250455 explains that you can use this attribute to control how the User and Contact creation wizards format the Full Name field and thus the *cn* attribute for new objects. The *createDialog* attribute isn't set by default, and this results in an order of first name, middle initials, and last name. To set a different format, modify the *createDialog* attribute of the display specifier. For example, to use the order last name, first name, use the following string:

%<sn>, %<givenName> %<initials>

The angle brackets are required and any attribute of the *user* or *contact* class can be used.

Each class has one or more instances of the *displaySpecifier* class that contains information about how to display objects of that class.

The *user* class, for example, includes a *user-Display displaySpecifier* object, located in a container in the configuration partition of Active Directory. The name of the object is derived by taking the name of the class object and appending "*-Display.*"

International Support

An important part of the *displaySpecifier* object is something we abbreviated as I18N at Microsoft—*internationalization.* Windows 2000 is available in dozens of languages and Active Directory must support each of those languages. The process of converting a software product into other languages is known as *localization.* All the Active Directory user interface elements are localized in each of the languages that Windows 2000 supports. Technically, "languages" is misleading; the correct term is *locale,* which is a term specifying a particular language and optional settings for a certain geographical or geopolitical region or cultural group.

Active Directory in Windows 2000 comes with support for 24 locales, which are listed in Table 8-4.

Locale	Language
0x0401	Arabic (Saudi Arabia)
0x0404	Chinese (Taiwan)
0x0405	Czech
0x0406	Danish
0x0407	German (Standard)
0x0408	Greek
0x0409	English (United States)
0x040B	Finnish
0x040C	French (Standard)
0x040D	Hebrew
0x040E	Hungarian
0x0410	Italian (Standard)
0x0411	Japanese
0x0412	Korean
0x413	Dutch

Table 8-4 Locales supported in Active Directory.

Locale	Language
0x414	Norwegian
0x0415	Polish
0x0416	Portuguese (Brazil)
0x0419	Russian
0x041D	Swedish
0x041F	Turkish
0x0804	Chinese (PRC)
0x0816	Portuguese (Standard)
0x0C0A	Spanish (Modern Sort)

IDsDisplaySpecifier

The *IDsDisplaySpecifier* interface is available to help applications work with objects of the *displaySpecifier* class. You use *IDsDisplaySpecifier* to avoid having to get the *displaySpecifier* object manually and figuring out its location based on the current locale.

The *IDsDisplaySpecifier* interface represents a *DsDisplaySpecifier* object, which must be instantiated using the COM *CoCreateInstance* function. Unlike the *IADsXXX* interfaces, *IDsDisplaySpecifier* is a utility interface and isn't bound to any particular object. In reality, it's a thin wrapper around Win32 API–style functions and not very COM-like in its implementation.

IDsDisplaySpecifier does not inherit from *IDispatch* and there is no type library available for it. This means it cannot be used from Visual Basic or the scripting languages. However, the regular *IADs* interface can be substituted to bind to the xxx-*Display* object and retrieve attribute values.

Table 8-5 lists the methods for the *IDsDisplaySpecifier* interface.

IDsDisplaySpecifier **Method**	**Description**
EnumClassAttributes	Uses a supplied callback function to enumerate each attribute of the class in order to retrieve the friendly attribute name.
GetAttributeADsType	Returns the *ADSTYPE* of a specified attribute.
GetClassCreationInfo	Retrieves the property pages of a class creation wizard.

Table 8-5 Methods of the *IDsDisplaySpecifier* interface. *(continued)*

Table 8-5 *continued*

IDsDisplaySpecifier Method	Description
GetDisplaySpecifier	Binds to a locale-dependent *displaySpecifier* object for the class specified. Must call the *SetServer* method beforehand to indicate where to find the object.
GetFriendlyAttributeName	Returns the localized version of the specified attribute name.
GetFriendlyClassName	Returns a localized name of the specified class.
GetIcon	Loads the resource containing the icon and returns a *HICON* handle to it.
GetIconLocation	Retrieves the filename and resource ID of the icon for the specified object class.
IsClassContainer	Tests whether a class is a container.
SetLanguageID	Sets the locale to use when retrieving display specifier information.
SetServer	Sets the preferred server to be used to gather display specifier information.

Display Specifier Sample

Listing 8-5 shows some sample code that puts display specifiers to work. In it, I gather information about an object class using the *IDsDisplaySpecifier* interface.

```
int WINAPI _tWinMain( HINSTANCE/*hInstance*/,
    HINSTANCE/*hPrevInstance*/,
    LPSTR/*lpCmdLine*/, int/*nCmdShow*/)
{

    // Initialize COM
    HRESULT hResult;
    CoInitialize( NULL );


    //---------------------------------------------
    // Browse to an object
    //---------------------------------------------


    // Set options for browsing dialog
    DSBROWSEINFO dsbInfo = { 0 };
    dsbInfo.cbStruct = sizeof( dsbInfo );  // Set size for version purpose
```

Listing 8-5 DsDisplaySpecifier.cpp showing how to use display specifiers.

```
dsbInfo.hwndOwner = NULL;  // Window handle
dsbInfo.pszCaption = _TEXT("Browse for object");  // Text for title bar
dsbInfo.pszTitle =
    _TEXT("Choose an object to display class information.");
dsbInfo.pszRoot = NULL;  // No root
dsbInfo.dwFlags =  // Option flags
//  DSBI_CHECKBOXES |  // Not currently used
    DSBI_ENTIREDIRECTORY |  // Include all trusted domains
    DSBI_EXPANDONOPEN |  // Expand tree to pszPath
    DSBI_IGNORETREATASLEAF |  // Show all possible containers
    DSBI_INCLUDEHIDDEN |  // Show hidden objects
//  DSBI_NOBUTTONS |  // Remove [+] [-] in tree view
//  DSBI_NOLINES |  // Don't draw lines
//  DSBI_NOLINESATROOT |  // Don't draw lines from root down
//  DSBI_NOROOT |  // Don't show the root object
//  DSBI_RETURN_FORMAT |  // Format paths based on ADS_FORMAT_*
    DSBI_RETURNOBJECTCLASS ;  // Fill in pszObject class
//  DSBI_SIMPLEAUTHENTICATE  // Don't use secure authenication
// Function to call back
dsbInfo.pfnCallback = NULL;
// Initialize message-specific data to 0
dsbInfo.lParam = 0;
// Format ADsPaths using X.500
dsbInfo.dwReturnFormat = ADS_FORMAT_X500;
// Specify current user name
dsbInfo.pUserName = NULL;
// Specify current user password
dsbInfo.pPassword = NULL;

// Must be wide string, not TCHAR
WCHAR pszObjectClass[MAX_PATH];
// Buffer to hold class name
dsbInfo.pszObjectClass = pszObjectClass;
// Size of classname buffer
dsbInfo.cchObjectClass = MAX_PATH;

// ADsPath to hold results
WCHAR pszResult[MAX_PATH] = { NULL };
// Place result in here
dsbInfo.pszPath = pszResult;
// Size of path buffer
dsbInfo.cchPath = MAX_PATH;

// Display browser dialog
hResult = DsBrowseForContainer( &dsbInfo );
```

(continued)

Listing 8-5 *continued*

```
if ( hResult == IDOK )
    {
    //-------------------------------------------
    // Create an instance of the DsDisplaySpecifier
    //-------------------------------------------
    IDsDisplaySpecifier *pobjDSDSpecifier = NULL;
    HRESULT hResult = CoCreateInstance( CLSID_DsDisplaySpecifier,
        NULL,
        CLSCTX_INPROC_SERVER,
        IID_IDsDisplaySpecifier,
        (void **) &pobjDSDSpecifier);
    // Ensure object was created
    if ( SUCCEEDED( hResult ) )
        {
        //-------------------------------------------
        // Initialize DsDisplaySpecifier parameters
        //-------------------------------------------

        // Set default locale to look up display specifiers.
        // 0=Current locale
        // Note:  Shown for example only, normally redundant.
        hResult = pobjDSDSpecifier->SetLanguageID( 0 );


        //-------------------------------------------
        // Get class information
        //-------------------------------------------

        // Get Friendly Class Name
        const int cchFriendlyName = 100;
        unsigned short pszFriendlyName[ cchFriendlyName ] = { NULL };
        hResult = pobjDSDSpecifier->GetFriendlyClassName(
            pszObjectClass,  // Name of class to look up
            pszFriendlyName,  // Buffer to store friendly name
            cchFriendlyName);  // Number of characters available

        // Get icon location
        // Must use GetIconLocation and LoadLibraryEx to
        // load the icon for use by MessageBoxIndirect
        INT residIcon;
        const int cchIconPathname = MAX_PATH;
        _TCHAR pszIconPathname[cchIconPathname] = { NULL };
        hResult = pobjDSDSpecifier->GetIconLocation(
            pszObjectClass,  // Name of class to look up
            DSGIF_ISNORMAL,  // Get the normal icon
            pszIconPathname,  // Pathname of file containing icon
            cchIconPathname,  // Number of characters available
            &residIcon); // Resource ID of icon in file
```

```
HINSTANCE hInstance = NULL;
if ( SUCCEEDED ( hResult ) )
    {
    // Load the file with the icon resource
    hInstance = LoadLibraryEx ( pszIconPathname,
        NULL,
        LOAD_LIBRARY_AS_DATAFILE);
    }


// Is Container?
_TCHAR *prgszBooleanText[2] = { _T("No"), _T("Yes") };
BOOL bIsContainer = FALSE;
bIsContainer = pobjDSDSpecifier->IsClassContainer(
    pszObjectClass,  // Name of class to lookup
    NULL,  // ???
    0 );   // Or DSICCF_IGNORETREATASLEAF


if (bIsContainer)
    bIsContainer = 1;
else
    bIsContainer = 0;


//-------------------------------------------
// Display class information
//-------------------------------------------


// Format information string
_TCHAR pszMessage[1024] = { NULL };
_stprintf( pszMessage,
    _T("ADsPath: \t%ws \nClass Name: \t%ws \nFriendly Name:
    \t%ws \nContainer: \t%ws \nIcon Location: \t%ws \nIcon
    ResID: \t%d"),
    pszResult,
    pszObjectClass,
    pszFriendlyName,
    prgszBooleanText[bIsContainer],
    pszIconPathname,
    -residIcon);


// Parameters for message box
MSGBOXPARAMS mbParameters;
mbParameters.cbSize = sizeof( MSGBOXPARAMS );
mbParameters.hwndOwner = NULL;
mbParameters.hInstance = hInstance;
mbParameters.lpszText = pszMessage;
mbParameters.lpszCaption = _T("Display Specifier Information");
mbParameters.dwStyle = MB_USERICON | MB_OK;
```

(continued)

Listing 8-5 *continued*

```
            mbParameters.lpszIcon = MAKEINTRESOURCE( -residIcon );
            mbParameters.dwContextHelpId = 0;
            mbParameters.lpfnMsgBoxCallback = NULL;
            mbParameters.dwLanguageId = 0;
            // Display message box with icon
            MessageBoxIndirect( &mbParameters );
            }
        }
    // Uninitialize COM
    CoUninitialize ();

    // Exit with any lingering hResult
    return ( hResult );
}
```

When you run this sample, select an object, and click OK, the display speci-fier information, along with the corresponding class icon, is displayed in a dia-log box as shown in Figure 8-7.

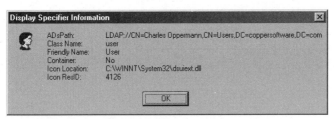

Figure 8-7 Output of the DsDisplaySpecifier sample for a selected object.

Summary

Many of the programs that you'll write for Active Directory will require you to provide a user interface with which to gather input from users and administra-tors. In this chapter, you've seen how you can make use of the interface elements provided by ADSI and Active Directory in your programs. In the next chapter, I'll describe a difficult but useful topic—how to extend and modify the Active Directory schema.

Part III

Special Topics

9

Active Directory Schema

In this chapter, I'll describe in more detail the makeup of the Active Directory schema. In the first part of the chapter, I'll explain how classes and attributes are structured and defined. Toward the end of the chapter, I'll show how to modify the default schema by adding a new attribute and a new class to the directory.

Understanding the Schema

The schema is the collection of class and attribute definitions in Active Directory. Active Directory has over 140 predefined types of classes and over 850 attributes. These classes and attributes define what data can be stored in the directory. In the following sections, I'll describe the base concepts of the schema and then provide a more detailed discussion of classes, attributes, and syntaxes.

Object Classes

The Active Directory schema contains objects that define each class that can be stored within the directory. Each class determines the rules to use when creating new objects of that class and the available attributes. For example, the Active Directory *person* class specifies that objects created using this class must have a *cn* (*Common-Name*) attribute and can optionally include a *sn* (*Surname*) and *telephoneNumber* attribute.

An Active Directory class also sets the rules for naming and containership. For example, every object has a naming attribute that is used to create its relative distinguished name (RDN). The naming attribute for new objects of the *organizationalUnit* class is the *ou* (*Organizational-Unit-Name*) attribute instead of the often-used *cn* attribute. Also, since any object can potentially be a container, you might expect the container to specify which classes of objects it can contain, but actually, the object class specifies what containers it's allowed to exist in. For example, *contact* class objects can exist only in *domainDNS* and *organizationalUnit* containers.

A class also sets the default security for new objects of the class. A default security descriptor is contained in the class and is copied to each object based on that class. I'll discuss security in more detail later in the chapter in the section "Security."

> **Note**   The terms *class* and *object* are overused in computer programming, so to make clear their usage in the context of Active Directory, remember that a *class* in Active Directory, sometimes called an *object class*, is a template that defines the type of object and what information is contained within it. An *object* is an instance of a class.

Object Attributes

The Active Directory schema also contains objects that define each attribute that can be stored within the directory. The definition of an attribute includes specifications for the name of the attribute, the type of data stored, and the range of values it can have. The definition also indicates whether attributes are mandatory or optional for a given object class. In Active Directory, attributes are defined only once and are available globally. This is different from COM objects, for which attributes (called *properties* in COM) are defined as part of the object.

An attribute can be defined and stored in the schema and used with one, many, or no classes. The class definition determines whether a particular attribute is available to objects of that class. Of course, you cannot create an instance of an attribute. It can exist only as part of its corresponding object.

Syntaxes

The type of value that an attribute can contain is defined by a *syntax*. Active Directory defines 26 syntaxes (although fewer are actually available). Examples of syntaxes are *Integer* for storing whole number values, and *Unicode String* for storing Unicode strings. A syntax serves two functions within Active Directory. First, it provides for validation to ensure data written to an attribute is the correct type, and second, a syntax provides *matching rules* that define how Active Directory compares values when searching. For example, the *CaseIgnoreString* syntax can be matched to a string containing uppercase and lowercase characters; however, the *CaseExactString* syntax requires that comparisons take the case of the characters into account.

Although syntaxes are part of the Active Directory schema, unlike classes and attributes, you cannot create new syntaxes or modify existing ones. Later in the chapter, I'll show how to use the *IADsSyntax* interface to discover information about a syntax and describe syntaxes in more detail.

> **Note**   While Active Directory supports many syntaxes, internally it ignores some of them. One such example is the *PrintableString* syntax, which should only contain printable characters and not include control code characters such as Tab (0x09). Care should be taken to design applications to set the desired syntax and validate the correctness of the data.

Object Identifiers

Each class, attribute, and syntax defined by Active Directory contains a unique number that is used to identify it and prevent naming conflicts. These unique numbers are known as *object identifiers* (OIDs). Their purpose is similar to globally unique identifiers (GUIDs), but whereas GUIDs are mathematically generated, the International Telecommunications Union (ITU) manages OIDs. Some examples of OIDs found in Active Directory are listed in Table 9-1.

OID	Defined For
1.2.840.113556.1.2.256	*streetAddress* attribute
1.2.840.113556.1.5.9	*user* class
2.5.5.9	*Integer* syntax

Table 9-1 Example object identifiers.

OIDs are segmented using branches, with each period separating a branch. In the preceding table, notice how both the *streetAddress* attribute and *user* class have 1.2.840.113556.1 in common. This is the Active Directory branch of the Microsoft tree. Table 9-2 shows what the numbers signify for the *user* class.

OID Branch	Branch Description
1	International Standards Organization (ISO)
2	ISO members
840	American National Standards Institute (ANSI) branch for organizations in the United States
113556	Microsoft
1	Active Directory
5	Classes
9	*user* class

Table 9-2 OID branches for the *user* class.

So why is the *Integer* syntax OID (2.5.5.9) so different? Because it's part of the X.500 standards published by the ITU and maintained by the ISO. The top-level branch, *2*, is maintained jointly by the ITU and ISO; the first *5* is the branch reserved for X.500 directory services, and the second *5* is for X.500 syntaxes. The *9* is reserved for the *Integer* syntax.

Unless you are extending the schema, you generally don't have to deal with OIDs. If you're curious, you can find more information in the LDAP RFCs; see Chapter 3 for a list.

Microsoft makes available a branch of OIDs for extensions. I'll describe these and other details about OIDs in the section "Obtaining an Object Identifier" later in the chapter.

Schema Structure

The schema itself is located within Active Directory in a container, known as the *Schema* container, that stores objects that define classes and attributes. Since the data definitions are contained within the directory, you can use the same methods to manipulate and extend the schema as you would with any other part of the directory.

The *Schema* container stores instances of the *classSchema* and *attribute-Schema* classes. Instances of the *classSchema* class exist for each class supported by Active Directory. Similarly, instances of the *attributeSchema* class exist for each supported attribute. This can be confusing from a terminology standpoint. An *attribute object* is an object in the *Schema* container that defines a particular attribute. In addition to the *attributeSchema* and *classSchema* objects, the *Schema* container also contains a single instance of a *subSchema* object that I'll discuss later in this chapter in the section "Abstract Schema."

Recall from the overview of Active Directory architecture in Chapter 2 that Active Directory is partitioned to reduce replication issues. These partitions consist of the domain partition, configuration partition, and schema partition. Each domain has a domain partition, but all the domains in an enterprise forest share a common configuration and schema partition. Each domain controller in the forest has a replica of the configuration and schema partitions. The schema has its own partition so that it can be referenced and replicated on a different schedule than the configuration partition.

Schema objects are stored in the *Schema* container. Its distinguished name (DN) has the following form:

CN=Schema,CN=Configuration,DC=*forest name*,DC=*forest root*

The values for *forest name* and *forest root* are the domain components for the enterprise Active Directory forest. For example, in the Copper Software business empire, the distinguished name of the *Schema* container would be:

CN=Schema,CN=Configuration,DC=coppersoftware,DC=com

Looking at the distinguished name for the *Schema* container, you can see that the *Schema* container is within the *Configuration* container. However, if you enumerate the configuration partition, you will not find a *Schema* container because the *Schema* container is a part of the schema partition.

Figure 9-1 shows the relationship between the *Configuration* and *Schema* containers and the configuration and schema partitions.

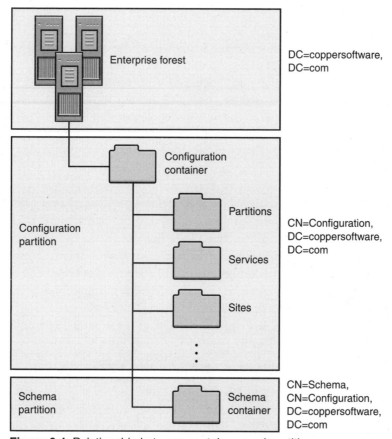

Enterprise forest — DC=coppersoftware, DC=com

Configuration container

Configuration partition

Partitions

Services — CN=Configuration, DC=coppersoftware, DC=com

Sites

Schema partition

Schema container — CN=Schema, CN=Configuration, DC=coppersoftware, DC=com

Figure 9-1 Relationship between containers and partitions.

The exact location of the *Schema* container can be obtained by looking at the *schemaNamingContext* property of the *RootDSE* object. The *schemaNamingContext* property contains the distinguished name for the *Schema* container. Listing 9-1, from the SchemaBrowser sample on the companion CD, shows how to obtain the location of the *Schema* container:

```
Public Function BindToSchemaPartition() As IADs

    ' Retrieve the RootDSE object from the nearest server
    Dim adsRootDSE As IADs
    Set adsRootDSE = GetObject("LDAP://RootDSE")

    ' Form an ADsPath string to the schema container
    Dim strSchemaADsPath As String
    strSchemaADsPath = _
        "LDAP://" & adsRootDSE.Get("schemaNamingContext")

    ' Get the root domain object
    Set BindToSchemaPartition = GetObject(strSchemaADsPath)

End Function
```

Listing 9-1 A function from the SchemaBrowser sample showing how to obtain the location of the *Schema* container.

Listing 9-2, from the ExtendSchema sample on the companion CD, shows the C++ version of obtaining the *Schema* container location.

```
//------------------------------------------------------------
// Function:      RetrieveSchemaPartition
// Description:   Retrieve the schema partition on any DC
//
// In:            IADs**    Empty IADs interface pointer
// Out:           IADs**    Bound to schema partition
// Returns:       HRESULT   COM/ADSI Error code
//
// Notes:         Caller must Release() interface when finished
//------------------------------------------------------------
HRESULT RetrieveSchemaPartition( IADs **padsSchema )
{
    HRESULT hResult;

    // Bind to the RootDSE
    IADs *padsRootDSE = NULL;
    hResult = ADsGetObject( L"LDAP://rootDSE",
                            IID_IADs,
                            (void**) &padsRootDSE );
```

Listing 9-2 A function from the ExtendSchema sample showing how to obtain the location of the *Schema* container.   *(continued)*

273

Listing 9-2 *continued*

```
    if( SUCCEEDED( hResult ) )
    {
    // Get the schema partition DN (AKA naming context)
    _variant_t varSchemaNC;
    hResult = padsRootDSE->Get( L"schemaNamingContext",
        &varSchemaNC );

    if( SUCCEEDED( hResult ) )
    {
        // Create ADsPath to the schema partition
        _bstr_t strSchemaPath = _bstr_t( "LDAP://" ) +
            _bstr_t(varSchemaNC);

        // Bind to the schema container, return IADs interface
        hResult = ADsGetObject( strSchemaPath,
                                IID_IADs,
                                (void**) padsSchema );
    }
    }
    // Free the RootDSE object
    if ( padsRootDSE )
        padsRootDSE->Release ();

    // Return the result code
    return hResult;
}
```

Abstract Schema

The LDAP recommendations do not specify exactly how a directory must implement its schema; they require only that information about the schema be available to applications in a prescribed format. Active Directory has an alternative representation of the schema in a *subSchema* object. This object is named the *Aggregate* object and is known as the *abstract schema*. The *Aggregate* object is contained in the *Schema* container, and in this single object, all the classes and attributes are made available. The reason for this alternative representation is to allow any client application to discover schema information independently of the implementation details. A client application uses the *subSchemaSubEntry* attribute of the *RootDSE* object to discover the distinguished name of the *subSchema* object.

The attributes of the *subSchema* class are listed in Table 9-3. Note that each and every class and attribute defined in the schema is contained in two multivalued attributes of the *Aggregate* object. Storing nearly 900 attribute values in a single attribute is remarkable.

subSchema Attribute	Description
attributeTypes	Each value contains information about an attribute defined in the schema, including the OID, name, and syntax of the attribute.
objectClasses	Each value contains information about a class defined in the schema, including the OID, name, and mandatory and optional attributes of the class.
extendedAttributeInfo	Each value contains extended information about an attribute defined in the schema, including the OID, name, GUID, and security information.
extendedClassInfo	Each value contains extended information about a class defined in the schema, including the OID, name, and GUID.
dITContentRules	This attribute is not required by RFC 2252, and its implementation by Active Directory is incomplete and undocumented.
modifyTimeStamp	A single-valued attribute that indicates the last time the schema was modified.

Table 9-3 Attributes of the *subSchema* class.

There is no need to work directly with the *Aggregate* object because ADSI exposes it as the abstract schema container. This special container is how ADSI allows easy access to the *subSchema* information. You can bind to the abstract schema using the following special ADsPath:

```
LDAP://schema
```

ADSI returns an *IADsContainer* interface. Each item in the virtual schema container is an attribute, class, or syntax defined by the schema. Accordingly, ADSI provides the *IADsProperty*, *IADsClass*, and *IADsSyntax* interfaces to allow access to the information provided.

Listing 9-3, from the SchemaBrowser sample on the companion CD, shows how to enumerate the objects of the abstract schema. For brevity, functions such as event handling that are unrelated to the schema have been omitted. See the sample on the companion CD for a complete listing.

```vb
' ADsClassList.frm - Main form for Schema Browser
' Shows binding to abstract schema
'
Option Explicit

Public Sub ListClasses(lstListBox As ListBox)
    '
    ' Enumerate all the classes in the schema container
    '
    Dim adsAbstractSchema As IADsContainer
    Set adsAbstractSchema = GetObject("LDAP://schema")

    ' Enumerate the classes of the schema
    adsAbstractSchema.Filter = Array("Class")

    Dim adsClass As IADsClass
    For Each adsClass In adsAbstractSchema

        ' Add the class name to the list box
        lstListBox.AddItem adsClass.Name

    Next adsClass

End Sub

Public Function BindToSchemaPartition() As IADs

    ' Retrieve the RootDSE object from the nearest server
    Dim adsRootDSE As IADs
    Set adsRootDSE = GetObject("LDAP://RootDSE")

    ' Form an ADsPath string to the schema container
    Dim strSchemaADsPath As String
    strSchemaADsPath = _
        "LDAP://" & adsRootDSE.Get("schemaNamingContext")
```

Listing 9-3 Code from the SchemaBrowser sample showing how to enumerate objects of the abstract schema.

```
        ' Get the root domain object
        Set BindToSchemaPartition = GetObject(strSchemaADsPath)

End Function
Private Sub Form_Load()

        ' Clear the list box and text box
        txtSchemaPath.Text = vbNull
        lstClasses.Clear

        ' Get the schema location, and display it
        Dim adsSchema As IADs
        Set adsSchema = BindToSchemaPartition()
        txtSchemaPath.Text = adsSchema.ADsPath

        ' Display each class in the list box
        Call ListClasses(lstClasses)

End Sub
```

The main window of the SchemaBrowser sample is shown in Figure 9-2. I'll expand on this sample and discuss the *IADsClass* and *IADsProperty* interfaces later in the chapter.

Figure 9-2 The main window of the SchemaBrowser sample showing the path to the *Schema* container and the classes contained within it.

Tools for Exploring the Schema

A good way to browse and learn about the schema is to use the Active Directory Schema snap-in for the Microsoft Management Console (MMC). This snap-in, introduced in Chapter 2, provides a tree-based view of the schema and allows you to view all available classes and attributes. Figure 9-3 shows an example of the Active Directory Schema snap-in.

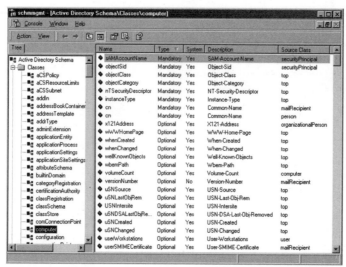

Figure 9-3 Active Directory Schema snap-in showing the attributes available in the *computer* class.

Since the schema is a technical and sensitive portion of Active Directory, the Schema snap-in is not among the list of Administrative Tools displayed in Control Panel. To start the Active Directory Schema snap-in, type *schmmgmt.msc* in the Run dialog box.

Although the actual schema is a single container, the Active Directory Schema snap-in displays two folders, one for classes and another for attributes. When a class is selected, the right pane displays a list of attributes available for that class. Double-click or press ALT+Enter to access the Properties dialog box for a selected class in the Classes folder or a selected attribute in the Attributes folder. Figure 9-4 shows the Properties dialog box for the *computer* class.

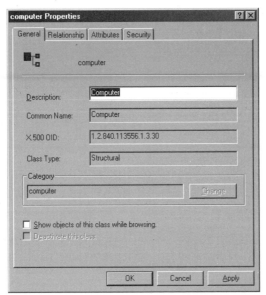

Figure 9-4 The Properties dialog box in the Active Directory Schema snap-in for the *computer* class.

The Base Directory Information Tree

The actual database that holds directory data is known as the *directory information tree* (DIT). The definition for the default entries that ship with Active Directory is sometimes referred to as the *base DIT*. The base DIT is an empty directory that contains only the schema objects and other entries, such as the default containers and display specifiers.

This initial content of Active Directory is specified in text form in the file %SystemRoot%\system32\schema.ini. This file is processed by Microsoft Windows 2000 when a server is promoted to a domain controller and a new directory is created. The entries in the Schema.ini file become the base DIT for the new Active Directory. Interestingly enough, the schema objects are not part of this file, but all other default entries in a new Active Directory are. A portion of the Schema.ini file is shown here.

```
;!--------------------------------------
;! The tree under the root of the domain.
;!--------------------------------------
[DEFAULTROOTDOMAIN]
objectClass = DomainDNS
objectCategory = Domain-DNS
```

(continued)

The Base Directory Information Tree *continued*

```
NTSecurityDescriptor=O:DAG:DAD:(A;;RP;;;WD)
(OA;;CR;1131f6aa-9c07-11d1-f79f-00c04fc2dcd2;;ED)
(OA;;CR;1131f6ab-9c07-11d1-f79f-00c04fc2dcd2;;ED)
(OA;;CR;1131f6ac-9c07-11d1-f79f-00c04fc2dcd2;;ED)
(OA;;CR;1131f6aa-9c07-11d1-f79f-00c04fc2dcd2;;BA)
(OA;;CR;1131f6ab-9c07-11d1-f79f-00c04fc2dcd2;;BA)
(OA;;CR;1131f6ac-9c07-11d1-f79f-00c04fc2dcd2;;BA)
(A;;RPLCLORC;;;AU)(A;;RPWPCRLCLOCCRCWDWOSW;;;DA)
(A;CI;RPWPCRLCLOCCRCWDWOSDSW;;;BA)(A;;RPWPCRLCLOCCDCRCWDWOSDDTSW;;;SY)
(A;CI;RPWPCRLCLOCCDCRCWDWOSDDTSW;;;EA)(A;CI;LC;;;RU)
(OA;CIIO;RP;037088f8-0ae1-11d2-b422-00a0c968f939;bf967aba-0de6-11d0-
a285-00aa003049e2;RU)
(OA;CIIO;RP;59ba2f42-79a2-11d0-9020-00c04fc2d3cf;bf967aba-0de6-11d0-
a285-00aa003049e2;RU)
(OA;CIIO;RP;bc0ac240-79a9-11d0-9020-00c04fc2d4cf;bf967aba-0de6-11d0-
a285-00aa003049e2;RU)
(OA;CIIO;RP;4c164200-20c0-11d0-a768-00aa006e0529;bf967aba-0de6-11d0-
a285-00aa003049e2;RU)
(OA;CIIO;RP;5f202010-79a5-11d0-9020-00c04fc2d4cf;bf967aba-0de6-11d0-
a285-00aa003049e2;RU)
(OA;CIIO;RPLCLORC;;bf967a9c-0de6-11d0-a285-00aa003049e2;RU)
(A;;RC;;;RU)
(OA;CIIO;RPLCLORC;;bf967aba-0de6-11d0-a285-00aa003049e2;RU)S:
(AU;CISAFA;WDWOSDDTWPCRCCDCSW;;;WD)
auditingPolicy=\x0001
nTMixedDomain=1
;Its a NC ROOT
instanceType=5
;Its the PDC, set FSMO role owner
fSMORoleOwner=$REGISTRY=Machine DN Name
wellKnownObjects=$EMBEDDED:32:a9d1ca15768811d1aded00c04fd8d5cd:
cn=Users,<Root Domain
wellKnownObjects=$EMBEDDED:32:aa312825768811d1aded00c04fd8d5cd:
cn=Computers,<Root Domain
wellKnownObjects=$EMBEDDED:32:a361b2ffffd211d1aa4b00c04fd7d83a:
ou=Domain Controllers,<Root Domain
wellKnownObjects=$EMBEDDED:32:ab1d30f3768811d1aded00c04fd8d5cd:
cn=System,<Root Domain
wellKnownObjects=$EMBEDDED:32:ab8153b7768811d1aded00c04fd8d5cd:
cn=LostAndFound,<Root Domain
wellKnownObjects=$EMBEDDED:32:2fbac1870ade11d297c400c04fd8d5cd:
cn=Infrastructure,<Root Domain
wellKnownObjects=$EMBEDDED:32:18e2ea80684f11d2b9aa00c04f79f805:
cn=Deleted Objects,<Root Domain
gPLink=$REGISTRY=GPODomainLink
mS-DS-MachineAccountQuota=10
isCriticalSystemObject=True
```

```
;systemFlags=FLAG_CONFIG_DISALLOW_RENAME            |
;                FLAG_CONFIG_DISALLOW_MOVE           |
;                FLAG_DISALLOW_DELETE
systemFlags=0x8C000000


;        every domain needs these in the root
CHILD= LostAndFound
CHILD= Deleted Objects
CHILD= Users
CHILD= Computers
CHILD= System
CHILD= Domain Controllers
CHILD= Infrastructure
CHILD= ForeignSecurityPrincipals
...
[Users]
nTSecurityDescriptor=O:DAG:DAD:(A;;RPWPCRCCDCLCLORCWOWDSDDTSW;;;SY)
(A;;RPWPCRCCDCLCLORCWOWDSW;;;DA)
(OA;;CCDC;bf967aba-0de6-11d0-a285-00aa003049e2;;AO)
(OA;;CCDC;bf967a9c-0de6-11d0-a285-00aa003049e2;;AO)
(OA;;CCDC;bf967aa8-0de6-11d0-a285-00aa003049e2;;PO)(A;;RPLCLORC;;;AU)
objectClass =Container
ObjectCategory =Container
description=Default container for upgraded user accounts
ShowInAdvancedViewOnly=False
isCriticalSystemObject=True
;systemFlags=FLAG_CONFIG_DISALLOW_RENAME            |
;                FLAG_CONFIG_DISALLOW_MOVE           |
;                FLAG_DISALLOW_DELETE
systemFlags=0x8C000000


[Computers]
nTSecurityDescriptor=O:DAG:DAD:(A;;RPWPCRCCDCLCLORCWOWDSDDTSW;;;SY)
(A;;RPWPCRCCDCLCLORCWOWDSW;;;DA)
(OA;;CCDC;bf967a86-0de6-11d0-a285-00aa003049e2;;AO)
(OA;;CCDC;bf967aba-0de6-11d0-a285-00aa003049e2;;AO)
(OA;;CCDC;bf967a9c-0de6-11d0-a285-00aa003049e2;;AO)
(OA;;CCDC;bf967aa8-0de6-11d0-a285-00aa003049e2;;PO)(A;;RPLCLORC;;;AU)
objectClass =Container
ObjectCategory =Container
description=Default container for upgraded computer accounts
ShowInAdvancedViewOnly=False
isCriticalSystemObject=True
;systemFlags=FLAG_CONFIG_DISALLOW_RENAME            |
;                FLAG_CONFIG_DISALLOW_MOVE           |
;                FLAG_DISALLOW_DELETE
systemFlags=0x8C000000
```

Working with Classes

Now that you have a basic understanding of the schema, let's look at classes in Active Directory in more detail. As mentioned, the *classSchema* class is a template for creating objects in Active Directory. Instances of the *classSchema* class exist for each class. Table 9-4 lists the attributes of the *classSchema* class.

classSchema Attribute	Mandatory or Optional	Syntax	Description
auxiliaryClass	Optional	*OID* Multivalued	List of auxiliary classes to be included with this class.
classDisplayName	Optional	*DirectoryString* Multivalued	Not used. It appears that this attribute is erroneously included in the *classSchema* class. This attribute is intended for the *displaySpecifier* class.
cn	Mandatory	*DirectoryString*	The common name for this class.
defaultHidingValue	Optional	*Boolean*	If True, new objects of this class will be hidden from view using the *showInAdvanced-ViewOnly* attribute.
defaultObjectCategory	Mandatory	*DN*	The DN of the most appropriate superclasses of this class.
defaultSecurityDescriptor	Optional	*DirectoryString*	The default security descriptor for objects of this class.
governsID	Mandatory	*OID*	The OID for this class. Must be unique in the schema.
isDefunct	Optional	Boolean	If True, the class has been disabled.
lDAPDisplayName	Optional	*DirectoryString*	The LDAP display name for this class.
mayContain	Optional	*OID* Multivalued	List of attribute names that can be contained within this class.
mustContain	Optional	*OID* Multivalued	List of attribute names that must be contained within this class.
objectClassCategory	Mandatory	*Enumeration*	Either 1, 2, or 3, for structural, abstract, or auxiliary class type.

Table 9-4 Attributes of the *classSchema* class.

classSchema Attribute	Mandatory or Optional	Syntax	Description
possSuperiors	Optional	OID Multivalued	List of classes that can contain this class.
rDNAttID	Optional	OID	The attribute is used to name objects of this class.
schemaFlagsEx	Optional	Integer	Internal use.
schemaIDGUID	Mandatory	OctetString	The GUID assigned by Active Directory to this class.
subClassOf	Mandatory	OID	The class name of the immediate superclass from which this class derives.
systemAuxiliaryClass	Optional	OID Multivalued	List of auxiliary classes that this class includes. Cannot be modified.
systemMayContain	Optional	OID Multivalued	List of attributes this class can contain. Cannot be modified.
systemMustContain	Optional	OID Multivalued	List of attributes this class must contain. Cannot be modified.
systemOnly	Optional	Boolean	If True, objects of this class cannot be modified.
systemPossSuperiors	Optional	OID Multivalued	List of classes that can contain this class. Cannot be modified.

Class Inheritance

Active Directory is designed to represent network resources and data for a company or an organization, and the resources or data often share common attributes. Instead of defining the same attributes in each class for a particular type, Active Directory allows one class to define the common characteristics and other classes to inherit those characteristics. By using inheritance, developers can make classes very specific and avoid redundant definitions.

When a new class is defined in the schema, a parent class must be specified. The parent class is also known as a *superclass,* and the inheriting, or child, class is known as the *subclass.* Through this inheritance model, attributes specified in the parent class are available to instances of the child class.

A common example of inheritance is the *user* class. In Active Directory, objects created from the *user* class represent a network account. The *user* class contains attributes such as the password, home directory location, and other pieces of information useful to operating on an Active Directory–enabled network. What's notable about the *user* class is that it does not include attributes for the user's name, e-mail address, and other personal information. However, the *organizationalPerson* class defines this information and includes many other attributes related to a person within a company or organization. Since the *user* class inherits from the *organizationalPerson* class, the *organizationalPerson* attributes are available to the *user* class. Figure 9-5 shows this inheritance.

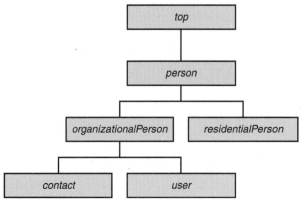

Figure 9-5 Class inheritance in Active Directory.

The inheritance model shown in this example is known as *single inheritance*. While the *user* class contains attributes defined in several classes, it inherits only from its immediate parent, *organizationalPerson*. Single inheritance contrasts with *multiple inheritance* (a feature available in the C++ language but not supported in Active Directory), in which a new class inherits directly from more than one parent class to form a sort of concatenated class. Personally, I believe that multiple inheritance in C++ is pure evil and should be avoided because it can exponentially increase the complexity of your program. However, multiple inheritance has some benefits, and Active Directory provides similar functionally using auxiliary classes, which I'll discuss later in this chapter in the section "Class Categories."

Which class a new class inherits from is set by using the *subClassOf* attribute of the *classSchema* object that represents the new class. The *subClassOf* attribute is a single-valued attribute, and only the immediate parent class is specified.

What attributes does a child class inherit from its parent class? The child class inherits all the possible attributes of the parent class, both optional and mandatory. When the same attribute is specified in both the child class and one of the parent classes, only one instance exists in objects of the child class, although the Active Directory Schema snap-in will list each parent class that includes it. A slight wrinkle to this rule is when the child class specifies that a particular attribute is optional but one of the parent classes specifies that the same attribute is required. Since at least one of the parent classes require the attribute, it is a required attribute in all child classes. For example, the *top* class specifies the *cn* attribute as optional because not all objects that inherit from *top* need that attribute. However, the *person* class specifies that *cn* is required because it is used as the naming attribute (*rDNAttID*) for the *person* class. All child classes that inherit from the *person* class will be required to contain the *cn* attribute.

Additionally, the child class inherits the list of possible superior classes from the parent class. A possible superior class is the class of object that is allowed to contain instances of the child class. This list is stored in the *possSuperiors* and *systemPossSuperiors* attributes of the *classSchema* object. For example, *contact* objects are allowed to be created only within a container of the *organizationalUnit* or *domainDNS* classes.

Security

Active Directory supports the robust Windows 2000 security subsystem. Each object class can define a default *security descriptor* (SD) that is applied to each new instance of that class. A security descriptor is a structure containing a security identifier (SID) for the owner of the object and one or more access control lists (ACL) to specify which users or groups are allowed (or denied) access to the object.

> **Note**   When an object is created in the directory, it inherits the security descriptor of its parent container in addition to having the default security descriptor of the object's class applied. This allows Active Directory to delegate or restrict permissions on a container-by-container basis.

Active Directory and ADSI help developers work with security descriptors by providing the *SecurityDescriptor* object and the associated *IADsSecurityDescriptor* interface. However, when specifying the default security descriptor for an object class, the *IADsSecurityDescriptor* interface is of no use because the attribute that stores the default security descriptor, *defaultSecurityDescriptor*, expects a Unicode string formatted in the Security Descriptor Definition Language (SDDL). An example SDDL is shown here:

```
O:AOG:DAD:(A;;RPWPCCDCLCSWRCWDWOGA;;;S-1-0-0)
```

This string contains a lot of information. Table 9-5 describes its components.

SDDL Component	Description
O:AO	The owner of the object is Account Operators group.
G:DA	The primary group for this object is the Domain Administrators group.
D:(...)	The discretionary access control list (DACL) with one access control entry (ACE).
A;;	Begins the list of rights that are allowed in this ACE.
RP	Read properties of the object.
WP	Write properties of the object.
CC	Create children of this object.
DC	Delete children of this object.
LC	List children of this object.
SW	Modify the group membership of a group object.
RC	Read Control.
WD	Modify DACL.
WO	Modify owner and assume ownership of the object.
GA	Generic all access rights.
;;;	This SD does not contain specific object GUIDs.
S-1-0-0	The SID string of the account for this DACL, in this case "Nobody".

Table 9-5 SDDL components of example string.

A security descriptor can be quite long as well, containing multiple access control entries and access control lists for auditing purposes. For example, the *defaultSecurityDescriptor* for the *user* class is shown below. I leave it as an exercise to the reader to figure out the permissions granted and denied.

```
D:(A;;RPWPCRCCDCLCLORCWOWDSDDTSW;;;DA)
(A;;RPWPCRCCDCLCLORCWOWDSDDTSW;;;SY)
(A;;RPWPCRCCDCLCLORCWOWDSDDTSW;;;AO)
(A;;RPLCLORC;;;PS)
(OA;;CR;ab721a53-1e2f-11d0-9819-00aa0040529b;;PS)
(OA;;CR;ab721a54-1e2f-11d0-9819-00aa0040529b;;PS)
(OA;;CR;ab721a56-1e2f-11d0-9819-00aa0040529b;;PS)
(OA;;RPWP;77B5B886-944A-11d1-AEBD-0000F80367C1;;PS)
(OA;;RPWP;E45795B2-9455-11d1-AEBD-0000F80367C1;;PS)
(OA;;RPWP;E45795B3-9455-11d1-AEBD-0000F80367C1;;PS)
(OA;;RP;037088f8-0ae1-11d2-b422-00a0c968f939;;RS)
(OA;;RP;4c164200-20c0-11d0-a768-00aa006e0529;;RS)
(OA;;RP;bc0ac240-79a9-11d0-9020-00c04fc2d4cf;;RS)
```

```
(A;;RC;;;AU)
(OA;;RP;59ba2f42-79a2-11d0-9020-00c04fc2d3cf;;AU)
(OA;;RP;77B5B886-944A-11d1-AEBD-0000F80367C1;;AU)
(OA;;RP;E45795B3-9455-11d1-AEBD-0000F80367C1;;AU)
(OA;;RP;e48d0154-bcf8-11d1-8702-00c04fb96050;;AU)
(OA;;CR;ab721a53-1e2f-11d0-9819-00aa0040529b;;WD)
(OA;;RP;5f202010-79a5-11d0-9020-00c04fc2d4cf;;RS)
(OA;;RPWP;bf967a7f-0de6-11d0-a285-00aa003049e2;;CA)
```

> **Note** The Windows security system is a complex and often confusing subject. I've found *Microsoft Windows 2000 Security Technical Reference* (Microsoft Press, 2000) invaluable for solving security-related issues. Chapter 7, "Access Control Model," provides excellent coverage of SIDs, ACEs, and ACLs. Additional information about security descriptors, SDDL, ACLs, and ACEs is available in the "Security" topic of the Microsoft Platform SDK.

Class Categories

Active Directory has three distinct categories of classes: *structural*, *abstract*, and *auxiliary*. I'll describe the use of each of these categories in the following sections.

The category for a class is specified in the *objectClassCategory* attribute of the *classSchema* object. This attribute is an integer that has one of four possible values. These are listed in Table 9-6.

Value	Description
0	88 Class
1	Structural
2	Abstract
3	Auxiliary

Table 9-6 Values for the *objectClassCategory* attribute.

I won't describe the 88 class, or type 88 class, category, as it is reserved for legacy classes that were defined before the 1993 X.500 recommendation. The name comes from the 1988 X.500 recommendation. (Reminds me of the time when languages were known by the year of their specification. COBOL 77 anyone?) Active Directory does not have any default classes that are part of the

88 class category. A class with an *objectClassCategory* of 0 does not receive as much consistency checking as do classes of other categories. As such, you should not create new schema objects within this category. It exists solely for potential backward compatibility.

Structural Classes

The structural class category is the most common. Structural classes define the objects that can actually be created within Active Directory. Structural classes must inherit from either another structural class or from an abstract class.

Abstract Classes

The abstract class category is used for high-level, generic definitions. An instance of an abstract class cannot be created within the directory itself. The purpose of an abstract class is to define a broad set of attributes that are then inherited by other classes that derive from it.

For example, the *top* class is at the top of the Active Directory class hierarchy. All other classes in the schema must derive from it. The *top* class is an abstract class that defines the common attributes that all classes within Active Directory must or may contain. The *top* class specifies that all child classes must contain the *instanceType*, *nTSecurityDescriptor*, *objectCategory*, and *objectClass* attributes. The set of optional attributes includes *cn*, *description*, and *createTimeStamp*.

Because the *top* class is an abstract class, you cannot create an instance of it in Active Directory. If you think about it, you would not need to because the *top* class, like all abstract classes, is too general in nature.

Abstract classes can inherit only from other abstract classes, with the exception of the special *top* class. The following is a list of abstract classes available in Active Directory:

- *applicationSettings*
- *applicationSiteSettings*
- *connectionPoint*
- *country*
- *device*
- *domain*
- *groupOfNames*
- *ipsecBase*
- *leaf*
- *organizationalPerson*

- *person*

- *rpcEntry*

- *securityObject*

- *top*

Auxiliary Classes

I mentioned earlier that Active Directory does not support C++ style multiple inheritance. However, the auxiliary class category provides a similar capability. Auxiliary classes are like abstract classes in that they define a set of attributes that become part of a child class. However, the attributes from auxiliary classes are included in the definition of a child class, whereas attributes from abstract classes are inherited.

This makes sense when two very different types of objects require a similar set of attributes. For example, the *group* and *user* classes. When used with Microsoft Exchange 2000 Server, *group* objects can be e-mail enabled and act as distribution lists. That means both *users* and *groups* require a common set of attributes related to e-mail, although that is about all they have in common. To provide a set of common attributes, Active Directory uses the *mailRecipient* auxiliary class, which is included in both the *user* and *group* objects.

An auxiliary class can inherit from another auxiliary class or an abstract class. The definition of an auxiliary class can also specify other auxiliary classes to be included.

The following is a list of auxiliary classes included with Active Directory. Note that server applications such as Exchange 2000 Server extend existing and add new auxiliary classes.

- *mailRecipient*

- *samDomain*

- *samDomainBase*

- *securityPrincipal*

Object Classes and Object Categories

Now that you know about inheritance and class categories, let's see how these pieces fit together to produce an instance of a class in the directory. Figure 9-6 shows an inheritance map for an instance of the *user* class. The *user* object represents a new user named John Doe. Note that not all the possible attributes (mandatory or optional) are shown, just a representative portion.

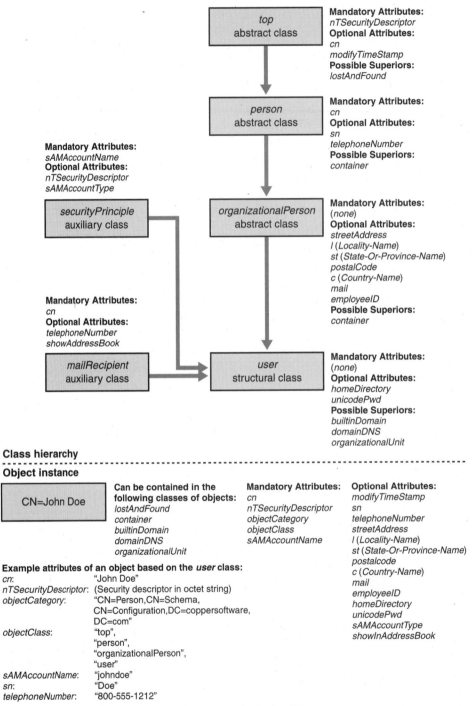

Mandatory Attributes:
nTSecurityDescriptor
Optional Attributes:
cn
modifyTimeStamp
Possible Superiors:
lostAndFound

top
abstract class

Mandatory Attributes:
cn
Optional Attributes:
sn
telephoneNumber
Possible Superiors:
container

person
abstract class

Mandatory Attributes:
sAMAccountName
Optional Attributes:
nTSecurityDescriptor
sAMAccountType

securityPrinciple
auxiliary class

organizationalPerson
abstract class

Mandatory Attributes:
(none)
Optional Attributes:
streetAddress
l (Locality-Name)
st (State-Or-Province-Name)
postalCode
c (Country-Name)
mail
employeeID
Possible Superiors:
container

Mandatory Attributes:
cn
Optional Attributes:
telephoneNumber
showAddressBook

mailRecipient
auxiliary class

user
structural class

Mandatory Attributes:
(none)
Optional Attributes:
homeDirectory
unicodePwd
Possible Superiors:
builtinDomain
domainDNS
organizationalUnit

Class hierarchy

- -

Object instance

CN=John Doe

Can be contained in the following classes of objects:
lostAndFound
container
builtinDomain
domainDNS
organizationalUnit

Mandatory Attributes:
cn
nTSecurityDescriptor
objectCategory
objectClass
sAMAccountName

Optional Attributes:
modifyTimeStamp
sn
telephoneNumber
streetAddress
l (Locality-Name)
st (State-Or-Province-Name)
postalcode
c (Country-Name)
mail
employeeID
homeDirectory
unicodePwd
sAMAccountType
showInAddressBook

Example attributes of an object based on the *user* class:

cn:	"John Doe"
nTSecurityDescriptor:	(Security descriptor in octet string)
objectCategory:	"CN=Person,CN=Schema, CN=Configuration,DC=coppersoftware, DC=com"
objectClass:	"top", "person", "organizationalPerson", "user"
sAMAccountName:	"johndoe"
sn:	"Doe"
telephoneNumber:	"800-555-1212"

Figure 9-6 Inheritance map of the *user* class in Active Directory.

In Figure 9-6, you'll notice that the *user* object inherits a mandatory attribute named *objectClass* from the *top* class. The *objectClass* attribute is a read-only, multivalued attribute that contains a value for each class that the object inherits from. For example, the *objectClass* for the *user* object is: *top*, *person*, *organizationalPerson*, and *user*. By examining the *objectClass* attribute of any object, you can readily tell which classes the object inherited from to form the object. Note, however, that the values in the *objectClass* attribute reflect only inherited classes, not included auxiliary classes.

Note   Since *objectClass* is a mandatory attribute of the *top* class, it is a required attribute for all classes. This means every object in Active Directory has this attribute. You can use this knowledge to build an LDAP query that searches every object. Use the "any" character (*) in the search:

```
(objectClass=*)
```

This query will always return every object within the search scope.

In addition to *objectClass*, the John Doe *user* object contains another mandatory attribute, *objectCategory*. What's interesting to note about the *objectCategory* attribute is that instead of being an integer value representing the class category, it's a distinguished name string. For example:

```
CN=Person,CN=Schema,CN=Configuration,DC=coppersoftware,DC=com
```

This distinguished name is pointing to the object in the schema that defines the *person* class. Huh? Didn't I just explain how a class category is either structural, abstract, or auxiliary?

This is a case of confusing terminology. *Classes* have categories that define the type of class (structural, abstract, or auxiliary). However, *objects* also have categories that define the type of object. Active Directory uses the *objectClassCategory* attribute of the class object to know how to treat the class. The *objectCategory* attribute is available for applications to deal with related objects.

Note   It's easy to confuse the *objectCategory* attribute with the *objectClassCategory* attribute. I tend to think of the class category as the "class type," which contains a value from a limited range (1, 2, or 3). Since the *objectCategory* is a distinguished name string, the range of possibilities is wider and it's easier for me to think of it as a category.

Having an attribute for the category of an object (as opposed to its class) is beneficial for two reasons. First, it allows related objects to be grouped in searches. Imagine that you want to find all the employees in your company with the last name Smith. You could use the following search query:

```
(&(objectClass=user)(sn=Smith))
```

This query would work, but the objects returned would only be the people named Smith who are network users. What about people who are not network users but are entered in the directory as contacts? You could write the following query to accommodate that case:

```
(&(|(objectClass=user)(objectClass=contact)))(sn=Smith))
```

However, this query is inefficient and won't accommodate extensions to the schema, for example, a class like *retiredEmployee*.

What you want to do is search for all the "people" in the directory. OK, so then this should work:

```
(&(objectClass=person)(sn=Smith))
```

This does work because the *person* value appears in the *objectClass* attribute of all objects of the *user* and *contact* classes. However, using the *objectCategory* attribute is more efficient because it's a single-valued attribute, as opposed to *objectClass*, which is multivalued. Such a query reduces the workload on the server and results in quicker searches.

The second major benefit of using *objectCategory* is that it's an *indexed attribute*, meaning that Active Directory can optimize itself to quickly search for objects based on that attribute. Contrast this with the *objectClass* attribute, which is not unique: every instance includes the *top* class. Searching multivalued attributes makes for inefficient indexing.

Normally, the *objectCategory* value is the distinguished name of the class object; however, it can point to any *classSchema* object in the schema. As we saw with the *user* object, the *objectCategory* value points to the *person* abstract class. This makes the common query for all objects representing people easy, for example:

```
(&(objectCategory=person)(sn=Smith))
```

The default value for an object's category is set in the *defaultObjectCategory* attribute of the class object. Applications cannot change the *objectCategory* attribute of an object, nor can the schema be modified to reflect a new value for *defaultObjectCategory*.

Object Naming

Developers new to Active Directory often ask me about object naming. Their question goes like this: "Why does the *Name* property of an object return something like *CN=John Doe*? Why can't it just return *John Doe*?"

The answer, which might not be satisfying, returns to the roots of LDAP and X.500. There is no fixed "name" attribute for any object. The string *CN=John Doe* is actually the RDN of the object. The RDN is made up of the *naming attribute* of the object, an equal sign, and the value of the naming attribute.

Generally, the naming attribute is the *cn* (*Common-Name*) attribute. Sometimes, however, a different attribute is chosen to be the naming attribute. The object named *DC=coppersoftware* is using the *dc* (*Domain-Component*) attribute as the naming attribute. Table 9-7 lists the classes that use a naming attribute other than *cn*.

Class	Naming Attribute
organization	o Organization-Name
organizationalUnit	ou Organizational-Unit-Name
country	c Country-Name
dnsNode	dc Domain-Component
dnsZone	dc Domain-Component
domain	dc Domain-Component
domainDNS	dc Domain-Component
locality	l Locality-Name

Table 9-7 Classes that use a naming attribute other than *cn*.

The naming attribute is set by the class using the *rDNAttID* attribute of the *classSchema* object. It contains the OID of the attribute to be used for the name of the object.

Creating Objects with the Same Name

I've heard from several network administrators who think it's impossible to have two people with the same name in the same container or organizational unit. This perceived problem reflects the design of the creation wizard for the *user* class more than the overall architecture of Active Directory.

When adding a new user to Active Directory, the New User Wizard automatically creates the Full Name field from the concatenation of the first name, middle initial, and last name of the person. The wizard uses the Full Name field as the value for the *cn* attribute. This attribute is the naming attribute for most classes, including the *user* class. So, if another user with the same *cn* value already exists in the container, an error will be presented to the user, as shown here:

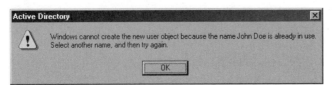

The solution is to create the user using a unique Full Name field by adding a relatively unique string. This illustration shows the name with the date appended.

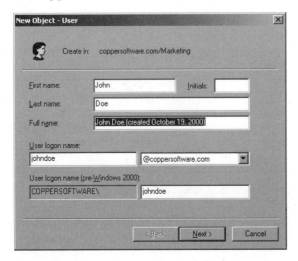

After the user is created, you can edit the *displayName* attribute to reflect the full name of the user. Modifying the *displayName* attribute will not affect the *cn* attribute, which is now unique in the container.

IADsClass

The *IADsClass* interface allows you to easily retrieve information about an object class. The interface is straightforward. Its properties are shown in Table 9-8. This ADSI interface is not specific to Active Directory, so not all its properties apply here. I've noted the relevant properties below.

IADsClass Property	Data Type	Description
Abstract	Boolean	True if the class is an abstract class.
AuxDerivedFrom	Variant array	Array of strings identifying the auxiliary classes that this class is derived from.
Auxiliary	Boolean	True if the class is an auxiliary class.
CLSID	String	The class ID GUID of the COM object that implements this class.
Container	Boolean	True if the class is a container.
Containment	Variant array	Array of strings identifying the classes this class can contain.
DerivedFrom	Variant array	Array of strings identifying the classes this class derives from. Under Active Directory, only the first derived class is listed.
HelpFileContext	Long	Context ID of the help file topic where information about this class can be found.
HelpFileName	String	Name of the help file that contains information about this class.
MandatoryProperties	Variant array	Array of strings, each with the name of the attributes that are required for this class.
NamingProperties	Variant array	Array of strings with the names of attributes that are used to name objects of this class. Under Active Directory, this property contains only one attribute.
OID	String	The object identifier for this class.
OptionalProperties	Variant array	Array of strings, each with the name of the attributes that are optional for this class.
PossibleSuperiors	Variant array	Array of strings identifying the classes that can contain instances of this class.
PrimaryInterface	String	The interface ID (IID) GUID of the primary interface for this class. For example, the *user* class would have the IID of the *IADsUser* interface.

Table 9-8 Properties of the *IADsClass* interface.

The *IADsClass* interface also defines a *Qualifiers* method that is not implemented with Active Directory.

Listing 9-4, from the SchemaBrowser sample, uses the *IADsClass* properties to display a dialog box with information about a particular class.

```
' ADsClassInfo.frm - Displays class information
' Shows the IADsClass interface
'
Private Sub Form_Load()

    ' Bind to the class object in the schema
    Dim adsClass As IADsClass
    Set adsClass = GetObject("LDAP://schema/" & frmClassList.Tag)

    ' Not all classes have these properties
    On Error Resume Next

    ' Fill in text fields with information from IADsClass
    txtDisplayName.Text = adsClass.Name
    txtOID.Text = adsClass.OID
    txtCLSID.Text = adsClass.CLSID
    txtPrimaryInterface.Text = adsClass.PrimaryInterface

    ' Set the type
    If adsClass.Abstract Then
        optAbstract.Value = True
        optAbstract.Enabled = True
    ElseIf adsClass.Auxiliary Then
        optAuxiliary.Value = True
        optAuxiliary.Enabled = True
    Else
        optStructural.Value = True
        optStructural.Enabled = True
    End If

    ' List Possible Superiors
    Call ListPossibleSuperiors(adsClass, lstPossSuperiors)

    ' Is this class a container?
    If adsClass.Container Then

        ' Set the container checkbox and enable
        chkIsContainer.Value = 1
        chkIsContainer.Enabled = True
```

Listing 9-4 Code from the SchemaBrowser sample showing how to use the *IADsClass* interface to obtain information about a class.

```
            ' List the objects that can be contained
            Call ListContainment(adsClass, lstContainment)

        Else
            ' Turn off container checkbox and disable
            chkIsContainer.Value = 0
            chkIsContainer.Enabled = False

        End If

        ' List derived classes
        Call ListDerivedClasses(adsClass, lstDerivedFrom)

        ' List derived auxiliary classes
        Call ListDerivedAuxClasses(adsClass, lstAuxDerivedFrom)

        ' List the attributes for this class
        Call ListAttributes(adsClass, lstAttributes)

        ' Set the naming attribute
        ' (just one under Active Directory)
        txtNamingAttribute.Text = adsClass.NamingProperties

        ' Restore error handling
        On Error GoTo 0

End Sub

Public Sub ListAttributes(adsClass As IADsClass, _
    lstListBox As ListBox)

' List mandatory attributes
With lstListBox

    Dim varProperty As Variant
    If IsArray(adsClass.MandatoryProperties) Then
        ' Enumerate each item
        For Each varProperty In adsClass.MandatoryProperties
            ' Add to list
            .AddItem varProperty
            .Selected(.NewIndex) = True
        Next
    Else
        .AddItem adsClass.MandatoryProperties
        .Selected(.NewIndex) = True
    End If
```

(continued)

Listing 9-4 *continued*

```
        ' List optional attributes
    If IsArray(adsClass.OptionalProperties) Then
        ' Enumerate each item
        For Each varProperty In adsClass.OptionalProperties
            ' Add to list
            .AddItem varProperty
            .Selected(.NewIndex) = False
        Next
    Else
        .AddItem adsClass.OptionalProperties
        .Selected(.NewIndex) = False
    End If

    .ListIndex = 0

End With

End Sub

Public Sub ListDerivedClasses(adsClass As IADsClass, _
    lstListBox As ListBox)

    ' List each derived class
    If IsArray(adsClass.DerivedFrom) Then

        ' Enumerate each item
        Dim varDerivedClass As Variant
        For Each varDerivedClass In adsClass.DerivedFrom
            ' Add to list
            lstListBox.AddItem varDerivedClass
        Next
    Else
        lstListBox.AddItem adsClass.DerivedFrom
    End If

End Sub

Public Sub ListDerivedAuxClasses(adsClass As IADsClass, _
    lstListBox As ListBox)

    ' List derived aux classes
    If IsArray(adsClass.AuxDerivedFrom) Then

        ' Enumerate each item
        Dim varDerivedClass As Variant
        For Each varDerivedClass In adsClass.AuxDerivedFrom
```

```
                    ' Add to list
                    lstListBox.AddItem varDerivedClass
            Next
        Else
            lstListBox.AddItem adsClass.AuxDerivedFrom
        End If

End Sub

Public Sub ListContainment(adsClass As IADsClass, _
    lstListBox As ListBox)

    ' List each item that can be contained
    If IsArray(adsClass.Container) Then

        ' Enumerate each item
        Dim varContainer As Variant
        For Each varContainer In adsClass.Containment
            ' Add to list
            lstListBox.AddItem varContainer
        Next
    Else
        lstListBox.AddItem adsClass.Containment
    End If

End Sub

Public Sub ListPossibleSuperiors(adsClass As IADsClass, _
    lstListBox As ListBox)

    If IsArray(adsClass.PossibleSuperiors) Then

        ' Enumerate each item
        Dim varContainer As Variant
        For Each varContainer In adsClass.PossibleSuperiors
            ' Add to list
            lstListBox.AddItem varContainer
        Next
    Else
        lstListBox.AddItem adsClass.PossibleSuperiors
    End If

End Sub
```

When you run the SchemaBrowser sample, select a class, and click the Properties button, a dialog box similar to Figure 9-7 is displayed.

Figure 9-7 The Class Properties dialog box showing information obtained using the *IADsClass* interface.

Working with Attributes

Like class objects in the schema, attributes are defined using objects. As mentioned earlier in this chapter, an *attribute object* is the object in the *Schema* container that defines a particular attribute. An attribute object is created from the *attributeSchema* class. Each *attributeSchema* object in the *Schema* container represents a single attribute definition.

The *attributeSchema* object defines the name, object identifier, and data type for an attribute. Like *classSchema* objects, an *attributeSchema* object has the naming attributes *cn* (*Common-Name*) and *lDAPDisplayName*. When referencing an attribute programmatically, always use *lDAPDisplayName*.

In addition to specifying the syntax to use for an attribute, the *attributeSchema* object defines whether the attribute accepts multiple values and the range of each value, including a minimum and maximum. Table 9-9 lists the attributes of the *attributeSchema* class.

attributeSchema Attribute	Mandatory or Optional	Syntax	Description
attributeID	Mandatory	OID	The OID for this attribute. This value Identifier must be unique among all the attributes defined in the schema.
attributeSecurityGUID	Optional	OctetString	A GUID stored as an octet string. This is an optional GUID that identifies the attribute as a member of an *attribute grouping* (also called a *property set*). You can use this GUID in access control entries to control access to all attributes in the property set; that is, to all attributes that have the specified GUID set in their *attributeSecurityGUID* property.
attributeSyntax	Mandatory	OID	The OID of the syntax for this attribute. The combination of the *attributeSyntax* and *oMSyntax* properties determines the type of data stored by instances of the attribute (the syntax).
classDisplayName	Optional	Directory-String Multivalued	Not used. It appears that this attribute is erroneously included in the *attributeSchema* class. This attribute is intended for the *displaySpecifier* class.
cn	Mandatory	Directory-String	The name of the attribute, in LDAP form (mixed-case, first letter lowercase, no dashes).
extendedChars-Allowed	Optional	Boolean	Not used. Exists for backward compatibility with Microsoft Exchange Server. If set, this attribute indicates that extended characters are allowed in attributes with a syntax of *String* (Teletex).
isDefunct	Optional	Boolean	Set to True to disable an attribute. Prevents new instances of an attribute from being created.
isEphemeral	Optional	Boolean	True if this object cannot be replicated.
isMemberOfPartial-AttributeSet	Optional	Boolean	True if the attribute is replicated to global catalog servers.

Table 9-9 Attributes of the *attributeSchema* class.   *(continued)*

Table 9-9 *continued*

attributeSchema Attribute	Mandatory or Optional	Syntax	Description
isSingleValued	Mandatory	*Boolean*	True if the attribute accepts only one value; False if the attribute is multivalued.
lDAPDisplayName	Mandatory	*Directory-String*	Name used by LDAP clients, including ADSI, to refer to this attribute.
linkID	Optional	*Integer*	A number that indicates that the attribute is part of a linked pair. An even number indicates a forward link; an odd number indicates a backward link.
mAPIID	Optional	*Integer*	Used by Messaging API (MAPI) clients to identify this attribute.
oMObjectClass	Optional	*OctetString*	When *oMSyntax* is 127, the correct OM class must be set here.
oMSyntax	Mandatory	*Integer*	The XDS/XOM syntax for this attribute.
rangeLower	Optional	*Integer*	Specifies the lowest value for numeric attribute types or the smallest size for string attribute types.
rangeUpper	Optional	*Integer*	Specifies the highest value for numeric attribute types or the largest size for string attribute types.
schemaFlagsEx	Optional	*Integer*	Internal use only.
schemaIDGUID	Mandatory	*OctetString*	GUID for this attribute.
searchFlags	Optional	*Enumeration*	Used to control indexing and other behavior. See the next section, "Types of Attributes," for more information.
systemOnly	Optional	*Boolean*	If True, this object cannot be modified.

Types of Attributes

Active Directory defines several types of attributes. Attributes that are to be included in the global catalog have the *isMemberOfPartialAttributeSet* attribute set to True. The *searchFlags* attribute uses the least significant bit to indicate whether the attribute should be indexed, which, as I've mentioned elsewhere, helps the server search for information more quickly.

Another attribute, *systemFlags,* defines additional characteristics for the attribute. These are defined with values from the *ADS_SYSTEMFLAG_ENUM* enumeration, shown here:

```
typedef enum {
    ADS_SYSTEMFLAG_DISALLOW_DELETE            = 0x80000000,
    ADS_SYSTEMFLAG_CONFIG_ALLOW_RENAME        = 0x40000000,
    ADS_SYSTEMFLAG_CONFIG_ALLOW_MOVE          = 0x20000000,
    ADS_SYSTEMFLAG_CONFIG_ALLOW_LIMITED_MOVE  = 0x10000000,
    ADS_SYSTEMFLAG_DOMAIN_DISALLOW_RENAME     = 0x08000000,
    ADS_SYSTEMFLAG_DOMAIN_DISALLOW_MOVE       = 0x04000000,
    ADS_SYSTEMFLAG_CR_NTDS_NC                 = 0x00000001,
    ADS_SYSTEMFLAG_CR_NTDS_DOMAIN             = 0x00000002,
    ADS_SYSTEMFLAG_ATTR_NOT_REPLICATED        = 0x00000001,
    ADS_SYSTEMFLAG_ATTR_IS_CONSTRUCTED        = 0x00000004
} ADS_SYSTEMFLAG_ENUM
```

Notable among these values are *ADS_SYSTEMFLAG_ATTR_NOT_REPLICATED,* which indicates that the attribute is not replicated to other domain controllers. For example, the attributes *lastLogon* and *lastLogoff* are not replicated between domain controllers since the information is relatively dynamic and changes frequently.

The *ADS_SYSTEMFLAG_ATTR_IS_CONSTRUCTED* flag denotes a special attribute that is not stored within an object but is one that the server will "construct" the value for when requested. Constructed attributes usually have values that the server must evaluate before returning. A good example is the *distinguishedName* attribute, which contains all the relative distinguished names for an object and its containers. Instead of storing the distinguished name in each attribute, Active Directory uses an internal method to figure out the object's location in the directory and returns that value when requested. Another example is the *modifyTimeStamp* attribute.

Not listed in the *ADS_SYSTEMFLAG_ENUM* enumeration are category 1 and category 2 attributes that are defined by Active Directory. Category 1 attributes have the 0x10 bit of the *systemFlags* value set. Category 2 attributes are extensions to the schema and do not have this bit set. You can't explicitly set this category bit.

IADsProperty

The *IADsProperty* interface is used to gather information about attributes. (ADSI uses the term *properties,* although it's more accurate to say attributes in this context). Most of the important information about an attribute is accessible through the *IADsProperty* interface, with the exception of information such as the system flags that are specific to Active Directory. Table 9-10 lists the properties of the *IADsProperty* interface.

IADsProperty Property	Data Type	Description
MaxRange	Long	The maximum value for this attribute. For an attribute containing a string, this value would be the maximum number of characters allowed.
MinRange	Long	The minimum value for this attribute.
MultiValued	Boolean	Is True if attribute accepts multiple values.
OID	String	The object identifier for this attribute.
Syntax	String	The name of the syntax object in the schema that this attribute uses.

Table 9-10 Properties of the *IADsProperty* interface.

The *IADsProperty* interface also defines a *Qualifiers* method that is not implemented with Active Directory.

Listing 9-5, from the SchemaBrowser sample, uses the properties of *IADsProperty* and *IADsSyntax* (discussed later in this chapter) to display a dialog box with information about a particular attribute.

```
' ADsAttributeInfo.frm - Attribute information for schema
' Shows the IADsProperty and IADsSyntax interfaces
'
'
Option Explicit

Private Sub Form_Load()

    On Error Resume Next

    ' Get information about the attribute to show
    ' Bind to the attribute object in the schema
    Dim adsProperty As IADsProperty
    Set adsProperty = GetObject("LDAP://schema/" & frmClassInfo.Tag)

    ' Fill in text fields with information from IADsClass
    txtDisplayName.Text = adsProperty.Name
    txtOID.Text = adsProperty.OID
```

Listing 9-5 Code from the SchemaBrowser sample showing how to use the *IADsProperty* and *IADsSyntax* interfaces to obtain information about an attribute.

```
        If adsProperty.MultiValued Then
            ' Set the checkbox field
            chkMultiValued.Enabled = True
            chkMultiValued.Value = 1
        Else
            chkMultiValued.Enabled = False
            chkMultiValued.Value = 0
        End If

        ' Set the syntax info
        txtSyntax.Text = adsProperty.Syntax

        ' Get the range values
        If adsProperty.MinRange Then
            txtMinValue.Enabled = True
            txtMinValue = adsProperty.MinRange
        Else
            txtMinValue.Enabled = False
        End If

        ' Get the range values
        If adsProperty.MaxRange Then
            txtMaxValue.Enabled = True
            txtMaxValue = adsProperty.MaxRange
        Else
            txtMaxValue.Enabled = False
        End If

        ' Set the syntax name
        txtSyntax.Text = adsProperty.Syntax

        ' Use IADsSyntax to return the data type
        Dim adsSyntax As IADsSyntax
        Set adsSyntax = GetObject("LDAP://schema/" & adsProperty.Syntax)

        txtDataType.Enabled = True
        txtDataType.Text = TypeName(adsSyntax.OleAutoDataType)

        ' Restore error handling
        On Error GoTo 0

End Sub
```

In the SchemaBrowser sample, when you select an attribute in the Class Properties dialog box and click the Properties button, a dialog box similar to Figure 9-8 is displayed.

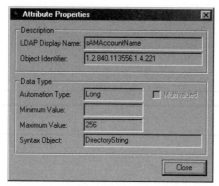

Figure 9-8 The Attribute Properties dialog box showing information obtained using the *IADsProperty* and *IADsSyntax* interfaces.

Attribute Syntaxes

As I mentioned earlier in this chapter, Active Directory uses syntaxes to validate the correct type of data being written for a particular attribute. Active Directory also uses syntaxes as a set of rules to compare attribute values. So, given a search query such as (*mail=*HOTMAIL.COM*), Active Directory will check the syntax of the *mail* attribute, which is a *DirectoryString*, and discover that it's a case-insensitive Unicode string. Therefore, an e-mail address such as chuckop@hotmail.com and ChuckOP@HoTMaiL.COM will correctly match the search query.

Several syntaxes have their roots in the X.500 specification, but some, like the *NTSecurityDescriptor* syntax are specific to Active Directory. Active Directory recognizes many of the syntaxes defined in the X.500 and LDAP specifications, but it makes no attempt to validate them. While the *PrintableString* syntax is designed to include characters of the printable character set, usually US-ASCII characters from 32 to 127, Active Directory does not enforce this syntax and will accept characters outside the 32 to 127 range. Future versions of Active Directory might enforce these syntaxes, so it's important that your application choose the correct syntax and work within the constraints defined for that syntax.

A program can enumerate the abstract schema for each syntax. Unlike classes and attributes, however, syntaxes are hard coded into Active Directory. It would be nice if there were a "syntaxSchema" object, but there isn't at the present time.

Table 9-11 lists the syntaxes that Active Directory recognizes. Each syntax is created by an *attributeSyntax* and *oMSyntax* pair. The *attributeSyntax* attribute specifies the OID for the syntax, and the *oMSyntax* attribute is an integer that supplies a more refined syntax definition. This definition is an alternative syntax description from the X/Open Object Model (XOM) and the X.400 API Association (XAPIA). Syntaxes with an *oMSyntax* value of 127 also include a value for the *oMObjectClass* attribute with an encoded object identifier. You don't have to worry about figuring out these values yourself. Just refer to Table 9-11 for the correct syntax and use the values provided. Note that the LDAP ADSI provider supports several more syntaxes than Active Directory does. Only the syntaxes recognized by Active Directory are listed.

Syntax	Identifiers and Data Types	Description
AccessPointDN	attributeSyntax: 2.5.5.14 oMSyntax: 127 oMObjectClass: 0x2B0C0287731C00853E	Used by X.400; not supported by Active Directory.
Boolean	attributeSyntax: 2.5.5.8 oMSyntax: 1 ADSTYPE: ADSTYPE_BOOLEAN VARTYPE: VT_BOOL	Boolean, either TRUE or FALSE.
CaseExactString	attributeSyntax: 2.5.5.3 oMSyntax: 27 ADSTYPE: ADSTYPE_CASE_ EXACT_STRING VARTYPE: VT_BSTR	Case-sensitive string.
CaseIgnoreString	attributeSyntax: 2.5.5.4 oMSyntax: 20 ADSTYPE: ADSTYPE_CASE_ IGNORE_STRING VARTYPE: VT_BSTR	Case-insensitive string; also known as a Teletex string.
DirectoryString	attributeSyntax: 2.5.5.12 oMSyntax: 64 ADSTYPE: ADSTYPE_CASE_ IGNORE_STRING VARTYPE: VT_BSTR	Case-insensitive Unicode string.
DN	attributeSyntax: 2.5.5.1 oMSyntax: 127 oMObjectClass: 0x2B0C0287731C00854A ADSTYPE: ADSTYPE_ DN_STRING VARTYPE: VT_BSTR	String containing a distinguished name.
DNWithBinary	attributeSyntax: 2.5.5.17 oMSyntax: 127 oMObjectClass: 0x2A864886F7140101010B ADSTYPE: ADSTYPE_DN_ WITH_BINARY VARTYPE: VT_DISPATCH to DNWithBinary object	Octet string containing binary data with a distinguished name maintained by Active Directory. Use IADsDNWithBinary to work with this syntax.

Table 9-11 Syntaxes recognized by Active Directory.

(continued)

Table 9-11 *continued*

Syntax	Identifiers and Data Types	Description
DNWithString	*attributeSyntax*: 2.5.5.14 *oMSyntax*: 127 *oMObjectClass*: 0x2A864886F7140101010C *ADSTYPE: ADSTYPE_DN_ WITH_STRING* *VARTYPE: VT_DISPATCH* to *DNWithString* object	String with a distinguished name value maintained by Active Directory. Use *IADsDNWithString* to work with this syntax.
Enumeration	*attributeSyntax*: 2.5.5.9 *oMSyntax*: 10 *ADSTYPE: ADSTYPE_INTEGER* *VARTYPE: VT_I4*	Defined by ITU, but not used in Active Directory.
GeneralizedTime	*attributeSyntax*: 2.5.5.11 *oMSyntax*: 24 *ADSTYPE: ADSTYPE_UTC_TIME* *VARTYPE: VT_DATE*	Time value in Generalized-Time format.
IA5String	*attributeSyntax*: 2.5.5.5 *oMSyntax*: 22 *ADSTYPE: ADSTYPE_ PRINTABLE_STRING* *VARTYPE: VT_BSTR*	IA5 String. The IA5 character set is defined in the T.50 specification of the ITU and is equivalent to the US-ASCII character set. Active Directory ignores this syntax.
Integer	*attributeSyntax*: 2.5.5.9 *oMSyntax*: 2 *ADSTYPE: ADSTYPE_INTEGER* *VARTYPE: VT_I4*	32-bit integer value.
INTEGER8	*attributeSyntax*: 2.5.5.16 *oMSyntax*: 65 *ADSTYPE: ADSTYPE_LARGE_ INTEGER* *VARTYPE: VT_DISPATCH* to *LargeInteger* object	64-bit integer value. Use *IADsLargeInteger* to work with this syntax.
NTSecurityDescriptor	*attributeSyntax*: 2.5.5.15 *oMSyntax*: 66 *ADSTYPE: ADSTYPE_NT_ SECURITY_DESCRIPTOR* *VARTYPE: VT_DISPATCH* to *SecurityDescriptor* object	Octet string containing a Windows NT security descriptor. Use *IADsSecurityDescriptor* to work with this syntax.
NumericString	*attributeSyntax*: 2.5.5.6 *oMSyntax*: 18 *ADSTYPE: ADSTYPE_ NUMERIC_STRING* *VARTYPE: VT_BSTR*	String containing numeric characters only. Active Directory ignores this syntax.

Syntax	Identifiers and Data Types	Description
OctetString	*attributeSyntax*: 2.5.5.10 *oMSyntax*: 4 *ADSTYPE*: *ADSTYPE_-OCTET_STRING* *VARTYPE*: *VT_UI1	VT_ARRAY*	Array of bytes for storing binary data.
OID	*attributeSyntax*: 2.5.5.2 *oMSyntax*: 6 *ADSTYPE*: *ADSTYPE_-CASE_IGNORE_STRING* *VARTYPE*: *VT_BSTR*	Object identifier string.
ORName	*attributeSyntax*: 2.5.5.7 *oMSyntax*: 127 *oMObjectClass*: 0x56060102050B1D	Used by X.400; not supported by Active Directory.
PresentationAddress	*attributeSyntax*: 2.5.5.13 *oMSyntax*: 127 *oMObjectClass*: 0x2B0C0287731C00855C *ADSTYPE*: *ADSTYPE_CASE_-IGNORE_STRING* *VARTYPE*: *VT_BSTR*	String containing an Open Systems Interconnection (OSI) presentation address (RFC 1278).
PrintableString	*attributeSyntax*: 2.5.5.5 *oMSyntax*: 19 *ADSTYPE*: *ADSTYPE_-PRINTABLE_STRING* *VARTYPE*: *VT_BSTR*	String containing printable characters.
ReplicaLink	*attributeSyntax*: 2.5.5.10 *oMSyntax*: 127 *oMObjectClass*: 0x2A864886F71401010106 *ADSTYPE*: *ADSTYPE_OCTET_STRING* *VARTYPE*: *VT_VARIANT*	Used internally by Active Directory.
Sid	*attributeSyntax*: 2.5.5.17 *oMSyntax*: 4 *ADSTYPE*: *ADSTYPE_-OCTET_STRING* *VARTYPE*: *VT_UI1	VT_ARRAY*	Octet string containing a Windows security identifier.
UTCTime	*attributeSyntax*: 2.5.5.11 *oMSyntax*: 23 *ADSTYPE*: *ADSTYPE_UTC_TIME* *VARTYPE*: *VT_DATE*	Time value in UTC-Time format.

IADsSyntax

The *IADsSyntax* interface is one of the simplest interfaces of the ADSI set. It contains just one property, *OleAutoDataType,* that returns a value representing the data type of the syntax. It's unfortunate that this interface does not return more information, such as the OID or the OM syntax number, but it's very useful for determining how ADSI will return values of a particular attribute. The value of *OleAutoDataType* is similar to the Visual Basic and VBScript *VarType* function and can be passed to the *TypeName* function to return a string with the name of the type. Table 9-12 lists the *IADsSyntax* property.

IADsSyntax Property	Data Type	Description
OleAutoDataType	Long	Returns the Automation data type. The value is defined by COM Automation as a *VARTYPE*. Pass this number to the Visual Basic *TypeName* function for a name string.

Table 9-12 Property of the *IADsSyntax* interface.

The SchemaBrowser sample uses the *IADsSyntax* interface when retrieving the information about an attribute. To place a descriptive string in the edit box for display, the program uses the Visual Basic *TypeName* function as follows:

```
txtDataType.Text = TypeName(adsSyntax.OleAutoDataType)
```

C and C++ developers can reference the *VARENUM* enumeration defined in the header file WTypes.h for the particular *VARTYPE*.

Extending the Schema

The Active Directory schema can be modified in several ways: new attributes and classes can be created, and existing ones can be disabled (but not deleted). You cannot disable core classes and attributes (called *system classes* or *system attributes*) that Active Directory needs. Adding classes and attributes is more common than disabling them.

Since Active Directory includes so many root classes and attributes, you don't often need to extend it. However, "never say never" is a good motto in the computer industry, and the designers of Active Directory, in classic Microsoft fashion, built a system in which modifying the schema is relatively easy.

But don't let the ease of modifying the schema entice you along a path of unnecessary work. Just because you can, doesn't mean you should. The purpose of this section is not only to show you how to modify the schema but to point out the impact and pitfalls of doing so.

The Process for Extending the Schema

The steps for extending the schema are as follows:

1. Decide whether to extend the schema.

2. Determine the method of extension.

3. Enable schema changes.

4. Obtain an OID.

5. Create schema objects.

6. Update the schema cache.

As an example, I'm going to design a schema extension that creates a new attribute and a new class that uses the new attribute. The example, which is very simple, provides a way for me to store the titles and authors of the many books I own.

When to Extend the Schema

You typically extend the schema when the existing classes and attributes do not fit with the type of data you want to store. Over the past year, I've worked with several developers who wanted to know how to extend the schema to fit some particular need they had. However, in many cases, Active Directory already contained a class or attribute in its default schema that fit the bill. Reviewing the existing schema carefully to see whether a class or attribute already exists is really important.

Of particular importance is the fact that schema additions are permanent. Let me say that again: Although you can add new attributes and classes, *you can never remove them from the schema*. You can disable classes and attributes, but they are not removed from the directory. Keep this in mind when testing your code.

What Data Is Best Stored in Active Directory?

Generally, directory services work best with data that is read more often than it is written. Since directory data must be replicated to other servers, an inherent latency is involved. If the data being stored is updated frequently and must be current on all the directory servers, Active Directory might not be the best place to store it.

> **Note**   The next release of Windows 2000, code-named Whistler, includes a new feature called *dynamic objects*. By using a new auxiliary class, a class can be created that contains a time-to-live (TTL) value. The TTL specifies, in seconds, how long the particular instance of an object remains in the directory. When the TTL reaches zero, the instance is deleted. See Chapter 11 for more information about this feature.

Another consideration when deciding whether to extend the schema is the size of the data you want to store. The smaller the better is the general rule. Microsoft recommends that no attribute value exceed 500 KB, including the sum of multivalued attributes. Additionally, no object should exceed 1 MB. I think these recommendations are excessively lenient. If you are considering adding an attribute that might contain 500 KB of data, maybe you should consider storing a pointer to the data in Active Directory and keep the data itself in a different store. Of course, you have to balance the maximum size of an attribute or class with the expectation of how many instances will be created in the directory. A 100-KB attribute might not be a big deal for a few objects. However, if you're attaching that attribute to, say, the *user* class, and there are 100,000 or more instances in the directory, watch out. The size of the data store might be prohibitive, and the replication traffic might swamp your network's available bandwidth.

Here is a real-world example. While working on Microsoft Exchange 2000 Server, I looked into the feasibility of storing short audio clips as an attribute of a *user* object. The idea was to provide an auditory version of a person's name when sending a message over a telephone voice-mail system. Even the most compressed audio clips took up at least 10 KB of space for each *user* object. Another problem was that the information was not streamed when it was needed; it had to be transferred in a block operation. This limitation resulted in small but noticeable delays at the client side. In the end, we decided to store the actual clip in the Exchange Web Storage System and provide an attribute with a URL pointer to the clip. The Web Storage System could use streaming techniques to efficiently provide multimedia content of any size without negatively affecting the performance of Active Directory.

Any time you want to create large attributes to store binary data, consider whether it would be better to use the attribute value as a pointer to the data and locate the data on a different server. Of course, the downside is making sure that the data is as widely available as Active Directory data.

Determining the Method of Extension

I cannot stress enough that you must carefully design your schema changes. Once you have done that, the next step is deciding which method to use to extend the schema. You can make schema changes using the following methods:

- Manually using the Active Directory Schema snap-in

- Manually using import files

- Programmatically using an installation program

Which method you use depends on the scope of the changes you want to make. For the addition of one or a few attributes or classes, the Active Directory Schema snap-in is easiest, as it presents a graphical user interface. If the changes are moderate, or you need to make them to a number of installations of Active Directory, using import files is a possibility. These files are in text format and can be easily edited. I discuss them in more detail later in the section "Using Import Files." A disadvantage of using import files is that they can be tampered with, and the ability to recover from errors is limited. You can solve those problems by extending the schema programmatically as part of your application's setup program. This is the method I recommend for directory-enabled applications.

Enabling Schema Changes

Regardless of the method you are using to modify the schema, you will need to enable schema changes. To ensure that changes to the schema are not made haphazardly, Windows 2000 imposes three safety interlocks that control modifications to the Active Directory schema.

- To prevent potential replication conflicts, only one domain controller in the organization is allowed to write to the schema. This server is known as the *schema operations master* or *schema master*. Changes can be made only to this domain controller's copy of the schema.

- The security permissions of the *Schema* container object are set so that only members of the Schema Admins group can modify the contents of the schema container.

■ A registry setting on all Windows 2000 domain controllers is used to enable schema changes. By default, this registry setting is set to prevent schema changes, even at the schema master.

The following sections describe each safety interlock and how to work with them in a program.

Connecting to the Schema Master

In many of the samples in this book, I use a practice known as *serverless binding*. Since Active Directory is distributed to all domain controllers, it doesn't matter which one you connect to. However, when updating the schema, you must connect to the domain controller that is acting in the role of schema master because only that domain controller is allowed to modify the schema. The first thing you need to know is which domain controller is performing that role, and then you need its full Domain Name System (DNS) address. With that information, you can bind directly to the schema on that domain controller and perform the modifications.

> **Note**   Some texts and articles on Active Directory recommend programmatically changing the schema master to be the one that is executing your code. That avoids having to figure out which domain controller is the schema master and remotely connecting to it. However, I think doing this is bad form. There might be a good reason why a particular domain controller is serving as the schema master and an application should not alter that, even if it restores the original settings afterward.

The process of figuring out the DNS name of the domain controller serving as the schema master involves several steps and is a little convoluted. ADSI provides some relief by providing the *ADSystemInfo* object and *IADsADSystemInfo* interface, which you can use to discover a number of pieces of information about the enterprise Active Directory.

The *SchemaRoleOwner* property of *ADSystemInfo* returns the distinguished name of the *NTDS Settings* object of the server that is acting as the schema master. By retrieving the parent of this object and binding to it, you can get the full address of the schema master domain controller. Listing 9-6, from the ExtendSchema sample on the companion CD, shows the *ReturnSchemaMaster* function, which retrieves the name of the schema master.

```
//------------------------------------------------------------
// Function:      ReturnSchemaMaster
// Description:   This function looks up the DC holding the schema
//                master FSMO role for the Active Directory forest
//                and returns its fully qualified DNS name.
//
// In/Out:        _bstr_t* String to hold schema master address
// Returns:       HRESULT  COM/ADSI error codes.
//
// Note:          ADSystemInfo only supported on Windows 2000
//------------------------------------------------------------
HRESULT ReturnSchemaMaster( _bstr_t *pbstrSchemaMasterFQDN )
{
HRESULT hResult;

// Create an ADSystemInfo object
IADsADSystemInfo *padsADSysInfo;
hResult = CoCreateInstance( CLSID_ADSystemInfo,
    NULL,
    CLSCTX_INPROC_SERVER,
    IID_IADsADSystemInfo,
    (void**) &padsADSysInfo );

if ( SUCCEEDED( hResult ) )
    {
    // Retrieve the SchemaRoleOwner attribute
    // The returned DN points to the NTDS Settings object for
    // the DC acting as the schema master.
    BSTR bstrSchemaDN;
    hResult = padsADSysInfo->get_SchemaRoleOwner ( &bstrSchemaDN );

    if( SUCCEEDED( hResult ) )
        {
        // Create ADsPath to the schema master NTDS object
        _bstr_t bstrSchemaMasterNTDS = _bstr_t( "LDAP://" ) +
            bstrSchemaDN;

        // Bind to the schema NTDS object
        IADs *padsSchemaNTDS = NULL;
        hResult = ADsGetObject( bstrSchemaMasterNTDS,
            IID_IADs,
            (void**) &padsSchemaNTDS );
```

Listing 9-6 The *ReturnSchemaMaster* function from the ExtendSchema   *(continued)*
sample showing how to retrieve the name of the schema master.

Listing 9-6 *continued*

```
        if ( SUCCEEDED ( hResult ) )
            {
            // Get the parent of the NTDS object
            BSTR bstrParent;
            hResult = padsSchemaNTDS->get_Parent ( &bstrParent );

            // The parent is the schema master
            IADs *padsSchemaMaster = NULL;
            hResult = ADsGetObject( bstrParent,
                IID_IADs,
                (void**) &padsSchemaMaster );

            if ( SUCCEEDED ( hResult ) )
                {
                // Get the actual DNS address
                _variant_t varDNS;
                hResult = padsSchemaMaster->Get ( L"dNSHostName",
                    &varDNS );
                // Return the FQDN address
                *pbstrSchemaMasterFQDN = _bstr_t( varDNS );
                }

            // Free the schema master object
            if ( padsSchemaMaster )
                padsSchemaMaster->Release ();

            // Free the parent string
            SysFreeString( bstrParent );
            }

        // Free the RootDSE object
        if ( padsSchemaNTDS )
            padsSchemaNTDS->Release ();
        }

    // Free the object-allocated string
    SysFreeString( bstrSchemaDN );
    }

// Release object
if ( padsADSysInfo )
    padsADSysInfo->Release ();

return hResult;
}
```

The *ReturnSchemaMaster* function is used by the *BindToSchemaMaster* function in Listing 9-7 to bind to the schema partition on the schema master domain controller:

```
//-------------------------------------------------------------------
// Function:       BindToSchemaMaster
// Description:    Bind to the schema container on the schema
//                 master server
//
// In/Out:         IADs**     Pointer to schema container
//                 _bstr_t*   String to hold server name
// Returns:        HRESULT    COM/ADSI error codes
//-------------------------------------------------------------------
HRESULT BindToSchemaMaster(IADs **padsSchema,
    _bstr_t *pbstrSchemaMasterFQDN )
{
HRESULT hResult;

// Bind to the RootDSE
IADs *padsRootDSE = NULL;
hResult = ADsGetObject( L"LDAP://rootDSE",
    IID_IADs,
    (void**) &padsRootDSE );

if( SUCCEEDED( hResult ) )
    {
    // Get the schema naming context DN
    _variant_t varSchemaNC;
    hResult = padsRootDSE->Get( L"schemaNamingContext", &varSchemaNC );
    if( SUCCEEDED( hResult ) )
        {
        // Retrieve the FQDN of the schema master
        ReturnSchemaMaster( pbstrSchemaMasterFQDN );

        // Create ADsPath to the schema NC on the schema master server
        _bstr_t strSchemaMasterPath = bstr_t( "LDAP://" ) +
            *pbstrSchemaMasterFQDN +
            _bstr_t( "/" ) +
            _bstr_t(varSchemaNC);
```

Listing 9-7 The *BindToSchemaMaster* function from the ExtendSchema *(continued)*
sample showing how to bind to the *Schema* container on the schema master.

Listing 9-7 *continued*

```
        // Bind to the schema container, return IADs interface
        hResult = ADsGetObject( strSchemaMasterPath,
            IID_IADs,
            (void**) padsSchema );
        }
    }
// Free the RootDSE object
if ( padsRootDSE )
    padsRootDSE->Release ();

// Return the result code
return hResult;
}
```

Verifying Correct Permissions

When preparing to extend the schema, your installation program must verify that it can actually create objects in the *Schema* container. The user executing the installation program, by default, must be a member of the Schema Admins group. (You could also run the installation program using the Run As command and provide the name and password of a user who is a member of Schema Admins.)

To prevent errors while creating schema objects, it's best to check early on whether sufficient privileges are available. Since system administrators might change the security settings for the Schema Admins group, verify the permissions by examining the *allowedChildClassesEffective* attribute of the *Schema* container. This multivalued attribute contains the names of each class of object that can be added by the current user. The two types of objects we're interested in creating are *attributeSchema* and *classSchema* objects to represent the additions we're making to the schema. If either or both of these objects are not part of *allowedChildClassesEffective*, the current execution context does not have sufficient privileges and the schema extension program should warn the user and exit. Alternatively, the installation program can prompt for a different set of credentials to be used and then verify against them.

Listing 9-8 shows the *VerifySchemaPermissions* function from the Extend-Schema sample on the companion CD. It demonstrates the method used to verify permissions, and it returns a result indicating whether the installation program has sufficient rights to modify the schema.

```
//-------------------------------------------------------------------
// Function:      VerifySchemaPermissions
// Description:   Verifies that current execution context has
//                proper permissions to update schema.
//
// In/Out:        IADs* IADs Pointer to schema container
// Returns:       HRESULT S_OK if allowed to modify schema
//                S_FALSE if not allowed to modify schema
//                E_POINTER if passed an invalid pointer
//                Other COM/ADSI result codes possible
//-------------------------------------------------------------------
HRESULT VerifySchemaPermissions( IADs *padsSchema )
{
HRESULT hResult;

// Verify that pointer is valid
if ( !padsSchema )
    return E_POINTER;

//------------------------------------------------
// Use GetInfoEx to retrieve constructed attribute
//------------------------------------------------

// Create variant array to hold attributes to retrieve
wchar_t* prgstrAttributes[] = { L"allowedChildClassesEffective" };
_variant_t varAttributes;
hResult = ADsBuildVarArrayStr( prgstrAttributes,
    ARRAYSIZE(prgstrAttributes),
    &varAttributes);

if (SUCCEEDED( hResult ) )
    {
    // Retrieve attribute and place in property cache
    hResult = padsSchema->GetInfoEx ( varAttributes, 0L );

    if ( SUCCEEDED( hResult ) )
        {
        // Get all the allowed classes
        _variant_t varAllowedClasses;
        hResult = padsSchema->GetEx( L"allowedChildClassesEffective",
            &varAllowedClasses);

        // Did we get values back?  Are they in an array?
        if ( SUCCEEDED ( hResult ) &&
            V_ISARRAY( &varAllowedClasses ) )
            {
            // Create a safe array
            SAFEARRAY *saClasses = V_ARRAY( &varAllowedClasses );
```

Listing 9-8 The *VerifySchemaPermissions* function from the ExtendSchema *(continued)*
sample showing how to verify whether the current user can update the schema.

Listing 9-8 *continued*

```
                    // Setup the upper and lower boundries of the array
                    long lMin;
                    long lMax;
                    SafeArrayGetLBound( saClasses, 1, &lMin );
                    SafeArrayGetUBound( saClasses, 1, &lMax );

                    // Variables are set when class found
                    bool bAttributeAllowed = false;
                    bool bClassAllowed = false;

                    // Enumrate each allowed class
                    for ( long nIndex = lMin;
                        nIndex <= lMax;
                        nIndex++ )
                        {
                        // Create a variant to hold the current value
                        _variant_t varClass;

                        // Use the Automation helper function to get the value
                        hResult = SafeArrayGetElement( saClasses,
                            &nIndex,
                            &varClass );

                        if ( SUCCEEDED( hResult ) )
                            {
                            // Is current value the attributeSchema class?
                            if ( _wcsicmp( L"attributeSchema",
                                _bstr_t(varClass) ) == 0)
                                {
                                bAttributeAllowed = true;
                                }
                            else
                                {
                                // Is current value the classSchema class?
                                if ( _wcsicmp( L"classSchema",
                                    _bstr_t(varClass) ) == 0)
                                    {
                                    bClassAllowed = true;
                                    }
                                }
                            }
                        }
                    // Return S_OK if both are allowed, otherwise S_FALSE
                    if ( bAttributeAllowed && bClassAllowed )
                        hResult = S_OK;
                    else
                        hResult = S_FALSE;
                    }
                }
            }
    // Return linger result
    return hResult;
    }
```

Modifying the Registry

The final step to enabling schema changes is to modify the *Schema Update Allowed* registry key on the schema master. You can use the Active Directory Schema snap-in or the Registry Editor, or you can change this setting programmatically. Using the Active Directory Schema snap-in is the easiest way to enable schema changes:

1. In the Active Directory Schema snap-in, select the root entry, named Active Directory Schema.

2. Click the Action menu, and then choose Operations Master. The Change Schema Master dialog box appears.

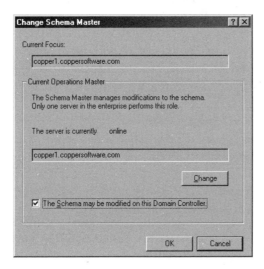

3. Select the check box titled The Schema May Be Modified On This Domain Controller.

4. Click OK.

If you are creating an application that extends the schema, you want to do this programmatically from your setup program. The specific value that forms the last safety interlock is in the registry of the schema master, at the following location:

```
HKEY_LOCAL_MACHINE\SYSTEM\CurrentControlSet\Services\NTDS\Parameters
```

The specific value is a *DWORD* and is named *Schema Update Allowed*. If *Schema Update Allowed* is not present or has a value of 0, updates are not allowed. A value of 1 enables schema changes for that domain controller. Only the domain controller that is acting as the schema master needs this value set. The other domain controllers will accept schema updates as part of the standard replication process.

Listing 9-9 shows the *EnableSchemaUpdates* function from the Extend-Schema sample on the companion CD. This function connects to the registry on the specified computer and returns the current value of *Schema Update Allowed*. Optionally, the function can set *Schema Update Allowed*, creating the value if necessary.

```
//-------------------------------------------------------------------
// Function:      EnableSchemaUpdates
// Description:   Connect to registry on remote computer and update
//                registry to enable Active Directory schema changes.
//
// In:            _bstr_t  Computer name (NetBIOS or FQDN address)
// In/Out:        DWORD*   0 to disable updates
//                1 to enable updates
//                -1 to read current value
//                On exit, contains the previous value of the key
// Returns:       HRESULT Win32 error code
//-------------------------------------------------------------------
HRESULT EnableSchemaUpdates( bstr_t bstrComputerName,
    DWORD *pdwEnableUpdates )
{
// Presume error until reset
long int lResult = E_FAIL;

// Save requested action
DWORD dwAction = *pdwEnableUpdates;

// Ensure string is valid
if ( bstrComputerName.length() == 0 )
    return E_INVALIDARG;

// Connect to registry on computer
HKEY hkHandle;
lResult = RegConnectRegistry( bstrComputerName,
    HKEY_LOCAL_MACHINE,
    &hkHandle);
if (lResult == ERROR_SUCCESS)
    {
    // Open the registry key for reading
    HKEY hkTarget;
    lResult = RegOpenKeyEx( hkHandle,
        _T("System\\CurrentControlSet\\Services\\NTDS\\Parameters"),
        0,
        KEY_READ,
        &hkTarget);
```

Listing 9-9 The *EnableSchemaUpdates* function from the ExtendSchema sample showing how to read or modify the *Schema Update Allowed* value in the registry.

```
    if (lResult == ERROR_SUCCESS)
        {
        // Query for the value
        DWORD dwType;
        DWORD dwSize = sizeof( DWORD );
        lResult = RegQueryValueEx( hkTarget,
            _T("Schema Update Allowed"),
            0,
            &dwType,
            (LPBYTE)pdwEnableUpdates,
            &dwSize);
        // Is update requested?
        if ( dwAction != -1 )
            {
            // Close handle to key because it's for read access only
            RegCloseKey( hkTarget );

            // Attempt to open key for writing
            lResult = RegOpenKeyEx( hkHandle,
                _T("System\\CurrentControlSet\\Services\\NTDS\\Parameters"),
                0,
                KEY_WRITE,
                &hkTarget);

            if ( lResult == ERROR_SUCCESS )
                {
                // Set the value as desired
                lResult = RegSetValueEx( hkTarget,
                    _T("Schema Update Allowed"),
                    0L,
                    REG_DWORD,
                    (LPBYTE)&dwAction,
                    dwSize);
                }
            }
        // Close the handle to the key
        RegCloseKey (hkTarget);
        }
    // Close the handle to the remote registry
    RegCloseKey (hkHandle);
    }
return lResult;
}
```

> **Important**   Do not leave the registry unlocked! When you are calling the *EnableSchemaUpdates* function to modify the registry, be sure to save the previous value, which is returned in the *pdwEnableUpdates* parameter. When finished with the schema modification, call *EnableSchemaUpdates* again with the previous value to return the registry to its previous state. The ExtendSchema sample shows how to do this.

Obtaining an Object Identifier

As I discussed at the beginning of this chapter, object identifiers (OIDs) are the unique identifiers for every attribute and class defined in the schema. For each new class and attribute you want to create, an OID must be obtained. There are two basic methods for obtaining an OID: getting a block of numbers from the Internet Assigned Number Authority (IANA) or using the numbers from the Microsoft-assigned block.

If you are going to be creating a lot of new classes or attributes, it's probably better to register with IANA and get your own branch of the global OID tree. IANA will assign numbers from the Private Enterprise Numbers branch of the OID tree. You can also register with ANSI in the United States to get a block of numbers for the US Organizations branch of the OID tree. ANSI charges a fee for this service, however. See the following Web sites for more information:

IANA	*http://www.iana.org/*
ANSI Registration	*http://web.ansi.org/public/services/reg_org.html*
For outside the United States, check the list of ISO members	*http://www.iso.ch/addresse/membodies.html*

The numbers you receive are yours to do with as you please. You can issue subtrees to others, but ultimately you are responsible for the management of this block of numbers. If you work with a lot of OIDs, take steps to manage your own numbers so that you don't accidentally reuse one. You could create a database of the numbers you assign and store them in a spreadsheet—or better yet, in Active Directory!

The easier and better way for making occasional schema extensions is to use a branch of numbers that Microsoft reserves for this purpose. Microsoft's branch of the OID tree for Active Directory purposes is 1.2.840.113556.1, and Microsoft has reserved two additional trees for Active Directory schema extensions. They are:

- 1.2.840.113556.1.4, for attributes

- 1.2.840.113556.1.5, for classes

The *Microsoft Windows 2000 Resource Kit* includes the Oidgen.exe utility for creating a unique number within the Microsoft branch. Of course, when *Microsoft* and *unique number* appear in the same sentence, a GUID isn't too far away. To keep themselves out of the business of managing all the numbers in their own branch of the OID tree, Microsoft uses GUIDs to create a unique number to tack onto the end of the Microsoft-allocated branch. The Oidgen utility actually creates two numbers, one for classes in the 1.2.840.113556.1.5 branch and another for attributes in the 1.2.840.113556.1.4 branch. Figure 9-9 shows the output of the Oidgen tool.

Figure 9-9 Using Oidgen to create unique base-object identifiers for new attributes and classes.

While in theory you could run Oidgen to generate a new OID every time you want to extend the schema, doing so is inefficient. Internally, Active Directory keeps a table of unique OID prefixes (the portion of the OID without the last branch). By doing so, it can quickly use the last branch number as an index value to speed up referencing of the entire OID. Creating a new branch for each new class or attribute will increase the size of the table and reduce Active Directory's performance.

A better solution is to simply use the Oidgen tool to set the number for your own branch and then assign numbers within that branch. For this sample, we need OIDs for one class and one attribute. Using the numbers assigned by Oidgen as a base, I'll use the OIDs listed in Table 9-13 for our new schema objects.

Object Identifier	Common Name
1.2.840.113556.1.5.7000.111.28688.28684.8.204138.830347.950265.1272930.1	coppersoft-Book
1.2.840.113556.1.4.7000.233.28688.28684.8.51404.1012371.312491.931313.1	coppersoft-Authors

Table 9-13 A class OID and an attribute OID generated with Oidgen.

Schema objects must have a name prefix that is unique, which is usually your company name or domain name. Microsoft keeps a registry of schema naming prefixes for companies that want to extend their schemas. If you want your application to be considered for the Certified for Windows logo program, you must register your naming prefix with Microsoft. For more information, refer to the Application Specification for Microsoft Windows 2000 included on the companion CD and the registration Web site at *http://msdn.microsoft.com/certification/ad-registration.asp*. The companion CD also includes the SchemaDoc tool to help you document your own schema extensions in XML.

Creating Schema Objects

The next step is to actually create the new schema objects. As mentioned earlier, this can be done in various ways. You can use the Active Directory Schema snap-in, use import files, or create the objects programmatically.

Using the Active Directory Schema Snap-in

Using the Active Directory Schema snap-in is the easiest way to create new schema objects. In the Active Directory Schema snap-in, select the Attributes folder or the Classes folder, click the Action menu, point to New, and select either Attribute or Class. After clicking Continue in the warning dialog box, the Create New Attribute or Create New Schema Class dialog box is displayed. Using these dialog boxes, you can add the necessary information and a new attribute or class will be created. Figure 9-10 shows the Create New Attribute dialog box.

Figure 9-10 Creating a new attribute object using the Active Directory Schema snap-in.

Using Import Files

Windows 2000 includes a command-line tool named Ldifde.exe that can be used to obtain detailed information about existing classes or attributes or to modify or create classes or attributes. You can find this tool in the %WinDir%\System32 folder of Windows 2000 Server or Windows 2000 Advanced Server. Ldifde.exe imports or exports text files that are in the LDAP Data Interchange Format (LDIF). Listing 9-10 shows a sample LDIF file that creates a new attribute named *coppersoft-Authors-v2* and a new class named *coppersoft-Book-v2*. The new attribute must be created first because the new class depends on its existence to be created.

```
# Create multi-valued attribute to hold author names
# (wrap lines using a single space after CR/LF)
dn: CN=coppersoft-Authors-v2,CN=Schema,CN=Configuration,
 DC=coppersoftware,DC=com
changetype: add
adminDisplayName: coppersoft-Authors-v2
attributeID:
 1.2.840.113556.1.4.7000.233.28688.28684.8.51404.1012371.312491.931313.2
attributeSyntax: 2.5.5.12
cn: coppersoft-Authors-v2
instanceType: 4
isSingleValued: FALSE
lDAPDisplayName: coppersoft-Authors-v2
distinguishedName: CN=coppersoft-Authors-v2,CN=Schema,CN=Configuration,
 DC=coppersoftware,DC=COM
objectCategory: CN=Attribute-Schema,CN=Schema,CN=Configuration,
 DC=coppersoftware,DC=COM
objectClass: attributeSchema
oMSyntax: 64
showInAdvancedViewOnly: TRUE

# Instruct Active Directory to reload the schema cache
# Must do this or creation of the class, below, will fail
# Use the schemaUpdateNow operational attribute of the RootDSE
DN:
changeType: modify
add: schemaUpdateNow
schemaUpdateNow: 1
-
```

Listing 9-10 ExtendSchema.ldf is an LDIF file that can be used with *(continued)* Ldifde to create a new attribute and a new class that uses the new attribute.

Listing 9-10 *continued*

```
# Add the Book class
dn: CN=coppersoft-Book-v2,CN=Schema,CN=Configuration,
 DC=coppersoftware,DC=COM
changetype: add
adminDisplayName: coppersoft-Book-v2
cn: coppersoft-Book-v2
defaultObjectCategory: CN=coppersoft-Book-v2,CN=Schema,CN=Configuration,
 DC=coppersoftware,DC=COM
governsID:
 1.2.840.113556.1.5.7000.111.28688.28684.8.2C4138.830347.950265.1272930.2
instanceType: 4
lDAPDisplayName: coppersoft-Book-v2
mayContain: coppersoft-Authors-v2
distinguishedName: CN=coppersoft-Book-v2,CN=Schema,CN=Configuration,
 DC=coppersoftware,DC=COM
objectCategory: CN=Class-Schema,CN=Schema,CN=Configuration,
 DC=coppersoftware,DC=COM
objectClass: classSchema
objectClassCategory: 0
possSuperiors: container
rDNAttID: cn
showInAdvancedViewOnly: TRUE
subClassOf: top
# Instruct Active Directory to reload the schema cache
# Do this if you need access to the class right away
DN:
changeType: modify
add: schemaUpdateNow
schemaUpdateNow: 1
-
```

Before you can create a new class that includes a newly created attribute, the in-memory schema cache on the schema master server must be refreshed. Normally this happens every 5 minutes, but it can be forced by writing a value of 1 to the *updateSchemaNow* operational attribute of the server's *RootDSE*. The sample LDIF file in Listing 9-10 updates the schema cache after creating the attribute and again after creating the class. See the "Updating the Schema Cache" section later in this chapter for more information.

To use this LDIF file with Ldifde, you would enter a command similar to the following:

```
ldifde -i -f authors.ldf -v
```

LDIF files are convenient, particularly for bulk importing and exporting of directory data. However, for schema modifications, I prefer using programmatic means that can respond to errors and notify the user of problems.

Using a Program

Actually creating the new schema objects is just like creating any other object in the directory. I'll use the *Create* method of the *IADsContainer* interface, bound to the *Schema* container. Then I'll set the required attributes using the *Put* method of the *IADs* interface. Finally, I'll call the *SetInfo* method to update the directory server.

If any errors occur, they'll generally be at the *SetInfo* method. If sufficient access permission doesn't exist, an access denied error occurs. Frequently, a constraint violation occurs if invalid data is specified, such as requesting a non-existent attribute name to be a required attribute for a new class.

> **Note**   The following *#define* statements are used by the code sample to hold the name and OID for the *coppersoft-Authors-v3* attribute and the *coppersoft-Book-v3* class. This way, they can be easily changed to include version numbers during the development and testing process. When the code is complete, remove the version numbers and add the objects to the schema and test again.
>
> If you change the name of an attribute or class, the OID must also be changed. I use a method of keeping the last number of the OID in synch with the number at the end of the object's name.
>
> ```
> // Name and OID for new attribute and class
>
> #define AUTHORS_ATTR_OID
> L"1.2.840.113556.1.4.7000.233.28688.28684.8.51404.1012371.312491.931313.3"
>
> #define AUTHORS_ATTR_NAME    L"coppersoft-Authors-v3"
>
> #define BOOK_CLASS_OID
> L"1.2.840.113556.1.5.7000.111.28688.28684.8.204138.830347.950265.1272930.3"
>
> #define BOOK_CLASS_NAME    L"coppersoft-Book-v3"
> ```

Creating a New Attribute   When creating a new attribute for the schema, the following attributes must be set before calling *SetInfo*: *lDAPDisplayName*, *oMSyntax*, *attributeID*, *attributeSyntax*, *isSingleValued*, *lDAPDisplayName*, and *oMSyntax*. See Table 9-9 for more information about these mandatory *attributeSchema* attributes, as well as optional *attributeSchema* attributes.

Listing 9-11 shows the *CreateDirectoryAttribute* function, which creates the *coppersoft-Authors* attribute in the schema. Note that when the *Create* method is called, an *IDispatch* interface is returned to the new object. I use the *QueryInterface* method to request the *IADs* interface so that I can make calls to the *Put* method.

```
//-----------------------------------------------------------------
// Function:      CreateDirectoryAttribute
// Description:   Create new attribute object in the schema
//
// In/Out:        IADsContainer* Pointer to schema container
// Returns:       HRESULT        COM/ADSI error code
//-----------------------------------------------------------------
HRESULT CreateDirectoryAttribute ( IADsContainer *padsSchema )
{
HRESULT hResult;

// Verify that pointer is valid
if ( !padsSchema )
    return E_POINTER;

// Create new attributeSchema object in the schema container
IDispatch *piDisp = NULL;
hResult = padsSchema->Create ( L"attributeSchema",
                               _bstr_t( L"CN=" ) +
                               _bstr_t( AUTHORS_ATTR_NAME ),
                               &piDisp );

if ( SUCCEEDED( hResult ) )
    {
    // Get IADs pointer to new object
    IADs *padsAttr = NULL;
    hResult = piDisp->QueryInterface ( IID_IADs,
                                       (void**) &padsAttr );
    if ( SUCCEEDED( hResult ) )
        {
```

Listing 9-11 The *CreateDirectoryAttribute* function from the ExtendSchema sample showing how to create a new attribute in the schema.

```
        //---------------------------------------------
        // Set the information for new attribute
        //---------------------------------------------

        // Indicate that this is a new attribute object
        hResult = padsAttr->Put ( L"objectClass",
            _variant_t( L"attributeSchema" ) );

        // Set the syntax to be a Unicode string
        hResult = padsAttr->Put ( L"attributeSyntax",
            _variant_t( L"2.5.5.12" ) );

        // Set the XOM syntax for Unicode string
        hResult = padsAttr->Put ( L"oMSyntax",
            _variant_t( L"64" ) );

        // Set the LDAP display name to match common name
        hResult = padsAttr->Put ( L"lDAPDisplayName",
            _variant_t( AUTHORS_ATTR_NAME ) );

        // Set the OID for this attribute
        hResult = padsAttr->Put ( L"attributeID",
            _variant_t( AUTHORS_ATTR_OID ) );

        // Indicate that this value is multivalued
        hResult = padsAttr->Put ( L"isSingleValued",
            _variant_t ( false ) );

        // Update the server with this object
        hResult = padsAttr->SetInfo ();
        }

    // Release the attribute pointer
    if ( padsAttr )
        padsAttr->Release ();
    }

// Release the IDispatch pointer
if ( piDisp )
    piDisp->Release ();

return hResult;
}
```

Creating a New Class   Creating a new class is similar to creating a new attribute. Listing 9-12 shows the *CreateDirectoryClass* function, which creates the *coppersoft-Book* class in the schema.

```
//----------------------------------------------------------------
// Function:       CreateDirectoryClass
// Description:    Create new class object in schema
//
// In/Out:         IADsContainer*  Pointer to schema container
// Returns:        HRESULT         COM/ADSI error code
//----------------------------------------------------------------
HRESULT CreateDirectoryClass ( IADsContainer *padsSchema )
{
HRESULT hResult;

// Verify that pointer is valid
if ( !padsSchema )
    return E_POINTER;

// Create new classSchema object in the schema container
IDispatch *piDisp = NULL;

hResult = padsSchema->Create ( L"classSchema",
                               _bstr_t( L"CN=" ) +
                               _bstr_t( BOOK_CLASS_NAME ),
                               &piDisp );

if ( SUCCEEDED( hResult ) )
    {
    // Get IADs pointer to new object
    IADs *padsClass = NULL;
    hResult = piDisp->QueryInterface ( IID_IADs,
                                       (void**) &padsClass );
    if ( SUCCEEDED( hResult ) )
        {
        //--------------------------------------------
        // Set the information for new class
        //--------------------------------------------

        // Indicate that this is a structural class
        hResult = padsClass->Put ( L"objectClassCategory",
            _variant_t( (short) 0x01 ) );

        // Set the LDAP display name to match common name
        hResult = padsClass->Put ( L"lDAPDisplayName",
            _variant_t( BOOK_CLASS_NAME ) );

        // Set the Admin display name to match common name
        hResult = padsClass->Put ( L"adminDisplayName",
            _variant_t( BOOK_CLASS_NAME ) );

        // Set the description
        hResult = padsClass->Put ( L"description",
            _variant_t( L"Example class" ) );
```

Listing 9-12 The *CreateDirectoryClass* function from the ExtendSchema sample showing how to create a new class in the schema.

```
        // Set the OID for this class
        hResult = padsClass->Put ( L"governsID",
            _variant_t( BOOK_CLASS_OID ) );

        // Indicate that this class inherits from the Top class
        hResult = padsClass->Put ( L"subClassOf",
            _variant_t( L"top" ) );

        // Set the new authors attribute to be part of this class
        hResult = padsClass->Put ( L"mayContain",
            _variant_t( AUTHORS_ATTR_NAME ) );

        // Update the server with this object
        hResult = padsClass->SetInfo();
        }

    // Release the class object pointer
    if ( padsClass )
        padsClass->Release ();
    }

// Release the IDispatch pointer
if ( piDisp )
    piDisp->Release ();

return hResult;
}
```

Updating the Schema Cache

After creating the new schema objects, if the application needs to take advantage of them right away, you must direct it to request the schema master server to update its in-memory cache. For performance reasons, a version of the schema is kept in memory and is not automatically updated when new classes and attributes are added.

Eventually, the schema master updates the cache, usually within 5 minutes, but if you require access to your objects before then, it's simple to trigger an update. There are two methods you can use to trigger an update of the schema cache. The first method is to use the *schemaUpdateNow* constructed attribute on the server's *RootDSE* object. When this attribute is updated with any value, the server automatically flushes and refreshes its cache. The second method is to use the *ADSystemInfo* object supplied by ADSI. The *RefreshSchemaCache* method triggers a refresh of the cache on the local computer only. This method is useful if you are running your installation program on the schema master. Although, as I mentioned earlier, you should not change the schema master role just to accommodate your installation program.

Listing 9-13 shows the *UpdateSchemaCache* function, which can trigger an update to the schema cache by using *schemaUpdateNow* or *RefreshSchemaCache*:

```
//------------------------------------------------------------------
// Function:       UpdateSchemaCache
// Description:    Triggers an update to the in-memory cache on the
//                 schema master
//
// In:             _bstr_t Computer name (NetBIOS or FQDN address)
//                 bool    True to update the cache on the local
//                         computer, regardless of the name passed.
//                         False to update cache on computer named.
// Returns:        HRESULT COM/ADSI error code
// Notes:          If program is running on schema master computer,
//                 use bUpdateLocal = True to use ADSystemInfo
//                 object to update local schema cache.
//                 ADSystemInfo only supported on Windows 2000
//------------------------------------------------------------------
HRESULT UpdateSchemaCache( bstr_t bstrComputerName, bool bUpdateLocal )
{
HRESULT hResult;

// Do we update the local schema cache?
if ( bUpdateLocal )
    {
    // Create an ADSystemInfo object
    IADsADSystemInfo *padsADSystemInfo;
    hResult = CoCreateInstance( CLSID_ADSystemInfo,
                                NULL,
                                CLSCTX_INPROC_SERVER,
                                IID_IADsADSystemInfo,
                                (void**) &padsADSystemInfo );

    if ( SUCCEEDED( hResult ) )
        {
        // Call method to refresh cache
        hResult = padsADSystemInfo->RefreshSchemaCache ();
        }
    }
```

Listing 9-13 The *UpdateSchemaCache* function from the ExtendSchema sample showing how to trigger an update of the in-memory cache on the schema master.

```
else
    {
    // Nonlocal update
    // Create ADsPath to the schema NC on the schema master server
    _bstr_t strSchemaRootDSE = _bstr_t( "LDAP://" ) +
        bstrComputerName +
        _bstr_t( "/RootDSE" );

    // Bind to the rootDSE on the schema master
    IADs *padsSchemaRootDSE = NULL;
    hResult = ADsGetObject( strSchemaRootDSE,
                            IID_IADs,
                            (void**) &padsSchemaRootDSE );

    if ( SUCCEEDED( hResult ))
        {
        // Trigger the update by writing a value of 1
        hResult = padsSchemaRootDSE->Put ( L"schemaUpdateNow",
            _variant_t( true ) );

        // Won't update cache until written
        hResult = padsSchemaRootDSE->SetInfo();
        }

    // Free the RootDSE pointer
    if ( padsSchemaRootDSE )
        padsSchemaRootDSE->Release ();
    }

return hResult;
}
```

Since updating the schema cache is time-consuming for the server, you should only do it when required. If you create several attributes, wait until all of them have been created before updating the cache. If you require access to the new class immediately, update the cache again after all the classes have been created.

ExtendSchema Sample

The main function of the ExtendSchema sample uses the functions described throughout this section to modify the schema. It's very straightforward, calling the respective functions to enable schema updates and verify permissions. Then it calls the function to create a new attribute and then the one to create a class that uses the attribute. Finally, it cleans up, refreshes the schema cache, and exits, as shown in Listing 9-14.

```c
int _tmain( int /* argc */, _TCHAR /* **argv */, _TCHAR /* **envp */
)
{
    // Initialize COM
    HRESULT hResult = CoInitialize ( NULL );


    //-----------------------------------------------
    // Bind to schema
    //-----------------------------------------------
    // Pointer to schema container on schema master
    IADs *padsSchema = NULL;

    // DNS name of schema master
    bstr_t bstrSchemaMaster;

    // Bind to schema and return IADs and name string
    hResult = BindToSchemaMaster( &padsSchema, &bstrSchemaMaster );

    // Display any error and exit
    if ( FAILED( hResult ) )
        DisplayErrorAndExit( hResult );
    else
        _tprintf( _T("Schema Master DNS address: %ls\n"),
            (wchar_t*)bstrSchemaMaster );


    //-----------------------------------------------
    // Verify Correct Permissions
    //-----------------------------------------------
    hResult = VerifySchemaPermissions( padsSchema );

    // S_FALSE means persmission not allowed
    if ( FAILED( hResult ) )
        DisplayErrorAndExit( hResult );
```

Listing 9-14 The main function from the ExtendSchema sample.

```
if ( hResult == S_FALSE )
    _tprintf( _T("Schema Permissions not okay.\n") );
else
    _tprintf( _T("Schema Permissions okay.\n") );

//---------------------------------------------
// Enable Schema Changes
//---------------------------------------------
DWORD dwEnableChanges = 1;
hResult = EnableSchemaUpdates( bstrSchemaMaster,
    &dwEnableChanges );

// Display any error and exit
if ( FAILED( hResult ) )
    DisplayErrorAndExit( hResult );
else
    _tprintf( _T("Registry unlocked, was %d\n"),
        dwEnableChanges );

// The following functions need an IADsContainer interface
IADsContainer *padsSchemaCont = NULL;
hResult = padsSchema->QueryInterface ( IID_IADsContainer,
    (void**) &padsSchemaCont );

// Display any error and exit
if ( FAILED( hResult ) )
    DisplayErrorAndExit( hResult );

//---------------------------------------------
// Create new attribute in the schema
//---------------------------------------------
hResult = CreateDirectoryAttribute ( padsSchemaCont );

// Display any error and exit
if ( FAILED( hResult ) )
    DisplayErrorAndExit( hResult );
else
    _tprintf( _T("Created Attribute.\n") );

//---------------------------------------------
// Must update cache after all attributes are
// created so they can be used by new classes
//---------------------------------------------
hResult = UpdateSchemaCache ( bstrSchemaMaster, false );
```

(continued)

Listing 9-14 *continued*

```
// Display any error and exit
if ( FAILED( hResult ) )
    DisplayErrorAndExit( hResult );
else
    _tprintf( _T("Schema Cache Updated.\n") );

//-------------------------------------------
// Create new class in the schema
//-------------------------------------------
hResult = CreateDirectoryClass ( padsSchemaCont );

// Display any error and exit
if ( FAILED( hResult ) )
    DisplayErrorAndExit( hResult );
else
    _tprintf( _TEXT("Created Class.\n") );

//-------------------------------------------
// Update schema master's in-memory cache
//-------------------------------------------
hResult = UpdateSchemaCache ( bstrSchemaMaster, false );

// Display any error and exit
if ( FAILED( hResult ) )
    DisplayErrorAndExit( hResult );
else
    _tprintf( _TEXT("Schema Cache Updated.\n") );

//-------------------------------------------
// Restore Original Registry value
//-------------------------------------------
hResult = EnableSchemaUpdates( bstrSchemaMaster,
    &dwEnableChanges );

// Display any error and exit
if ( FAILED( hResult ) )
    DisplayErrorAndExit( hResult );
else
    _tprintf( _TEXT("Registry restored, was %d\n"),
    dwEnableChanges );

//-------------------------------------------
// Release objects and exit
//-------------------------------------------

// Release the schema container interface
if ( padsSchemaCont )
    padsSchema->Release ();
```

```
    // Release the schema pointer
    if ( padsSchema )
        padsSchema->Release ();

    // Uninitialize COM and exit
    CoUninitialize ();

    // Exit with any lingering hResult
    return hResult;
}
```

Listing 9-15 shows the *DisplayErrorAndExit* function. This function executes when an error occurs, displays a formatted error string, and exits the application.

```
//--------------------------------------------------------------------
// Function:     DisplayErrorAndExit
// Description:  Displays error message and exits application
//
// In/Out:       DWORD containing error code
// Returns:      Does not return
//--------------------------------------------------------------------
void DisplayErrorAndExit ( DWORD dwError )
{
    // Create error string
    PTSTR pszErrorMessage = NULL;
    FormatMessage( FORMAT_MESSAGE_ALLOCATE_BUFFER |
                   FORMAT_MESSAGE_FROM_SYSTEM |
                   FORMAT_MESSAGE_IGNORE_INSERTS,
                   NULL,
                   dwError,
                   MAKELANGID(LANG_NEUTRAL, SUBLANG_DEFAULT),
                   (PTSTR) &pszErrorMessage,
                   0,
                   NULL );
    // Print error
    _tprintf( pszErrorMessage );

    // Free the buffer.
    LocalFree( pszErrorMessage );

    // Close application and return error
    exit( dwError );
}
```

Listing 9-15 The *DisplayErrorAndExit* function from the ExtendSchema sample, which displays an error string and exits the application when an error occurs.

Summary

The schema is the most complex part of Active Directory. The abstract schema is helpful for casual browsing and inspection of object and property types. However, working directly with Active Directory's implementation of the schema is often necessary to fully understand the behavior of the directory.

Extending the directory is not as difficult as it might seem. In fact, the ease with which it's accomplished should remind you of the importance of carefully assessing the impact such extensions will have on the size of the directory, client access traffic, and bandwidth issues related to replication.

In the next chapter, I'll look at performing common network administration tasks using Windows Script.

10

Active Directory Administration Using Windows Script

In developing programs for Active Directory, you'll often work with common directory objects such as users, groups, computers, and printers. Active Directory Service Interfaces (ADSI) makes your work easier by supplying interfaces designed specifically for the type of object you want to work with. The Windows scripting environment makes a network administrator's life easier by providing access to Active Directory through ADSI using relatively simple programming languages. This chapter contains a lot of sample source code, mostly in small functions, that illustrates how to perform a specific task. You can copy and modify this code to use as part of your own administration toolkit.

Windows Scripting

For many years, network administrators and "power users" used MS-DOS batch files (.bat) to automate certain tasks. When Windows came along, the need to automate some tasks still existed, but Microsoft didn't include any scripting capability in Windows itself.

Not until the development of Automation, which allowed scripting languages to access COM objects, was real scripting possible in the Windows environment. Automation allows scripting languages to create instances of COM objects and access the properties and methods of those objects at runtime.

Basically, the first script hosts were Microsoft applications, Word and Excel, among others. These applications also included Microsoft Visual Basic for Applications (VBA), a slightly trimmed down version of the popular language that ships as part of the Visual Basic programming environment.

As the Internet became more popular, Microsoft included support for VBScript, an even more trimmed down version of Visual Basic than VBA, and JScript, Microsoft's implementation of JavaScript, in Microsoft Internet Explorer and Microsoft Internet Information Server (IIS).

A proliferation of languages, including VBA, VBScript, JScript, large applications such as Word, client Web browsers, and Web servers, all can make use of COM objects that support Automation.

Windows Script Host

The missing piece is an execution environment independent of an application, which is where Windows Script Host comes in. In 1998, Microsoft made Windows Script Host 1.0 available for download and included it in the Windows NT 4.0 Option Pack and Windows 98. Windows Script Host doesn't actually execute the scripts themselves; it provides a means for a *script engine* to execute a particular script.

The script engine is specific to a programming language. The Windows Script components include engines for VBScript and JScript. Other languages, such as Perl and Python, also have engines available. The ability to code in the language of your choice and have your program execute across the Windows platform is extremely powerful. Each script engine provides the features native to the languages, such as VBScript's *For Each* statement or JScript's C/C++ style comments (*/* */* and *//*). Many Perl scripts written as CGI Web server scripts can now be easily ported and run independently of a Web server.

Windows Script Files

Version 1.0 of Windows Script Host loads a particular script engine based on the filename extension of the file containing the script code. For example, a file named Simple.vbs would instruct Windows Script Host to load the VBScript engine, whereas Simple.js would indicate that the JScript engine is required. Starting with Windows Script Host 2.0, available in Windows 2000, Windows Script Host adds support for a new file type, a Windows Script file (.wsf), that uses XML tags to define various sections. A major benefit of a Windows Script file is that it can contain multiple scripts, in any supported language. A practical example of this capability would be a system administrator's toolkit. These tools are likely to be written in various languages. With a Windows Script file, these tools can be collected and bundled into a single .wsf file. The scripts contained in a .wsf file can also invoke procedures contained in the same or in another .wsf file.

The other major benefit of Windows Script Host 2.0 is its ability to create Windows Script Components. A Windows Script Component is a COM object created by a program written in one of the Windows Script languages. Let's say you've developed a nifty script that gathers the names of all the users logged onto the network. Now, instead of cutting and pasting that code into each script in which you need to perform that task, you can publish it as a Windows Script Component and any script, or any application that uses COM, can take advantage of your code! That is true code reuse, enabled by Windows Script.

A Windows Script file is structured differently from a .vbs or .js file. A Windows Script file is actually an XML file. This format allows for a lot of flexibility in the creation of scripts, such as including multiple scripts in a single file and handling events. The XML elements I'll use are *job*, *script*, and *reference*. The *job* element tells Windows Script Host to treat its content as one task. Multiple jobs can be included in a single file and referenced using a command-line argument. The *script* element specifies which language the script is written in. This is used by Windows Script Host to load the correct scripting engine. The *reference* element specifies a type library, which I'll discuss in more detail later in this chapter.

> **Note**   The naming and versioning of Windows Script can be a little hairy. Microsoft uses the term *Windows Script*, which is a collection of the various Windows scripting components. At the time of this writing, the current version of Windows Script is 5.5, and includes Windows Script Host and Windows Script Components 2.0, VBScript 5.5, JScript 5.5, and the Windows Script Run-Time 5.1. The next version of Windows will ship with Windows Script 5.6, which has a wealth of new features including improved argument handling, comment blocks, remote scripting, and object model improvements. Windows Script 5.6 also includes support for documenting and digitally signing scripts.

Windows Script Object Model

Windows Script provides an object model that can be used by any script engine. The *WScript* object provides access to information about the execution environment, whereas the *WshArguments* object contains information and methods to retrieve command-line arguments—a requirement of scripting. Other objects in the model include *WshShell*, an interface to the user interface shell of Windows, and *WshNetwork*, which allows scripts to use file and print resources on a network.

The model also includes objects that represent drives, folders, and files. Any script running under Window Script Host can use these objects. Table 10-1 lists the Windows Script Host objects along with objects supplied by the Windows Script runtime engine.

Object	Description	Supplied By
WScript	Data and methods that represent the current execution environment	Windows Script Host
WshArguments	Collection of command-line arguments	Windows Script Host
WshEnviroment	Collection of named system environment variables	Windows Script Host
WshNetwork	Properties and methods to work with networking	Windows Script Host
WshShell	Methods to control processes and the registry and to create new shortcuts	Windows Script Host
WshShortcut	Represents a shortcut file	Windows Script Host
WshSpecialFolder	Collection of special Windows folders such as Desktop, Control Panel, and Start Menu	Windows Script Host
WshUrlShortcut	Represents a shortcut to a URL	Windows Script Host
Dictionary	Simple database array	Windows Script runtime
Drive	Properties related to logical disk drives	Windows Script runtime
Drives collection	Collection of *Drive* objects available	Windows Script runtime
Encoder	Mechanism to encode script files so that they can't be easily read	Windows Script runtime
File	Properties of a file and methods to copy, move, or delete	Windows Script runtime
Files collection	Collection of *File* objects within a folder	Windows Script runtime
FileSystemObject	Properties and methods related to the file system	Windows Script runtime
Folder	Properties of a single folder within the file system	Windows Script runtime
Folders collection	Collection of *Folder* objects within a Folder	Windows Script runtime
TextStream	Provides read/write access to a text file	Windows Script runtime

Table 10-1 Windows Script objects.

Type Libraries

A *type library* is a definition of one or more COM objects that includes information about the objects' interfaces such as properties, methods, parameters, and data types. A type library allows compilers like Microsoft Visual C++ and Visual Basic to perform type checking, for example, verifying that the data type being passed to a method is correct. It also improves performance because the compiler can create code that directly invokes a method, rather than perform a series of steps at runtime. This is called *early binding* and is discussed in Chapter 3.

Type libraries also contain the definitions for constants, enumerations, and structures. A constant is simply a named value. For example the *ADS_USE_SSL* constant has a value of 2. By using constants, it's easier to write and understand the source code. Enumerations are a group of related constants. The *ADS_USE_SSL* constant is part of the *ADS_AUTHENTICATION_ENUM* enumeration that defines the various authentication options available with the *ADsOpenObject* function and *IADsOpenDSObject* interface.

Until recently, Windows Script developers could not utilize type libraries. The original version of Windows Script Host did not support type libraries, and constants had to be explicitly defined, which hampered the porting of source code from Visual Basic to VBScript. However, Windows Script Host 2.0 can be instructed to load a type library so that constants defined in that type library can be accessed. Listing 10-1 shows a script available on the companion CD that uses the ADSI type library, named the Active DS Type Library (ActiveDS.tlb), in conjunction with the handy ADSI *Pathname* object.

> **Note** Unlike in Visual Basic, referencing a type library in a script does not mean you can declare variables of a specific data type. Also, objects in a script that reference a type library are still late bound. However, referencing a type library does allow a script to use the constants defined in the type library.

```
<job id="UseTypeLib">
<reference guid="{97D25DB0-0363-11CF-ABC4-02608C9E7553}"/>
<script language="VBScript">
' Bind to the local global catalog server
Set adsRootDSE = GetObject( "LDAP://RootDSE" )

' Create ADsPath to the default directory partition
strADsPath = "LDAP://" & adsRootDSE.Get( "defaultNamingContext" )
```

Listing 10-1 UseTypeLib.wsf shows how to reference the ADSI type library   *(continued)* and how to use constants defined in that type library.

Listing 10-1 *continued*

```
' Create an ADSI Pathname object
Set adsPathname = CreateObject("Pathname")

' Provide the Pathname object with our ADsPath
adsPathname.Set strADsPath, ADS_SETTYPE_FULL

' Retrieve various formats of the ADsPath
strWindows  = adsPathname.Retrieve(ADS_FORMAT_WINDOWS)
strX500     = adsPathname.Retrieve(ADS_FORMAT_X500)
strProvider = adsPathname.Retrieve(ADS_FORMAT_PROVIDER)

' Prepare strings and display
strADsPath  = "Original ADsPath:" & vbTab & strADsPath  & vbNewLine
strWindows  = "Windows format:"   & vbTab & strWindows  & vbNewLine
strX500     = "X.500 format:"      & vbTab & strX500     & vbNewLine
strProvider = "Provider only:"     & vbTab & strProvider & vbNewLine
WScript.Echo strADsPath & strWindows & strX500 & strProvider
</script>
</job>
```

Figure 10-1 shows an example of the output when you run the UseTypeLib script.

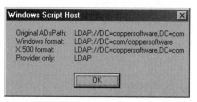

Figure 10-1 Output of UseTypeLib.wsf script, using the *Pathname* object and constants defined in the ADSI type library.

The *reference* element is used to tell Windows Script Host to load the ADSI type library. The string "{97D25DB0-0363-11CF-ABC4-02608C9E7553}" is the GUID of the type library. Windows Script Host uses this number to look up the actual type library file, ActiveDS.tlb, in the computer's registry, normally installed in the %SystemRoot%\System32 folder.

The UseTypeLib sample uses several constants defined in the Active DS Type Library file. For maximum effect, I chose the ADSI *Pathname* object, because it uses many of the *ADS_XXX* constants. The *Pathname* object helps to work with paths in ADSI. Once a path for the *Pathname* object is specified via the *Set* method, different formats for the path can be retrieved using the *Retrieve* method. The Windows format is sometimes known as OSF-style or the canonical format and is commonly used by the Exchange 5.5 directory. The X.500 format uses the familiar distinguished name (DN) style you've seen throughout this book. A sample, named Pathname.wsf, that demonstrates some of the capabilities of the *Pathname* object is available on the companion CD.

The *reference* element can also identify a type library by using a program identifier (ProgID) stored in the registry. Some COM components, such as ActiveX Data Objects (ADO), incorporate a type library within the component. Unfortunately, with ADSI, you must reference a GUID to identify the Active DS Type Library.

Type Libraries: More Than You Want To Know

Type libraries are created by the developer of the COM component using the Object Definition Language (ODL). A special compiler, MIDL, is used to create the type library file (.tlb). This file can then be distributed with the component or embedded in the binary code as a resource. Visual Basic developers use the References command to instruct the compiler to load and use a type library. Visual C++ (5.0 and later) developers can instruct the compiler to reference a type library by using the *#import* directive.

Creating and Editing Scripts

Although creating simple scripts is easy, scripting does have its drawbacks. Currently the development environments available from Microsoft for creating scripts are limited. Programmers accustomed to working with the rich editors and debuggers in Visual C++ 6.0 and Visual Basic 6.0 are stuck using Notepad to create many scripts. Even the script editor in Microsoft Visual InterDev 6.0 only recognizes scripts designed for its specific environment. While Visual InterDev 6.0 can be tweaked to provide syntax coloring and IntelliSense statement completion, you cannot use the built-in debugger easily. Many script developers use Notepad and the Microsoft Script Debugger to create small scripting applications.

The upcoming release of Microsoft's development environment, Visual Studio.NET, brings welcome relief to script developers. You can create a Windows Script file using the new XML editing environment and take advantage of Visual Studio's IntelliSense feature to provide statement completion and use drop-down lists of properties and methods. Debugging Windows Script files, a bane for many, is also integrated into Visual Studio.NET.

For more information on scripting in Windows, you can refer to an excellent book, *Microsoft Windows Script Host 2.0 Developer's Guide* by Günter Born (Microsoft Press, 2000).

Let's turn our attention now to using Windows Script to actually manage network resources in Active Directory.

Managing Users

The most visible and common administrative task in Active Directory is managing user accounts. Prior to Active Directory, user accounts existed primarily for authorization and security purposes. With Active Directory, the focus has shifted to representing actual people. Information about people in Active Directory is represented in two forms: users and contacts. An object of the *user* class represents a single person and contains naming, contact, and security information. An object of the *contact* class is similar, but it omits security information. Contacts are used to keep track of people in an organization who are not network users. Contacts can also represent people external to the organization, such as customers.

The *IADsUser* Interface

When ADSI binds to any object, it does a quick check of the object's schema class. ADSI then determines whether the class includes an appropriate interface. In the case of objects of the *user* or *contact* classes, ADSI provides the *IADsUser* interface, which encapsulates the information common to both users and contacts. Tables 10-2 and 10-3 show the properties and methods of *IADsUser*.

IADsUser Property	Data Type	Matching Attribute in Active Directory	Description
AccountDisabled	Boolean	*userAccountControl* (*UF_ACCOUNTDISABLE* flag)	If True, the account is disabled.
AccountExpirationDate	Date	*accountExpires*	The date and time when an account expires.
BadLoginAddress	String	Not supported under Active Directory	The address of the computer that caused an account lockout.
BadLoginCount	Long	*badPwdCount*	The number of failed login attempts.
Department	String	*department*	The name of the department the user is associated with.

Table 10-2 Properties of the *IADsUser* interface.

IADsUser Property	Data Type	Matching Attribute in Active Directory	Description
Description	String	description	A description of the user.
Division	String	division	The organizational division the user is associated with.
EmailAddress	String	mail	The user's e-mail address.
EmployeeID	String	employeeID	The employee identification number associated with the user.
FaxNumber	Variant array of strings	facsimileTelephone-Number	List of fax telephone numbers for the user. In Active Directory, the list has a single string.
FirstName	String	givenName	The first, or given, name of the user.
FullName	String	displayName	The full name of the user, including given and last names.
GraceLogins-Allowed	Long	Not supported under Active Directory	The number of times a user can log on after his or her password has expired.
GraceLogins-Remaining	Long	Not supported under Active Directory	The number of grace logins left before account lock out.
HomeDirectory	String	homeDirectory	The UNC path to the user's home directory.
HomePage	String	wWWHomePage	The URL to the user's Web page.
IsAccountLocked	Boolean	Not supported under Active Directory	Is True if account is locked.
Languages	Variant array of strings	Not supported under Active Directory	An array of names of the languages associated with the user.
LastFailedLogin	Date	badPasswordTime	The date and time of the most recent failed login attempt.
LastLogin	Date	lastLogon	The date and time of the most recent network login.
LastLogoff	Date	lastLogoff	The date and time of the most recent network login.
LastName	String	sn	The last name of the user.
LoginHours	Variant array of Booleans	logonHours	The time periods during each day of the week indicating valid login periods.

(continued)

Table 10-2 *continued*

IADsUser Property	Data Type	Matching Attribute in Active Directory	Description
LoginScript	String	*scriptPath*	The path of user's login script.
LoginWork-stations	Variant array of strings	*userWorkstations*	The network addresses of allowed workstations for the user.
Manager	String	*manager*	The distinguished name of the *Manager* object for this user.
MaxLogins	Long	Not supported under Active Directory	The maximum number of simultaneous logins.
MaxStorage	Long	*maxStorage*	The maximum amount of disk space allowed for the user.
NamePrefix	String	*personalTitle*	The name prefix, such as Mr. Ms., or Hon., of the user.
NameSuffix	String	*generationQualifier*	The name suffix (Jr., III) of the user.
OfficeLocations	Variant array of strings	*physicalDelivery-OfficeName*	The array of end-user locations.
OtherName	String	*middleName*	The middle name of the user.
Password-ExpirationDate	Date	Not supported under Active Directory	The date and time when the password will expire.
PasswordLast-Changed	Date	*pwdLastSet*	The date and time when the password was last set.
PasswordMini-mumLength	Long	Not supported under Active Directory	The minimum number of characters allowed in a password.
Password-Required	Boolean	*userAccountControl* (*UF_PASSWD_NOTREQD* flag)	If True, a password is required.
Picture	Variant array of bytes	*thumbnailPhoto*	Image of the user.
PostalAddresses	Variant array of strings	*postalAddress* Supported but not used by Active Directory	An array of strings with street, city, state, and postal code.
PostalCodes	Variant array of strings	*postalCode*	The postal code for the user.
Profile	String	*profilePath*	The user's profile path.
RequireUnique-Password	Boolean	Not supported under Active Directory	If True, user is required to supply unique passwords.

IADsUser Property	Data Type	Matching Attribute in Active Directory	Description
SeeAlso	Variant array of strings	seeAlso	An array of ADsPaths of other objects related to this user.
TelephoneHome	Variant array of strings	homePhone	A list of home telephone numbers.
TelephoneMobile	Variant array of strings	mobile	A list of mobile telephone numbers.
TelephoneNumber	Variant array of strings	telephoneNumber	A list of work-related telephone numbers.
TelephonePager	Variant array of strings	pager	A list of pager telephone numbers.
Title	String	title	The user's title within the organization.

IADsUser Method	Description
ChangePassword	Changes the users password. The new and current passwords must be supplied
Groups	Returns a collection of groups the user belongs to.
SetPassword	Sets the password for the user's account.

Table 10-3 Methods of the *IADsUser* interface.

The *IADsUser* interface was created while Active Directory was still being designed, so the properties of the *IADsUser* interface don't always match the attributes available in a *user* object very well. I'll discuss this in the next section.

Creating Users

Several important items should be considered when creating users. First, you need to understand which attributes are required when the object is created. Second, you need to know what information to put into which attribute. Unfortunately, Active Directory poses several "gotchas" that are compounded by the differences between the *IADsUser* properties and the Active Directory attributes they are mapped to.

One such "gotcha" is the address attributes for a user. While the *IADsUser* interface provides the *PostalAddress* property, using this property to access the postal address of a user will not work under Active Directory. You shouldn't use the *PostalAddress* property because Active Directory uses separate attributes for street (*streetAddress*), city (*l*), state (*st*), and postal code (*postalCode*). With Active Directory, you must use the *Get* method of the *IADs* interface to access these attributes.

Naming Attributes

Active Directory requires two attributes to be set when creating a new *user* object. The first is the *cn* (*Common-Name*) attribute. This is simply the name of the object and may or may not relate to the name of the user. As with all objects in Active Directory, the name of the object must be unique within its container. If a user is added to a container that already has an object with the same name, the create operation fails.

As I mentioned in Chapter 9, I've talked with several administrators who think that users with the same name cannot be represented in the same Active Directory container. This misperception is created by the behavior of the New User wizard in the Active Directory Users and Computers snap-in. The New User wizard uses the text in the Full Name field as the value for the *cn* attribute. The Full Name field is dynamically created as information is typed into the First Name, Initials, and Last Name fields.

In practice, the *cn* value is the full name of the user, but any unique string can be used, including the logon name. (See the next paragraph). A limitation of using a unique string is that the Active Directory user interface uses the *cn* attribute value in several places instead of the more appropriate *displayName* attribute. Exchange 2000 Server, however, does use the *displayName* attribute correctly in its various user interface components such as the Address Book.

The second required attribute, and a potential source of conflict, is the *sAMAccountName* attribute. This is the logon name used by versions of Windows prior to Windows 2000. With Active Directory, the string the user types in at the log-on prompt can be the *sAMAccountName* value or a user principal name (UPN). The UPN is more flexible than the *sAMAccountName* attribute in that it consists of two parts—the first being a user name followed by the at-sign (@), and the second a Domain Name System (DNS) address known as the UPN suffix. Generally, the UPN of a user will be their e-mail address, charles@coppersoftware.com or charles.oppermann@coppersoftware.com, for example. The UPN is useful because it gives users a common and easy-to-remember identifier—their e-mail address—to log onto the network.

Regardless of the UPN, the *sAMAccountName* attribute must still be unique in the domain. There are two ways to avoid a conflict with duplicate values for the *sAMAccountName attribute*. A simple method is to attempt to add the user and detect whether an error has occurred. Another way is to query the local global catalog (GC) server with the proposed value for *sAMAccountName*, as the *sAMAccountName* attribute is among those included in the global catalog subset. The LDAP query string would be (*sAMAccountName*=proposedvalue). Since the *sAMAccountName* attribute is also an indexed attribute, the global catalog server can perform an efficient search. If an object is returned by the search, the proposed name is already used. With either method, if a name conflict is detected, the script can then prompt for another account name or attempt to generate a unique one. Account names must be 20 characters or less, and generally do not contain spaces.

Create User Script

Listing 10-2 shows a script, available on the companion CD, that adds a user to Active Directory. You can easily modify this sample to read in the information from a text file or a database to create multiple users at one time. The script shows how to create a *user* object in the *Users* container and set various attributes using the *IADs* and *IADsUser* interfaces. Notice that the *Create* method of the *IADsContainer* interface, which was discussed in Chapter 6, is used to create the *user* object. All new objects in Active Directory are created with the *Create* method of *IADsContainer*.

```
<job id="CreateUser">
<reference guid="{97D25DB0-0363-11CF-ABC4-02608C9E7553}"/>
<script language="VBScript">
'
' CreateUser - Creates example user
'
' Strings used to identify and describe the new user
' Logon name
strUserAcct = "JAUser"
strFullName = "Joe A. User"
strFirstName = "Joe"
strLastName = "User"
strPassword = "mypassword"
' Lots of confusion on these.  Wizard uses initials as a "middle initial"
strMiddleName = "Average"
strInitials = "A"
' Descriptive info
strUserDesc = "Example user for testing purposes."
strTelephone = "888-555-1212"
strStreet = "One Microsoft Way"
strCity = "Redmond"
strState = "WA"
strZIPCode = "98052"
```

Listing 10-2 CreateUser.wsf shows how to create an example user.   *(continued)*

Listing 10-2 *continued*

```
' Display info
WScript.Echo "Creating new user '" & strFullName & "'..."

' Bind to the rootDSE and get the default domain partition
Set adsRootDSE = GetObject("LDAP://rootDSE")
strDomainDN = adsRootDSE.Get("defaultNamingContext")

' Bind to the Users container of the domain
strADsPath = "LDAP://CN=Users," & strDomainDN
Set adsContainer = GetObject(strADsPath)

' Go to the next line if an error occurs
On Error Resume Next

' Create the object in the container using the full user name
Set adsUser = adsContainer.Create("user", "cn=" + strFullName)

' Set the down-level account name for the user (<20 characters)
adsUser.Put "sAMAccountName", strUserAcct

' Set the UPN for the user
adsUser.Put "userPrincipalName", strUserAcct

' Update server with required properties
adsUser.SetInfo

' Check for errors
If Err.Number <> 0 Then
    ' Check to see whether user already exists error
    If Err.Number = &H80071392 Then
        ' Display error message and exit
        WScript.Echo "The user name '" & strFullName & "' already exists."
        WScript.Quit 1
    Else
        WScript.Echo "Unexpected error creating user." & vbNewLine & _
            Err.Description & " (" & Hex(Err.Number) & ")"
        WScript.Quit 1
    End If
End If

' Turn off error handling
On Error GoTo 0

' Use IADsUser properties to set other pieces of data
' Refresh the local property cache with new user info
adsUser.GetInfo
```

```
' Set the user password.  SetInfo must be called beforehand (above)
adsUser.SetPassword strPassword

' Require the user to change password on login
adsUser.Put "pwdLastSet", 0

' Enable the account (the default when created is disabled)
adsUser.AccountDisabled = False

' Set the display name of the user
adsUser.FullName = strFullName

' Set name information of the user
adsUser.FirstName = strFirstName
adsUser.LastName = strLastName
adsUser.OtherName = strMiddleName
adsUser.Put "initials", strInitials

' Set the description using the Description property
adsUser.Description = strUserDesc

' Set the telephone number
adsUser.TelephoneNumber = strTelephone

' Set the address information
' Must use Active Directory attributes, not PostalAddress property.
adsUser.Put "streetAddress", strStreet
adsUser.Put "l", strCity
adsUser.Put "st", strState
adsUser.Put "postalCode", strZIPCode

' Apply the properties to the directory
adsUser.SetInfo

' Release objects
Set adsUser = Nothing
Set adsContainer = Nothing

' Finish
WScript.Echo "User created successfully."
</script>
</job>
```

When you run the CreateUser script, a user named "Joe A. User" is created in the *Users* container. Figure 10-2 shows the Properties dialog box for the new user in Active Directory Users and Computers.

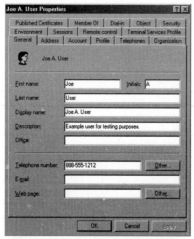

Figure 10-2 Properties dialog box for the new user created with the CreateUser script.

Default User Values

If you do not explicitly set the properties and attributes listed in Tables 10-4 and 10-5 when creating a new user, Active Directory will use default values.

IADsUser Property	Default Value
AccountDisabled	True
AccountExpirationDate	1/1/1970. This indicates that the account never expires.
PasswordLastChanged	Default is 0, which means the user must change the password at next logon.
PasswordRequired	False

Table 10-4 Default property values for a *user* object.

User Attribute	Default Value
memberOf	If not specified, this attribute remains empty; however the Domain Users group is set as the primary group for the user.
nTSecurityDescriptor	A security descriptor is created from the combination of the *user* class and parent object's security descriptors.
objectCategory	Set to Person. This attribute is automatically set by Active Directory and cannot be modified.

Table 10-5 Default attribute values for a *user* object.

Passwords

The password for a user account is contained in the *unicodePwd* attribute of the *user* object. The actual password is stored in the directory using an encryption technique known as *one-way format* (OWF). You cannot directly read or write to the *unicodePwd* attribute even if you have the appropriate security privileges. This restriction prevents the password from being transmitted in clear text over the network.

In order to set or change a user's password, you must use the *SetPassword* or *ChangePassword* methods of the *IADsUser* interface. The specific method to use depends on the security context of the application.

The *SetPassword* method accepts a string parameter and uses it to replace the current password. This method can be used by administrators to reset a user's password. When *SetPassword* is used in a program that creates a *user* object, the *pwdLastSet* attribute should be set to 0, which indicates that the user must change her password the next time she logs on. In Active Directory Users and Computers, this option is available on the Account tab of the user's Properties dialog box, in a check box named User Must Change Password At Next Logon. It's good security practice to require users to change their password to something of their own choosing, rather than use a default password, which could be compromised. The CreateUser script shown in Listing 10-2 sets the *pwdLastSet* attribute to 0.

The *ChangePassword* method accepts two parameters: the old password and the new password. Because it requires knowledge of the existing password, this method can be used by end users.

Listing 10-3 shows a script available on the companion CD that can be used to change a password. It accepts three command-line parameters. The first is the name of the user, for example, "Joe A. User". Any format recognized by Windows can be used, such as domainname\username or username@domainname.com. The second and third parameters are the current and new passwords, respectively. Note that quotation marks are required for any parameters that have spaces. Here's an example:

```
changepassword "Joe A. User" mypassword mynewpassword
```

> **Note**   This script uses the ADSI object named *NameTranslate* to retrieve the user's distinguished name in the directory. Retrieving this information allows us to avoid searching the directory for the *user* object. *NameTranslate* uses the *DsCrackNames* API. *NameTranslate* is part of Windows 2000; other platforms require the Active Directory Client to be installed to use it.

```
<job id="ChangePassword">
<reference guid="{97D25DB0-0363-11CF-ABC4-02608C9E7553}"/>
<script language="VBScript">
'
' ChangePassword
  Accepts a name and prompts for old and new passwords
'
' Accepts a username and resets the password
' Name must be full name ("Charles Oppermann") or be in
' domainname\username format ("coppersoftware\charles")
'
' Check whether there is a command-line argument
Set wshArguments = WScript.Arguments

If (wshArguments.Count = 3) Then

    ' Treat the command-line argument as the name to use
    strUser = wshArguments(0)
    strOldPassword = wshArguments(1)
    strNewPassword = wshArguments(2)

Else
    WScript.Echo "Incorrect number of arguments." & vbNewLine & _
        "Usage:  ChangePassword.wsf username " & _
        "oldpassword newpassword"
    WScript.Quit 1
End If

' Use NameTranslate to look up the computer in the directory
Set adsNameTranslate = CreateObject("NameTranslate")
adsNameTranslate.Init ADS_NAME_INITTYPE_GC, vbNullString

' Set the user name into nametranslate
' Specify unknown format, so that system will guess
adsNameTranslate.Set ADS_NAME_TYPE_UNKNOWN, strUser

' Get the DN of the object
strDN = adsNameTranslate.Get(ADS_NAME_TYPE_1779)

' Make DN an ADsPath by prefixing the ADSI provider
strADsPath = "LDAP://" & strDN

' Bind to user object
Set adsUser = GetObject(strADsPath)
```

Listing 10-3 ChangePassword.wsf shows how to change the password for an existing user.

```
' Confirm change
strPrompt = "Change password for " & adsUser.FullName & " from '" & _
    strOldPassword & "' to '" & strNewPassword & "'?"
nConfirmed = MsgBox(strPrompt, vbYesNo, "Change Password")

If nConfirmed = vbYes Then
    ' Go to the next line if an error occurs
    On Error Resume Next

    ' Change the password
    adsUser.ChangePassword strOldPassword, strNewPassword

    ' Check for errors
    If Err.Number <> 0 Then
        ' Display error message
        Select Case (Err.Number)
            Case &H80070056
                WScript.Echo "The specified password for " & _
                    adsUser.FullName & " is not correct."
            Case &H800708C5
                WScript.Echo "The specified password does not " & _
                    "meet policy requirements."
            Case Else
                WScript.Echo "Unexpected error changing password." & _
                    vbNewLine & Err.Description & " (" & _
                    Hex(Err.Number) & ")"
        End Select
    Else
        WScript.Echo "Password successfully changed for " & _
            adsUser.FullName
    End If
End If

</script>
</job>
```

> **Note**   The *userPassword* attribute, part of the *person* object class, is not used in Active Directory.

Working with Exchange 2000 Server

Microsoft Exchange 2000 Sever is Microsoft's latest version of its enterprise e-mail server. Exchange 2000 uses Active Directory to store configuration data for itself and extends many classes with new attributes and display specifiers. When a user or contact is *mailbox-enabled*, Exchange 2000 has a mailbox for the user or contact and has updated the person's information in Active Directory to indicate their e-mail address and the location of their mailbox.

A common task when creating users is to create an Exchange 2000 mailbox at the same time. Exchange 2000 makes this easy by providing management interfaces that aggregate some existing ADSI interfaces. This is done by using the ADSI Extension feature. While I won't go into the details, suffice to say that the properties and methods of the Exchange 2000 *IMailboxStore* and *IMailRecipient* interfaces are available when bound to a *user* or *contact* class object.

The *IMailboxStore* and *IMailRecipient* interfaces are part of the Collaboration Data Objects for Exchange Management (CDOEXM). CDOEXM extends ADSI and Collaboration Data Objects (CDO) to include properties and methods to manage Exchange 2000. Although CDO and CDOEXM are not covered in this book, I wanted to mention these technologies so that you are aware of them.

For more information about creating mailboxes and sending e-mail programmatically in Exchange 2000 Server, along with sample scripts, see the Exchange folder on the companion CD. To learn more about CDO, CDOEXM, and Exchange 2000 development, I suggest the Microsoft Press book *Programming Collaborative Web Applications with Microsoft Exchange 2000 Server*, by Mindy Martin. (And you thought the title of *this* book was long!)

Managing Groups

High on the list of common administrative tasks is managing groups. A group is simply a list of related objects. Generally, a group contains a list of users, computers, or other groups. An example of a group is all the managers in an organization. Adding each manager's *user* object to the group provides centralized administration and easier communication with all the managers. The chairman of a company can then send e-mail to a single address, such as managers@coppersoftware.com, to reach all the managers at once. Network administrators can assign specific security privileges to a group that enables group members to perform specific tasks. For example, the manager's group might be given access to restricted shared folders or files.

Types of Groups

Active Directory represents a group as a single object of the *group* class. This object contains attributes describing group properties and group members. There are two types of groups: *distribution* and *security.*

A distribution group is used for e-mail distribution lists or other, nonsecurity related purposes. For example, the list of people to receive the company newsletter could be contained in a distribution group named Newsletter Readers. If you've worked with Microsoft Exchange Server 5.5 or earlier, you probably created distribution lists. A distribution group in Active Directory is the same in concept and is used by Microsoft Exchange 2000 Server for the same purpose.

A security group is used to apply a common set of access permissions to the members of the group. Security groups have the same benefits as distribution groups but also provide security information. The permissions assigned to the group are applied to the members of the group when they log on to the network.

Distribution and security groups in Active Directory have a scope that determines how security permissions are set. A group has one of three scopes: *universal, global,* or *domain local.* A universal group covers all the domains within a group. Users can be added from any domain, and the group's permissions apply to all the domains in the forest. A global group applies to the domain in which the group was created. Only users in the same domain can be added, but permissions apply to all the domains in the forest. The domain local scope is the opposite of the global scope. A domain local group can have members from anywhere in the forest, but permissions are applied only to the domain that the group was created in.

In most cases, global groups are sufficient. Changing the members in a universal group triggers replication between domains and global catalog servers. If a universal group is required, consider creating global groups in each domain and adding members for that domain. Then add each global group to the universal group. This will prevent unnecessary replication each time the global group changes membership. Domain local groups are best for assigning special permissions on a per-domain basis and for controlling access to nondirectory objects such as files and shared folders.

Real-World Advice

Andy Webb, cofounder of Simpler-Webb, Inc. is an experienced developer working with Active Directory and Microsoft Exchange Server. He confirms the potential replication issues with universal groups, saying: "The group membership is a single multivalued property on the group object. Whenever a member is added or removed, this property is updated and must be replicated to global catalog servers. It is possible to make a change to the group on more than one global catalog. For example, someone is added to a group in one domain. That change is reflected in the local global catalog quickly. However, if in another domain someone is removed from the same group, a replication conflict occurs because that domain doesn't have the change from the first domain yet. The first change is going to be lost in favor of the second change, which occurred later in time. With just two global catalogs it's unlikely that this would happen since replication will be pretty simple and quick. With a large, highly distributed set of global catalogs, the 'window' of risk gets much bigger."

Because of the potential of replication conflicts and changes being lost, developers and administrators working with Active Directory should avoid creating universal groups with memberships that change often. Since changes to global groups do not force global catalog updates, using global groups as members of a universal group effectively avoids this problem.

The next release of Active Directory is expected to improve its support of group handling and replication issues. Of course, careful planning will reap benefits now and in the future.

ADSI Group Interfaces

ADSI includes an interface for working with groups, appropriately named *IADsGroup*. This interface contains *Add* and *Remove* methods to manage the list of group members. The properties and methods of *IADsGroup* are listed in Tables 10-6 and 10-7.

IADsGroup Property	Data Type	Description
Description	String	A description of the group

Table 10-6 Properties of the *IADsGroup* interface.

IADsGroup Method	Description
Add	Adds a user or other security principle to the group
IsMember	Checks to see whether the specified object is a member of the group
Members	Returns a collection of member objects of the group by using the *IADsMember* interface
Remove	Removes a member from the group

Table 10-7 Methods of the *IADsGroup* interface.

Creating a Group

To create a group, start by calling the *Create* method of the *IADsContainer* interface. The *Create* method of the *IADsContainer* interface was used earlier in the CreateUser script to create a *user* object, and using it to create a group is no different. Then fill in the necessary information about the group.

For a group, Active Directory requires that the *cn*, *groupType*, and *sAMAccountName* attributes be filled in before a program or script calls *SetInfo*. The *cn* attribute is simply the name of the group. The *groupType* attribute is the combination of constants from the *ADS_GROUP_TYPE_ENUM* enumeration. The *sAMAccountName* is the name used by down-level (older) clients such as Windows 95, Windows 98, and Windows NT 4.0 to access the group using the SAM API functions such as *NetGroupGetInfo*. The *sAMAccountName* for groups can be up to 256 characters long. As mentioned earlier, the limit for users is 20 characters.

After all the required properties are filled in with values, the *SetInfo* method of *IADs* is called to update the directory server. A new group object isn't actually saved to the directory until the *SetInfo* method is called.

Listing 10-4 shows a script, available on the companion CD, that creates a security-enabled group with global scope. Once the group is created and the required properties are specified, the *SetInfo* method is called. The script checks for any errors that might have occurred. If any do occur, the script displays the error information and exits. If no errors occur, the script continues setting descriptive properties of the group and then updates the server with a final call to *SetInfo*.

```
<job id="CreateGroup">
<reference guid="{97D25DB0-0363-11CF-ABC4-02608C9E7553}"/>
<script language="VBScript">
' CreateGroup.wsf - Creates an example group in the Users container
'
' Strings used to identify and describe the new group
strGroupName = "Example Group"
strGroupDesc = "Example group for testing purposes."
strGroupInfo = "This is an example group, safe to delete."

' Display info
WScript.Echo "Creating group '" & strGroupName & "'..."

' Bind to the RootDSE and get the default domain partition
Set adsRootDSE = GetObject("LDAP://RootDSE")
strDomainDN = adsRootDSE.Get("defaultNamingContext")

' Bind to the Users container of the domain
strADsPath = "LDAP://CN=Users," & strDomainDN
Set adsContainer = GetObject(strADsPath)

' Go to the next line if an error occurs
On Error Resume Next

' Create the group object in the container
Set adsGroup = adsContainer.Create("group", "CN=" + strGroupName)

' Set type as security and scope to global
lGroupType = ADS_GROUP_TYPE_SECURITY_ENABLED Or _
        ADS_GROUP_TYPE_GLOBAL_GROUP
adsGroup.Put "groupType", lGroupType

' Set the account name for the group
' Can be same as full group name (<256 characters)
adsGroup.Put "sAMAccountName", strGroupName

' Update server with required properties
adsGroup.SetInfo

' Check for errors
If Err.Number <> 0 Then
    ' Check to see whether group already exists error
    If Err.Number = &H80071392 Then
        ' Display error message and exit
            WScript.Echo "The group '" & strGroupName & _
                "' already exists."
            WScript.Quit 1
```

Listing 10-4 CreateGroup.wsf shows how to create a security-enabled group with global scope.

```
      Else
          WScript.Echo "Unexpected error creating group." & vbNewLine & _
              Err.Description & " (" & Hex(Err.Number) & ")"
          WScript.Quit 1
      End If
  End If

  ' Turn off error handling
  On Error Goto 0

  ' Set the description using the Description property
  adsGroup.Description = strGroupDesc

  ' Set the notes field using the info attribute
  adsGroup.Put "info", strGroupInfo

  ' Apply the properties to the group entry
  adsGroup.SetInfo

  ' Release objects
  Set adsGroup = Nothing
  Set adsContainer = Nothing

  ' Finish
  WScript.Echo "Group created successfully."
</script>
</job>
```

When you run the CreateGroup script, a group named "Example Group" is created in the *Users* container. Figure 10-3 shows the Properties dialog box for the new group in Active Directory Users and Computers.

An important caveat when creating groups is to avoid hard coding a particular location or container name. Placing fixed addresses or names in applications is generally a bad practice and it's particularly true for Active Directory–enabled applications because each domain may be configured differently. The CreateGroup script creates the example group in the *Users* container. A better approach would be to use the well-known GUID for the *Users* container. In addition, applications should not depend on groups always being in the same location because an administrator might move the group or rename one of its containers. Applications can search for the group or use the *otherWellKnownObjects* attribute to track the object's location in the directory regardless of name or location. The Create-Computer sample shown in the next section uses the well-known GUID to locate the *Computers* container. See Chapter 4 for more information about binding to objects with well-known GUIDs.

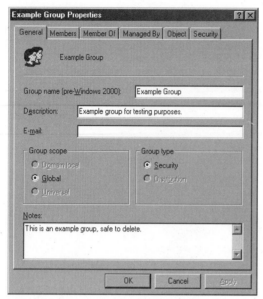

Figure 10-3 Properties dialog box for the new group created with the CreateGroup script.

Enumerating Groups

Using the *IADsGroup* interface, you can obtain the list of members of a group. When you call the *Members* method of *IADsGroup*, you receive an *IADsMembers* interface, which exposes the collection of members. *IADsMembers* is very similar in both function and purpose to *IADsContainer*. Both allow enumeration using the *For Each* statement in Visual Basic and VBScript. Table 10-8 shows the properties of *IADsMembers*.

IADsMembers Property	Data Type	Description
Count	Long	Number of members in the collection.
Filter	Variant array of strings	Array of class names used to filter the enumeration of members. Same as the *Filter* method of the *IADsContainer* interface.
get__NewEnum (Not exposed in Visual Basic)	Object	Creates a new enumerator object that supports the *IEnumVARIANT* interface. Called indirectly from Visual Basic by using the *For Each* statement. Returns an *IUnknown* interface pointer. Note that there are two underscore () characters in the name.

Table 10-8 Properties of the *IADsMembers* interface.

The following code illustrates how to enumerate the members of a group.

```
' Get the members collection
Set adsMembers = adsGroup.Members

' Enumerate each member
For Each adsMember In adsMembers

    ' Display the full name of the member
    WScript.Echo adsMember.Get("name")
Next
```

Modifying Group Membership

The *Add* and *Remove* methods of *IADsGroup* are used to modify the membership of a group. Listing 10-5 shows the ModifyGroup script, available on the companion CD, that shows how to add, remove, verify, and list members in a group. The ModifyGroup script runs at the command prompt and accepts a group name, an action (*add*, *del*, *test*, or *list*), and a user name. Based on the input, the script will add the user to the group, remove the user from the group, use the *IsMember* method to confirm membership, or list the group members. Here are some examples of its usage:

```
cscript modifygroup.wsf "coppersoftware\Example Group" /add "Joe A. User"
cscript modifygroup.wsf "coppersoftware\Example Group" /test "Joe A. User"
cscript modifygroup.wsf "coppersoftware\Example Group" /list
cscript modifygroup.wsf "coppersoftware\Example Group" /del "Joe A. User"
```

To list the members of the group, the *Members* method is called to return a collection of members, which is enumerated using the *For Each* statement.

```
<job id="ModifyGroup">
<reference guid="{97D25DB0-0363-11CF-ABC4-02608C9E7553}"/>
<script language="VBScript">
'
' ModifyGroup
' Can add, remove, verify, and list members of a group
'
' Check whether there is a command-line argument
Set wshArguments = WScript.Arguments

' Get parameters based on number of arguments
Select Case wshArguments.Count
```

Listing 10-5 ModifyGroup.wsf shows how to add, remove, verify, and list   *(continued)*
members of a group.

Listing 10-5 *continued*

```
Case 1
        strGroup = wshArguments(0)

    Case 2
        strGroup = wshArguments(0)
        strAction = wshArguments(1)

    Case 3
        strGroup = wshArguments(0)
        strAction = wshArguments(1)
        strUser = wshArguments(2)
End Select

' Check for no group name or help request
If strGroup = "" Or InStr(1, strGroup, "?", vbTextCompare) > 0 Then

    ' Show usage and quit
    strUsage = "Usage: modifygroup 'groupname'"
    strUsage = strUsage & vbCrLf & "                    [ /add  username ]"
    strUsage = strUsage & vbCrLf & "                    [ /del  username ]"
    strUsage = strUsage & vbCrLf & "                    [ /test username ]"
    strUsage = strUsage & vbCrLf & "                    [ /list ]"
    '
    strUsage = strUsage & vbCrLf & _
        "Where username is either UPN (charles@coppersoftware.com) "
    strUsage = strUsage & vbCrLf & "or Domain (domainname\username)"
    WScript.Echo strUsage
    WScript.Quit (1)
End If

' Figure out action requested
' Take the left-most 2 characters of the parameter and
' check whether they match into the argument list
nAction = InStr(1, "/t/l/a/d", Left(strAction, 2), vbTextCompare)

' Use NameTranslate to look up the group in the directory
Set adsNameTranslate = CreateObject("NameTranslate")

' Specify the GC for quick lookups
adsNameTranslate.Init ADS_NAME_INITTYPE_GC, vbNull

' Set the group name into NameTranslate
' Specify unknown format to have object determine
adsNameTranslate.Set ADS_NAME_TYPE_UNKNOWN, strGroup

' Get the DN of the group
strGroupDN = adsNameTranslate.Get(ADS_NAME_TYPE_1779)
```

```
' Bind to group object
Set adsGroup = GetObject("LDAP://" & strGroupDN)

' If a user was specified, get their information
If strUser <> "" Then

    ' Set the user name into NameTranslate
    adsNameTranslate.Set ADS_NAME_TYPE_UNKNOWN, strUser

    ' Get the DN of the user
    strUserDN = adsNameTranslate.Get(ADS_NAME_TYPE_1779)

    ' Bind to the user object
    Set adsUser = GetObject("LDAP://" & strUserDN)
Else

    ' If no user specified, can only list
    nAction = 3
End If

' Perform an action
Select Case nAction

    Case 1
        ' Test for membership
        If adsGroup.IsMember(adsUser.ADsPath) Then

            ' Display if member
            WScript.Echo adsUser.FullName & " is a member of the " & _
                adsGroup.Get("name") & " group."
        Else

            ' Display if not member
            WScript.Echo adsUser.FullName & " is not a member of the " & _
                adsGroup.Get("name") & " group."
        End If

    Case 5
        ' Add action
        WScript.Echo "Adding " & adsUser.FullName & " to group " & _
            adsGroup.Get("name")

        ' Add user to group
        adsGroup.Add adsUser.ADsPath

    Case 7
        ' Remove action, get confirmation
        strPrompt = strAction & adsUser.FullName & strVerb & _
            adsGroup.Get("name") & "?"
```

(continued)

Listing 10-5 *continued*

```
            If MsgBox(strPrompt, vbYesNo, "Modify Group") = vbYes Then

                WScript.Echo "Removing " & adsUser.FullName & _
                    " from group " & adsGroup.Get("name")

                ' Remove user from group
                adsGroup.Remove adsUser.ADsPath
            End If

        Case Else
            ' Some other action, list membership
            WScript.Echo "Listing all members in group " & adsGroup.Name

            ' Skip to the next line on errors
            On Error Resume Next

            ' Get the description
            strDescription = adsGroup.Description

            ' If something was returned, display it
            If strDescription <> "" Then

                ' Creation description string
                strDescription = "Description: " & strDescription
                WScript.Echo strDescription

            End If

            ' Display separator
            WScript.Echo String(Len(strDescription), "-")

            ' Get the members collection
            Set adsMembers = adsGroup.Members

            ' Enumerate each member
            For Each adsMember In adsMembers

                ' Display the name of the member
                WScript.Echo adsMember.Get("name")
            Next

            ' Turn error handling back on
            On Error GoTo 0
    End Select
```

```
WScript.Echo "Finished."

</script>
</job>
```

Note   If you attempt to use the ModifyGroup script or any interface to
Active Directory to list the members of the Domain Users group, you will
find that none are listed. Since every user created in the domain is automatically a member of the Domain Users group, Microsoft realized that
thousands of values could be written to the members attribute of the
group. This would cause problems with replication and performance, so
Active Directory simply doesn't bother trying to keep the Domain Users
group updated. However, Active Directory maintains an association between the Domain Users group and its members via the *primaryGroupID*
attribute of the *user* object. When a new user is created, this attribute
is given the security identifier of the Domain Users group.

Managing Computers

Like users, computers also have accounts in Active Directory. In fact, the *computer* class inherits from the *user* class. Computer accounts are treated like user
accounts for purposes of security and access permissions to the network and
domain. A computer account is used to validate a computer to the network separately from a user in order to access shared resources.

A computer name can be 15 characters or less and is also followed with a
dollar sign ($). This is an old LAN Manager convention to separate machine ac-
counts from user accounts. Computer accounts can be set with passwords, but
the passwords are used only until the computer is validated by the domain and
a secure channel is created. This is known as *joining* a computer to a domain.
A new password is established when the computer joins the domain. Computers are generally placed in the *Computers* container, although network administrators may place them in an organizational unit.

Listing 10-6 shows a script, available on the companion CD, that creates a
computer account in the *Computers* container. Since I've been harping about not
hard coding paths into your scripts, I use the well-known GUID for the *Computers* container. Since the actual GUID value for the *Computers* container is not

in the ActiveDS.tlb type library, I use a *Const* statement to hold its value. The same is true for the user flags (*UF_**) that also need to be defined.

```
<job id="CreateComputer">
<reference guid="{97D25DB0-0363-11CF-ABC4-02608C9E7553}"/>
<script language="VBScript">
'
' CreateComputer - Creates a computer account
'
' Constants from Active Directory not included in type library
Const ADS_GUID_COMPUTRS_CONTAINER = "aa312825768811d1aded00c04fd8d5cd"
Const UF_WORKSTATION_TRUST_ACCOUNT = &H1000
Const UF_ACCOUNTDISABLE = &H2
Const UF_PASSWD_NOTREQD = &H20


' Computer name
strCompName = "Test1"

' Display info
WScript.Echo "Creating new computer account '" & strCompName & "'..."

' Bind to the RootDSE and get the default domain partition
Set adsRootDSE = GetObject("LDAP://RootDSE")
strDomainDN = adsRootDSE.Get("defaultNamingContext")

' Use WKGUID to bind to Computers container
strGUIDPath = "LDAP://"
strGUIDPath = strGUIDPath & "<WKGUID="
strGUIDPath = strGUIDPath & ADS_GUID_COMPUTRS_CONTAINER
strGUIDPath = strGUIDPath & ","
strGUIDPath = strGUIDPath & strDomainDN
strGUIDPath = strGUIDPath & ">"

' Bind to Computers container
Set adsContainer = GetObject(strGUIDPath)

' GUID binding is very limited, so rebind not using GUID
strADsPath = "LDAP://" & adsContainer.Get("distinguishedName")
Set adsContainer = GetObject(strADsPath)

' Go to the next line if an error occurs
On Error Resume Next

' Create the object in the container
Set adsComputer = adsContainer.Create("computer", "cn=" + strCompName)
```

Listing 10-6 CreateComputer.wsf shows how to create a computer account.

```
' Set the account name for the computer
' Must be 15 characters or less and have a trailing dollar sign
adsComputer.Put "sAMAccountName", strCompName & "$"


' Must specify userAccountControl before applying changes
' since it's read-only after creation


' Set account flag to indicate this is a machine account
adsComputer.Put "userAccountControl", UF_WORKSTATION_TRUST_ACCOUNT Or _
    UF_ACCOUNTDISABLE Or UF_PASSWD_NOTREQD


' Update server with required properties
adsComputer.SetInfo


' Check for errors
If Err.Number <> 0 Then
    ' Check to see whether computer already exists error
    If Err.Number = &H80071392 Then
        ' Display error message and exit
        WScript.Echo "The computer '" & strCompName & "' already exists."
        WScript.Quit 1
    Else
        WScript.Echo "Unexpected error creating computer." & _
            vbNewLine & Err.Description & " (" & Hex(Err.Number) & ")"
        WScript.Quit 1
    End If
End If


' Turn off error handling
On Error GoTo 0


' Set other attributes for the computer object
' Refresh the local cache
adsComputer.GetInfo


' Set a default password. Used only until computer joins domain.
' Must be lowercase
strPassword = strCompName & "$"
strPassword = LCase(strPassword)
adsComputer.SetPassword strPassword


' Enable the account
' Note: IADsUser properties work on computer accounts
adsComputer.AccountDisabled = False


' Apply the properties to the directory
adsComputer.SetInfo
```

(continued)

Listing 10-6 *continued*

```
' Release objects
Set adsComputer = Nothing
Set adsContainer = Nothing

' Finish
WScript.Echo "Computer created successfully."

</script>
</job>
```

When you run the CreateComputer script, a computer account named "Test1" is created in the *Computers* container. Figure 10-4 shows the Properties dialog box for the new computer account in Active Directory Users and Computers.

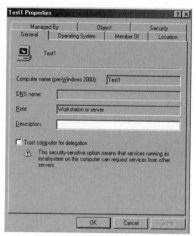

Figure 10-4 Properties dialog box for the new computer account created with the CreateComputer script.

Managing Services

Active Directory uses the concept of a *connection point* to allow services to advertise themselves throughout a network. A connection point is a simple object that represents an instance of a particular service. Many features of Windows 2000 take advantage of connection points, including print queues, shared folder volumes, Windows Sockets, and the Remote Procedure Call (RPC) naming service. Here are some more details about managing the most common services, printer and file sharing.

Managing Print Queues

Listing 10-7 shows the PrintOps script, available on the companion CD, which is a complete printer control tool. The code is self-explanatory, but with it you can list all the print queues and print jobs on a computer and optionally pause and resume printing. You can also purge all print jobs. Here are some examples of its usage:

```
cscript printops.wsf coppersoftware\copper1 /list
cscript printops.wsf coppersoftware\copper1 /pause
cscript printops.wsf coppersoftware\copper1 /resume
cscript printops.wsf coppersoftware\copper1 /flush
```

```
<job id="PrintOps">
<reference guid="{97D25DB0-0363-11CF-ABC4-02608C9E7553}"/>
<script language="VBScript">
'
' PrintOps
' List, pause, resume, and purge print queues
'
Set wshArguments = WScript.Arguments

' Get parameters based on number of arguments
Select Case wshArguments.Count

    Case 1
        strComputer = wshArguments(0)

    Case 2
        strComputer = wshArguments(0)
        strAction = wshArguments(1)

End Select

' Check for no group name or help request
If strComputer = "" Or InStr(1, strGroup, "?", vbTextCompare) > 0 Then

    ' Show usage And quit
    strUsage = "Usage: PrintOps 'domain\computername'"
    strUsage = strUsage & vbCrLf & "                       [ /list   ]"
    strUsage = strUsage & vbCrLf & "                       [ /flush  ]"
    strUsage = strUsage & vbCrLf & "                       [ /pause  ]"
    strUsage = strUsage & vbCrLf & "                       [ /resume ]"
    WScript.Echo strUsage
    WScript.Quit (1)
End If
```

Listing 10-7 PrintOps.wsf shows how to list, pause, resume, and purge jobs   *(continued)*
in print queues.

Listing 10-7 *continued*

```
If strAction = "" Then
    strAction = "/list"
End If

' Figure out action
' Take the left-most 2 characters of the parameter and
' check whether they match into the argument list
nAction = InStr(1, "/f/p/r/l", Left(strAction, 2), vbTextCompare)

' Use NameTranslate to look up the computer in the directory
Set adsNameTranslate = CreateObject("NameTranslate")

' Specify the GC for quick lookups
adsNameTranslate.Init ADS_NAME_INITTYPE_GC, vbNull

' Set the computer name into NameTranslate
' Specify unknown format to have object determine
' Add a dollar sign to indicate a computer account
adsNameTranslate.Set ADS_NAME_TYPE_UNKNOWN, strComputer & "$"

' Get the DN of the computer
strComputerDN = adsNameTranslate.Get(ADS_NAME_TYPE_1779)

' Bind to computer object
Set adsComputer = GetObject("LDAP://" & strComputerDN)

' Enumerate the print queues of this computer
adsComputer.Filter = Array("PrintQueue")

WScript.Echo "Print queues on " & adsComputer.Get("name") & "..."

For Each varPrintQueue In adsComputer

    Set adsPrintQueue = GetObject(varPrintQueue.ADsPath)

    strQueue = adsPrintQueue.Get("Name")
    strQueue = strQueue & vbCrLf & "Model: " & vbTab & _
        adsPrintQueue.Model
    strQueue = strQueue & vbCrLf & "Description: " & vbTab & _
        adsPrintQueue.Description
    strQueue = strQueue & vbCrLf & "Location: " & vbTab & _
        adsPrintQueue.Location
    strQueue = strQueue & vbCrLf & "Path: " & vbTab & _
        adsPrintQueue.PrinterPath
    WScript.Echo strQueue
```

```
' Get an interface to the queue ops
Set adsPrintQueueOps = adsPrintQueue

' Perform an action
Select Case nAction

    Case 1
        ' Flush printer queues
        WScript.Echo "Removing all print jobs from queue..."

        adsPrintQueueOps.Purge

    Case 3
        ' Pause the print queue
        WScript.Echo "Pausing print jobs..."

        adsPrintQueueOps.Pause

    Case 5
        ' Resume the print queue
        WScript.Echo "Resuming print jobs..."

        adsPrintQueueOps.Resume

    Case Else
        ' Some other action, list jobs in queue
        strAction = "Listing all jobs in queues " & adsComputer.Name
        WScript.Echo strAction

        ' Display separator
        WScript.Echo String(Len(strAction), "-")

        ' Skip to the next line on errors
        On Error Resume Next

        For Each adsPrintJob In adsPrintQueueOps.PrintJobs

            strJob = "Job: " & adsPrintJob.Description
            strJob = strJob & vbCrLf & "User: " & adsPrintJob.User
            strJob = strJob & vbCrLf &  "Priority: " & _
                adsPrintJob.Priority
            strJob = strJob & vbCrLf &  "Pages: " & _
                adsPrintJob.TotalPages
            strJob = strJob & vbCrLf &  "Size: " & adsPrintJob.Size
            WScript.Echo strJob
```

(continued)

Listing 10-7 *continued*

```
        Next

        ' Turn error handling back on
        On Error GoTo 0
End Select

' Display Queue Status
Select Case adsPrintQueueOps.status
    Case 0
        strStatus = "Normal"
    Case 1
        strStatus = "Paused "
    Case 2
        strStatus = "Error "
    Case 3
        strStatus = "Pending Deletion "
    Case 4
        strStatus = "Paper Jam "
    Case 5
        strStatus = "Paper Out "
    Case 6
        strStatus = "Manual Feed "
    Case 7
        strStatus = "Paper Problem "
    Case 8
        strStatus = "Offline "
    Case &H100
        strStatus = "I/O Active "
    Case &H200
        strStatus = "Busy "
    Case &H400
        strStatus = "Printing "
    Case &H800
        strStatus = "Output Bin Full "
    Case &H1000
        strStatus = "Not Available "
    Case &H2000
        strStatus = "Waiting "
    Case &H4000
        strStatus = "Processing "
    Case &H8000
        strStatus = "Initializing "
    Case &H1000
        strStatus = "Warming Up "
    Case &H2000
        strStatus = "Toner Low "
```

```
            Case &H4000
                strStatus = "No Toner "
            Case &H8000
                strStatus = "Page Punt"
            Case &H100000
                strStatus = "User Intervention Required"
            Case &H200000
                strStatus = "Out Of Memory "
            Case &H400000
                strStatus = "Door Open "
            Case &H800000
                strStatus = "Server Unknown "
            Case &H1000000
                strStatus = "Power Save "
            Case Else
                strStatus = "Unknown status (" & adsPrintQueueOps.status & ")"
        End Select

WScript.Echo "Status: " & strStatus

Next

WScript.Echo "Finished."

</script>
</job>
```

Volumes

A feature in Active Directory that doesn't get the attention it deserves is *volume* objects. These objects represent shared folders. For example, you can tell someone to access a shared folder on a particular computer using a UNC name such as \\server1\applications. This path works great until \\server1 is taken off line and replaced with \\server2. Users could browse and search the network for shared folders, but that might become incredibly tedious in a large organization with dozens, or even hundreds, of computers.

Just as with printers, Active Directory allows the publishing of shared folders. Unlike printers, however, a shared folder is not contained in a *computer* object hierarchy. Shared folders are represented in Active Directory with objects of the *volume* class. Objects of the *volume* class are very simple, containing just six attributes beyond those specified by the *top* class. Three of the attributes are inherited from the *connectionPoint* class, and three are specified by the *volume* class. Table 10-9 lists these attributes.

Volume Attribute	Source Class	Description
cn	*connectionPoint*	Mandatory single-valued common name
keywords	*connectionPoint*	Multivalued strings indicating keywords to be associated with this volume
managedBy	*connectionPoint*	A DN string pointing to the user managing this volume
contentIndexing-Allowed	*volume*	Boolean value indicating whether content is indexed on this volume
lastContentIndexed	*volume*	Timestamp for when volume content was last indexed
uNCName	*volume*	Mandatory string value containing the UNC path of the volume, for example: \\servername\foldername

Table 10-9 Attributes of the *volume* class.

Publishing and Using Shared Folders

Unlike printers, there is no provision to automatically publish a shared folder in Active Directory. The *volume* objects representing shared folders can be created only at the domain root or within an organizational unit. This makes sense because administrators can group all the required resources for a department into a single organizational unit. Using the Find option in the Directory folder of My Network Places, users can query for available shared folders. Users can also browse the Directory namespace looking for shared folders, which is much faster than scanning lists of servers. Once a shared folder is found you can open a window or map a drive letter to the folder. You can map a drive letter to a shared folder programmatically by using the *WshNetwork* object provided by Windows Script.

Mapping Drive Letters to Shared Folders

Listing 10-8 shows a script, available on the companion CD, that enumerates shared folders that are published in Active Directory and maps them to drive letters. The sample is not picky; it maps all the shared folders it can find in the root of the directory. The script uses the *uNCName* attribute of the *volume* object to discover the UNC pathname of the shared folder. The *WshNetwork* object uses this pathname to perform the mapping operation between a drive letter and the folder.

Windows Management Instrumentation

Although ADSI was designed for directory management, it also includes a number of network management features. Network management is usually concerned with enumeration of the devices connected to the network and the administration of those devices. To aid network management, Microsoft is focusing on a technology, similar in architecture to ADSI, called *Windows Management Instrumentation* (*WMI*).

WMI is Microsoft's implementation of the Web-Based Enterprise Management (WBEM) initiative of the Distributed Management Task Force (DMTF), an industry coalition formed to provide industry standards and recommendations to reduce enterprise management costs. What that means for developers is an object model that enables easier management of network resources. While primarily targeted to network administrators, WMI is useful to all developers of directory-aware products.

With WMI, you can access and manipulate not only network device information on servers but on individual workstations as well. With the object model, you can access information about a computer's hard disks, getting information about file formats, free space, and security information, for example. Setting security on computer and network objects programmatically is made much easier. As an example, network administrators can use WMI to enumerate all the computers in the enterprise that have a particular video driver that needs updating.

WMI is extremely powerful and, while outside the scope of this book, it warrants review by developers of network and directory-aware applications.

```vbscript
<job id="MapSharedFolders">
<reference guid="{97D25DB0-0363-11CF-ABC4-02608C9E7553}"/>
<script language="VBScript">
'
' MapSharedFolders - Enumerates all the volume objects at
' the root of the directory and maps them to drive letters
'
' Create the WSH Network object that will perform the mapping
Set objWshNetwork = WScript.CreateObject("WScript.Network")

' Connect to the LDAP server's root object
Set objADsRootDSE = GetObject("LDAP://RootDSE")
```

Listing 10-8 MapSharedFolder.wsf shows how to enumerate shared folders   *(continued)*
and map them to drive letters.

Listing 10-8 *continued*

```
' Form an ADsPath string to the name of the default domain
strPath = "LDAP://" + objADsRootDSE.Get("defaultNamingContext")

' Connect to the directory specified in the path
Set objADsContainer = GetObject(strPath)

' Only enumerate shared folders
objADsContainer.Filter = Array("volume")

' For performance reasons, retrieve only the uNCName attribute
objADsContainer.Hints = Array("uNCName")

' Display ADsPath being used
WScript.Echo "Enumerating all shared folders in " & objADsContainer.Name

' Enumerate through all the existing drives to find the last drive letter
Set objFileSystem = CreateObject("Scripting.FileSystemObject")

For Each objDrive in objFileSystem.Drives
    strLastDriveLetter = objDrive.DriveLetter
Next

' Loop through each object in the container
For Each objADs In objADsContainer
    ' Get the UNC path and store it
    strSharePath = objADs.Get("uNCName")

    ' Display the name of the object and the path
    WScript.Echo objADs.Name & vbTab & strSharePath

    ' Increment the drive letter
    ' BUGBUG:  Will fail after Z!
    strLastDriveLetter = chr( 1 + Asc(strLastDriveLetter) )

    ' Append a colon to the drive letter
    strDriveLetter = strLastDriveLetter & ":"

    ' Map the share to a drive letter
    objWshNetwork.MapNetworkDrive strDriveLetter, strSharePath
Next

' Display all current network drive mappings
WScript.Echo "Current network drive mappings:"

' Enumerate drives (0 is letter, 0+1 is UNC path)
Set objWshNetworkDrives = objWshNetwork.EnumNetworkDrives
```

```
For numDrive = 0 to objWshNetworkDrives.Count - 1 Step 2
' Display the drive letter and path
    WScript.Echo objWshNetworkDrives.Item(numDrive) & vbTab & _
        objWshNetworkDrives.Item(numDrive + 1)
Next

' Finished
WScript.Echo "Finished."
</script>
</job>
```

The Net Use command allows you to map a shared folder to the next available drive letter using an asterisk (*). In the MapSharedFolder script, however, you must supply a drive letter and colon character (i.e., F:) when calling the *MapNetworkDrive* method.

Summary

In this chapter I hope you have learned the power of using Windows Script and ADSI to perform everyday management of Active Directory. In the next and final chapter, I'll show how Active Directory can be accessed from a Web browser. Throughout this book, I've mentioned some of the changes and improvements that are being planned for the next version of Active Directory, and I'll cover those in more detail in the next chapter as well.

11

The Web and Beyond

As more companies manage information such as expense reports, time reporting, sick leave, and vacation requests through e-mail and corporate intranets, the need for secure and robust Web database applications increases. With Active Directory, redundant databases can be eliminated, and with the security features of Microsoft Windows 2000, a "single sign-on" can be achieved so that a user can easily access information stored remotely. When you combine Active Directory, the robust security and authentication features in Windows 2000, and the capabilities of Active Server Pages (ASP), you can create useful applications that use a Web browser as a common client.

In this final chapter I want to apply what I've covered in this book to the ASP programming environment. Up till now, I've shown applications for Active Directory written in C++, Visual Basic, or VBScript. In this chapter, I'll take the VBScript Phone sample shown in Chapter 5 and move it to the ASP environment. Also in this chapter, I'll describe issues related to working with Active Directory on versions of Windows before Windows 2000 and then look ahead at what's up for Active Directory in the next release of Windows.

Active Directory and ASP

ASP is the technology used in Microsoft Internet Information Services (IIS) that allows HTML pages to be created programmatically on the server. Developing an ASP application consists of creating .asp files that contain script code mixed with HTML. When a client requests an .asp file, IIS processes the script code on the server and returns HTML to the client.

ASP can work with any language that is supported by Windows Script. Traditionally, VBScript is preferred for server-side scripts, and JScript is used for client-side scripting because more browsers support it. For creating scripts on the server you can use whichever language you please. I've used VBScript in the sample for this chapter.

As with Windows Script, ASP allows you to access any COM object on the server that supports Automation—for example ActiveX Data Objects (ADO). The ability to access functionality and data on the server and return results as plain HTML is a powerful model. All the client needs to interact with the server is a modern browser. This capability makes ASP well suited for working with Active Directory.

Listings 11-1 and 11-2 show the .asp files included on the companion CD that are used to create an ASP version of the Phone sample presented in Chapter 5, "Searching Active Directory." This sample searches Active Directory for *user* or *contact* objects that match a given last name. For the objects that match, the full name and telephone number are displayed.

I've spilt the ASP version of the Phone sample into two pages. The first page, Default.asp, uses a simple form in which a user can enter the last name to look up. The second page, Results.asp, performs the search and displays the results in a table. Here is the code for the two pages:

```
<%@ Language=VBScript %>
<HTML>
<HEAD>
<TITLE>Phone Number Search</TITLE>
<LINK rel="stylesheet" type="text/css" href="styles.css">
</HEAD>
<BODY>
<H1>Search for Phone Number</H1>
<FORM method=GET action="results.asp" id="frmSearch">
<P>Enter the last name of the person to look up.</P>
<P>
    Name:
    <INPUT id="txtName"
           name="Name"
           title="Enter the last name of the person to look up"
           >
    <INPUT id="btnSearch"
           type="submit"
           title="Search for matching names"
           value="Search"
           >
</P>
</FORM>
</HTML>
```

Listing 11-1 Default.asp asks the user for a name to search for.

```
<%@ Language=VBScript %>
<HTML>
<HEAD>
<TITLE>Phone Number Search Results</TITLE>
<LINK rel="stylesheet" type="text/css" href="styles.css">
</HEAD>
<BODY>
<h1>Phone Number Search Results</h1>
<P>Search results for "<%=Request.QueryString ("Name")%>"</P>
<P><A href="default.asp">Search again</A></P>
<TABLE class=ResultsTable>
    <THEAD>
    <TR>
        <TH>Name</TH>
        <TH>Phone Number</TH></TR>
    </THEAD>
    <TBODY>
<%
' Build the query string
' First, need to discover the local global catalog server
Set adsRootDSE = GetObject("GC://RootDSE")

' Form an ADsPath string to the DN of the root of the
' Active Directory forest
strADsPath = "GC://" & adsRootDSE.Get("rootDomainNamingContext")

' Wrap the ADsPath with angle brackets to form the base string
strBase = "<" & strADsPath & ">"

' Release the ADSI object, no longer needed
Set adsRootDSE = Nothing

' Specify the LDAP filter
' First, indicate the category of objects to be searched
' (all people, not just users)
strObjects = "(objectCategory=person)"

' Get the name to search for from the URL
strPerson = Request.QueryString("Name")

' If the given name is blank, then filter on all people
If (strPerson = "") Then
    strName = "(sn=*)"
Else
```

Listing 11-2 Results.asp retrieves the name to search for and uses ADO *(continued)* to search the directory and display matching names and telephone numbers.

Listing 11-2 *continued*

```
      strName = "(sn=" & strPerson & "*)"
End If

' Add the two filters together
strFilter = "(&" & strObjects & strName & ")"

' Set the attributes for the recordset to contain
' We're interested in the common name and telephone number
strAttributes = "cn,telephoneNumber"

' Specify the scope (base, onelevel, subtree)
strScope = "subtree"

' Create ADO connection using the ADSI OLE DB provider
Set adoConnection = Server.CreateObject ("ADODB.Connection")
adoConnection.Open "Provider=ADsDSOObject;"

' Create ADO commmand object and associate with the connection
Set adoCommand = Server.CreateObject ("ADODB.Command")
adoCommand.ActiveConnection = adoConnection

' Create the command string using the four parts
adoCommand.CommandText = strBase & ";" & strFilter & ";" & _
    strAttributes & ";" & strScope

' Set the number of records in the recordset logical page
adoCommand.Properties("Page Size") = 20

' Set the maximum result size
adoCommand.Properties("Size Limit") = 20

' Sort the results based on the cn attribute
adoCommand.Properties("Sort On") = "cn"

' Execute the query for the user in the directory
Set adoRecordSet = adoCommand.Execute

If adoRecordSet.EOF Then
    Response.Write "</TBODY><THEAD><TH>No names found</TH></THEAD>"
Else
```

```
    ' Loop through all the returned records
    While Not adoRecordSet.EOF
        ' Display the row using the selected fields
        Response.Write "<TR>"
        Response.Write "<TD>" & adoRecordSet.Fields("cn") & "</TD>"

        ' Check to see if telephone number field is null
        If IsNull( adoRecordSet.Fields("telephoneNumber") ) Then
            Response.Write "<TD>(number not listed)</TD>"
        Else
        ' Retrieve the telephone number and add to the display line
        Response.Write "<TD>" & _
            adoRecordSet.Fields("telephoneNumber") & "</TD>"
        End If

        ' End the row
        Response.Write "</TR>"

        ' Advance to the next record
        adoRecordSet.MoveNext
    Wend
End If

' Close the ADO connection
adoConnection.Close
%>
</TBODY>
</TABLE>
</BODY>
</HTML>
```

As you can tell from these listings, writing VBScript for ASP pages is not much different from writing it for the Windows Script Host environment. Essentially these listings are HTML code with script code enclosed within <% %> tags. Output is generated using the *Write* method of the *Response* object. The statement <%=expression%> is a shortcut to using the *Response.Write* method. This statement indicates to ASP that it should evaluate the expression and output the results. The output is placed in the resulting page, which is then downloaded to the browser. In this example, the name and telephone number are displayed in an HTML table.

Figure 11-1 shows how this sample looks when hosted on a server running IIS.

Figure 11-1 ASP version of the Phone sample.

You should consider several issues when creating ASP pages, some general and others specific to ADSI and Active Directory.

■ **Understand the security context.** Unless authenticated, scripts processed by ASP are executed in the context of the user account specified in the IIS Web site configuration. Usually this is the IUSR_*machinename* account, which has limited security privileges. These security limitations can generate errors when attempting to modify Active Directory objects. I'll discuss authentication in more detail in the next section.

■ **Use *Server.CreateObject* instead of *CreateObject*.** While either method will work, the *CreateObject* method of the *Server* object is more efficient because with it, ASP can track the object and is aware of the threading model that the object uses. Using *Server.CreateObject* prevents the blocking of threads that occurs when the VBScript *CreateObject* function is used.

- ■ **Minimize Context Switches.** The server processes each script block within an ASP page before the page is downloaded to the client. Each script block loads and then unloads the scripting engine, a process that can be inefficient when it's required many times. Grouping server-side scripts into large blocks using the *<SCRIPT RUNAT=SERVER> </SCRIPT>* or *<% %>* tags results in faster processing and less overhead on the server.

Authentication

As I mentioned earlier, the execution context for ASP pages is generally the IUSR_*machinename* account, where *machinename* is the name of the Web server. To protect itself from outside attack, this account usually has limited security privileges. In the ASP Phone sample, the security privileges for this account are not an issue because the Domain Users group (of which the IUSR_*machinename* account is a member) has privileges to read *user* and *contact* data. However, the ability to read the data is just a default setting. Some Active Directory configurations may have tighter security that requires higher privileges. More commonly, while reading data is allowed, changing Active Directory data is restricted to members of the appropriate administrators group or other designated accounts. In the case of displaying a *user* object, the person represented by that object is allowed to update his or her own personal properties.

The problem you face is figuring out which user is accessing the ASP page. The process of validating the user or client, known as *authentication,* allows IIS to execute ASP pages in the security context of the user or client requesting the page.

Integrated Windows Authentication

By default, IIS 5 in Windows 2000 uses *anonymous authentication*, which uses the IUSR_*machinename* security context. To force IIS to authenticate a remote user securely, you set the properties for the Web site (or directory or page) in the Authentication Methods dialog box for IIS Web site properties. Clear the Anonymous Access check box and select the Integrated Windows Authentication check box, as shown in Figure 11-2.

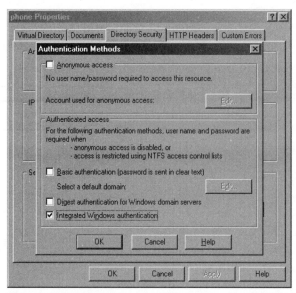

Figure 11-2 Using Integrated Windows authentication for Web sites.

Integrated Windows authentication was previously known as NT LAN Manager (NTLM) and Windows NT Challenge/Response authentication. Windows 2000 and IIS 5 support both NTLM Challenge/Response authentication and the native Kerberos v5 security protocol. Incorporating Kerberos is easier and has the added advantage of verifying the server to the client to ensure the server is not being impersonated.

Figure 11-3 shows an overview of the steps involved with Web authentication using NTLM Challenge/Response.

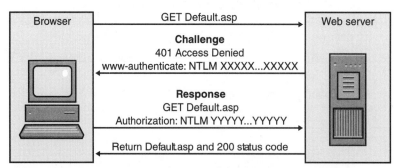

Figure 11-3 Web authentication using NTLM Challenge/Response.

First the browser client makes a request for a resource such as a Web page. The request is made as an HTTP *GET* request. If the resource is restricted and requires authentication, the Web server returns an HTTP *error response* to the browser. In this case, a 401 Access Denied response is sent along with two HTTP header packets—one package is a negotiate request, and the other is an NTLM challenge header. The browser creates a response on the basis of the supported authentication methods and the challenge. The response includes the credentials of the current user, but it does not include the user's password. This means that anyone sniffing the network packets cannot gain access to the actual password. This response is included in another HTTP *GET* request. The server processes the request and authenticates the response. If the credentials of the user allow access to the selected resource, the HTTP request is accepted and the page is returned to the browser. If the user does not have access, a 403 error response is returned to the browser, which means the credentials were valid but not sufficient to allow access. Depending on the browser, a password dialog box might be displayed to the user, as shown in Figure 11-4.

Figure 11-4 Enter Network Password dialog box.

Integrated Windows authentication has some limitations, namely that only Microsoft Internet Explorer supports it. Also, it cannot be used when a firewall or proxy server re-creates the HTTP headers because to do so would compromise the security of the authentication. For corporate intranets, re-creating HTTP headers is generally not a problem, but when creating ADSI applications for use outside a corporate network, other methods must be used.

Introduction to Kerberos

Windows 2000 introduced a new security protocol to the Windows family, *Kerberos*. Originally developed at the Massachusetts Institute of Technology and defined in RFC 1510 and RFC 1964, Kerberos is the default authentication protocol for Windows 2000 workstations and servers. Windows 2000 implements version 5 of Kerberos.

A notable difference between the Kerberos and NTLM protocols (also supported in Windows 2000) is the concept of *mutual authentication*. With NTLM, the client application sends the user's credentials to the server. If the credentials match what's stored in the security database (Active Directory in Windows 2000, or the Security Accounts Manger in Windows NT 4.0), the user is authenticated. Thus, the server "knows" who the client is, but the client does not know who the server is. A rouge server could request credentials from the user and retain them for future malicious use. With mutual authentication under Kerberos, the server must authenticate itself to the client before the client presents the user's credentials.

Electronic security works best when it's kept simple. Simplicity provides fewer weak spots to exploit. Kerberos works on a simple "ticket" scheme. When a client presents credentials to the authentication service (AS) running on a Windows 2000 domain controller, the AS verifies the credentials with Active Directory. If they match, the AS sends a *ticket* back to the client. A ticket is just a packet of data that the Kerberos subsystems understand. The ticket contains, among other things, the client's identity (not the credentials, however), a session key, and a timestamp. All the sensitive parts of a ticket are encrypted with the server's key.

The first ticket issued by the AS is a special ticket, known as the *ticket granting ticket* (TGT). This ticket is used to access the Key Distribution Center (KDC). The KDC is another security subsystem of Windows 2000. Its role is to validate access to the services available on the server and supply cryptography keys to clients to secure their communications. ·

After the client has been authenticated by the server and holds a TGT, it can then submit that ticket to the KDC when it wants to access a secure service, such as IIS on another server. When the KDC gets the service request and TGT from the client, it issues a *service ticket* (ST) that contains a session key. The ST is sort of a "hall pass" that allows the client to validate itself to the service on another server. Service tickets can expire, in which case the client asks the KDC to issue a new ticket.

The client presents the ST to IIS and, in return, IIS sends back an authentication packet that is used by the client to validate the service. Then the client can communicate with the service normally—in this case issuing HTTP requests. The Kerberos Tray tool, part of the *Microsoft Windows 2000 Server Resource Kit*, is useful for viewing what tickets the current client holds. Here's an example of Kerberos Tray.

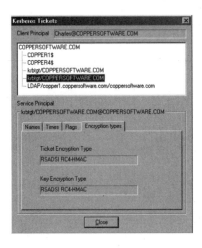

Basic Authentication

Windows 2000 and IIS 5 support *Basic authentication* as another way to validate a user. This method uses the HTTP header to send the user name and password to the server for validation. Most Web browsers support Basic authentication as part of the HTTP protocol defined in RFC 2617. The password is encoded using the simple binary BASE64 encoding scheme. While not exactly readable, this scheme is easy to decode by someone trying to get at your password. As such, Windows 2000 considers the password to be sent in "clear text," which can be dangerous if compromised.

By combining Basic authentication with the Secure Sockets Layer (SSL) and the Transport Layer Security (TLS) protocols, you can achieve a moderate degree of protection. Nonetheless, there are issues with Basic authentication and site design resulting in the browser continuing to send the clear text password after the initial authentication without using the SSL channel for protection. Because the integrity of the account password is vital to Windows security, I can't recommend Basic authentication, particularly when more secure methods exists.

COM+ Components

Sometimes, regardless of who is requesting an operation, you need to execute a script in a high-level security context. Operations such as creating or deleting users require Administrator access by default. Instead of assigning permissions to users to perform restricted operations, you can create a COM+ component with high-level access on the Web server to work on behalf of the user.

COM+ allows developers to partition their application into components and give each its own security context in a transaction managed environment on a server. By encapsulating the functionality of the application into a component, you can instruct Windows to execute the component using *impersonation*. The component is registered with COM+ and given a user account and password that's used only to execute that component. The ASP page creates an instance of the component and uses it to access directory data. Using a component like this is handy when you need to circumvent the built-in security in an isolated fashion.

For example, you could create a COM+ component that allows the creation of computer accounts over an intranet application. When someone needs to add a new computer to the forest, he or she could use a Web site that asks for the computer account name and offers to reset an existing account or add a new one. Because the user might be using an older operating system to make the request (after all, they are creating a new computer account!), secure forms of authentication may not be available.

The solution would be to take the program that creates or resets computer accounts and add it as a COM+ component to the Web server that provides the interface. The COM+ application is assigned to a user account with sufficient rights to create or reset computer accounts. The ASP code can then reference the component, passing it the computer name and other information provided by the user and returning the status of the operation when complete.

Tip   The Domain Admins group by default is allowed to create computer accounts and many other tasks in Active Directory. Assigning a high level of access to a process that only creates computer accounts is probably overkill, and the application might intentionally, or unintentionally, wreak havoc. A better solution is to create a specific user account named Computer Accounts Manager and give that account only the rights necessary to create and reset computer accounts. Use that account and its password when setting up the COM+ application.

You'll rarely need to create a COM+ component. Through delegation and careful security planning, it's usually not necessary to impersonate high-level accounts to perform directory operations. Understanding and using the built-in security features of Windows will meet most requirements.

Note   While I'd like to cover all the many cool and interesting things that ASP and COM+ offer developers of directory-enabled applications, I can't do so and still publish this book in a reasonable time frame. A book that I've found useful is *Alex Homer's Professional ASP 3.0 Web Techniques* by (guess who) Alex Homer (WROX, 2000). Another good source of information is *Designing Secure Web-Based Applications for Microsoft Windows 2000* by Michael Howard (Microsoft Press, 2000). This book is particularly helpful for understanding the issues of security and authentication for Web-based ADSI applications.

Windows Platform Considerations

Developers of Active Directory applications need to ensure that their applications run on various versions of Windows. In a perfect world, everyone would use the latest version of Windows and whenever a new version was released it would be instantly propagated to all computers. The reality is that many organizations still run Windows 98 or even Windows 95 on most of their desktop computers. Upgrading these machines to Windows 2000 would give network administrators more stability and better management of resources, but upgrades aren't always practical.

In many cases, applications developed to work with Active Directory will need to run on various versions of Windows, and the developers of those applications must take into account the different levels of API support that are available with older versions of Windows.

Installing new technologies on older versions of Windows is one of the toughest tasks that Microsoft faces. Trust me, I dealt with this issue when I was working on Active Accessibility. Because of the naming of ADSI, many developers believe that installing the ADSI package is all that is required to work with Active Directory. However, ADSI provides only a portion of what's needed.

Active Directory has its own set of components, which includes the various administrative programming interfaces, user interface resources such as dialog boxes and menus, and functions that support low-level access to Active Directory (*DsXXX* functions) and extend the Windows shell namespace to allow browsing the directory. These components and ADSI are part of Windows 2000 and the forthcoming release of Windows, code-named "Whistler."

You can download the latest version of ADSI for various platforms and languages at *http://www.microsoft.com/adsi/* or *http://www.microsoft.com/windows2000/*. However, this download includes only the ADSI components and the LDAP provider; it does not include the modules for the Active Directory functions.

To solve this problem, Microsoft provides the Active Directory Client. This package updates previous versions of Windows to include the ADSI components and Active Directory components. This package also contains components that rely on Active Directory to function—the Distributed File System, for example—and provides a specialized user interface designed to search for Active Directory objects. An example of this UI is the Find Printer tool on the Find option on the Start menu.

The package for Windows 95 and Windows 98, named DSClient.exe, is available in the Clients\Win9x folder on the Windows 2000 Server and Windows 2000 Advanced Server CD-ROMs. DSClient.exe is also available on this book's companion CD in the DSClients folder.

Consumer Versions of Windows

With Windows Millennium Edition (Me), the recent upgrade to Windows 98, Microsoft made a major change to its support policy. Windows Me marks a clear separation between business and consumer operating systems. Officially, Microsoft does not support ADSI on Windows Me. That's not to say ADSI won't work, but since Windows Me is intended for home use only, there isn't specific ADSI support available.

If you are planning on using Windows Me at home and dialing into your company's network via RAS or VPN, be aware of this limitation.

Windows XP Home Edition is slated to be the replacement for Windows Me. Although Windows XP Home Edition is in beta testing as of this writing, I would expect that ADSI will remain unsupported for this and future releases of consumer-oriented versions of Windows.

A version of the Active Directory Client for Windows NT 4.0 was released in February 2001 and is included on the book's companion CD in the DSClients folder. It is also expected to be included in Service Pack 7 for Windows NT 4.0. The latest version of the Active Directory Client can be found at *http://www.microsoft.com/windows2000/*.

Using the WinNT Provider with Active Directory

In Windows NT 4.0, domain data was contained in the Security Account Manager (SAM) database. This data includes information about computers and users, groups, security settings, and shared printers and folders.

Before ADSI was available, applications could call various APIs to create users, manipulate printers, and perform other operations on items contained in the SAM database. In fact, the WinNT provider calls these APIs (which have the format *Net*XXX) to perform the actions required. This use of the WinNT provider is a good example of how ADSI provides a common, object-oriented programming model on top of language-specific, monolithic APIs.

Now that ADSI is established, a lot of code, particularly network administration scripts and ASP-based applications, use the WinNT provider to work with Windows NT 4.0 domains. That code will continue to work with Active Directory under Windows 2000 because Active Directory is backward compatible with Windows NT 4.0. However, new features in Active Directory are not available through the *Net*XXX APIs, so applications using the WinNT provider cannot access them.

While it's not necessary to rush out and start converting your code that uses the *Net*XXX APIs or the WinNT provider, you should follow the example in this book and use the LDAP provider exclusively to access Active Directory. Obviously, in a mixed Windows NT and Windows 2000 environment, you must use the WinNT provider, but be sure to let the IT department know of all the nifty features you could have in your application if it didn't have to limit itself.

ADSI Versions

Windows 2000 includes an updated version of ADSI 2.5. This version includes support for Active Directory tombstone objects and various bug fixes.

The Windows 2000 version of ADSI also includes support for the *NameTranslate*, *WinNTSystemInfo*, and *ADSystemInfo* objects. This support is not included in the basic ADSI 2.5 package for Windows 95, Windows 98, and Windows NT 4.0 because the necessary Directory Service (*Ds*XXX) APIs are not available. Installing the Active Directory Client provides support for the *NameTranslate* object.

Windows 2000 Service Pack 1 contains a new option that speeds access to known directory objects. In a program using the LDAP provider, if the binding string includes a server name, you can improve performance by using the *ADS_SERVER_BIND* flag with the *ADsOpenObject* function or the *OpenDSObject* method of the *IADsOpenDSObject* interface. This option is discussed in Chapter 4.

Note A *tombstone* is the information left behind when Active Directory is told to delete an object. Instead of deleting an object's entire content, Active Directory moves it to a Deleted Objects folder and sets the *isDeleted* attribute to True. Although most of the object's attributes are deleted to save space, others that uniquely identify the object, such as *objectGUID* and *RDN,* are retained. After 60 days (the default value), the object is completely removed from the directory. By not deleting the object immediately, Active Directory prevents fragmentation of the NTDS.dit file, which improves performance for very large directories.

Determining the ADSI Version

How do you know whether the computer your application is running on has the correct components? The ADSI resource kit, part of the ADSI 2.5 SDK included on the companion CD, comes with an unsupported but useful component, contained in the file ADsVersion.dll, that you can use to determine the version of ADSI. This component exposes the *ADsVersion* object and associated *IADsVersion* interface. This interface includes properties that contain ADSI version information. These properties are listed in Table 11-1.

IADsVersion Property	Data Type	Description
GetVersion	String	Complete ADSI version number in text form
GetMajorVersion	Long	ADSI major version number
GetMinorVersion	Long	ADSI minor version number
GetLocale	String	Current locale identifier (two-character string)

Table 11-1 The properties of the *IADsVersion* interface, used to obtain version information about ADSI.

The *IADsVersion* interface also contains a *Connect* method for gathering the information remotely. *Connect* specifies which computer to retrieve ADSI version information from. No error is generated when a remote computer cannot be contacted.

Listing 11-3 shows code from the VBScript sample included on the companion CD that uses the *ADsVersion* object and displays the information available. In order for this script to run properly, the file ADsVersion.dll must be registered using Regsvr32.exe.

```
' ADsVersion.vbs
' Display ADSI version information
' Requires AdsVersion.dll to be registered

' Create ADsVersion object and catch any errors
On Error Resume Next
Set objADsVersion = CreateObject("ADsVersion")

' Check for error
If Err.Number <> 0 Then
    ' CreateObject failed
    WScript.Echo "Error getting ADSI version information." & _
        vbNewLine & "Ensure AdsVersion.dll is registered."
Else
    ' Prompt for computer to query
    strComputer = InputBox( _
        "Computer Name to get ADSI version:" & vbCrLf & _
        "(enter * for local machine):", "ADSI Version", "*")

    If strComputer <> "" Then

        If strComputer = "*" Then
            strComputer = ""
        End If
        ' Query the computer
        ' Note: If the remote computer cannot be contacted, no error
        ' is generated and version data will be incorrect
        objADsVersion.Connect strComputer

        ' Build string with version data
        strVersionInfo = "ADSI Version Information" & vbNewLine
        strVersionInfo = strVersionInfo & "Computer: " & strComputer & _
            vbNewLine
        strVersionInfo = strVersionInfo & "Version String: " & _
            objADsVersion.GetVersion & vbNewLine
```

Listing 11-3 ADsVersion.vbs uses the *ADsVersion* object to determine the ADSI version installed on the specified computer.   *(continued)*

Listing 11-3 *continued*

```
        strVersionInfo = strVersionInfo & "Major Version Number: " & _
            objADsVersion.GetMajorVersion & vbNewLine
        strVersionInfo = strVersionInfo & "Minor Version Number: " & _
            objADsVersion.GetMinorVersion & vbNewLine
        strVersionInfo = strVersionInfo & "Locale: " & _
            objADsVersion.GetLocale


        ' Display the string
        WScript.Echo strVersionInfo
    End If
End If
```

Figure 11-5 shows the information that is displayed when you run this script.

Figure 11-5 Output of the ADsVersion.vbs sample.

A modified version of this program, named ADsClientVersion.wsf, is also included on the companion CD. In addition to determining ADSI version information, this expanded version gathers Windows Script and operating system information.

Whistler

The next version of Windows 2000, code-named "Whistler," is in beta testing as of this writing. The server editions of Whistler will contain a new release of Active Directory that is expected to contain a number of enhancements and new features. Here is a partial list of what Whistler is expected to include as far as ADSI and Active Directory support is concerned:

- **Dynamic objects and dynamic auxiliary classes**   Provides support for directory objects that have a specified lifetime.

- **Application Directory Partitions**   New partitions (or naming-contexts) can be created within Active Directory that have their own replication properties and schedule.

- **A new object class named *inetOrgPerson***   This new class, defined in RFC 2798, allows for better interoperability between Active Directory and third-party LDAP directories and also provides secure validatation of e-commerce customers.

- **Virtual list view (VLV) searches**   VLV searches instruct Active Directory to return a portion of an entire result set.

- **Attribute Scoped Query searches**   Attribute Scoped Query searches return objects referenced in a multivalued attribute stored in the base object.

- **Ability to turn off referral generation by the server**   By using the extended LDAP control *LDAP_SERVER_DOMAIN_SCOPE_OID* when a search is conducted against Active Directory in Whistler, the server will not bother to generate referrals. In most cases referrals will be ignored by the client, so this can improve search performance. ADSI will automatically use this extended control when searches specify the *ADS_CHASE_REFERRALS_NEVER* flag.

- **Ability to reverse, or roll-back, schema modifications**

- **Improved universal groups**   Groups are no longer limited to 5,000 members. In addition, replication issues are eased by replicating group membership changes on a *per-value* basis rather than a *per-attribute* basis. However, this improvement requires that all the domain controllers in a forest are running Whistler.

- **User interface improvements**   Whistler includes a radical change to the object picker dialog box that makes it more efficient for large networks. Administrators can pick multiple objects in the snap-ins and edit them as a group. Also, common queries such as finding printers can be saved.

- **New security protocols**   LDAP, and thus ADSI, now support the TLS and Digest Authentication (DIGEST-MD5 SASL) methods for better integration with the Windows security system. Additionally, the default security for many directory objects is increased

I'd love to discuss all of these new features in depth, but they are still being tested, and how they appear in the final product might be different from how I've described them above. However, I do want to cover a few of these changes in more detail—dynamic objects, application partitions, the *inetOrgPerson* class, virtual list view searching, and user interface enhancements.

Dynamic Objects

At the beginning of this book, I mentioned that directory data is relatively static. Directories traditionally have been poor hosts to data that is changed frequently or has a limited lifetime. With the release of Whistler, however, Active Directory will provide more support for dynamic data using a feature named *dynamic objects*. By using a new auxiliary class, you can create a class that contains a time-to-live (TTL) value for a directory object. The TTL specifies, in seconds, how long the particular instance of the object should remain in the directory. When the TTL reaches zero, the instance is deleted.

The network service that requires the dynamic data is, in effect, off-loading garbage collection to Active Directory. A good example of this might be a DHCP address lease. When a networked computer requests a TCP/IP address, the DHCP server could create a dynamic object that contains information about the address being leased and set an expiration value. Unless the machine refreshed the lease, and the DHCP server in turn refreshed the dynamic object, the object would be deleted. Clients could refresh the TTL by directly updating the attribute or by performing an LDAP extended operation.

Classes of dynamic objects are created by including a new auxiliary class in the schema when the class is created. This auxiliary class is called *dynamicObject*. This auxiliary class adds an optional attribute to the newly created class called *entryTTL,* which is the time-to-live value expressed in seconds. Since it's impractical to have Active Directory update the value of this attribute every second, *entryTTL* is implemented as a constructed attribute, meaning that its value is computed. When a client accesses *entryTTL*, Active Directory looks at another attribute of the *dynamicObject* class, *ms-DS-Entry-Time-To-Die*, which is the absolute time for when the object will be deleted (unless refreshed). Active Directory then subtracts the current time from the absolute time and returns the difference as the number of seconds.

Not only can new classes be dynamic, but existing objects can be made dynamic as well. You do this by adding the *dynamicObject* auxiliary class name to the existing object's *objectClass* attribute. At the same time, you also set the value for the TTL.

Dynamic objects are much like ordinary objects with regard to searching or enumeration. A minor difference is that when the TTL expires and the object is deleted by Active Directory, no tombstone is left behind. Also, you can create dynamic container objects, but they may contain only dynamic objects. This makes sense because you wouldn't want Active Directory deleting your static directory object just because the dynamic container got blown away.

> **Note**   While the *dynamicObject* auxiliary class is usually added to make a limited-lifetime object, Active Directory in Whistler will allow any auxiliary class to be attached to an existing object. This feature is known as *dynamic auxiliary classes.* The new auxiliary class is added as a value to the *objectClass* attribute. To keep track of just the structural classes, a new optional attribute, *structuralObjectClass,* is defined as an optional attribute of the *top* class. This attribute contains nothing but the names of the structural classes that define the object.

Refreshing Dynamic Objects

The TTL value for dynamic objects can range from 1 second to 1 year. However, the object can stay in the directory indefinitely as long as it's refreshed before the TTL value is 0 and the object expires. The object is refreshed either by directly modifying the *entryTTL* attribute with a new value or by using an extended LDAP control.

You can find out whether the server you're communicating with can refresh dynamic objects by checking the *supportedExtension* attribute of the *RootDSE* object. This multivalued attribute lists the extended operations that the server supports. The dynamic refresh operation is listed with the object identifier (OID) of 1.3.6.1.4.1.1466.101.119.1. When the object is refreshed using the extended operation, a value is sent from the client to the server specifying the new TTL. As stipulated in RFC 2589, however, the server can reject the client-specified value and return instead a value that it assigns. A rejection such as this might occur because of the server's workload or because the TTL value requested by the client is outside the minimum and maximum limits defined for the server.

> **Note** More information about dynamic objects can be found in RFC 2589, "Lightweight Directory Access Protocol (v3): Extensions for Dynamic Directory Services."

Application Partitions

I bet you're thinking about the replication impact of dynamic data. Wouldn't the constant creation and deletion of short-lived objects generate a lot of replication traffic? Generally, yes, but Whistler also includes a feature named *application partitions* (also known as *non-domain naming contexts*, or NDNC) that can be used to cordon off dynamic data from more traditional and static directory data.

In Whistler, you cannot create dynamic objects in the configuration or the schema partition. This limitation makes perfect sense because those partitions replicate to all the domain controllers in the forest. You wouldn't want data that changes frequently to be replicated to hundreds of domain controllers, often in remote locations and connected by slow links.

By using application partitions, a directory-enabled application can store static or dynamic data and finely control or prevent its replication throughout the forest. This allows data to be located only where it's needed, reducing the effect of replication traffic on the network. The use of an application partition is particularly well suited to dynamic data that changes more often than the average replication latency of the configuration partition. You can still take advantage of Active Directory's replication infrastructure, but you set the rules.

An application partition can contain any type of object with the exception of security principal objects such as *users*, *groups*, or *computers*. Windows must ensure that those kinds of objects are available throughout the network. Objects in application partitions are also not replicated to the global catalog.

inetOrgPerson

Active Directory in Whistler includes support for the common *inetOrgPerson* class. Many early adopters of Active Directory were users of other directory products, such as Netscape Directory Server and Novell NDS. Both of these products, as well as other third-party LDAP directories, supported the *inetOrgPerson* class that was used to keep track of people with access to networking resources. While Active Directory has the *organizationalPerson* class, this class was an abstract class, and objects could not be created from it.

To ease the burden of migrating from and synchronizing with another directory service, the Whistler release of Active Directory implements the *inetOrgPerson* class. The *inetOrgPerson* class is defined in RFC 2798, which is an informational RFC, not a mandatory one. All the attributes defined in RFC 2798 are included as part of the Active Directory *inetOrgPerson* class. Table 11-2 lists those attributes.

inetOrgPerson Attribute	Syntax	Defined In	Description
audio	Octet string	RFC 1274	An audio recording. Format is not defined. Multivalued.
businessCategory	Directory string	RFC 2256	The category of business for this person. Multivalued.
carLicense	Directory string	RFC 2798	The license or registration plate associated with the person's vehicle. Multivalued.
departmentNumber	Directory string	RFC 2798	Numeric or alphanumeric code for the department to which a person belongs. Multivalued.
displayName	Directory string	RFC 2798	Printable version of the person's name.
employeeNumber	Directory string	RFC 2798	Numeric or alphanumeric identifier assigned to a person.
employeeType	Directory string	RFC 2798	Identifies the employer-to-employee relationship; for example, "full time," "contractor," "intern," and so on.
givenName	Directory string	RFC 2256	The first name of the person.
homePhone	Directory string	RFC 1274	The home telephone number for the person.
homePostalAddress	Directory string	RFC 1274	The postal mailing address for the person.
initials	Directory string	RFC 2256	Active Directory uses this attribute for the person's middle initial, although it can be used for the combination of the first letters of each name of the user.
jpegPhoto	Octet string	RFC 2798	Image of the person in JPEG File Interchange Format (JFIF). Multivalued.
labeledURI	Directory string	RFC 2079	Uniform Resource Identifier (URI) with a label. Multivalued.
mail	Directory string	RFC 2798	The e-mail address of the person.
manager	Distinguished name	RFC 1274	The distinguished name of the object associated with the manager or supervisor of the person.

Table 11-2 Attributes that are defined for the new *inetOrgPerson* class in Whistler. *(continued)* This table does not include attributes that are inherited from other classes.

Table 11-2 *continued*

inetOrgPerson Attribute	Syntax	Defined In	Description
mobile	Directory string	RFC 1274	The phone number for the mobile telephone for the person.
o	Directory string	RFC 2256	The name of the organization associated with the person. Multivalued.
pager	Directory string	RFC 1274	The phone number of the pager device used by the person.
photo	Octet string	RFC 1274	Photograph of the person in G3 fax format. Multivalued.
preferredLanguage	Directory string	RFC 2798	The person's preferred written or spoken language. Values for this attribute conform to the Accept-Language header field defined by HTTP in RFC 2068.
roomNumber	Directory string	RFC 1274	The room number associated with the person's primary location. Multivalued.
secretary	Distinguished name	RFC 1274	The distinguished name of the object representing the secretary or assistant to the person. Multivalued.
uid	Directory string	RFC 2798	The user identification used for computer network access. Multivalued.
userCertificate	Octet string	RFC 2256	A security certificate for the person. Format is undefined. Multivalued.
userPKCS12	Octet string	RFC 2798	Contains the person's personal identity information in the Public Key Cryptography Systems #12 (PKCS #12) standard format. Multivalued.
userSMIMECertificate	Octet string	RFC 2798	The person's S/MIME certificate encoded with PKCS #7 (RFC2315) standard format. Multivalued.
x500UniqueIdentifier	Octet string	RFC 2256	Used to distinguish between objects when a distinguished name has been reused. Multivalued.

An important feature of Active Directory implementation of the *inetOrgPerson* class is that it inherits from the *user* class. Since the *user* class includes the *securityPrincipal* auxiliary class, this allows *inetOrgPerson* objects to be equal to other users with respect to security and access control. Having this equality is particularly important with e-commerce applications that must securely authenticate remote users to allow access to databases and process transactions. Now customers can be represented with *inetOrgPerson* classes and can be authenticated using the same security methods available to intranet and LAN users.

There is no need to move all your users to the new *inetOrgClass* because Whistler adds the same attributes to its version of the *user* class. This helps retain compatibility with existing deployments of Active Directory.

Virtual List View Searching

The release of Active Directory in Whistler supports a new type of searching called *virtual list view* (VLV). A VLV search relies on the directory server to provide a virtual "view" into the entire result set. The server manages the data, while the client retrieves only the portion of the result set that is currently displayed to the user.

This mechanism is similar in nature to the virtual list-view style for list-view controls. It's best used for address box style applications in which a search can return many hundreds or thousands of results. Normally, to indicate to the user the relative position of the entries shown, the client needs to know the total number of results from a particular search. In a VLV search, the search can quickly return an estimate of the total number of entries along with the first result set so that the user can gauge the current view in relation to the total.

Imagine you are creating an address book application for an organization with thousands of people listed in the directory. The user invokes the application, which shows the first dozen or so people returned. Now imagine that the user wants to quickly move to the middle of the list to see entries that start with the letter O. In most list views, the user can press the O key and that event will move the focus to the first item starting with O.

Without a VLV search, the application would have to do one of two things: it could abandon the current search and request a new one with all the entries starting with O, or the application could retrieve all the entries (remember, there are thousands) and cache them locally. Doing the latter allows the user to move quickly between the various entries but only after the server has returned A through Z, which could take an unacceptably long time.

The VLV search provides the benefits of both methods without the network traffic and delay associated with returning all the results to the client. The client also doesn't have to allocate large amounts of memory to cache the results.

However, the server does return an estimate of the total number of results, so the application appears to have all the results available and the scroll bar or slider can indicate the relative position of the current view within the entire result set.

To provide support for VLV searches, Whistler defines two LDAPv3 extended controls, which are additions to the LDAP API and protocol that support new functionality. Both controls contain information about the view.

The process of performing a VLV search is similar to a regular search using the *IDirectorySearch* interface. You supply an *ADS_VLV* structure, which is placed in the *ADS_SEARCHPREF_INFO* array. You must also specify a sorted result using the *ADS_SORTKEY* structure.

The *ADS_VLV* structure specifies how many rows to return in the search and at what offset. For example, if you searched a container that has 1,000 items, but you only want the first 20 to be returned, the *dwOffset* member would be zero, and the *dwAfterCount* would be 20. VLV also allows you to guess at the number of items you need to view in a result set. If you don't know how many items the search will return, but you want to show the middle 50, you can indicate to Active Directory that you think 100 items are part of the search, and you want the offset to be 50. Active Directory will take the ratio you supply (100/50) and apply it to the estimate that the server comes up with. It may not be exact, but if the folder contains 1200 items, the search offset will be 600.

Similarly, if you want to display the last 10 items of a container, set your estimate to 100 (or any positive value) and set the offset to the same value. Then put the value 10 into *dwBeforeCount* so that Active Directory will return 10 rows.

When you're ready to retrieve the results, execute the search normally using the *ExecuteSearch* method of the *IDirectorySearch* interface. However, not until the *GetFirstRow* method is called or the *GetNextRow* method is called for the first time is the server contacted and a VLV response returned along with the number of results you specify (*dwBeforeCount* + *dwAfterCount* + the target).

The VLV response is returned as a column. The server returns a pointer to the *ADS_VLV* structure that is updated with an estimated count of the total number of results and the adjusted offset. The application can then apply a new offset and perform the search again. Since it's only a few results at a time, the server can process it very quickly.

Listing 11-4 uses the VLV searching method in Whistler to return all the objects in the schema container. The search starts at the end of the container and displays the records in blocks of 40, each moving backward until all the items have been shown.

> **Note**   The code below is based on the Beta 2 version of Whistler and may not function correctly or at all in the final version.

```
//------------------------------------------------------------------
// VLVSearch.cpp
//
// Description:
// Display the contents of the schema container in blocks of 40
// items, going backward.  Shows how virtual list view searches
// work under Whistler.
//
// Platform: Win32 Console Mode Application
//------------------------------------------------------------------
// C++ and Compiler Support
#include <tchar.h>
#include <string.h>
#include <stdio.h>
#include <comdef.h>
// Windows Platform Support
#include <objbase.h>
// Active Directory Support
#include <prerelease\activeds.h>
// Warning level 4 for this code
#pragma warning( push, 4 )
// Includes ADSI libraries
#pragma comment( lib, "activeds.lib" )
#pragma comment( lib, "adsiid.lib"   )
// Returns number of elements in array (good for strings)
#define ARRAYSIZE(a)    (sizeof(a)/sizeof(a[0]))


// Function prototype
HRESULT VLVSearchAndDisplay(IDirectorySearch* padsSearch,
    PADS_VLV padsVLVPref );


//------------------------------------------------------------------
// Function:  wmain
// Inputs:    int argc         Number of command line arguments
//            wchar_t *argv[]  Pointer to argument string array
//            wchar_t *envp[]  Pointer to enviroment string array
// Returns:   int              Program exit code
//                             0 = no errors, otherwise HRESULT
//------------------------------------------------------------------
```

Listing 11-4 VLVSearch.cpp uses the VLV searching method of Whistler   *(continued)*
to return all the objects in the schema container in blocks of 40 items.

Listing 11-4 *continued*

```
int wmain( int /*argc*/, wchar_t* /*argv[]*/, wchar_t* /*envp[]*/)
{
//Initialize COM
HRESULT hResult = CoInitialize(NULL);

// Get a base IADs object
IADs *padsRootDSE;
hResult = ADsGetObject( L"LDAP://RootDSE",
                        IID_IADs,
                        (void**) &padsRootDSE );

// Use the Get method to get the schema partition
_variant_t varDomain;
hResult = padsRootDSE->Get(L"schemaNamingContext",
                           &varDomain);

//Build LDAP path to the domain
_bstr_t bstrDirectoryPath =_bstr_t( "LDAP://" ) +
                           _bstr_t( varDomain );

_tprintf( _T("Searching %ls\n"), (wchar_t*)bstrDirectoryPath);

// Get the directory search interface to the domain
IDirectorySearch *padsSearchContainer = NULL;
hResult = ADsGetObject( bstrDirectoryPath,
                        IID_IDirectorySearch,
                        (void **) &padsSearchContainer );

// Allocate space for the VLV preferences
// Recommend initializing all members to zero
ADS_VLV adsVLVPref = { NULL };

// Show one block at a time (before + target + after)
DWORD dwBlockSize = 40;
bool bLastBlock = false;

// Set the initial VLV preferences
adsVLVPref.dwContextIDLength = 0;
adsVLVPref.lpContextID = NULL;
// Initial estimate of number of entries
adsVLVPref.dwContentCount = 100;
// Start at the end
adsVLVPref.dwOffset = adsVLVPref.dwContentCount;
```

```
adsVLVPref.dwBeforeCount = dwBlockSize;
adsVLVPref.dwAfterCount = 1;

// Loop backward through the container
while (true)
    {
    _tprintf( _T("---Offset %d of %d---\n"),
              adsVLVPref.dwOffset,
              adsVLVPref.dwContentCount );

    // Get the next block
    hResult = VLVSearchAndDisplay( padsSearchContainer, &adsVLVPref );

    // Move backward through the container (with overlap)
    adsVLVPref.dwOffset -= dwBlockSize;

    // Less than zero?  Go once more with 0 as offset
    if ((signed int)adsVLVPref.dwOffset < 0)
        {
        if (bLastBlock = false)
            {
            bLastBlock = true;
            adsVLVPref.dwOffset = 0;
            adsVLVPref.dwBeforeCount = 0;
            adsVLVPref.dwAfterCount = dwBlockSize;
            }
        else
            // If last block was set, break out of loop
            break;
        }
    }

// Clean up objects
if ( padsSearchContainer )
    padsSearchContainer->Release();

if ( padsRootDSE )
    padsRootDSE->Release();

// Uninitialize COM
CoUninitialize();

return hResult;
}
```

(continued)

Listing 11-4 *continued*

```
//------------------------------------------------------------------
// Function: VLVSearchAndDisplay
// Inputs:    IDirectorySearch* Object reference to search container
//            PADS_VLV           VLV search preferences, updated on exit
// Returns:  HRESULT            Program exit code
//                              0 = no errors, otherwise HRESULT
//------------------------------------------------------------------
HRESULT VLVSearchAndDisplay(IDirectorySearch* padsSearch,
                            PADS_VLV padsVLVPref )
{
HRESULT hResult;

// Create search preferences structure
ADS_SEARCHPREF_INFO arSearchPrefs[3];

// Set the VLV search preferences into the array
arSearchPrefs[0].dwSearchPref = ADS_SEARCHPREF_VLV;
arSearchPrefs[0].vValue.dwType = ADSTYPE_PROV_SPECIFIC;
arSearchPrefs[0].vValue.ProviderSpecific.dwLength = sizeof( ADS_VLV );
arSearchPrefs[0].vValue.ProviderSpecific.lpValue = (LPBYTE)padsVLVPref;

// Set a subtree search
arSearchPrefs[1].dwSearchPref  = ADS_SEARCHPREF_SEARCH_SCOPE;
arSearchPrefs[1].vValue.dwType  = ADSTYPE_INTEGER;
arSearchPrefs[1].vValue.Integer = ADS_SCOPE_SUBTREE;

// Create a sort key using the cn attribute
ADS_SORTKEY adsSortKey = { NULL };
adsSortKey.pszAttrType = L"cn";
adsSortKey.fReverseorder = 0;

// Create the search sort search preference
arSearchPrefs[2].dwSearchPref = ADS_SEARCHPREF_SORT_ON;
arSearchPrefs[2].vValue.dwType = ADSTYPE_PROV_SPECIFIC;
arSearchPrefs[2].vValue.ProviderSpecific.dwLength = sizeof(ADS_SORTKEY);
arSearchPrefs[2].vValue.ProviderSpecific.lpValue = (LPBYTE) &adsSortKey;

// Set the search preferences
hResult = padsSearch->SetSearchPreference( arSearchPrefs, 3 );

// Execute search and request all attributes
// Returns handle to search
ADS_SEARCH_HANDLE hSearch;
hResult = padsSearch->ExecuteSearch( L"(objectClass=*)",
                                     NULL,
                                     -1,
                                     &hSearch);
```

```
if ( SUCCEEDED(hResult) )
    {
    // GetFirstRow to actually run the search
    hResult = padsSearch->GetFirstRow(hSearch);

    if (SUCCEEDED(hResult))
        {
        ADS_SEARCH_COLUMN colSearchColumn;

        // Loop through each row returned
        while (hResult != S_ADS_NOMORE_ROWS)
            {
            // Get first attribute
            hResult = padsSearch->GetColumn(hSearch,
                                            L"Name",
                                            &colSearchColumn);

            if (SUCCEEDED(hResult))
                {
                // Display the attribute
                _tprintf( _T("%ls\t\n"),
                          colSearchColumn.pADsValues->CaseIgnoreString);

                // Must free the column each time
                padsSearch->FreeColumn( &colSearchColumn );
                }

            //Get the next row
            hResult = padsSearch->GetNextRow( hSearch );
            }

        // Get the VLV response metadata as a column
        hResult = padsSearch->GetColumn(hSearch,
                                        ADS_VLV_RESPONSE,
                                        &colSearchColumn );

        // Verify that it is VLV data
        // ADsType is set to ADSTYPE_PROV_SPECIFIC
        // and the number of values is 1
        if (colSearchColumn.dwADsType == ADSTYPE_PROV_SPECIFIC &&
            colSearchColumn.dwNumValues == 1 )
            {
            // Retrieve the metadata into a ADSVALUE structure
            ADSVALUE adsValue = colSearchColumn.pADsValues[0];
            PADS_VLV pVlv = (PADS_VLV)(adsValue.ProviderSpecific.lpValue);
```

(continued)

415

Listing 11-4 *continued*

```
            // Update the passed in structure with the new values
            padsVLVPref->dwContentCount = pVlv->dwContentCount;
            padsVLVPref->dwOffset = pVlv->dwOffset;
            }
        else
            _tprintf( _T("Error retrieving Virtual List View Response
                from Active Directory.\n"));

            // Must free the VLV metabase column like any other
            padsSearch->FreeColumn( &colSearchColumn );
            }

        // Close the search handle to clean up
        padsSearch->CloseSearchHandle(hSearch);
        }

    return hResult;
    }
```

User Interface Enhancements

Whistler also contains a number of changes to the user interface for Active Directory. A goal of the new design is to reduce network traffic for large organizations. For example, a new object picker dialog box is available that enables searches. When showing a list of users, the Windows 2000 object picker dialog box would query the server for all the users, even though only one would be required.

The Whistler version of the object picker dialog box, shown in Figure 11-6, reminds me of an e-mail interface. When searching for a name, you can type it in and click the Check Names button to resolve any ambiguities. The Advanced button displays the new query dialog box, shown in Figure 11-7. While this user interface is still being worked on, the ability to start a search from within the object picker is very powerful.

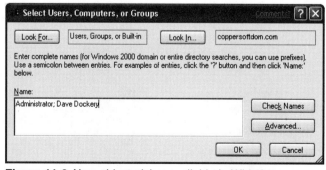

Figure 11-6 New object picker available in Whistler.

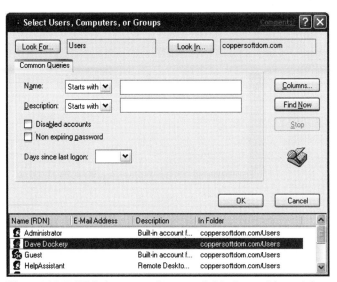

Figure 11-7 Whistler query form available from object picker.

> **Note** I'm happy to report that all the user interface code presented in Chapter 8 works as expected with the Beta 2 version of Whistler.

Summary

First with Windows 2000 and now with Whistler, Microsoft is expanding the role of directory services. In the process, it is breaking the traditional mold of directory-enabled networks.

I hope this book has spurred your imagination and given you the knowledge to create your own great applications that use Active Directory. Thank you for reading.

Appendix

Active Directory Resources

The following compilation lists resources that provide information about programming with Active Directory and related topics. These resources are available on *www.microsoft.com* and other Internet sites.

> **Note** Internet addresses change often. If you experience any difficulty finding the information presented in this appendix, go to the root site (for example, *www.microsoft.com*) and try searching for the information. Also, the links to third-party sites are not under the control of Microsoft, and Microsoft is not responsible for the contents of or changes to these sites.

http://msdn.microsoft.com

MSDN, the Microsoft Developers Network. This site is an invaluable resource with a tremendous amount of information on Microsoft technology. Regular columns written by the developers of the technology provide unique insight. The entire MSDN Library is available online, including the complete Active Directory, Active Directory Service Interfaces (ADSI), and Lightweight Directory Access Protocol (LDAP) documentation set. A number of articles are devoted to Active Directory and ADSI, including a chat transcript with the ADSI development team. This is my favorite jumping-off point for anything to do with Microsoft technologies.

http://msdn.microsoft.com/downloads/

MSDN Online Downloads. Some of the C++ code samples for this book require header and library files from the Microsoft Platform SDK. The files that you need should be included on the companion CD, but if you are missing files, you should check this link to download the appropriate components from the Platform SDK.

http://search.support.microsoft.com/kb/

Microsoft Knowledge Base. This is the first place to go when you are having a problem. You can research the problem and the fixes for it that are documented in Knowledge Base articles. And here's a tip: When searching the Knowledge Base, use the advanced features to find information quickly. For example, to get a list of articles related to Active Directory bugs or fixes, use a Boolean search and type *bug OR fix AND "Active Directory"*

http://www.microsoft.com/adsi/

The semiofficial Microsoft page for ADSI. Unfortunately, at the time of this writing, the page was not actively maintained and is somewhat outdated.

http://www.microsoft.com/windows2000/news/bulletins/ adextension.asp

Active Directory Client Extensions. This page hosts the latest Active Directory Clients for Windows 95, Windows 98, and Windows NT Workstation 4.0. Although these components are included on the companion CD, newer versions will be available on this site when they are released.

news://msnews.microsoft.com/

Microsoft newsgroups cover many topics, including Active Directory and ADSI. These "peer-to-peer" newsgroups are useful for learning about the problems other users have and for finding common solutions. The newsgroups are currently not staffed or monitored by Microsoft support engineers. Here's a list of relevant newsgroup addresses that you can access with Outlook Express or another newsgroup viewer:

news://msnews.microsoft.com/microsoft.public.active.directory.interfaces
news://msnews.microsoft.com/microsoft.public.adsi.general
news://msnews.microsoft.com/microsoft.public.exchange2000.active.
  directory.integration
news://msnews.microsoft.com/microsoft.public.platformsdk.active.directory
news://msnews.microsoft.com/microsoft.public.platformsdk.adsi
news://msnews.microsoft.com/microsoft.public.win2000.active_directory
news://msnews.microsoft.com/microsoft.public.metadirectory

http://msdn.microsoft.com/newsgroups/

All the Microsoft newsgroups cited above, available using a Web interface.

http://www.microsoft.com/windows2000/

The Microsoft Windows 2000 home page. From this page, you can reach a number of resources, including much of the Windows 2000 Professional and Windows 2000 Server resource kits, which I consider invaluable for developers and administrators alike. The Download, Support, and Technical Library sections are also excellent.

http://www.ietf.org/

The Internet Engineering Task Force (IETF). Home of all the RFC documents.

http://www.ietf.org/html.charters/ldapbis-charter.html
http://www.ietf.org/html.charters/ldup-charter.html
http://www.ietf.org/html.charters/ldapext-charter.html

IETF working groups for LDAP. These working groups are defining the future of LDAP and Active Directory.

http://www.itu.int/

International Telecommunications Union. The X.500 specifications are available for purchase here.

http://www.alvestrand.no/objectid/

Unofficial registry of object identifiers (OIDs). This site is useful for viewing what branches of the OID tree contain and who manages them.

http://mysite.directlink.net/gbarr/perl-ldap/

This site contains a collection of perl modules that provide an object-oriented interface to LDAP.

http://www.oblix.com/pointofentry/ldap/l

An excellent starting point for LDAP information and resources. The site is not specific to Active Directory, but it still contains some applicable information.

http://www.ldapguru.com/

Comprehensive site with message boards, downloads, and a wealth of technical articles.

http://www.learnasp.com/

An excellent resource for developers working with Active Server Pages (ASP). Charles Carroll provides a number of articles, sample code, and tutorials for developers starting to working with ASP and ASP.NET.

http://www.asplists.com/
http://www.asplists.com/asplists/adsi.asp

Hundreds of high-quality moderated e-mail lists related to ASP. This site also includes a number of ADSI mailing lists, plus information about Microsoft .NET technologies. A personal favorite of mine.

http://www.activedir.org/

Supports a mailing list for Active Directory issues.

http://www.15Seconds.com

15Seconds offers a mailing list that's used by a number of knowledgeable professionals. The 15Seconds ADSI Web page is out-of-date, however.

http://www.win2000mag.com/

Windows 2000 Magazine. A number of articles about administering Windows 2000.

http://msdn.microsoft.com/scripting/

Microsoft Scripting technologies. The latest documentation, downloads, and resources for Windows Scripting, including VBScript, JScript, Windows Script Host, and Windows Script Components.

http://www.win32scripting.com/

Windows Scripting Solutions. High-quality articles about scripting, including information on ADSI, CDO, and WMI.

http://www.labmice.net/activedirectory/

Another comprehensive site with a number of articles related to Active Directory and Windows 2000 administration.

http://www.coppersoftware.com/activedir/

My page for Active Directory resources, sample source code, and articles.

Index

Note: Italicized page references indicate figures, tables, or code listings.

Index

Index

About the Author

Charles Oppermann is the founder and president of Copper Software, a software engineering and design firm specializing in directory services, user interface design, and the training of software developers. Charles recently retired from Microsoft Corporation, where he worked as a program manager and developer for several products, including Windows 95, Internet Explorer (versions 3 and 4), Windows 2000, and Exchange  2000 Server. For 5 years at Microsoft, Charles focused on creating adaptive and accessible user interfaces for people with disabilities and was the program manager and coinventor of the Microsoft Active Accessibility technology. Before joining Microsoft, Charles was vice president of development for Henter-Joyce, a company specializing in text-to-speech products for the visually impaired.

When not working at his computer, Charles enjoys hiking and flying his small plane, "Charlie Whiskey," around the beautiful Pacific Northwest. His next project is to earn an instrument rating for his pilot's license so he can fly during the rare rainy weather in the Seattle area.

You can e-mail Charles at charles@coppersoftware.com and visit his Web site at *http://www.coppersoftware.com/*.

Hooks on a Sling

The hooks illustrated on the cover are a component of a set of tools known as *slings*. Literally thousands of configurations of slings are used in many industries for moving heavy loads. The size of the sling and the hook are determined by the weight, shape, and size of the load to be moved or lifted. Wire rope is the most commonly used sling. This type of sling can easily accept a large hook and also has the lowest cost per ton of lift. It is frequently used in the construction industry where heavy loads and rugged conditions exist. Chains are another common sling used with hooks and are usually found in steel mills, foundries, and heavy machine operations that require repetitive lifts.

Tools are central to the progress of the human race. People are adept at building and using tools to accomplish important (and unimportant) tasks. Software is among the most powerful of tools moving us forward, and Microsoft is proud to create tools used by millions worldwide and to contribute to continuing innovation.

The manuscript for this book was prepared and galleyed using Microsoft Word 2000. Pages were composed by Microsoft Press using Adobe PageMaker 6.52 for Windows, with text in Garamond and display type in Helvetica Condensed. Composed pages were delivered to the printer as electronic prepress files.

Cover Designer:	Methodologie, Inc.
Interior Graphic Designer:	James D. Kramer
Principal Compositor:	Paula Gorelick
Interior Artist:	Michael Kloepfer
Copy Editor:	Cheryl Penner
Indexer:	Julie Kawabata

The definitive guide
to the architecture
and internals of
Microsoft's premier
operating system

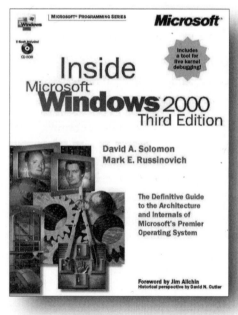

U.S.A. **$49.99**
U.K. £32.99 [V.A.T. included]
Canada $72.99

ISBN: 0-7356-1021-5

Master the inner workings of Microsoft's premier operating system with this newly updated guide to the Microsoft® Windows® 2000 core architecture and internals. Written in partnership with the product development team and with full access to the Windows 2000 source code, this book provides a detailed look beneath the surface of Windows 2000. It's packed with the latest concepts and terms, kernel and source code specifics, undocumented interfaces, component and tool descriptions, and architectural perspectives that reveal the inner workings of Windows 2000. In short, it delivers all the minute details that developers need to debug code and to make better design decisions. Administrators also will find this book invaluable for understanding system performance and troubleshooting problems.

Microsoft®

mspress.microsoft.com

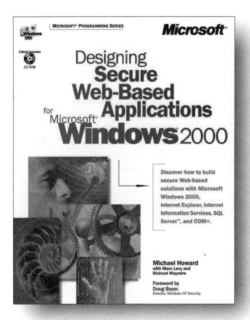

Get a **Free**
e-mail newsletter, updates,
special offers, links to related books,
and more when you
register on line!

Register your Microsoft Press® title on our Web site and you'll get a FREE subscription to our e-mail newsletter, *Microsoft Press Book Connections.* You'll find out about newly released and upcoming books and learning tools, online events, software downloads, special offers and coupons for Microsoft Press customers, and information about major Microsoft® product releases. You can also read useful additional information about all the titles we publish, such as detailed book descriptions, tables of contents and indexes, sample chapters, links to related books and book series, author biographies, and reviews by other customers.

Registration is easy. Just visit this Web page and fill in your information:

http://mspress.microsoft.com/register

Microsoft®

Proof of Purchase

Use this page as proof of purchase if participating in a promotion or rebate offer on this title. Proof of purchase must be used in conjunction with other proof(s) of payment such as your dated sales receipt—see offer details.

Microsoft® Windows® 2000 Active Directory™ Programming
0-7356-1037-1

CUSTOMER NAME

Microsoft Press, PO Box 97017, Redmond, WA 98073-9830

MICROSOFT LICENSE AGREEMENT

Book Companion CD

IMPORTANT—READ CAREFULLY: This Microsoft End-User License Agreement ("EULA") is a legal agreement between you (either an individual or an entity) and Microsoft Corporation for the Microsoft product identified above, which includes computer software and may include associated media, printed materials, and "online" or electronic documentation ("SOFTWARE PRODUCT"). Any component included within the SOFTWARE PRODUCT that is accompanied by a separate End-User License Agreement shall be governed by such agreement and not the terms set forth below. By installing, copying, or otherwise using the SOFTWARE PRODUCT, you agree to be bound by the terms of this EULA. If you do not agree to the terms of this EULA, you are not authorized to install, copy, or otherwise use the SOFTWARE PRODUCT; you may, however, return the SOFTWARE PRODUCT, along with all printed materials and other items that form a part of the Microsoft product that includes the SOFTWARE PRODUCT, to the place you obtained them for a full refund.

SOFTWARE PRODUCT LICENSE

The SOFTWARE PRODUCT is protected by United States copyright laws and international copyright treaties, as well as other intellectual property laws and treaties. The SOFTWARE PRODUCT is licensed, not sold.

1. GRANT OF LICENSE. This EULA grants you the following rights:

a. Software Product. You may install and use one copy of the SOFTWARE PRODUCT on a single computer. The primary user of the computer on which the SOFTWARE PRODUCT is installed may make a second copy for his or her exclusive use on a portable computer.

b. Storage/Network Use. You may also store or install a copy of the SOFTWARE PRODUCT on a storage device, such as a network server, used only to install or run the SOFTWARE PRODUCT on your other computers over an internal network; however, you must acquire and dedicate a license for each separate computer on which the SOFTWARE PRODUCT is installed or run from the storage device. A license for the SOFTWARE PRODUCT may not be shared or used concurrently on different computers.

c. License Pak. If you have acquired this EULA in a Microsoft License Pak, you may make the number of additional copies of the computer software portion of the SOFTWARE PRODUCT authorized on the printed copy of this EULA, and you may use each copy in the manner specified above. You are also entitled to make a corresponding number of secondary copies for portable computer use as specified above.

d. Sample Code. Solely with respect to portions, if any, of the SOFTWARE PRODUCT that are identified within the SOFTWARE PRODUCT as sample code (the "SAMPLE CODE"):

  i. Use and Modification. Microsoft grants you the right to use and modify the source code version of the SAMPLE CODE, *provided* you comply with subsection (d)(iii) below. You may not distribute the SAMPLE CODE, or any modified version of the SAMPLE CODE, in source code form.

  ii. Redistributable Files. Provided you comply with subsection (d)(iii) below, Microsoft grants you a nonexclusive, royalty-free right to reproduce and distribute the object code version of the SAMPLE CODE and of any modified SAMPLE CODE, other than SAMPLE CODE (or any modified version thereof) designated as not redistributable in the Readme file that forms a part of the SOFTWARE PRODUCT (the "Non-Redistributable Sample Code"). All SAMPLE CODE other than the Non-Redistributable Sample Code is collectively referred to as the "REDISTRIBUTABLES."

  iii. Redistribution Requirements. If you redistribute the REDISTRIBUTABLES, you agree to: (i) distribute the REDISTRIBUTABLES in object code form only in conjunction with and as a part of your software application product; (ii) not use Microsoft's name, logo, or trademarks to market your software application product; (iii) include a valid copyright notice on your software application product; (iv) indemnify, hold harmless, and defend Microsoft from and against any claims or lawsuits, including attorney's fees, that arise or result from the use or distribution of your software application product; and (v) not permit further distribution of the REDISTRIBUTABLES by your end user. Contact Microsoft for the applicable royalties due and other licensing terms for all other uses and/or distribution of the REDISTRIBUTABLES.

2. DESCRIPTION OF OTHER RIGHTS AND LIMITATIONS.

- **Limitations on Reverse Engineering, Decompilation, and Disassembly.** You may not reverse engineer, decompile, or disassemble the SOFTWARE PRODUCT, except and only to the extent that such activity is expressly permitted by applicable law notwithstanding this limitation.

- **Separation of Components.** The SOFTWARE PRODUCT is licensed as a single product. Its component parts may not be separated for use on more than one computer.

- **Rental.** You may not rent, lease, or lend the SOFTWARE PRODUCT.

- **Support Services.** Microsoft may, but is not obligated to, provide you with support services related to the SOFTWARE PRODUCT ("Support Services"). Use of Support Services is governed by the Microsoft policies and programs described in the user manual, in "online" documentation, and/or in other Microsoft-provided materials. Any supplemental software code provided to you as part of the Support Services shall be considered part of the SOFTWARE PRODUCT and subject to the terms and conditions of this EULA. With respect to technical information you provide to Microsoft as part of the Support Services, Microsoft may use such information for its business purposes, including for product support and development. Microsoft will not utilize such technical information in a form that personally identifies you.

- **Software Transfer.** You may permanently transfer all of your rights under this EULA, provided you retain no copies, you transfer all of the SOFTWARE PRODUCT (including all component parts, the media and printed materials, any upgrades, this EULA, and, if applicable, the Certificate of Authenticity), **and** the recipient agrees to the terms of this EULA.

- **Termination.** Without prejudice to any other rights, Microsoft may terminate this EULA if you fail to comply with the terms and conditions of this EULA. In such event, you must destroy all copies of the SOFTWARE PRODUCT and all of its component parts.

3. **COPYRIGHT.** All title and copyrights in and to the SOFTWARE PRODUCT (including but not limited to any images, photographs, animations, video, audio, music, text, SAMPLE CODE, REDISTRIBUTABLES, and "applets" incorporated into the SOFTWARE PRODUCT) and any copies of the SOFTWARE PRODUCT are owned by Microsoft or its suppliers. The SOFTWARE PRODUCT is protected by copyright laws and international treaty provisions. Therefore, you must treat the SOFTWARE PRODUCT like any other copyrighted material **except** that you may install the SOFTWARE PRODUCT on a single computer provided you keep the original solely for backup or archival purposes. You may not copy the printed materials accompanying the SOFTWARE PRODUCT.

4. **U.S. GOVERNMENT RESTRICTED RIGHTS.** The SOFTWARE PRODUCT and documentation are provided with RESTRICTED RIGHTS. Use, duplication, or disclosure by the Government is subject to restrictions as set forth in subparagraph (c)(1)(ii) of the Rights in Technical Data and Computer Software clause at DFARS 252.227-7013 or subparagraphs (c)(1) and (2) of the Commercial Computer Software—Restricted Rights at 48 CFR 52.227-19, as applicable. Manufacturer is Microsoft Corporation/One Microsoft Way/Redmond, WA 98052-6399.

5. **EXPORT RESTRICTIONS.** You agree that you will not export or re-export the SOFTWARE PRODUCT, any part thereof, or any process or service that is the direct product of the SOFTWARE PRODUCT (the foregoing collectively referred to as the "Restricted Components"), to any country, person, entity, or end user subject to U.S. export restrictions. You specifically agree not to export or re-export any of the Restricted Components (i) to any country to which the U.S. has embargoed or restricted the export of goods or services, which currently include, but are not necessarily limited to, Cuba, Iran, Iraq, Libya, North Korea, Sudan, and Syria, or to any national of any such country, wherever located, who intends to transmit or transport the Restricted Components back to such country; (ii) to any end user who you know or have reason to know will utilize the Restricted Components in the design, development, or production of nuclear, chemical, or biological weapons; or (iii) to any end user who has been prohibited from participating in U.S. export transactions by any federal agency of the U.S. government. You warrant and represent that neither the BXA nor any other U.S. federal agency has suspended, revoked, or denied your export privileges.

6. **NOTE ON JAVA SUPPORT.** THE SOFTWARE PRODUCT MAY CONTAIN SUPPORT FOR PROGRAMS WRITTEN IN JAVA. JAVA TECHNOLOGY IS NOT FAULT TOLERANT AND IS NOT DESIGNED, MANUFACTURED, OR INTENDED FOR USE OR RESALE AS ON-LINE CONTROL EQUIPMENT IN HAZARDOUS ENVIRONMENTS REQUIRING FAIL-SAFE PERFORMANCE, SUCH AS IN THE OPERATION OF NUCLEAR FACILITIES, AIRCRAFT NAVIGATION OR COMMUNICATION SYSTEMS, AIR TRAFFIC CONTROL, DIRECT LIFE SUPPORT MACHINES, OR WEAPONS SYSTEMS, IN WHICH THE FAILURE OF JAVA TECHNOLOGY COULD LEAD DIRECTLY TO DEATH, PERSONAL INJURY, OR SEVERE PHYSICAL OR ENVIRONMENTAL DAMAGE. SUN MICROSYSTEMS, INC. HAS CONTRACTUALLY OBLIGATED MICROSOFT TO MAKE THIS DISCLAIMER.

DISCLAIMER OF WARRANTY

NO WARRANTIES OR CONDITIONS. MICROSOFT EXPRESSLY DISCLAIMS ANY WARRANTY OR CONDITION FOR THE SOFTWARE PRODUCT. THE SOFTWARE PRODUCT AND ANY RELATED DOCUMENTATION ARE PROVIDED "AS IS" WITHOUT WARRANTY OR CONDITION OF ANY KIND, EITHER EXPRESS OR IMPLIED, INCLUDING, WITHOUT LIMITATION, THE IMPLIED WARRANTIES OF MERCHANTABILITY, FITNESS FOR A PARTICULAR PURPOSE, OR NONINFRINGEMENT. THE ENTIRE RISK ARISING OUT OF USE OR PERFORMANCE OF THE SOFTWARE PRODUCT REMAINS WITH YOU.

LIMITATION OF LIABILITY. TO THE MAXIMUM EXTENT PERMITTED BY APPLICABLE LAW, IN NO EVENT SHALL MICROSOFT OR ITS SUPPLIERS BE LIABLE FOR ANY SPECIAL, INCIDENTAL, INDIRECT, OR CONSEQUENTIAL DAMAGES WHATSOEVER (INCLUDING, WITHOUT LIMITATION, DAMAGES FOR LOSS OF BUSINESS PROFITS, BUSINESS INTERRUPTION, LOSS OF BUSINESS INFORMATION, OR ANY OTHER PECUNIARY LOSS) ARISING OUT OF THE USE OF OR INABILITY TO USE THE SOFTWARE PRODUCT OR THE PROVISION OF OR FAILURE TO PROVIDE SUPPORT SERVICES, EVEN IF MICROSOFT HAS BEEN ADVISED OF THE POSSIBILITY OF SUCH DAMAGES. IN ANY CASE, MICROSOFT'S ENTIRE LIABILITY UNDER ANY PROVISION OF THIS EULA SHALL BE LIMITED TO THE GREATER OF THE AMOUNT ACTUALLY PAID BY YOU FOR THE SOFTWARE PRODUCT OR US$5.00; PROVIDED, HOWEVER, IF YOU HAVE ENTERED INTO A MICROSOFT SUPPORT SERVICES AGREEMENT, MICROSOFT'S ENTIRE LIABILITY REGARDING SUPPORT SERVICES SHALL BE GOVERNED BY THE TERMS OF THAT AGREEMENT. BECAUSE SOME STATES AND JURISDICTIONS DO NOT ALLOW THE EXCLUSION OR LIMITATION OF LIABILITY, THE ABOVE LIMITATION MAY NOT APPLY TO YOU.

MISCELLANEOUS

This EULA is governed by the laws of the State of Washington USA, except and only to the extent that applicable law mandates governing law of a different jurisdiction.

Should you have any questions concerning this EULA, or if you desire to contact Microsoft for any reason, please contact the Microsoft subsidiary serving your country, or write: Microsoft Sales Information Center/One Microsoft Way/Redmond, WA 98052-6399.